Principles of Food, Beverage, and Labor Cost Controls

for Hotels and Restaurants

Fourth Edition

Principles of Food, Beverage, and Labor Cost Controls
for Hotels and Restaurants
Fourth Edition

PAUL R. DITTMER

Chair, Hotel and Restaurant Management Department
New Hampshire College
Manchester, New Hampshire

GERALD G. GRIFFIN

Chair, Hotel and Restaurant Management Department
New York City Technical College
The City University of New York
Brooklyn, New York

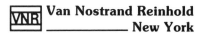

VNR **Van Nostrand Reinhold**
_____ **New York**

To our wives
Barbara and Charlene
in appreciation of their faith
and forbearance.

Copyright © 1989 by Van Nostrand Reinhold

Library of Congress Catalog Card Number 89-30619
ISBN 0-442-23432-5

I(T)P   Van Nostrand Reinhold is an International Thomson Publishing company.
        ITP logo is a trademark under license.

Printed in the United States of America

Van Nostrand Reinhold
115 Fifth Avenue
New York, NY 10003

International Thomson Publishing GmbH
Konigswinterer Str. 518
5300 Bonn 3
Germany

International Thomson Publishing
Berkshire House,168-173
High Holborn, London WC1V 7AA
England

International Thomson Publishing Asia
38 Kim Tian Rd., #0105
Kim Tian Plaza
Singapore 0316

Thomas Nelson Australia
102 Dodds Street
South Melbourne 3205
Victoria, Australia

International Thomson Publishing Japan
Kyowa Building, 3F
2-2-1 Hirakawacho
Chiyada-Ku, Tokyo 102
Japan

Nelson Canada
1120 Birchmount Road
Scarborough, Ontario
M1K 5G4, Canada

16 15 14 13 12 11 10 9 8 7 6 5

Library of Congress Cataloging-in-Publication Data
Dittmer, Paul, R.
    Principles of food, beverage & labor cost controls for hotels and
restaurants / Paul R. Dittmer, Gerald G. Griffin.—4th ed.
        p.   cm.
    Includes index.
    ISBN 0-442-23432-5
    1. Restaurants, lunch rooms, etc.—Finance. 2. Hotels, taverns,
etc.—Finance. I. Griffin, Gerald G. II. Title.
III. Title: Principles of food, beverage, and labor cost controls
for hotels and restaurants.
TX911.3.F5D57   1989
647.95'0681—dc19   89-30619
                                                CIP

Contents

Preface

Over the years, the authors have taught many courses whose titles have included such words as "food," "beverage," "labor," "cost," and "control" in a variety of combinations. Each teaching assignment has brought with it the responsibility for selecting an appropriate text for student use. In preparing this work, our objective has been to present the principles of control in a clear, direct, and logical manner. We have attempted throughout to present these principles in sufficient detail for the student whose experience in the industry may be somewhat limited.

Not suprisingly, a wealth of information about control has been available for some time, both in books and in periodicals. However, until recently, most of it has been written primarily for the practicing professional, not for the student. The amount addressed to students—the professionals of the future—has been entirely insufficient. Many educators have found it necessary to rely on these materials, even though they were not prepared primarily for student use. Valuable as they have been to the professional audience, these materials have been of limited use in the classroom. Particular articles from periodicals and certain chapters from books have been useful, especially when presented by an able instructor, but their use has tended to leave gaps, many of which have been filled chiefly by lecture—not always an entirely successful approach with students.

There has clearly been a need for a text—one that would present the principles of control in a cogent manner, and would simultaneously instill in the student an awareness of the increasing need for controls in this highly diversified industry. In our efforts to fill this need, we have tried always to keep in mind that any discussion of principles and theory must be grounded in practical, everyday terms whenever possible. To attempt such a text without this view would be to risk leaving the student ill-prepared to face the realities of the complex foodservice industry.

With these ends in mind, we have designed and written the text in four parts. Part One is a general introduction to the subjects of cost, sales, and control, the study of which will provide the student with necessary background information for mastering the topics covered in the remaining three parts: food control, beverage control, and labor control. Part One is written to be congruent with each of the other parts. Thus, the book can be used in its entirety as the text for a single course in food, beverage, and labor controls. Alternatively, use of Part One, and one or more of the other parts, results in suitable text for schools with some or all of the topics in two or three separate courses.

Over the years, changes in the role of women in the workforce have occasioned changes in the language, especially in the use of the pronouns "he" and "she." Today, everyone knows that managers, food controllers, employees, and customers may be either male or female, and this can present problems for writers. Some choose to use the term "he/she" to solve the problem. We prefer to alternate "he" and "she" through the text to indicate that the job title cited may be held by a man or woman.

Finally, the techniques and procedures illustrated in this text are intended to serve as examples of the wide range of those used in industry. We do not intend to imply that these are the only techniques and procedures used, nor do we mean to suggest that they are appropriate in all situations. They are merely examples. Experienced managers will recognize that techniques and procedures for control must be developed for particular settings and circumstances. We hope that those illustrated in the following chapters will help readers develop appropriate techniques and procedures to meet the control needs of their establishments.

Introduction

THE RUSH HOUR INN

Until two years ago when he purchased the restaurant, Larry Rusher had been a successful salesman of heavy machinery. His annual income was substantial, and he augmented it by investing in some profitable real estate ventures with his brother. However, his job as a salesman required that he travel most of the time, and his feeling that he was a stranger to his own children made him decide to give it up in favor of operating his own business.

On the advice of his brother, he decided to go into the restaurant business, even though he lacked previous experience in the field. After all his years of travel, he felt he knew more about restaurants from the customer's point of view than most restaurateurs. So he began to look around for an appropriate property. Fortunately, he soon found a place just twelve miles from his home, located on a main road on the outskirts of a city of 75,000 people. The building and equipment were only six years old and apparently in fine condition, and the retiring owner was anxious to sell at a very fair price. The owner's books revealed a successful operation, with a net income of approximately $40,000 per year. Larry Rusher decided to buy.

The restaurant contained 100 seats. It was open seven days a week from 6:00 A.M. to 10:00 P.M., and it served a varied menu of standard American fare. Larry felt that he would be able to run it successfully with the dedicated assistance of his wife and a few loyal employees.

In the first year, profits were less than those the previous owner had achieved. After two years, Larry found profits continuing to decline. The restaurant was simply not showing an adequate profit, even though he had increased the volume of business over that of the previous owner. The place was reasonably busy. His customers often complimented him on the food. His employees appeared to be loyal and helpful in every way. However, Larry Rusher found himself operating a popular, but not very profitable, food and beverage business. At the end of the second full year of operation, the income statement prepared by his accountant revealed a profit of $9, 870 before income taxes (see Fig. I.1). It was apparent to Larry, his family, and his accountant, that unless something could be done to improve the profit, continued operation would not be worth the effort required.

THE GRADUATE RESTAURANT

Just a few miles down the road from the Rush Hour Inn. Jim Young owns and operates the Graduate Restaurant. After spending four years in the Air Force, Jim worked for an insurance company for a few years before enrolling in a nearby college to study hotel and restaurant management. His interest in the food and beverage sector of the hospitality industry had grown steadily since his high school days. Still, it took considerable courage for him to give up a fairly promising

FIGURE I.1
The Rush Hour Inn
Income Statement
For the Year Ending December 31, 19XX

Sales		
Food Sales	559,300.00	
Beverage Sales	98,700.00	
Total		658,000.00
Cost of Sales		
Cost of Food Sold	223,720.00	
Cost of Beverages Sold	29,610.00	
Total		253,330.00
Gross Profit on Sales		404,670.00
Controllable Expenses		
Payroll	157,920.00	
Payroll Taxes and Employee Benefits	39,480.00	
Other Controllable Expenses	98,700.00	
Total		296,100.00
Profit Before Occupation Costs		108,570.00
Occupation Costs		65,800.00
Profit Before Depreciation		42,770.00
Depreciation		32,900.00
Profit Before Income Taxes		9,870.00

insurance career to go back to school. He received a degree for his study and then went to work as an assistant manager of a local restaurant. Over a period of several years, he had worked in three food and beverage operations in the area (the Rush Hour Inn among them) before he decided that he was ready to try one on his own. With the help of his family and a local bank, he was able to purchase the Graduate Restaurant, a fairly popular establishment with the same type of menu as the Rush Hour Inn and comparable prices and hours of operation. In fact, the only differences to the casual observer were size and location: the Graduate Restaurant had only fifty seats and was in a somewhat less favorable location.

Under the previous owner, the restaurant had shown a profit of $18,000 per year. But Jim felt sure he could improve that figure over a period of time by applying the principles he had learned in the college's hotel and restaurant management program. The employees he inherited with the restaurant were both loyal and cooperative, and he found them receptive to the changes that he made gradually over the first year of operation. None of the changes were dramatically apparent to the customers, and at the end of the first year, most had not noticed any changes at all. In general, they were as pleased with the establishment as they had been when Jim first took it over, and they continued to return. In addition, newcomers tried the restaurant, liked what they found, and became regular customers. At the end of the first full year of operation, Jim's accountant presented him with an income statement showing $37,375 profit before income taxes (see Fig. I.2).

The statement confirmed Jim's expectations. It proved to him that his management of the operation was effective in the ways he had anticipated. At the end of his first year, he looked to the future with confidence.

A comparison of the two restaurants' statements reveals some very important facts. As one might expect, the Rush Hour Inn, with twice as many seats as the Graduate Restaurant, as well as a comparable menu and comparable prices, shows approximately twice the dollar volume of sales. However, in spite of the apparently favorable sales comparison, the Rush Hour Inn's profit is only a small fraction of the profit generated by the Graduate Restaurant. Since the difference between sales and profit on each income statement is represented by costs of various kinds, we can infer that part of the difficulty with the Rush Hour Inn has something to do with cost. The costs of operation are somehow in more favorable proportion to sales in the Graduate Restaurant. Initially, it is to the nature of these costs, and their relations to sales, that we must look to uncover the differences between the two establishments. It is possible that the costs of operation are not well regulated, or controlled, in the Rush Hour Inn. It is also possible that sales are not well controlled, and that if Larry Rusher is going to increase his profit to a desirable level, he must begin by exercising greater control over the several kinds of operating costs, as well as over sales.

The statement of income from the Graduate Restaurant suggests that Jim Young has kept both costs and sales under control, and, as we shall see, this is critically important to the success of his business. Comparative investigation of the

FIGURE I.2
The Graduate Restaurant
Income Statement
For the Year Ending December 31, 19XX

Sales		
Food Sales	276,250.00	
Beverage Sales	48,750.00	
Total		325,000.00
Cost of Sales		
Cost of Food Sold	96,687.00	
Cost of Beverages Sold	12,188.00	
Total		108,875.00
Gross Profit on Sales		216,125.00
Controllable Expenses		
Payroll	65,000.00	
Payroll Taxes and Employee Benefits	16,250.00	
Other Controllable Expenses	48,750.00	
Total		130,000.00
Profit Before Occupation Costs		86,125.00
Occupation Costs		32,500.00
Profit Before Depreciation		53,625.00
Depreciation		16,250.00
Profit Before Income Taxes		37,375.00

two restaurants would reveal that Jim Young had instituted various controls in the Graduate Restuarant that would be found noticeably absent in Larry Rusher's business. These have enabled Jim to manage his business more effectively. It will be important, therefore, to look closely at the nature and effect of succeeding chapters. However, it will first be useful to define clearly what we mean by the words **cost**, **sales**, and **control**. These will be the subjects of the first two chapters.

Principles of
Food, Beverage,
and Labor
Cost Controls

for Hotels and Restaurants

Fourth Edition

part one

Introduction to Food, Beverage, and Labor Controls

chapter 1

Cost and Sales Concepts

Learning Objectives

After reading and studying this chapter, the student should be able to:

1. Define both cost and sales.
2. Define and distinguish between the various types of costs.
3. Define the cost-to-sales ratio and cite formulas used in its calculation.
4. Perform various calculations using the cost percentage formulas.
5. List and explain factors that cause variations in cost-to-sales relationships.
6. Explain and show the importance of matching costs with sales.

COST CONCEPTS

Definition of Cost

Accountants define a **cost** as a reduction in the value of an asset for the purpose of securing benefit or gain. That definition, while technically correct, is not very useful to a discussion of controls, so we will modify it somewhat.

As we use the term in our discussion of cost control in the food and beverage business, cost will mean *the price to the hotel or restaurant of goods or services when the goods are consumed or the services rendered.* Food and beverage items are consumed when they have been used up, wastefully or otherwise, and are no longer available for the purposes for which they were acquired. Thus, the cost of a piece of meat is incurred when the piece is sold, or thrown away because it has spoiled, or when it has been stolen and is no longer available for the purpose for which it was purchased. The cost of labor is incurred when services are rendered, whether the person rendering the service is paid at that point or at a later date.

The cost of any item may be expressed in a variety of ways—in units of weight, or volume, or total value. The cost of meat, for example, can be expressed as a value per pound or as a value per individual portion. The cost of liquor can be discussed in terms of the cost per bottle, per drink, or per ounce. Labor costs can be expressed in terms of an hourly wage or a weekly wage.

Costs can be divided into several different categories, and it is necessary to distinguish between them.

Fixed and Variable Costs

The terms **fixed** and **variable** are used to distinguish between those costs that have a direct relationship to business volume and those that do not.

Fixed Costs

Fixed costs are those that are normally unaffected by changes in sales volume. They are said to have little direct relationship to the volume of business because they do not change significantly when sales volume increases or decreases. Insurance premiums, real estate taxes, and depreciation on equipment are all examples of fixed costs. Real estate taxes, after all, are set by governmental authorities and are based on government's need for a determined amount of total revenue. The taxes for an individual establishment are based in part on total square footage of assessed property, and they do not vary depending on whether the establishment is empty or full.

All fixed costs change over time, sometimes increasing, sometimes decreasing. However, changes in fixed costs are only indirectly related to changes in business volume. For example, an increase in insurance premiums may be attributable to an insurance company's perception of increased risk accompanying higher volume, but this apparent relationship between volume and cost should be viewed as an indirect. Even though the increase in the insurance cost might be distantly traceable to an increase in volume, the cost of insurance would still be considered fixed. Advertising expense would be another example: larger establishments tend to spend more on advertising because their volume is greater and they have greater numbers of dollars available for the purpose, but their advertising expense is still considered a fixed cost.

The term "fixed" should never be taken to mean static or unchanging, but merely to indicate that any changes that may occur in such costs are related only indirectly or distantly to changes in volume. Sometimes, in fact, changes in fixed costs are wholly unrelated to changes in volume, as with real estate taxes based on square footage. Other examples of costs that are generally considered fixed include repairs and maintenance, rent or occupation costs, most utility costs, and such professional services as accounting.

Variable Costs

Variable costs are clearly related to business volume. As business volume increases, variable costs will increase; as volume decreases, variable costs should decrease, too. The obvious examples of variable costs are food, beverages, and labor. However, there are significant differences between the behavior of food and beverage costs on the one hand, and labor costs on the other.

Food and beverage costs are considered directly variable costs. **Directly variable costs** are those that are directly related to volume of business, such that *every* increase or decrease in volume brings a corresponding increase or decrease in cost. Every time a restaurant sells an order of roast beef, it incurs a cost for the meat sold. Each sale of a bottle of beer at the bar brings about a monetary cost for the beer sold. Total directly variable costs, then, increase or decrease, or at least *should* increase or decrease, in direct proportion to sales volume.

Payroll costs, often referred to as **labor costs**, present an interesting contrast. Restaurant employees may be divided into two categories—first, those whose numbers will remain constant through normal fluctuations in business volume; second, those whose numbers and consequent total costs should logically, and often will, vary with normal changes in volume. The first category includes such personnel as the manager, bookkeeper, chef, and cashier. In terms of the above definition, they are fixed-cost personnel. Their salaries may change, but not as a direct result of changes in business volume. The second category would include serving personnel as the most obvious example. As business volume changes, their numbers and total costs will change appropriately.

Both fixed-cost and variable-cost employees are included in one category on the income statement—"Payroll." Because payroll cost has both the fixed element and the variable element, it is categorized as a **semivariable cost**, meaning that a portion of it should remain constant with changes in business volume, and another portion should not.

It must be noted that each individual establishment must make its own determination of which employees shall be fixed-cost employees and which variable cost. In some specialized cases, it is possible for payroll to consist entirely of either fixed-cost or variable-cost personnel. For example, there are restaurants whose entire staffs work for an hourly wage, and whose working hours and consequent cost are almost wholly related to business volume. Conversely, in some smaller restaurants employees may all be on a regular salary, in which case labor cost would be considered fixed.

Controllable and Noncontrollable Costs

Costs may also be labeled **controllable** and **noncontrollable. Controllable costs** are those that can be changed in the short term. Variable costs are normally controllable. The cost of food or beverages sold can be changed, for example, by varying portion sizes or by varying ingredients, or both, either immediately or when the supply is replenished. The cost of labor can be increased or decreased in the short run by hiring or laying off workers, or by increasing or decreasing working hours or, in some instances, by increasing or decreasing wages.

In addition, certain fixed costs are controllable, including advertising and promotion, utilities, repairs and maintenance, and administrative and general expenses, a category which includes office supplies, postage, and telephone expenses, among others.

By contrast, **noncontrollable costs** are those that cannot be changed in the short term. These are usually fixed costs, and a list of the common ones would include rent, interest on a mortgage, real estate taxes, license fees, and depreciation. Changes in any of these are normally beyond management's immediate power.

Unit and Total Costs

It is important to distinguish between **unit costs** and **total costs.** The units may be food or beverage portions, as in the cost of one steak or one martini, or units of work, as in the hourly rate for an employee.

On the other hand, it is sometimes useful to discuss costs in terms of totals, as in the total cost of all food served in one period,—such as a week or a month, or the total cost of labor for one period. These, of course, are how costs are expressed on the income statement.

Some examples will be useful to illustrate the above. A restaurant cutting steaks from a strip loin purchases one strip loin for $52.50. If all of the strip is consumed in one day, the total cost is $52.50. However, the cost per unit, the steak, will depend on the number of steaks cut from the strip. If fifteen steaks are cut, the unit cost is an average of $3.50. However, each steak will vary in cost because it is not normally possible for a butcher to cut all steaks exactly the same weight. In the food and beverage business we usually deal with **average** unit costs, rather than **actual** unit costs. Nevertheless, it is necessary to know unit costs for purposes of pricing and determining unit profitability. Total costs, including those that appear in income statements, are normally used for broader purposes, including overall relationships between costs and sales, as will be discussed later in this chapter, and for determining overall profitability of operations.

It is significant to note that as business volume changes, the effects on various costs change. Let us assume that a restaurant has a fixed cost for rent of $2,000 per month. If 2,000 customers were served during a period of one month, the average unit rental cost to the restaurant would be $1 for each customer served. If in the succeeding month the number of customers increased to 4,000, the total fixed cost for rent would not change, but the fixed cost per unit (customer) would be reduced from $1.00 to $.50.

The same analysis may be done with variable costs. The variable cost for the steak described above was $3.50 per unit. If 2,000 customers in a given month order steak, the total variable cost would be $7,000 at $3.50 average unit cost per steak. If in the following month 4,000 customers ordered steak, the variable cost per unit (the steak) should remain $3.50, while the total variable cost for 4,000 steaks increases to $14,000.

While the foregoing illustrates behavior with increase in business volume, the same relationships hold true as business volume decreases. Figure 1.1 illustrates the

FIGURE 1.1
Cost Behavior as Business Volume Changes*

	Unit Cost	Total Cost
Fixed Cost	Changes	Does not change
Variable Cost	Does not change	Changes

*It must be noted that not all will agree with this. The point must be made that actual variable costs per unit tend to decrease as volume increases. Labor becomes more productive with greater time utilization, and food purchasing at greater volume can reduce cost.

above behavior of fixed and variable costs per unit and in total. It is important to understand these relationships when dealing with cost-volume-profit analysis and the calculation of break-even points, which are discussed in Chapter 3.

Prime Cost

Prime cost is a term our industry uses to refer to the combined total costs of food and beverages sold, plus payroll, payroll taxes, and employee benefits. These last three, taken together, represent the largest portion of all operating costs for virtually all foodservice operations. Consequently, prime cost is of the greatest interest to most owners and managers because the control of prime cost will play a large part in determining whether or not an establishment meets its financial goals. In this text, we will therefore concentrate on those controllable costs that are most important in determining profit—food cost, beverage cost, and labor cost.

Historical and Planned Costs

Two additional cost concepts are important for a deeper understanding of cost control. First, the definition of cost at the beginning of this chapter carries with it the implication that all costs are **historical**, that is, that they can be documented through such records as invoices, wage rates, and contractual agreements, such as a lease. These documents are used for various purposes, such as establishing unit costs, menu prices, and total wages for past periods. Generally, when we speak of costs we are using the term in this historical sense. However, cost control is a management tool, and it is not sensible for management merely to wait until historical costs for any period are available. Hence, **planning** is always a vital management function, and in order to be effective, a manager must often use historical costs to infer what costs will be or should be for a coming period. Thus, historical costs are necessary for effective planning. Such planning is often called **budgeting,** a topic to be discussed in Chapter 2.

Costs fluctuate considerably in the food and beverage business for several reasons: (1) most food costs change seasonally, depending on supply and demand conditions; (2) inflation has been evident in the United States economy, especially in the past, and (3) legislated minimum wage rates and negotiated labor agreements also affect labor costs over time. Management must somehow keep these anticipated, though not necessarily accurately predictable, changes in mind when planning for future costs. For example, many banquet functions are booked substantially in advance with menus and prices agreed on. Anticipated, yet inexact, changes in cost must be factored into the agreed-on prices if adequate profits are to be derived.

COST TO SALES RATIO: THE COST PERCENTAGE

Raw dollar figures for directly variable and semivariable costs are seldom, if ever, of any particular significance for control purposes. Because these costs vary to some extent with business volume, they become significant only when expressed in relation to that volume with which they vary. We calculate costs in dollars and compare those costs to sales in dollars. This enables us to discuss the relationship between costs and sales, sometimes described as the cost per dollar of sale, but more often as the cost percentage, or the ratio of costs to sales. The formula common to the industry that we will use throughout this book is:

$$\frac{\text{Cost}}{\text{Sales}} = \text{Cost per Dollar of Sale}$$

The division problem implicit in the formula always results in a decimal answer, and any decimal can be converted to a percentage by moving the decimal point two places to the right and adding a % sign. For this reason, the formula is often written as:

$$\frac{\text{Cost}}{\text{Sales}} = \text{Cost \%}$$

This formula can then be extended to show the following relationships:

$$\frac{\text{Food Cost}}{\text{Food Sales}} = \text{Food Cost \%}$$

$$\frac{\text{Beverage Cost}}{\text{Beverage Sales}} = \text{Beverage Cost \%}$$

$$\frac{\text{Labor Cost}}{\text{Total Sales}} = \text{Labor Cost \%}$$

Let us go back to the income statements for the Rush Hour Inn and the Graduate Restaurant in the Introduction. In the case of the Graduate Restaurant, we saw that food costing $96,687 ultimately resulted in sales of $276,250. In order to determine the percentage of sales represented by cost, we divide the cost by the sales, as in the preceding formula, and multiply the resulting decimal answer by 100 in order to convert it to a percentage.

$$\frac{\$96,687}{\$276,250} = .34999 \times 100 = 34.99\%,$$
$$\text{or } 35\%, \text{ rounded off}$$

Thus we learn that the food cost percentage, or the cost-to-sales ratio, in the Graduate Restaurant over the past year has been 35%. This tells us that 35% of the income from food sales over the year has gone to cover the cost of the food sold. Expressed another way, the cost of food sold represents $.35 out of each $1.00 in sales. Following the same formula, we may now take the figures for food costs and food sales from the income statement of the Rush Hour Inn and calculate the food cost percentage, or cost per dollar of sale, for purposes of comparison.

$$\frac{\$223,720}{\$559,300} = .4 \times 100 = 40\%$$

So in the case of the Rush Hour Inn, the food cost per dollar of sale is $.40, and the food cost percentage is 40%.

Cost percentages are useful to management in at least two ways. They provide a means of comparing costs relative to sales for two or more periods of time, and they provide a means of comparing two or more operations. When comparing cost percentages for two or more operations, it is important to note that the comparisons are valid only if the operations are similar. Thus, one could compare two fast-food restaurants with similar products, but one could not compare a French restaurant with a local diner and expect the comparison to be meaningful.

A comparison that will reveal some useful information now can be established for our two restaurants (Fig. 1.2). It is only at this point that the figures can begin to take on some real meaning for us and that we can begin to compare them intelligently. Significantly, we learn that one of the principal differences between the two restaurants lies in the fact that the food cost per dollar of sale is $.05 higher in

FIGURE 1.2
Comparison of Costs and Sales/Rush Hour Inn
and Graduate Restaurant

	Rush Hour Inn	Graduate Restaurant
Food sales	$559,300	$276,250
Cost of food sold	223,720	96,687
Cost per dollar of sale	$.40	$.35
Food cost percentage	40%	35%

one. Expressed another way, we can say that the cost-to-sales ratio for food is 5% higher in the Rush Hour Inn. It is not until we have converted the raw dollar figures to this form that we have any useful way of comparing them.

Because food is a variable cost, it will increase and decrease with sales volume. It would not be possible to establish useful comparisons between operating periods for one restaurant or between comparable restaurants (as in a chain, for example) unless we were to work with the cost percentages, or the costs per dollar of sale. Since cost-control figures in the hospitality industry are most commonly expressed in terms of the cost percentage, we will deal with percentage figures in this text. In addition, because dollar figures in real restaurant operations seldom result in round numbers, we will express our percentages in tenths of one percent, for example, 35.9% or 36.2%. This, too, is common to the hospitality industry and permits a greater degree of accuracy. After all, in the case of the Rush Hour Inn, one tenth of one percent of sales is $559.30, which is a considerable quantity of real dollars.

Using the formula above, it is now possible to establish a chart comparing the two restaurants from the point of view of costs as percentages of sales (see Fig. 1.3). It is both interesting and significant that the cost percentages for the components of prime cost—food, beverages, and labor—are all higher at the Rush Hour Inn than at the Graduate Restaurant. The remaining costs are the same in both establishments when expressed as percentages of sales. These remaining costs are often referred to by food service operators as overhead costs. In this text, we will use the term **overhead** cost to mean all costs other than the prime cost. These are normally all of the fixed costs associated with operating the business.

Sometimes the formula Cost/Sales = Cost % is rearranged algebraically to facilitate other calculations—for instance, when a banquet manager has been directed by upper management to ensure that all functions operate at a preestablished food cost percentage, and this manager wants to quote a sales price for a particular menu item, the cost of which is known. The calculation of sales price is simplified if the formula is rearranged in the form Cost/Cost % = Sales (or Sales Price). If preestablished cost percentage were 30.0%, and the food cost for the item were $3.60, the appropriate sales price would be $12.00, as illustrated below.

FIGURE 1.3
Comparison of Cost Percentages/Rush Hour Inn and Graduate Restaurant

	Rush Hour Inn	Graduate Restaurant
Food cost as a % of food sales	40.0%	35.0%
Beverage cost as a % of beverage sales	30.0%	25.0%
Combined food and beverage costs as a % of total sales	38.5%	33.5%
Payroll, payroll taxes, and employee benefits as a % of sales	30.0%	25.0%
Overhead as a % of sales	30.0%	30.0%

$$\frac{\$3.60}{0.3} = \$12.00$$

In another instance, consider this banquet manager dealing with a group that is willing to spend $15.00 per person for a banquet, and the same preestablished 30.0% cost percentage is to apply. Calculation of the maximum permissible cost per person is facilitated by arranging the formula as Sales (or Sales Price) multiplied by Cost %, so the cost per person can be calculated at $4.50, as illustrated:

$$\$15.00 \times 0.3 = \$4.50$$

In summary, the so-called cost percentage formula is found and used in any one of three possible forms:

$$\frac{\text{Cost}}{\text{Sales}} = \text{Cost \%}$$

$$\frac{\text{Cost}}{\text{Cost \%}} = \text{Sales}$$

$$\text{Sales} \times \text{Cost \%} = \text{Cost}$$

The foregoing has assumed that costs are stable for prices quoted. However, it is often necessary to quote prices for functions to be held some months in the future. To do so with a greater degree of accuracy, one should consider both seasonal fluctuations in costs and inflation rates. For example, the price of most shellfish is highest in New England during the winter months when the catch is smallest, and this fact should be taken into account when quoting prices in July for a function to be held in January. Moreover, in times of inflation, food costs increase at various rates. These can frequently be approximated by management from published information and should be taken into account when quoting future sales prices. One possible example would be the case of an establishment quoting a banquet price for a date six months in the future when the current rate of inflation is 10% on an annual basis. If the current food cost for the function is calculated to be $4.00, the manager could be reasonably sure that the cost would be somewhat higher in six months. While it is not possible to predict the future cost with perfect accuracy, it is possible to approximate it. One simple way would be to assume that one half of the annual rate would apply to the first six months of the upcoming year, and thus to use 5% (one half of 10%) as the approximate future cost, which in this case would be $4.20. Assuming a preestablished food cost percentage of 30%, sales price would be increased from $13.33 to $14.00, as illustrated here:

$$\frac{\$4.00}{0.3} = \$13.33 \text{ versus } \frac{\$4.20}{0.3} = \$14.00$$

Mathematicians would immediately recognize that this procedure is less than wholly accurate. However, it does offer a simple system for taking inflation into some account, which is preferable to ignoring it.

INDUSTRYWIDE VARIATIONS IN COSTS

As percentage of sales, the costs for food and beverage operations vary considerably. Some of the factors contributing to these variations would type of service, location, price structure, and type of menu.

In very broad terms, there are two types of restaurants:

- Those that operate at a low margin of profit per item served and depend on a relatively high volume of business to make a profit.
- Those that operate at a relatively high margin of profit per item and therefore do not need to rely on such a high volume of business in order to show a profit.

It is apparent that if the two were to have any menu items in common, the menu price would tend to be lower in restaurants of the first category.

The following examples of the cost structures of hypothetical restaurants in each of these two categories are intended to serve only as illustrations of relative costs. The examples should not be taken to imply either that these are standards for the industry or that any particular restaurant should have the illustrated cost structure. The cost structure for each individual restaurant must be determined for that restaurant alone, the obvious point being that as percentages of sales, costs must always total less than 100.0% if the operation is to be profitable.

Restaurants that depend principally on convenience foods—the so-called fast-food operations—are generally in the first (low margin) category above. Because of relatively lower menu prices, the food cost percentages in such establishments tend to be higher. Because they are often able to operate with less highly skilled, highly paid personnel, and often with fewer personnel, they are able to offset the high food cost percentage with a low labor cost. A typical cost analysis for such a restaurant might be as seen in Figure 1.4.

FIGURE 1.4
Cost Analysis/Typical Low-Margin Restaurant

Cost of food and beverages	40.0%
Labor cost, including payroll, payroll taxes, and employee benefits	20.0%
Other controllable and noncontrollable costs	30.0%
Profit before income taxes	10.0%
Total	100.0%

FIGURE 1.5
Cost Analysis/Typical High-Margin Restaurant

Cost of food and beverages	25.0%
Labor cost, including payroll, payroll taxes, and employee benefits	35.0%
Other controllable and noncontrollable costs	30.0%
Profit before income taxes	10.0%
Total	100.0%

Restaurants in the second (high margin) category tend to depend less on convenience foods and to cater to customers who are looking for fresh foods, often prepared gourmet-style, and more service. This type of food preparation and service usually requires a greater number of personnel who are more highly skilled and often better paid. This tends to keep the cost of labor higher than in the first example, but the food cost percentage in such establishments will tend to be lower, partly because of higher menu prices. An analysis of the costs for such a restaurant might resemble those in Figure 1.5.

It is important to note that operations in the first category require greater numbers of customers to achieve a given dollar volume of sales. In the second example, partly because of higher menu prices, fewer customers are required to reach a given dollar volume. In general, it is possible to achieve a profit with fewer customers if menu prices are high.

In the two examples cited above, profit as a percentage of sales is shown at 10.0%. We must emphasize that these figures are not to be taken as industry standards, or even as necessarily desirable standards. Some experts feel that 5.0% profit is desirable, and others feel that a lower percentage of profit will help ensure customer return and lengthen the business life of a restaurant. The percentage of profit for any restaurant must be based on other factors, such as return on investment, the risk of being in business as opposed to other forms of investment, the return one might get in some other business, and a whole range of considerations involving the competition. In the last analysis, cost and profit determinations must be made on an individual establishment basis.

Now that we have taken a brief look at the types of costs involved in food and beverage operations and have found that some of them are controllable, it is time to take a closer look at what we mean by control and at what factors must be established before management can institute systems for keeping costs under control. However, before we do so, it will be useful to arrive at a working definition of a word that we have taken for granted thus far: **sales**.

SALES CONCEPTS

The term "sales" is used in a number of ways among professionals in the food service industry. In order for the term to be meaningful, one must be specific about the context in which it is used. It will therefore be useful to define the term and its various uses in the industry.

Monetary Sales Concepts

In general, a **sale** is the revenue resulting from a restaurateur's exchanging his or her products and services for value. We normally think of a sale in monetary terms, although there are other possibilities. The most commonly encountered uses of the term are the following.

Total Dollar Sales:

Total dollar sales is a term used to refer to the total dollar volume of sales in any given time period, such as a week, a month, or a year. For example, total dollar sales for the Rush Hour Inn amounted to $658,000 for the year ending December 31, 19—.

Total Dollar Sales by Category:

Examples of total dollar sales by category are total food sales or total beverage sales, referring to the total dollar volume of sales for all items in one category. By extension, we might see such terms as total steak sales, or total seafood sales, referring to the total dollar volume of sales for all items in those particular categories.

Sales Price:

Sales price refers to the amount charged a customer for each unit sold. The unit may be one item—an appetizer or an entree—or an entire meal, depending on how a restaurant prices its products. The sum of all sales prices charged for all items sold in a given time period will be total dollar sales for that time period.

Average Dollar Sale:

The average dollar sale (sometimes referred to as **average cover**) is determined by dividing total dollar sales by the number of customers. For example, if total dollar sales for a given day in a restaurant were $1,258, and the restaurant had served 183 customers, the average dollar sale would be $6.87. The concept is sometimes expressed as the average check, the average check price, or the average cover, all of which terms tend to be synonymous in our industry. The average dollar sale is used by food service operators for comparative purposes, to identify trends in sales, and to make judgments about the comparative effectiveness of various menus or menu listings, or even of sales promotions.

Sales per Server:

Sales per server is total dollar volume of sales for which a given server has been responsible in a given time period, such as a meal period, a day, or a week. These figures are sometimes used by management to make judgments about the comparative sales effectiveness of individual employees. It might be helpful to be able to identify those servers responsible for the greatest and for the least dollar sales in a given period.

Average Sales per Server:

Average Sales per Serving Person is total dollar sales for an individual server divided by the number of customers served by that individual. This too is a figure used for comparative purposes, and it is usually considered a better indicator of the sales ability of a particular individual because, unlike total sales per serving person, it eliminates differences caused by the fact of different numbers of persons served.

Sales per Seat:

Sales per seat is total dollar sales for a given time period divided by the number of seats in the restaurant. The normal time period used is one year. This figure is most frequently calculated by chain operations in order to compare sales results from one unit to another. In addition, the National Restaurant Association determines this average nationally so that individual operators may compare their results to those of other restaurants.

Nonmonetary Sales Concepts

All of the above sales concepts are related to dollar sales and will be encountered by those entering the food and beverage industry. At the same time, there are a number of nonmonetary sales concepts and terms that should be understood.

Quantity of Items Sold:

Quantity of items sold, often expressed as number sold, refers to the particular number of steaks, or shrimp cocktails, or any other menu item sold in a given time period. This figure is useful in a number of ways. For example, a restaurateur could use number sold to identify those menu items unpopular with customers, in order to eliminate such items from the menu. Additionally, historical records of number of particular items sold help in forecasting likely sales, and such forecasts are useful for controlling purchasing and production. The figure is also used in a variety of ways in controlling inventory and reconciling sales, as we will see in later chapters.

Average Number of Covers:

Cover is a term used in our industry to describe one diner, regardless of the quantity of food he or she consumes. At breakfast, one cover might be an individual consuming a continental breakfast, while another might be someone who ordered a full breakfast of eggs, bacon, toast, and so on. The average number of covers is determined by dividing the total number of customers, or covers, for a given time period by another number. There are several possibilities for that other number, depending on our objective. The following suggest several possibilities.

$$\text{Covers per Hour} = \frac{\text{Total Covers}}{\text{Number of Hours of Operation}}$$

$$\text{Covers per Day} = \frac{\text{Total Covers}}{\text{Number of Days of Operation}}$$

$$\text{Covers per Server} = \frac{\text{Total Covers}}{\text{Number of Servers}}$$

The figures so derived can be of considerable help to management in making such judgments as the suitability of a particular employee schedule or the effectiveness of a particular server.

Seat Turnover:

Seat turnover, most often called simply **turnover** or **turns,** refers to the number of seats occupied during a given period, or the number of customers served during that period divided by the number of seats available. For example, if 150 persons were served luncheon in a dining room with 50 seats, seat turnover would be calculated as 3, obviously meaning that on average, each seat had been used three times during the period. This may be calculated for any given time period, but is most often determined per meal per day.

Sales Mix:

This term is used to describe the relative quantities sold of any menu item compared to other items in the same category. The relative quantities are normally percentages of total unit sales and always total 100%. For example, assume a menu with five entree items represented by the letters A, B, C, D, and E. If total sales for all entree items in a given time period were 8,000—1,000 portions of A; 1,200 of B; 1,800 of C; 2,400 of D; and 1,600 of E—item A represents 12.5% of total unit sales, item B, 15%, item C, 22.5%, item D, 30%, and item E, 20%. That is the sales mix for this establishment, based on historical records.

MATCHING COSTS WITH SALES

For the restaurateur to stay in business profitably, total sales must be greater than total costs. If costs exceed sales for an extended period of time, the restaurateur will confront bankruptcy, or at the very least will have to put additional funds into the business to keep it going. It is the job of the cost controller and manager to be continually aware of the costs of operating the business and to keep them below sales. Cost information is gathered in many operations daily and compared with sales information for that day to determine the ratio of the various types of costs to sales. These ratios are compared to the same ratios from previous periods, and judgments are made as to whether the ratios are satisfactory. If not, remedial steps are taken to bring costs down to the point at which the ratios are satisfactory. It is important that the comparative cost and sales information be from like periods. Customarily, comparisons are made for specific days of the week—Monday last week with Monday this week, for example. Comparisons sometimes are made of like weeks in two different months—for example, the first week in June compared with the first week in July. However, this information may not be valid if there is a normal seasonal fluctuation in business for those two months. Often, last week and this week are compared, so that trends can be established.

In many establishments, cost and sales information is compared only periodically. However, it is obvious that remedial action will be more effective if the cost and sales information is current. Establishments that gather cost and sales information only monthly, quarterly, or annually are oftentimes unable to take effective remedial action, because the information is too old to shed light on current problems.

CHAPTER ESSENTIALS

In this chapter, we defined "cost" as the term is used in the food service industry and showed that all industry-related costs can be viewed from several perspectives, including fixed versus variable costs (with some variable costs being directly variable and others being semivariable), controllable versus noncontrollable costs, total versus unit costs, and historical versus planned or budgeted costs. We explained the term prime cost and showed how the components of the prime cost relate to one another as well as to total sales. We defined the cost-to-sales ratio and provided the formulas by which various calculations are accomplished. We also showed how cost-to-sales ratios may vary from one establishment to another throughout the industry.

We defined sales and illustrated a number of special terms commonly used in the industry to discuss and compare sales, including total volume of dollar sales, total dollar sales by category, sales prices, average dollar sales per customer, per server, and per seat, as well as quantity of items sold, and turnover. Finally, we illustrated the matching principle of accounting as it relates to the foodservice industry: matching costs with sales.

An understanding of these concepts will be necessary to anyone seeking to comprehend the control process in the foodservice industry.

KEY TERMS IN THIS CHAPTER

Cost	Cost per dollar sale
Fixed cost	Overhead
Variable cost	Sale
Directly variable cost	Total dollar sales
Semivariable cost	Sales price
Controllable cost	Average dollar sale
Noncontrollable cost	Sales per serving person
Unit cost	Average sale per serving person
Total cost	Sales per seat
Prime cost	Cover
Historical cost	Covers per hour
Planned cost	Seat turnover
Budgeted cost	Sales mix
Cost percentage	

QUESTIONS AND PROBLEMS

1. Calculate the cost percentages. Express your answers to the nearest tenth of a percent.
    a. Cost $200.00   Sales $500.00
    b. Cost $150.00   Sales $500.00
    c. Cost $178.50   Sales $700.00
    d. Cost $216.80   Sales $800.00
    e. Cost $127.80   Sales $450.00
    f. Cost $610.00   Sales $2,000.00

2. Calculate cost when the cost percentage and sales are given.
    a. Cost % 28.0%   Sales $500.00
    b. Cost % 34.5%   Sales $2,400.00
    c. Cost % 24.8%   Sales $225.00

    d. Cost % 31.6% Sales $1,065.00

    e. Cost % 29.7% Sales $790.00

    f. Cost % 21.2% Sales $4,100.00

3. Calculate sales when cost percentage and cost are given.

    a. Cost % 30.0% Cost $90.00

    b. Cost % 25.0% Cost $500.00

    c. Cost % 33.3% Cost $1,000.00

    d. Cost % 27.3% Cost $1,300.40

    e. Cost % 24.5% Cost $88.20

    f. Cost % 34.8% Cost $1,113.60

4. List three examples of costs in a restaurant that are fixed. Are they controllable? Explain your answers.

5. List three examples of costs in a restaurant that are variable. Are they controllable? Explain your answers.

6. Define:

a. Labor cost	e. Controllable cost
b. Food cost	f. Variable cost
c. Profit	g. Unit cost
d. Beverage cost percentage	h. Prime cost

7. Write a short paragraph illustrating why a comparison of raw costs in two restaurants would not be meaningful, but a comparison of significant cost percentages might be.

8. Present cost for one a la carte steak is $3.20. This cost is 40.0% of the menu sales price.

    a. What is the present sales price?

    b. At an annual inflation rate of 11%, what will this steak cost one year from today?

    c. Using the cost calculated in (b) above, what should the menu sales price be for this item if the cost percentage is to be 38%?

    d. If you were a banquet manager planning a function six months from now, using this item, what unit cost would you plan for?

    e. The banquet manager in (d) above has already calculated that the other items included in this banquet menu will have increased in cost in six months from $2.00 to $2.11. What should the sales price per person be for this banquet if the desired cost percentage is 40%?

9. In the Downtowner Restaurant, total fixed costs for October 19—were $28,422.80. In that month, 14,228 covers were served.

    a. What was fixed cost per cover for October?

    b. Assume that fixed costs will increase by 2% in November. Determine fixed cost per cover if the number of covers decreases by 10% in November.

10. A certain restaurant purchased domestic burgundy wine at $4.20 per bottle. Each bottle contains three liters, the equivalent of 101 ounces. The wine is served in five-ounce glasses, and management allows for one ounce of spillage per three-liter bottle.

    a. What is the average unit cost per drink?

    b. What is the total cost of sixty glasses of wine?

    c. The banquet manager is planning a function for 120 persons for next Friday evening. Each guest will receive one glass of wine. How many bottles should be ordered for the party?

    d. What will be the unit cost of the wine? The total cost?

11. Sales records for luncheon in the Newmarket Restaurant for a recent week were:

        Item A—196
        Item B— 72
        Item C—142
        Item D— 24
        Item E—112
        Item F—224
        Item G—162

    Given this information, calculate sales mix.

12. Calculate the average dollar sale per customer from the following:

    a. Sales: $1,000.00; number of customers: 125.

    b. Sales: $1,300.00; number of customers: 158.

    c. Sales: $8,720.53; number of customers: 976.

13. A certain restaurant served covers and had gross sales for a three-hour period as illustrated in the following table. Determine (a) the average number of covers served per hour per server, and (b) the average sale in dollars per server for the three-hour period.

Server	Covers served	Gross sales per server
A	71	$237.40
B	66	$263.95
C	58	$188.25

14. In Question 13 above:

    a. Calculate the average dollar sale.

    b. Calculate the turnover for the three-hour period if there are sixty-five seats in the restaurant.

15. In Questions 13 and 14 above, if there were 85,629 customers per year and gross sales were $352,783.40:

    a. Calculate average dollar sale per customer.

    b. Calculate sales per seat for the year.

16. The financial records of the Colonial Restaurant reveal the following figures for the year ending December 31, 19XX:

Depreciation	$25,000
Food sales	$375,000
Cost of beverages sold	$30,000
Other controllable expenses	$60,000
Payroll	$130,000
Beverage sales	$125,000
Payroll taxes and employee benefits	$20,000
Cost of food sold	$127,500
Occupancy costs	$55,000

    a. Following the form illustrated in the introductory chapter, prepare an income statement for the business.

    b. Determine the following percentages:

        1. Food cost percent
        2. Labor cost percent (payroll, plus payroll taxes and employee benefits)
        3. Beverage cost percent
        4. Combined food and beverage cost percent
        5. Percentage of profit before income taxes

    c. Assume that the restaurant has seventy-five seats. Determine food sales per seat for the year.

chapter 2

Control

Learning Objectives

After reading and studying this chapter, the student should be able to:

1. Define and illustrate what is meant by control.
2. Pinpoint responsiblity for control in a food and beverage operation.
3. Give examples of various techniques used in food, beverage, and labor control.
4. Define the following terms as used in food, beverage, and labor control:

standards	sales control
procedures	standard costs
standard procedures	quality standards
budget	quantity standards
cost control	

5. Prepare an operating budget.
6. List the steps in the control process.
7. Describe the significance of the cost–benefit ratio in control decisions.

A considerable part of the previous chapter on costs and sales was devoted to developing basic understanding of the meaning of those terms as they relate to the food and beverage industry. This chapter will define control, discuss the relationship of control to costs and sales, and outline how a manager institutes control in an enterprise. While later chapters will go into specific procedures used in food, beverage, and labor control, this chapter will primarily discuss control and the control process in general terms.

Before beginning the discussion, it will be well to point out that control really means controlling people rather than things. Obviously, cans of food do not disappear all by themselves, excess amount of liquor are not used unless a bartender allows it, incorrect hours of work are generally not recorded except to the extent that a paymaster has incorrect information, food is not consumed by rodents unless human beings make that food accessible, revenues will not be missing if patrons are not allowed to leave without paying for what they have consumed. In all these cases, the difficulties that can arise are the result of human action, or lack of it, and if a business is to proceed profitably according to plan, people's actions must be controlled.

The people involved may not be simply the personnel of the food and beverage operation; "people" may include guests and patrons of the establishment, and, in some cases, intruders who may seek to avail themselves of the resources of the establishment without the knowledge and agreement of the management. Thus putting locks on both the front and back doors is one of the most basic control devices to prevent intruders from entering and probably stealing food, beverages, equipment, and even cash while the operation is closed. Another simple control procedure is to locate the cashier near the front door in an effort to prevent customers from leaving without paying their bills. A time clock for employees serves many purposes, one of which is to develop an accurate set of records of the numbers of hours worked by each of the hourly wage employees, and this is another kind of control. Still another good example is the bartender's amount of a particular alcoholic ingredient. Interestingly enough, the concept of control refers to nonhumans too. For example, the institution of various sanitation procedures serves effectively to control infestation by various insects and rodents; loss of food to nonhuman invaders surely constitutes unwarranted additional cost to any restaurant.

DEFINITION OF CONTROL

Control is a process by means of which managers attempt to direct, regulate, and restrain the actions of people in order to achieve desired goals.

An obvious first step is to establish goals for the enterprise. Probably the most common goal for all private enterprises is financial success, although this is by no means the only long-range goal of business. Other goals might relate to preserving the environment, promoting better health among the population, or aiding in the integration of minority groups into national economic life.

To achieve these goals, management must set up any number of subgoals compatible with its long-range plans. These tend to be more specific and usually more immediate in nature. For example, to achieve the goal of preserving the environment, it would be necessary to make rather immediate plans to process or dispose of waste materials in appropriate ways. A full discussion of general business goals and the planning for their achievement is not within the scope of this text. Rather, we will restrict ourselves to a discussion of the control processes employed by managers in the hospitality industry to achieve the goal of profitable operation. This will entail a discussion of how costs and sales are controlled in food and beverage operations—the means employed by foodservice managers to direct, regulate, and restrain the actions of people, both directly and indirectly, in order to keep costs within acceptable bounds, to account for revenues properly, and to make profits.

COST CONTROL

The process whereby managers attempt to regulate costs and guard against excessive costs is known as **cost control**. It is an ongoing process and involves every step in the chain of purchasing, receiving, storing, issuing, and preparing food and beverages for sale, as well as scheduling the personnel involved. Exact methods for cost control will vary from place to place, depending in part on the nature and scope of operation, but the principle behind the varying methods will be constant. The obvious goal is to eliminate excessive costs for food and beverages and labor—to exercise governing power over costs in all areas in order to ensure that the business will operate at a profit.

Two of the principal causes of excessive costs are inefficiency and waste. For example, storing food in refrigerators that are not cold enough, or liquor in bottles that are not tightly closed, will lead to spoilage and hence to excessive cost. So will the preparation of an inedible beef stew or an undrinkable martini. When the stew is thrown into the garbage can or the martini poured down the drain, costs of operation are increased but sales are not. Since profit is essentially the difference between sales and costs, it is apparent that any increase in costs that does not lead to corresponding increases in sales can only have the effect of reducing profits. Clearly, management must take steps to guard against the occurrence of these excessive costs.

SALES CONTROL

While cost control is critically important to the profitable operation of any business, it alone will not ensure profitability. Additional steps must be taken to ensure that all sales result in appropriate income to the business. For example, profits will be adversely affected if a steak listed in the menu for $8.95 is sold to a customer for $7.95, or the cocktail that is supposed to sell for $1.35 is sold for $1.15. Therefore, it is important in most instances to insist that employees record each sale clearly on a check.

In addition, it is useful to check recorded sales against produciton records to ensure that all quantities produced are accounted for. Various methods for ensuring that all portions that have left the kitchen or bar have been recorded as sales on checks will be discussed in Chapter 13, which will include a more thorough treatment of this complex topic.

Although it is unfortunate that not all employees are completely honest, it is a fact of life that must be taken into account in food and beverage operations. Therefore, guest checks are usually numbered to ensure accountability. Sometimes duplicate copies of the checks, clearly identified as duplicates so they are not confused with the originals, are used to reconcile kitchen production with recorded sales. When the checks and duplicates are numbered sequentially, missing numbers can be noted and investigated at once.

RESPONSIBILITY FOR CONTROL

The total responsibility for the operation of any food and beverage enterprise rests ultimately with management. A number of factors, including nature and scope of operations, will determine the extent to which the manager exercises direct control as opposed to delegating responsibility to a subordinate. In general, the larger the operation, the more likely it is that one or more subordinates will supervise and direct control procedures.

For the purpose of this text, the authors will assume the existence of both a food controller and a beverage controller, each of whom will be responsible for the supervision of all control procedures in that single area. By the same token, we will assume that the manager will personally retain direct control over labor cost. While we recognize that this is not the case in all operations, such assumptions do facilitate discussion of the principles of control. Given the variety and number of different types of food and beverage operations in existence, it would be all but impossible to pinpoint just who is responsible for what controls in which type of restaurant, and in our view such a discussion would require considerably more space than it would be worth. The important point to remember is that ultimate responsibility rests with management.

NEED FOR CONTROL

The food and beverage business can be characterized as one that involves raw materials purchased, received, stored, and issued for the purpose of manufacturing products for sale. In these respects, many similarities exist between the food and beverage business and other manufacturing businesses. As an example, let us look at the steps involved in the production of wood furniture.

The furniture manufacturer must determine what kinds of woods are best suited to the types of furniture he or she intends to manufacture and must purchase appropriate numbers of board feet of lumber at favorable prices. When the wood is delivered, the shipment must be checked to ensure that the material delivered is exactly what was ordered. Then it must be moved into appropriate storage facilities, partly to prevent theft and partly to ensure that the characteristics of the wood will not be adversely affected by climate. The wood must then be issued in appropriate amounts for the production of various kinds of tables and chairs. During the manufacturing process, some effort must be made to maintain a balance in the production, so that, for example, one table top is made for each four legs. When the manufacturing process is completed and the furniture is sold to customers, care must be taken to ensure that each sale is properly recorded, that the correct price is charged for each piece of furniture sold and delivered, and that the total dollar value of each sale is collected.

A great number of similarities exist between the manufacturing industries and the food and beverage business. The motel coffee shop, the school cafeteria, the hotel dining room, the resort cocktail lounge—all these have in common with other manufacturing businesses the responsibilities for purchasing, receiving, storing, and issuing raw materials for the production of finished products for sale. In the food and beverage business, we talk about fruits, vegetables, meat, poultry, and a large number of other foods—fresh, frozen, and canned—but these really serve the same purposes in our business that wood serves in the manufacture of furniture. Similarly, we deal with wines, spirits, and a number of other beverages, both alcoholic and nonalcoholic, which constitute the raw materials from which drinks are produced for sale.

These raw materials must be carefully selected, always with the desired final products in mind, and appropriate quantities of each must be ordered to meet expected production needs. In each case, the order for any raw materials should be placed with the vendor who will deliver it at the most favorable price. As food and beverage items are received, they must be checked to see that the restaurant or bar is getting what it pays for. Then the materials must be stored appropriately with respect to temperature and security until needed. When a chef or a head bartender requests materials from storage, the raw food or beverage item must be made available for the production of menu items for sale.

At each stage of operation it is necessary to institute control in order to prevent the kinds of problems mentioned earlier. Control may be accomplished in a variety of ways, and anyone who atttempts to manage a food and beverage operation should be aware of the techniques and devices available for use.

The selection of particular techniques and devices depends on the nature of the difficulty to be controlled and on the situation in which the difficulty exists, as well as on the management style of the individual making the selection. Thus selection of the means of control is not always simple, and the student should be aware of some of the options available.

CONTROL TECHNIQUES

The variety of control techniques available to a manager includes the following:

1. establishing standards
2. establishing procedures
3. training
4. setting examples
5. observing and correcting employee actions
6. requiring records and reports
7. censuring and disciplining employees
8. preparing and following budgets

Establishing Standards

Standards may be defined as rules or measures established for making comparisons and judgments. In business, these standards are set by management and are used for judging the extent to which results meet expectations. Several types of standards set by knowledgeable food and beverage managers are useful in establishing control over operations. It will be important to develop a working understanding of the several kinds of standards before proceeding.

Quality standards refer to the degree of excellence of raw materials, finished products, and, by extension, work. In one sense, establishing quality standards is a grading process. Most food items are graded according to degree of excellence—many of them by the United States Department of Agriculture—and management must establish a standard of quality for each item for purposes of purchasing. Beef, for example, is generally available in a number of different grades for restaurant and insitutional use, and it is important to determine which grade will be used for the preparation of a particular menu item.

Beverage items may also be differentiated by quality. For example, some spirits improve with age, and a twelve-year-old scotch whickey is generally considered to be of a higher qulaity than another that is only eight years old. Management in beverage operations must determine which beverage items are of appropriate quality to ensure customer satisfaction.

Quality standards must also be determined for the work force. In some hotels and fine restaurants, higher degrees of skill are required for the production and service of elaborate menu items than would be necessary in the average roadside diner.

Quantity standards refer to measures of weight, count, or volume. Thus management must establish such quantity standards as portion sizes for menu items and drinks and, in many instances, work output for employees.

The portion size for every food item served must be clearly established. Each shrimp cocktail should contain a predetermined number of shrimp of specified size, and a certain measure of sauce, as well as clearly identified measures of garnishes. An order of soup should be identified as to size of bowl or cup to be used, or the size ladle to be used in dishing it out, and the quantity of garnish to be included. Entree items must be established as being of a certain number of ounces or pieces. Surrounding items such as vegetables should be served with a certain size spoon, as with peas, or be measured by count, as with asparagus spears.

In bar operations, management must establish a standard quantity (in ounces) for each shot of liquor used. In many instances, bars operate with standard drink recipes indicating the quantities of ingredients to be used in preparing a particular drink.

Quantity standards are often important in the control of labor costs as well. It is useful to know when staffing, for example, how many tables or seats a server can cover during a given period, or how many sandwiches a pantry worker can make per hour when planning a luncheon schedule for the staff.

In addition to quality and quantity standards, it is ultimately necessary to determine and set cost standards for operation. Cost standards are usually referred to as standard costs.

A **standard cost** is the agreed-upon cost of goods or service used to measure other costs. Paradoxically, it is simultaneously both realistic and ideal. For example, if one quart of liquor costs $6.40 to purchase, each and every ounce has a real cost of $.20, the standard cost of one ounce. If the entire bottle is used to prepare drinks, each of which contains one ounce, the standard cost of each should be $.20. However, this price is an ideal, since it does not allow for spillage or evaporation, both of which are likely to occur in bar operations. Standard costs are determined in several important ways, each of which will be discussed in detail in succeeding chapters. In the case of labor, these standard costs may be determined by obtaining averages over a period of time. In the case of foods and beverages, they may be determined by actual test, the simplest form of which has been previously illustrated in the discussion of the standard cost of one ounce of liquor.

Standard costs are useful in measuring an operation's effectiveness. As we shall see, comparing standard costs with actual costs can help determine how effectively food and beverage materials and labor resources are being deployed in a business operation. Cost standards are necessary in cost control because they provide a means of comparing what we are doing with what we should be doing.

Establishing Procedures

In addition to establishing standards for quality and quantity, food and beverage managers must establish standard procedures. **Procedures** are the methods employed to prepare a product or perform a job, and **standard procedures** are those that have been established as the correct methods, routines, and techniques for day-to-day operations. As we shall see in later chapters, for management to achieve effective control over food, beverage, and labor costs, the establishment of these standard procedures at every stage of the "manufacturing" process is necessary.

Ordering and purchasing procedures must be standardized to ensure that the raw food and beverage materials are purchased in needed quantities and qualities at favorable prices and at appropriate times. Receiving procedures must be standardized so that all goods received conform in quality, quantity, and cost to those ordered. Standard storing procedures must be put into effect to guard against both spoilage and theft, either of which will lead to excessive costs.

Issuing must be standardized so that food and beverage items will be used in the order they are received, thus preventing spoilage and the resulting excess costs. To further guard against spoilage and theft, issuance must accord with carefully determined production needs. Moreover, records of issues must be maintained in order to calculate a cost per item produced; such costs can then be compared to standard costs to determine the effectiveness of operation.

Production procedures must be standardized for a number of reasons. In order to satisfy customers, any given item must be produced by the same method and with the same ingredients every time it is served. It should also be served in the same quantities each time, partly so that customers will not feel cheated and partly to maintain cost standards.

When standards have been instituted in each of these categories—quality, quantity, and procedure—it then becomes possible to measure each aspect of the business. The day-to-day operating realities can be compared to the standards established, significant variations noted, and changes made to bring products and practices more nearly in line with the standards set. To the extent to which realities compare favorably with the standards set, effective controls exist.

Training

While etablishing standards and standard procedures is highly important, it is really only a first step in the process of control. None of the standards are of any significance unless the employees are aware of them, and they will become aware of such standards only if management is willing to commit itself to training, a process by means of which managers teach employees how work is to be done, given the standards and standard procedures established. If, for example, management has established that hamburgers are to be prepared in four-ounce portions, then those employees who are to produce portions of hamburgers must be made aware of the fact that four ounces is the correct portion size. Moreover, each person must be trained to produce portions of that size at his or her work station, using whatever equipment and supplies are to be provided. Obviously, failure to make all employees aware of the relevant standards and standard procedures established for their work renders the standards useless.

Any food service manager who trains employees would doubtless agree that training is difficult, frustrating, time-consuming, and, in short run, costly. Perhaps that is why a substantial number of poor managers ignore it and simply put new employees to work without devoting any time to demontrating and explaining what they are to do. Sometimes the new employee is introduced to a co-worker who is expected to train the newly hired individual. Occasionally this works reasonably well; more often it does not, frequently because the co-worker is either unwilling or unable to train the new employee. After all, the typical restaurant employee is not hired for his or her ability to train others.

If employees are not suitably trained in the use of the standards and standard procedures, the control aspects of the manager's job become difficult, at best; sometimes control becomes impossible. Further discussion of this topic will be deferred to suitable sections of the text and the chapters on labor control.

Setting Examples

Often, establishing standards and standard procedures is not quite as formal as the foregoing sections might suggest. In many instances, they are actually established informally when the employees in an operation follow the examples set by the manager's overt behavior, responses to questions, and even by the manager's failure to speak or take action in some situation. In general, the behavior of individuals in a group tends to be influenced by the actions, statements, and attitudes of their leaders. Thus by instructing personnel in the particulars of how their jobs are to be done, managers are in effect controlling: since their particular goals are presumable consistent with their long-range business objectives, their instructions reflect the standards and procedures which they expect will lead to those goals. At the same time, the manager's behavior in performing any task will influence the manner in which an employee will perform that same task. If the manager who has occasion to work with employees plating food for the dining room serves excessive portion sizes, employees will be inclined to do the same when the manager is not there. Similarly, if a manager is inclined to wrap up parcels of food to take home for personal use, employees will be so inclined as well. And if the manager observes them doing so and fails to end the practice, the amount of food leaving the premises will usually increase.

It must be noted that any manager must be consistent in setting examples as well as in directing, regulating, and restraining employees and their actions. In far too many cases managers appear not to have long-range and short-range goals clearly in mind as they go about the business of managing, and their examples, actions, directions, and responses to employee quesions do not offer a clear picture to subordinates. Such inconsistency confuses employees and has the effect of breaking down whatever control might otherwise exist.

Observing and Correcting Employee Actions

If management observes a bartender mixing drinks without measuring ingredients and fails to direct the individual to measure quantities carefully then the bartender could reasonably assume that such work was acceptable and the manager would be missing an opportunity to control behavior. Should the manager observe the receiving clerk failing to verify that quantities of meat received agree with the quantity on the invoice and not correct the practice, the employee could not possibly know that his or her performance was unacceptable.

One of the manager's important tasks is to observe the actions of all employees continually as they go about their daily jobs, to judge those actions in the light of what the employees should be doing, and to correct them to the extent necessary at appropriate times.

Requiring Records and Reports

Obviously the manager cannot be in all places at all times to observe employees' actions. The owner/manager of a small operation can observe employee actions to a far greater extent than can the manager of a larger operation consisting of one or more bars and dining rooms seating hundreds of people and employing hundreds of personnel. The larger the establishment, the more likely it is that management observations cannot be direct but must be abstracted and inferred from a variety of records and reports. The variety and extent of these will be discussed in great detail in later chapters. One such report already discussed is the income statement, which summarizes cost and sales information for a particular period and from which can be determined such factors as cost-to-sales ratios of various kinds. If the ratios are acceptable to management, this implies in general terms that the performance of employees has been acceptable during the period covered by the statement. If these ratios are not acceptable, the implication is that the employees have not followed some or all of the standards and standard procedures formally or informally established. The manager may not be able to pinpoint specific problems from such a general report as the income statement; other more specific and more timely reports and records are often required. Some of these may be developed daily, others, weekly and monthly, as will be seen in succeeding chapters. Of significance is that the manager needs timely information to determine whether or not long-range and short-range goals and subgoals are being met. If not, the timeliness affords the opportunity of taking corrective action.

Censuring and Disciplining Employees

Censure and disciplinary action are two commonly employed control techniques. For example, the manager whose financial performance did not compare favorably with plans may have this fact pointed out to him by top management in any number of ways. The possibilities may range from quiet discussion to heated admonition, or from demotion or transfer to termination. On another level, an employee who has been informed about performance standards and who then does not meet these expectations is likely to learn about it from a supervisor or manager. At first, this might be simply called to his attention in an objective and unemotional way, and he could be given an opportunity to improve performance. If that improvement is not forthcoming in a reasonable period, then admonition on a second occasion is likely to be more severe. Most responsible managers would hope that a second such occasion would be the last and would bring about the necessary improvement. However, if it did not, then a manager would find it necessary to take progressively more forceful actions, the last of which would be termination. This should normally be used only if it is simply impossible to control and modify the employee's job performance. After all, if an employee was worth hiring, he should be worth keeping, and all suitable efforts should be made to bring his job performance into line. In addition, a high rate of employee turnover because of excessive firings can be very costly, leading perhaps to such additional costs as classified advertising for new help, increasing rates of unemployment insurance contributions in some states, lower rates of productivity, higher training costs, and others.

On the one hand, it must be understood that the object of censuring and disciplining employees is to change or modify their job performance—to control performance in such a way that the job activity of each employee is consistent with the standards and procedures that management has determined are likely to enhance the firm's goals and objectives. On the other hand, it should be apparent that censure and disciplinary action generally have negative connotations in the minds of employees, most of whom would normally prefer to avoid any such unpleasantness. If certain behavior patterns—those that follow the standards and procedures established by management—lead to positive and pleasant rewards, and others—those that ignore management's standards and procedures—bring the negative and unpleasant rewards of censure and disciplinary action, then most employees will generally prefer to strive toward the former and to avoid the latter. The very fact that employees know that transgressions lead to unpleasantness tends to have the desirable effect of making job activity conform with management's planned standards and procedures.

Preparing and Following Budgets

Perhaps the most common technique for controlling business operations is the use of budgets. A budget is a realistic expression of management's goals and objectives expressed in financial terms. Large businesses establish budgets for specific aspects of operation—such as sales budgets, cash flow budgets, capital equipment budgets, and advertising budgets, as well as others.

Restaurants need many of these budgets too. Capital equipment budgets, for example, are often prepared because of the ongoing need to replace equipment that wears out and purchase new types of equipment that come on the market. Capital equipment is typically very costly, and plans must be made to provide the necessary cash to purchase it. Advertising budgets are established so that expected sales can be generated without excess spending that will either cause the restaurant to lose money or cause a decline in profits.

The most important type of budget a restaurant can prepare is the **operating budget**. Stated in dollar terms, it is a forecast of sales activity and an estimate of costs that will be incurred in the process of generating those sales. By extension, the budget suggests the profit that should result after the costs of producing those sales have been met, and also represents a financial plan for operations for the period it covers. In this text, we will restrict our discussion to the preparation of an operating budget, because it is most closely aligned with the subject of food, beverage, and labor control. For established restaurants, the operating budget is prepared with the help of historical information coupled with anticipated changes in the various categories in the budget and in the business environment as well. Thus, if federal or state legislation will affect wage rates paid to employees in the period covered by the budget in preparation, this information must be used in planning. If the establishment's real estate tax rates have been increased or decreased, this information too should be reflected in the budget. More difficult to deal with, but equally important, are the effects of poor weather conditions on future crops, anticipated shortages of beef due to cattlemen's reduction in herds, and general conditions in the economy that may affect the size of the restaurant's clientele.

In new establishments that do not have previous financial statements, information from a market analysis and from a manager's previous experience provides the best alternative source of data for budget preparation. When no market analysis is available, when the manager is not widely experienced in the food and beverage business, or when both of these are true, budgets are often not prepared at all, and management misses an opportunity to employ one of the most useful of all control techniques.

PREPARING THE OPERATING BUDGET

As previously stated, the operating budget is normally prepared using historical information from previous budgets and other financial records. This information, together with anticipated changes in sales and costs, provides the data needed to prepare the operating budget for the coming period. Operating budgets can be prepared for any period of time—a day, a week, a month, a quarter of a year, six months, or a full year. Typically, the yearly budget is prepared first and then broken down into smaller time periods. Time periods will not reflect the same sales and costs because of the seasonality of the restaurant business. Thus, for example, if the budget for a restaurant forecasts $400,000 in sales for the year, each quarter would not necessarily forecast sales of $100,000. The first and fourth quarters may be the busy time for the restaurant and the second and third the slowest. So the restaurant may forecast $125,000 in sales for the first and fourth quarters and only $75,000 in sales for each of the second and third quarters. In addition, the restaurant might forecast sizable profits for the busy quarters and break-even for the slow quarters.

The following illustration of budget preparation is a **static budget**. That is, it is a budget prepared assuming only one given level of business activity for the year (i.e., $400,000 in sales). One must recognize, however, that budget projections are often not correct. Sales levels can be higher or lower than projections because managers and people who prepare budgets often are not very good at seeing into the future, or they do not take all of the information at hand into account when preparing the budget. A new office building down the street may generate additional luncheon business not anticipated, or planned advertising may bring in additional customers; conversely, road construction out front may cause business to drop off for a period of time, or a factory down the road may close and cause a loss in business. To counteract such possibilities, managers often prepare budgets for different levels of business activity. These are called **flexible budgets** and are prepared for business volume above and below the expected sales level. When sales levels appear to have changed from expectations, management is prepared with a new set of budgeted cost figures for that sales level.

To illustrate the preparation of a budget, let us use as the example the Graduate Restaurant described in the Introduction. The income statement and relevant percentages are reproduced in Figure 2.1.

FIGURE 2.1
The Graduate Restaurant Income Statement For the Year Ending December 31, 19XX

			Percentages of Sales
Sales			
Food sales	$276,250		85%
Beverage sales	48,750		15%
Total		$325,000	100%
Cost of sales			
Cost of food sold	$ 96,687		35% (of food sales)
Cost of beverage	12,188		25% (of bev. sales)
Total		$108,875	35.5% (of total sales)
Gross profit on sales		$216,125	66.5%
Controllable expenses			
Payroll	$ 65,000		20%
Payroll taxes, etc.	16,250		5% (25% of payroll)
Other controllable expenses	48,750		15%
Total		$130,000	40%
Profit before occupancy costs		$ 86,125	26.5%
Occupancy costs		$ 32,500	10%
Profit before depreciation		$ 53,625	16.5%
Depreciation		$ 16,250	5%
Profit before income tax		$ 37,375	11.5%

Previous discussion has also distinguished between controllable and noncontrollable costs, and between fixed and variable costs. To prepare an operating budget, it is necessary to determine which categories of expenses are fixed and which are variable. Each restaurant must make its own determination. For purposes of this illustration the following assumptions will be made.

Fixed costs	
Depreciation	$ 16,250
Occupancy costs	32,500
Other controllable costs	48,750
Fixed labor	39,000 (60% of 65,000 labor costs)*
Payroll taxes on fixed labor	9,750 (25% of 39,000)
Total fixed costs	$146,250
Variable costs	
Cost of food	35% of food sales
Cost of beverage	25% of beverage sales
Payroll costs	9.4% of food sales**
Payroll taxes	25% of variable payroll

* Payroll is a semivariable cost, so it must be broken down into its fixed and variable components. The illustration has assumed that 60% of the total payroll cost is fixed and that the remainder is variable.

** Given total payroll cost of $65,000 and assuming that 60% of this is for fixed labor, the balance of 40% is for variable labor. As a dollar figure, this is $26,000 (40% of $65,000). As a percentage of food sales, this $26,000 is 9.4%. This is done on the assumption that in this particular restaurant, increases or decreases in labor cost are the result of increases or decreases in food sales volume, not beverage sales volume.

It is now possible to begin preparation of the budget for the Graduate Restaurant for the coming fiscal year. The initial step in this process is to examine sales figures from the recent past to note any trends that may be evident. In some establishments, such examination of sales records might reveal regular increases in sales from year to year; in others, decreases might be evident; in still others, changes from year to year might show no discernible pattern. In any case, it is the job of the owner or manager to analyze past sales performance and to identify reasons for that performance. Information proceeding from such analysis will be of great value in projecting sales levels for the period to be covered by the budget.

The next step in the budgeting process would be to look at the external climate surrounding the business and assess those factors that may affect sales volume in the coming year. Such factors would probably include general economic conditions in the nation and in the immediate geographical area; population changes; changes that could affect transportation to the establishment, including new highways, bus routes, and so on; and any number of others.

Another important step is to review the operation's internal conditions, planned changes in which will affect sales volume. For example, any plans to increase or decrease menu prices will clearly affect sales volume, and the impact of such changes must be clearly assessed. So must such varied possibilities as anticipated changes in the number of seats in the restaurant, in the items listed in the menu, and in levels of advertising.

After investigating sales as discussed above, the next logical procedure is to determine the nature and extent of changes in cost levels, some of which will be dictated by anticipated changes in sales volume, and others of which will occur independent of volume changes. Variable costs are sure to be affected by changes in volume but may also be affected by other factors. Increased sales volume may necessitate hiring additional servers, but a union labor contract may include a new hourly wage figure for all employees. There are many other possibilities for cost increases, including a clause in a lease dictating a rent increase effective on a particular date, higher utility rates, or anticipated increases in the costs of particular foods. Any anticipated changes in cost and sales levels must be considered and factored into the new budget.

Let us assume that the management of the Graduate Restaurant has carefully examined past cost and sales figures and has assessed the impact of various anticipated changes in both internal and external conditions on those figures. The following changes are anticipated:

1. Both food and beverage sales are expected to increase by 10%.
2. Fixed payroll costs will increase by 8%.
3. Variable payroll will continue to be the same percentage of sales.
4. Payroll taxes will increase proportionately with the increase in payroll costs.
5. Other controllable costs will increase by $6,500.

6. Occupancy costs will increase by $2,000.
7. Food and beverage cost percentages will remain the same.

Based on these anticipated changes, the budget for the Graduate Restaurant for the coming fiscal year would be as illustrated in Figure 2.2. Assuming that projections for sales, costs, and profits are were acceptable to management, the budget would be adopted as the plan of action for the covered period. If the projections were unacceptable, management would reexamine both the assumptions on which the budget was based and the budget figures themselves. Such reexamination might suggest the desirability of additional changes affecting sales or costs that might lead to more acceptable results. Before the adoption of the budget, the effects of such potential changes could be tested by means of the techniques of cost/volume/profit analysis, to be discussed in the following chapter.

Once an acceptable budget is adopted for an upcoming period, it becomes a standard against which operating performance is measured as the fiscal year progresses. To use it effectively for this purpose, management often apportions sales and cost figures into quarterly or monthly segments, which serve as standards

FIGURE 2.2
The Graduate Restaurant Operating Budget For Fiscal Year Ending December 31, 19XX

Sales	Previous Year	Change	Upcoming Year
Food sales	$276,250	+ $27,625	303,875
Beverage sales	48,750	+ 4,875	53,625
Total	325,000	+ 32,500	357,500
Cost of Sales			
Cost of food sold	$ 96,687	+ $ 9,669	$106,356
Cost of beverages sold	12,188	+ 1,218	13,406
Total	108,875	+ 10,887	119,762
Gross profit	216,125		237,738
Controllable expenses			
Fixed payroll	39,000	+ 3,120	42,120
Variable payroll	26,000	+ 2,600	28,600
Total payroll	65,000	+ 5,720	70,720
Payroll taxes	16,250	+ 1,430	17,680
Other controllable expenses	48,750	+ 6,500	55,250
Total	130,000	+ 13,650	143,650
Profit before occupancy costs	86,125		94,088
Occupation costs	32,500	+ 2,000	34,500
Profit before depreciation	53,625		59,588
Depreciation	16,250		16,250
Profit before income taxes	$ 37,375		$ 43,338

or targets for the covered periods. If cost and sales figures do not meet expectations as identified in the budget for a given period, investigation into the causes of such differences will be made. Once the causes have been identified, it is possible and desirable to take remedial actions to ensure better performance in the next operating period. If, for example, sales do not increase to the extent predicted, it will be necessary to adjust costs so that desired profit levels may be maintained. If payroll or any other controllable cost is greater than the amount budgeted, then management will attempt to determine the reasons for the excessive amounts and take appropriate measures to control future costs at more suitable levels.

THE CONTROL PROCESS

From the foregoing discussion of the techniques of control, it is possible to generalize four basic steps that lie at the heart of the control process:

1. Establish standards and standard procedures for operation.
2. Train all individuals to follow established standards and standard procedures.
3. Monitor performance and compare actual performance with established standards.
4. Take appropriate action to correct deviations from standards.*

To illustrate the manner in which the control process follows these steps, let us assume a restaurant whose owner wants to serve the finest food. To reach this goal, the owner must establish those standards and standard procedures that will define the meaning of "the finest." In the case of one menu item—prime sirloin steak—the standard is *prime,* a term that specifies certain identifiable characteristics. The instructions to appropriate employees must reflect the fact that only prime beef is to be purchased for the production of this menu item. Whoever receives beef from the purveyor should check to see that it is the correct quality by examining the meat and checking for the USDA grade stamp on the outside fat. From time to time, the manager must make some observations to see that the meat purchased meets the standards set. This may require either examining raw meat hanging in the refrigerator or sitting down in the dining room and ordering a steak. If the manager is lax, customers will often note the divergence in quality from their past experiences there, and some will undoubtedly complain; others will merely not return. If the manager finds that the beef purchased is not in compliance with the standards set, then some remedial action is called for if the goal of offering the finest food is to be met.

---

* It should be noted that investigation will sometimes reveal that an established standard is unrealistic or inappropriate. In those instances, it will probably be desirable to change the standard.

It is possible to develop a set of analogous circumstances in virtually any other area of the operation where control must be instituted. Wherever control is needed in restaurant operations, it can best be accomplished by means of following the four aforementioned steps.

CONTROL SYSTEMS

A **control system** is the sum of all control techniques and the means by which they are implemented. In the past, such systems were principally based on paper-and-pencil methods and often required difficult and lengthy calculations. In more recent years, sophisticated devices have been introduced to decrease the reliance on paper calculations and records. These have included cash registers that keep records of numbers of portions sold and print out simple reports to management at the end of a day. However, in some establishments, even these are now being replaced by elaborate, extraordinarily useful computers and computer programs designed to assist management in maintaining control over operations in ways that were not previously possible. For example, one popular computer system, when properly used, makes it impossible for servers to obtain food from a kitchen or drinks from a bar without recording those items in computer memory for future reference. Using the data recorded, the computer then prepares an accurate check for each guest and summarizes sales at the end of a day—item sales, average cover, average sale per server, and sales mix, to name but a few of the possibilities.

Today, one cannot discuss control systems for food and beverage operations without taking computers into account. They are integral parts of the control systems in many establishments; in others, they constitute almost the entire control system. Use of computers in food and beverage operations will be treated in detail in Chapter 4.

COST/BENEFIT RATIO

One additional important concept must be introduced before leaving the general subject of control: the **cost/benefit ratio**, or the relationship between the cost incurred in instituting and maintaining a control or control system, and the benefits or savings that the control or control system can generate.

The student can appreciate that all control measures bring some cost to a business, sometimes relatively insignificant, at other times great, and occasionally even prohibitive. A relatively insignificant cost is required to institute the simple control measure of locking the front and back doors at night to prevent burglary. Relocating a cashier's desk to a position judged more suitable for preventing customers from leaving without paying costs somewhat more. Establishing a system of the time clocks presided over by timekeepers is an even greater and ongoing cost. Establishing a control department within the restaurant and hiring a food controller and a beverage controller, with appropriate secretarial and other assistance, together with all the paper, supplies, and equipment these individuals would need, would surely entail large and possibly prohibitive sums of money.

One must remember that the purpose of cost and sales control measures is to guard against excessive costs and to ensure that all sales result in appropriate income. In other words, the business must benefit from the introduction of any control device, procedure, or personnel. For example, if recent telephone bills have reached unwarranted levels because of nonbusiness-related long-distance calls placed on the office telephone, a simple control expenditure for a telephone lock might result in considerable savings. In similar fashion, hiring a cashier to record sales and collect cash would probably go further toward ensuring that sales resulted in income than could a procedure that permitted servers to collect for the food and beverages they served. In each of these cases, as in all examples of incurring cost for purposes of control, the amount of such cost incurred should be exceeded by the benefits derived by the business.

Before instituting any new procedures for control, management must first determine that the anticipated savings will be greater than the cost of the new procedures. Any manager must look critically at the various methods and procedures available for improving control to determine whether their imposition will save more than they cost. If the control procedures cost more than the benefits anticipated, they will eventually weaken the restaurant's financial position. It is usually unwise in business to attempt controls whose cost exceeds their benefits. In its simplest form, this is to say that no one in business should spend a dollar if the expected savings is less than a dollar. This is particularly true with computer systems, which may cost $30,000 or more, depending on the perceived needs of the restaurant and the equipment selected. One would have to be certain that the annualized cost of the system, including supplies, personnel, and maintenance, would be less than the anticipated benefits derived each year.

Other Considerations

Before instituting any control procedure and incurring the consequent dollar costs, one must look at the nonquantifiable effects, beneficial and otherwise. Control systems and procedures generally affect many aspects of the operation, sometime in negative ways not anticipated by management. For example, a system that verifies that all food going from the kitchen to the dining room is appropriately recorded in computer memory may slow down service, reduce seat turnover, and even result in cold food being served to guests. Similarly, the installation of a time clock to develop accurate payroll records might cause resentment among long-time, loyal, and valued employees, some of whom might seek other employment rather than punch a time clock. Thus, in addition to monetary considerations, management should carefully evaluate the nonmonetary effects of instituting any control system or procedure.

CHAPTER ESSENTIALS

In this chapter we established working definitions of the important terms control, cost control, and sales control. We fixed responsibility for control and demonstrated the need for control through all operating phases in a successful enterprise. Eight commonly used control techniques were defined and illustrated. Managers frequently employ one or all of them in implementing the four-step process of control. Particular emphasis was given to the preparation and use of the operating budget as a control technique. Finally, we described the significance of the cost/benefit ratio in determining the extent to which control measures are to be implemented.

KEY TERMS IN THIS CHAPTER

Control	Standard procedures
Cost control	Budget
Sales control	Operating budget
Standards	Static budget
Quality standards	Flexible budget
Quantity standards	Control process
Standard cost	Control systems
Procedures	Cost/benefit ratio

QUESTIONS AND PROBLEMS

1. Using one standard portion of chicken for an example, compare the quality standards one might find in use for that item in a school cafeteria with those one might expect to find in a fine restaurant.

2. How would the quality standards for labor in a fine restaurant compare with those in a school cafeteria? Why?

3. Are censure and discipline the only control techniques that have negative connotations? Why?

4. For purposes of establishing control, the management of a cocktail lounge has directed a bartender, who was formerly permitted to mix drinks without measuring, to use a device that automatically measures quantities poured. What positive and negative effects can this new procedure have on bar operation?

5. From your own experience, cite an instance in which a manager's inconsistency in setting examples or giving directions has led to confusion in day-to-day operations.

6. How can budgets be used as control devices in food and beverage operations?

7. What is the purpose of cost control? Of sales control?

8. Imagine that you are the manager of a fine restaurant and are confronted with the problem of a server who refuses to follow the service standards and techniques established by the owner. It is apparent to you that the server's approach results in faster but sloppy service. Two of the owner's goals are profitability and fine service. Discuss the possible actions that you might take under these conditions to control the employee's behavior and to work toward achieving the owner's goals.

9. A restaurant offers chopped steak as one of the items on the menu, and each cook who prepares it has her own ideas as to what constitutes chopped steak. Using the four steps in the control process as the basis for your response, show how a new manager might eliminate this problem.

10. The manager of a restaurant decides that all employees should be searched before they leave the premises each day because he believes this will reduce the problem of employee theft. Discuss the possible costs and potential benefits the manager should consider before instituting this policy.

11. If the standard cost of a one-ounce drink (excluding mixer) is $.25 and the actual cost averages out to $.27 per drink, calculate the amount of excess cost in thirty-two drinks. How much liquor does that additional cost represent?

12. If the standard cost of a 1½-ounce drink is $.40 and the real cost is $.43, calculate the amount of money wasted in thirty-two drinks. How much liquor does it represent?

13. If the standard cost of a 1¼-ounce drink is $.30 and the real cost is $.35, calculate the additional cost in thirty-two drinks and the amount of the liquor the additional cost represents.

14. Calculate the following standard costs if the liter bottle costs $6.76:

    a. For a 1-ounce drink.

    b. For 1¼-ounce drink.

    c. For a 1½-ounce drink.

15. Define standard procedures in your own words and give two examples from your own experience.

16. Given the following information reflecting the manager's expectations for the coming year's operation of the Market Restaurant, prepare the operating budget for the year, using the illustration provided in this chapter.

    Food sales: $420,000
    Beverage sales: $90,000
    Cost of food: 36.0% of food sales
    Cost of beverages: 24.0% of beverage sales

Variable payroll: 20.0% of food sales
Fixed payroll: $42,000
Payroll taxes and employee benefits: 25.0% of total payroll
Other controllable expenses: $63,000
Depreciation: $25,500
Occupancy costs: $36,000

17. The manager of the Downtown Restaurant has been following an operating budget for the current year; it is reproduced below:

Sales:		
Food sales	$630,000	
Beverage sales	140,000	
Total sales		$770,000
Cost of sales:		
Cost of food sold	$252,000	
Cost of beverages sold	35,000	
Total costs		287,000
Gross profit on sales		$483,000
Controllable expenses:		
Payroll	$173,250	
Payroll taxes and		
employee benefits	45,045	
Other controllable expenses	82,000	
Total controllable expenses	$300,295	$300,295
Profit before occupancy costs		$182,705
Occupancy costs		64,000
Profit before depreciation		118,705
Depreciation		38,500
Profit before income taxes		$ 80,205

For the upcoming year, the following changes are expected:

Food sales will increase by 10%.
Beverage sales will increase by 6%.
Food cost percentage and beverage cost percentage will remain the same.
Fixed payroll—$69,300 for this year—will increase by $8,000.
Variable payroll will be 16% of expected food sales.
Payroll taxes and employee benefits will remain the same percentage of payroll.
Controllable expenses will increase by $12,000.
Occupancy costs will increase by $5,000.
Depreciation will remain the same.

Given these expected changes, prepare the operating budget for the coming year.

18. Referring to Question 17, assume that the prepared operating budget has been adopted. After the first six months of operation, financial records reveal the following:

Food sales have increased by 12% rather than by 10%.

Beverage sales have increased by 5% rather than by 6%.

Food cost percentage is 1% lower than budgeted, but beverage cost percentage is 2% higher.

Variable payroll is 14% of food sales, rather than the expected 16%.

Assuming that the trends evident in the first six months continue for the balance of the year, and that both sales and expenses are equally divided between the two halves of the year, prepare a revision of the budget for the second six-month period.

chapter 3

Cost/Volume/Profit Relationships

Learning Objectives

After reading and studying this chapter, the student should be able to:

Part A

1. Explain the importance of the cost/volume/profit relationship to cost control.
2. Solve problems to determine:

Sales in dollars and units	Contribution rate
Variable costs	Contribution margin
Fixed cost	Variable rate
Profit	Break-even point

Part B

3. Graphically illustrate break-even computation.
4. List and illustrate ways in which the break-even point can be changed.

No discussion of costs, sales, and control would be complete without an understanding of cost/volume/profit relationships. In Part A of this chapter, these relationships are explained. Part B, designed for more advanced study, deals with more complex applications of cost/volume/profit analysis in food and beverage management and control.

PART A

In the Introduction, we pointed out the substantial profit made by the Graduate Restaurant, noting that the cost percentages were in more favorable relation to sales than that of the Rush Hour Inn. We should not assume, however, that good cost-to-sales relationships automatically result in profit for a restaurant or that

FIGURE 3.1
The Graduate Restaurant

Sales	$325,000	100.0%
Cost of sales	108,875	33.5%
Cost of labor	81,250	25.0%
Cost of overhead	97,500	30.0%
Profit	37,375	11.5%

higher or lower cost percentages are necessarily desirable for a given restaurant. Indeed, it is possible that a higher cost percentage (which means lower menu prices or more food given each customer) might result in sufficient additional customers to provide a substantial profit even with high cost percents. Nevertheless, it is obvious that the sum of the cost percents cannot exceed 100% if the operation is to be profitable. It will be useful to examine illustrations from the examples in the Introduction (see Fig. 3.1). At the given level of sales and costs, satisfactory profit has been earned.

It is possible to earn acceptable profit at sales levels other than $325,000 even though prime cost, as percentage of sales, increases. Figure 3.2 illustrates how this may be possible.

Although the cost-to-sales ratios for the components of the prime cost have increased (cost of sales from 35.5% to 40%, and cost of labor from 25% to 30%), a satisfactory profit was still realized, because overhead has accounted for the same number of dollars in both cases. Consequently, as sales volume increases, this number of dollars has represented a smaller percentage of sales.

Now let us hypothesize a decrease in sales in the restaurant, as illustrated in Figure 3.3. In this instance, cost percents for the components of the prime cost were the same as they had been at sales level $325,000. However, the operation shows a loss rather than a profit, because the fixed element for overhead, still $97,500, now accounts for 48.75% of sales dollars, rather than the 30% it represented in Figure 3.1.

The key to understanding the cost/volume/profit relationship lies in understanding that fixed costs exist in an operation regardless of sales volume, and that it is necessary to generate sufficient total volume to cover both fixed and variable costs. This is not say, however, that variable cost percents are to be ignored. In fact,

FIGURE 3.2
The Graduate Restaurant

Sales	$500,000	100.0%
Cost of sales	200,000	40.0%
Cost of labor	150,000	30.0%
Cost of overhead	97,500	19.5%
Profit	52,500	10.5%

FIGURE 3.3
The Graduate Restaurant

Sales	$200,000	100.0%
Cost of sales	67,000	33.5%
Cost of labor	50,000	25.0%
Cost of overhead	97,500	48.75%
Profit (loss)	(14,500)	(7.25%)

if variable cost percentage is high, it may not be possible to generate sufficient volume to cover fixed costs. After all, a dining room can be turned over only a limited number of times in any given meal period. On the other hand, if variable cost percentages are too low, it may not be possible to generate sales volume, simply because potential customers perceive prices as too high for value received and thus dine elsewhere.

THE COST/VOLUME/PROFIT EQUATION

From the foregoing, it should be apparent that some sort of relationships exist among sales, cost of sales, cost of labor, cost of overhead, and profit. In fact, these relationship can be expressed as follows:

$$\text{Sales} = \text{Cost of Sales} + \text{Cost of Labor} + \text{Cost of Overhead} + \text{Profit (or minus Loss)}*$$

Because cost of sales is variable, cost of labor includes both fixed and variable elements, and cost of overhead is fixed, one could shorten and simplify the above equation to:

$$\text{Sales} = \text{Variable Cost} + \text{Fixed Cost} + \text{Profit}$$

This is the basic equation of cost/volume/profit analysis.

By letting the first letters of the terms stand for those terms, this could be written as a formula:

$$S = VC + FC + P$$

For the balance of this work, then

$$S = \text{Sales}$$
$$VC = \text{Variable Cost}$$
$$FC = \text{Fixed Cost}$$
$$P = \text{Profit}$$

---

* The effect on loss will be implicit in all future statements of this formula and will not be restated each time.

In proceeding with the chapter, the reader will do well to keep three points in mind.

1. Within the normal range of restaurant operations, a relationship exists between variable costs and sales that tends to remain relatively constant. That relationship is normally expressed as either a percentage or a decimal and tends to be stable.
2. Fixed costs, on the other hand, tend to account for stable numbers of dollars regardless of dollar sales volume. Consequently, expressed as either a percentage or a decimal, the relationship between fixed costs and sales changes as sales volume increases and decreases.
3. Once acceptable levels are determined for costs, they must be controlled at those levels if the operation is to be profitable.

Before attempting detailed discussion of cost/volume/profit relationships, it will be necessary to introduce and define some important terms, concepts, and abbreviations. These will be illustrated using figures from the income statement for the Graduate Restaurant, because they are now familiar to the student. The figures from the income statement as reproduced in Figure 3.4.

We will first determine total variable cost for the Graduate Restaurant, which consists of cost of food sold, cost of beverage, and the variable portion of the cost of labor (the cost of labor includes both a fixed element and a variable element; see Chapter 2). In the Graduate Restaurant, labor costs are 40% variable and 60% fixed. These figures will be used in the illustration that follows.

By referring to Figure 3.4, one can determine that cost of food sold is $96,687 and cost of beverage sold is $12,188. The variable portion of labor cost will be 40% of total payroll expense (payroll, plus payroll taxes, etc.). Total payroll expense is $81,250, and 40% of that figure is $32,500. By addition, we can determine total variable cost.

Next, we will determine total fixed cost for the restaurant, which will consist of all costs other than the variable costs. From Figure 3.4, these are the fixed portion of the labor cost (60% of $81,250, or $48,750), other controllable expenses ($48,750, coincidentally), occupancy costs ($32,500), and depreciation ($16,250).

Given the above, the basic cost/volume/profit equation for the Graduate Restaurant is:

Sales ($325,000) = Variable Cost $141,375 ($96,687 + $12,188 + $32,500) + Fixed Cost $146,250 ($48,750 + $48,750 + 32,500 + 16,250) + Profit $37,375

or

S ($325,000) = VC ($141,375) + FC ($146,250) + P ($37,375)

FIGURE 3.4
The Graduate Restaurant Income Statement for the Year Ending December 31, 19XX

Sales			Percentages of Sales
Food sales	$276,250		85%
Beverage sales	48,750		15%
Total		$325,000	100%
Cost of sales			
Cost of food sold	$ 96,687		35% (of food sales)
Cost of beverage	12,188		25% (of bev. sales)
Total		$108,875	35.5% (of total sales)
Gross profit on sales		$216,125	66.5%
Controllable expenses			
Payroll	$ 65,000		20%
Payroll taxes, etc.	16,250		5% (25% of payroll)
Other controllable expenses	48,750		15%
Total		$130,000	40%
Profit before occupancy costs		$ 86,125	26.5%
Occupancy costs		$ 32,500	10%
Profit before depreciation		$ 53,625	16.5%
Depreciation		$ 16,250	5%
Profit before income tax		$ 37,375	11.5%

VARIABLE RATE AND CONTRIBUTION RATE

Variable rate and contribution rate are two additional terms that must be defined before discussion and analysis can proceed.

Variable Rate

A **variable rate** is similar to a cost percentage, but it is expressed in decimal form. It is the ratio of variable cost to dollar sales, and is determined by dividing variable cost by sales.

$$\text{Variable Rate} = \frac{\text{Variable Cost}}{\text{Sales}}$$

Variable rate is normally abbreviated as VR, so this can be written

$$VR = \frac{VC}{S}$$

In the example above, variable cost (VC) is $141,375, and sales (S) is $325,000.

Therefore

$$\text{Variable Rate} = \frac{\text{Variable Cost } \$141{,}375}{\text{Sales } \$325{,}000}$$

$$VR = .435$$

This is much the same as saying that 43.5% of the dollar sales is needed to cover the variable costs, or that $.435 of each dollar of sales is required for that purpose.

Contribution Rate

If 43.5% of dollar sales are needed to cover the variable costs, then the remainder of 56.5% is available for other purposes. Those other purposes are meeting fixed costs and providing for profit. Thus $.565 of each dollar of sales is available to contribute to covering fixed costs and providing profit. This percentage (or ratio, or rate) is known as the contribution rate, and is abbreviated as CR. Thus,

$$CR = \text{Contribution Rate}$$

The CR is determined by subtracting the VR from 1:

$$CR = 1 - VR$$

In the case of the Graduate Restaurant, the CR is .565, found by subtracting the VR of .435 from 1.

$$1 - .435 = .565$$

BREAK-EVEN POINT

The student will recognize at once that there can be no profit until all of the fixed costs have been met. If dollar sales volume is insufficient to cover both variable and fixed costs, the business will operate at a loss. If dollar sales are sufficient to cover both variable and fixed costs exactly, but insufficient to provide any profit (i.e., profit is zero), the business is said to be operating at the break-even point, usually abbreviated as BE. Thus,

$$BE = \text{Break-even Point}$$

COST/VOLUME/PROFIT ANALYSIS FOR THE
GRADUATE RESTAURANT

For the Graduate Restaurant, we now have the following figures available:

Sales $325,000
Variable costs $141,375
Fixed costs $146,250
Profit $37,375
Variable rate .435
Contribution rate .565

An additional formula must be introduced at this point:

$$\text{Sales} = \frac{\text{Fixed Cost} + \text{Profit}}{\text{Contribution Rate}}$$

which is abbreviated as

$$S = \frac{FC + P}{CR}$$

To prove that the formula works, we will substitute figures above in this formula, as follows:

$$\$325,000 = \frac{\$146,250 + \$37,375}{.565}$$

or

$$\$325,000 = \$325,000.$$

This formula can be used to determine sales levels required to earn any profit one might choose to put into the equation. For example, one might be interested in determining the break-even point for the Graduate Restaurant, the point at which Profit would be equal to zero dollars. One would simply let P = 0, and solve the equation as follows:

$$S = \frac{FC + P}{CR}$$

$$S = \frac{\$146{,}250 + 0}{.565}$$

$$S = \$258{,}849.56,$$

which we will round off to $258,850.

At that level of sales, variable costs (VC) will be $112,599.75, or 43.5% of sales. We round this off to $112,600. This, added to FC of $146,250, totals $258,850, leaving no profit.

$$S\ (\$258{,}850) = VC\ (\$112{,}600) + FC\ (\$146{,}250) + P\ (0)$$

However, the Graduate Restaurant did not operate at BE. The sales level achieved was $325,000, which is $66,150 beyond BE. While there were no fixed costs to cover beyond BE, each dollar of sale above it does have variable costs associated with it, here found to have been $.435 for each dollar of sale, or .435 VR multiplied by S (sales). If we multiply the dollar sales of $66,150 by VR .435, we find variable costs associated with those sales beyond BE to be $28,775.25, rounded off to $28,755.

$$VC\ (\$28{,}775) = S\ (\$66{,}150) \times VR\ (.435)$$

If the variable cost of $28,775 is subtracted from sales of $66,150, the result ($37,375) is equal to the profit (P) for the period, and is made up of $.565 out of each dollar sale beyond BE.

$$P\ (\$37{,}375) = S\ (\$66{,}160) \times CR\ (.565)$$

It should be stressed that this is true only for sales beyond BE: before reaching BE, there is no profit.

CONTRIBUTION MARGIN

Each dollar of sales, then, may be divided imaginatively into two portions: that which must be used to cover variable costs associated with the item sold and that which remains to cover fixed costs and to provide profit. The dollar amount remaining after variable costs have been subtracted from the sales dollar is defined as the contribution margin, and is abbreviated as CM. Thus

$$CM = \text{Contribution Margin}$$

When sales reach a level sufficient to cover all variable and fixed costs with an additional amount left over, that additional amount is obviously profit. Moreover, since contribution margin is going to cover fixed costs until break-even is reached, after break-even is reached, contribution margin becomes profit.

The importance of contribution margin in food and beverage management cannot be overemphasized. Clearly, any item sold for which variable cost exceeds sales price results immediately in a negative contribution margin, which is an immediate financial loss to the business. A prime sirloin steak with variable cost of $4.00 must be sold for an amount greater than $4.00, or there will be such a loss. Furthermore, in establishing a sales price for the steak, provision must be made for each sale to result in an adequate contribution margin. An adequate contribution margin is one which, when taken with all other contribution margins from all other sales, will be sufficient not only to cover fixed costs of operation but also to provide for an additional amount beyond break-even that will be the desired profit.

Detailed discussion of the techniques for analyzing and evaluating the contribution margin for individual menu items will be found in Chapter 13.

COST CONTROL AND THE COST/VOLUME/PROFIT EQUATION

Earlier in this chapter, we emphasized that for operations to achieve planned profits, cost must be kept under control by means described in Chapter 2. It will be useful now to illustrate what happens to planned profits when costs are not kept under control. For illustration, we will refer to the operating budget for the Graduate Restaurant for the coming year, as developed in Chapter 2 and reproduced in Figure 3.5.

In order to determine the variable rate (VR) for the coming year, we must add the budgeted variable costs for food and beverages ($119,762) and the variable portions of both payroll, and payroll taxes and employee benefits.

In the discussion of the budget for the Graduate Restaurant for the coming year in Chapter 2, it was stated that sales were to increase by 10% and that variable costs would remain the same percentages as before. Therefore, the ratio of variable costs to sales (the variable rate, or VR), calculated as .435 from figures in the income statement earlier in this chapter, is budgeted to remain the same for the coming year. Since this is true, the contribution rate (CR), defined as 1 - VR, will also be the same, or .565. Budgeted fixed costs for the coming year are:

Fixed payroll	$42,120
Fixed payroll taxes and employee benefits	10,530
Other controllable expenses	55,250
Occupancy costs	34,500
Depreciation	16,250
Total fixed costs	$158,650

FIGURE 3.5
The Graduate Restaurant
Operating Budget

Sales		
Food sales	$303,875	
Beverage sales	53,625	
Total sales		$357,500
Cost of sales		
Cost of food sold	106,356	
Cost of beverages sold	13,406	
Total cost		119,762
Gross profit		237,738
Controllable expenses		
Payroll	70,720	
Payroll taxes and employee		
benefits	17,680	
Other controllable expenses	55,250	
Total controllable expenses		143,650
Profit before occupation costs		94,088
Occupation costs		34,500
Profit before depreciation		59,588
Depreciation		16,250
Profit before income taxes		43,338

Assume that the new year has begun under the budget and that the manager fails to control variable costs adequately. Excessive variable costs develop because of this lack of control, largely through inefficiency and waste. Such problems as spoilage of raw materials and poor scheduling of staff are common causes of these excessive costs.

Now assume that these excessive variable costs have had the effect of increasing the variable rate from the .435 to .515, which is to say that the amount needed to cover variable costs has risen from a planned 43.5% of each sales dollar to 51.5%.

We will now use the formula developed earlier in the chapter to determine the sales level required to earn the $43,338 profit if variable rate is .515

$$S = \frac{FC + P}{CR}$$

Substituting in the formula, we find that

$$\text{Sales} = \frac{\$158,650 + \$43,383}{.485\,(1 - .515)}$$

which equals $416,562.98 in dollar sales required, an additional $59,062.89 in sales.

It should be obvious that these additional sales are required to earn the planned profit simply because of the excessive variable costs that have had the effect of unnecessarily increasing the variable rate. The planned profit could have been earned at the sales level of $357,500 if management had done a better job of controlling variable costs. And this could have been done, conceivably, without any change in quality or quantity standards, and without raising prices.

Thus an understanding of cost/volume/profit relationships is central to full comprehension of the problems inherent in controlling food and beverage costs and sales. For example, one must understand that lowering contribution margins will necessitate increasing volume in order to achieve a given target profit. Sometimes the higher volume may not be attainable in a given restaurant, because of seat capacity, or realistic turnover rates, or even the size of the market. On the other hand, higher contribution margins, while requiring fewer customers, may not be an adequate answer because of the need to raise sales prices beyond the capacity or willingness of customers to pay. Some establishments with low menu prices and low contribution margins are very successful because they are able to maintain high volume. Others with similar prices, contribution margins, and volume may be unsuccessful because of their higher fixed costs. There are other food and beverage operations with high contribution margins and low volume, some of which are successful while others are not. The difference is normally to be found in the differences in their fixed costs. Arguably, the ideal restaurant would have high contribution margins, high volume, and low fixed costs.

Once satisfactory levels of costs, sales, and volume are found, it is clearly necessary for management to maintain those levels—to control costs and sales—for the establishment to maintain a suitable degree of profitability.

CHAPTER ESSENTIALS: PART A

In this portion of the chapter, we have shown how an understanding of cost/volume/profit relationships is useful to those who attempt to institute control by illustrating the effect of excessive or uncontrolled costs on profits. We have provided the essential formulas required for cost/volume/profit analysis and illustrated their use. We have defined the terms break-even point, variable rate, contribution rate, and contribution margin. Finally, we have pointed out the necessity for understanding cost/volume/profit relationships.

KEY TERMS: PART A

Cost/volume/profit equation

Variable rate

Contribution rate

Break-even point

Contribution margin

PART B

The foregoing discussion was the briefest introduction possible to the basic concepts of cost/volume/profit relationships. However, there are several additional points that should be treated in an introductory chapter, points that are not critical to the student's comprehension of material in the following chapters but that will round out the student's understanding of these topics. These will be discussed in Part B.

It is important to note the analyses in Part A, as well as those that follow in Part B, are based on certain assumptions that an owner or manager must understand before attempting cost/volume/profit analysis. The assumptions are that:

1. Costs in a particular establishment can be classified as fixed or variable with reasonable accuracy.
2. Variable costs are directly variable, as defined in Chapter 1.
3. Fixed costs are relatively stable and will remain so within the relevant range.
4. Sales prices will remain constant for the period covered by the analysis.
5. The sales mix in the restaurant will remain relatively constant.

To the extent that these assumptions are not correct for a particular establishment, any analysis attempted will be less than accurate. However, even if they are less that wholly correct, the analysis can be useful. For most establishments, the inaccuracies within the normal business volume range do not seriously inhibit the use of such analyses.

To an owner or manager who attempts cost/volume/profit analysis is seeking answers there are many questions: What profit will the establishment earn at a given sales level? What level of sales will be required to earn a given profit? How many sales (or covers) will be required to reach the breakeven point? These questions, and many others like them, always divide into two categories: those solved with dollar formulas, and those solved with unit formulas.

DOLLAR CALCULATIONS

We have established a formula for determining the dollar sales level required to earn any planned or targeted profit, given a dollar amount of fixed cost and an expected variable rate, summarized as

$$S = \frac{FC + P}{1 - VR \text{ (or CR)}} \qquad \text{(Formula \#1)}$$

This formula may also be applied when seeking the break-even point, merely by letting $P = 0$.

Algebraically, this formula may be restated in several ways, such as those listed below, in order to solve for any unknown component.

$$CR = \frac{FC + P}{S} \qquad \text{(Formula \#2)}$$

$$P = (S \times CR) - FC \qquad \text{(Formula \#3)}$$

$$FC = (S \times CR) - P \qquad \text{(Formula \#4)}$$

These formulas have useful applications for restaurateurs. For example, suppose that an owner knows the fixed costs and the anticipated sales level for a given restaurant, has particular profit target in mind, and wants to determine what variable rate must be maintained to achieve the targeted profit. Assume the following figures:

Fixed costs	$160,000
Sales potential	500,000
Profit target	40,000

Using Formula #2, we can determine a projected CR of

$$\frac{FC\ \$160,000 + P\ \$40,000}{S\ \$500,000} = .4\ CR$$

Since CR = 1 − VR, then VR must be .6, which is to say that variable costs may not exceed 60% of the sales dollars at the expected sales level, or that $.60 out of every dollar of sales is the maximum that can be used to cover variable costs.

Using figures selected from those above, we might then use Formula #3 to solve for potential profit in a restaurant with fixed costs of $160,000, sales of $500,000, and a projected variable rate of .6. Thus,

$$(S\ \$500,000. \times CR.4) - \$160,000. = P\ \$40,000.$$

Using Formula #4, solving for FC, we see that

$$(S\ \$500,000 \times CR.4) - P\ \$40,000. = FC\ \$160,000.$$

All of the foregoing problems and discussions of cost/volume/profit relationships have addressed questions of dollars, either dollar costs, dollar sales, or dollar profits. However, there are occasions when owners and managers are interested in determining numbers of sales (covers) or customers required to achieve a given goal. On these occasions, unit calculations are used.

UNIT CALCULATIONS

In general, determining the numbers of sales needed to cover given fixed costs is possible if one also knows average sales price per unit sold and average variable cost per unit. Average sales price per unit may be determined by dividing total dollar sales for a period of time by the number of customers served in the period. This is commonly known as the **average cover**. Average variable cost may be determined by dividing total variable costs by this same number of customers. For example, if a small restaurant recorded sales of $24,000 and variable costs of $15,000 in a period when 3,000 customers had been served, then:

$$\frac{\$24,000 \text{ Sales}}{3,000 \text{ Customers}} = \$8.00 \text{ Average Sale or Cover}$$

Similarly,

$$\frac{\$15,000 \text{ Variable Cost}}{3,000 \text{ Customers}} = \$5.00 \text{ Average Variable Cost}$$

With this information, it is possible to determine average contribution margin (CM), defined previously as average sale minus average variable cost. Thus,

Average sale	$8.00
− Average VC	−5.00
Average CM	$3.00

Before using this figure to complete calculations to determine required unit sales levels, one important limitation on its use must be noted. An establishment with a stable sales mix will gain more reliable data from the ensuing calculations than will one with wide fluctuations in the sales mix. Fluctuations in the sales mix typically cause fluctuations in the variable cost structure, and wide fluctuations may introduce serious distortions.

Mathematically, sales volume required to break even may be calculated by means of the following formula:

$$\text{Unit Sales Required} = \frac{\text{Fixed Costs}}{\text{Contribution Margin/Unit}}$$

For example, suppose that the small restaurant referred to is selling one item only for $8 on the menu and that the variable cost for that item is $5. This particular establishment has total fixed costs to be covered of $9,000. Each time one order of this item is sold, the sale generates a contribution margin (sales price − variable cost) of $3.00. Therefore, in order to cover the $9,000 fixed cost, the restaurant must sell 3,000 units of the item, each producing its $3.00 contribution margin. This may be calculated as follows:

$$\text{Unit Sales Required} = \frac{\text{FC \$9,000}}{\text{CM \$3.00}}$$

$$\text{Unit Sales Required} = 3,000$$

This is further illustrated in Figure 3.6, a graphic representation of the cost/volume/ profit equation, often referred to as break-even analysis. Note that dollar costs and sales are plotted on the vertical axis, while sales volume, or unit sales, are plotted on the horizontal axis. Note the line for fixed cost—a perfectly horizontal line, because fixed costs do not change as sales volume increases or decreases. Next, examine

FIGURE 3.6
Break-even Analysis

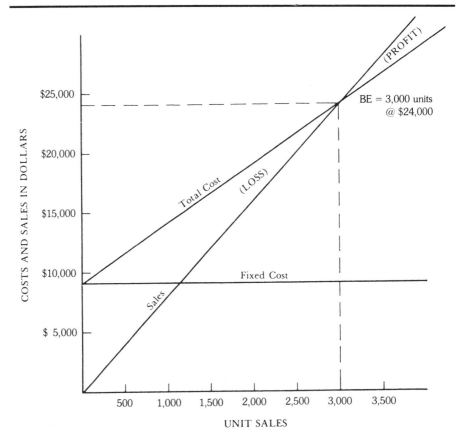

the line for total cost, the sum of all fixed and variable costs at each level of sales volume. At volume level zero (if such a level were possible) there would be no variable costs. Total costs would be the same as fixed costs. As volume increases, variable costs increase accordingly. These are added to fixed costs and result in the total cost line. The sales line begins at zero. As sales volume increases, dollar sales obviously increase. At each sales level, dollar sales are equal to unit sales multiplied by the average sale. If average sale is $8.00, then 1,000 sales are plotted as $8,000 and 3,000 sales are plotted as $24,000.

The point at which the sales line and the total cost line meet is the break-even point, previously described as the point at which all costs are exactly covered by revenue, with neither profit nor loss resulting. In the present case, break-even point occurs at $24,000 in sales, with 3,000 units sold. Sales volume of less than 3,000 units will result in financial loss, while greater sales volume will bring profit. Note that the amount of the loss at each level of sales volume is represented by the space between the total cost and the total sales lines to the left of the break-even point. The amount of profit is described by those same two lines, but to the right of the break-even point.

CALCULATING AVERAGE VARIABLE RATE

It is apparent that food and beverage operations do not offer one product, as in the preceding analysis, but rather have a large number of products with varying sales prices and costs. Consequently, each product's contribution margin is different from that of the other products on the menu. The application of cost/volume/profit analysis to restaurant operations is therefore more complex than has been suggested by the foregoing discussion.

This problem is resolved by establishing an average variable rate for an individual operation, recognizing that if the average rate is too high, an unrealistic or impossible number of customers or unit sales may be required for the operation to be profitable. For example, a hypothetical small restaurant without a liquor license may sell four items with the variable costs and sales prices given in Figure 3.7.

To arrive at an average variable rate, it is first necessary to make some assumptions about the percentage of revenue likely for each of these items during a

FIGURE 3.7

	VC	S	VR
Steak	5.00	8.00	.625
Scallops	3.00	6.00	.5
Chicken	2.00	5.00	.4
Spaghetti	1.00	4.00	.25

given period. If past records of sales are available, this information will be more accurate. If none are available, estimates must be made. For simplicity, we will assume that each of the items will be ordered by 25% of the customers. If that is true, then the relationship between dollar sales for any item and total sales for all items will hold constant, regardless of whether the restaurant has 40, 200, or 300 customers in a given period. To illustrate at the forty-customer level:

> Ten will order steak at total variable cost of $50 and total sales of $80.
>
> Another ten will order scallops at total VC of $30 and total S of $60.
>
> Still another ten will order chicken at total VC of $20, bringing in total dollar S of $50.
>
> The final ten will order spaghetti at total VC of $10, bringing sales up by another $40.
>
> Total VC for all items will be the sum of the above, or $110, while total S will be $230 (see Fig. 3.8).
>
> Since VR equals VC/S in this instance, the calculation is:

$$\frac{\$110 \text{ VC}}{\$230 \text{ S}}, \text{ or a } 47.8\% \text{ average variable rate.}$$

If the total anticipated number of customers were to increase from 40 to 200, and the proportion of persons ordering each item were to remain unchanged, calculations would reveal a total anticipated variable cost of $550 and total anticipated sales of $1,150. These figures also reveal an average variable rate of .478.

Another way of determining average VR, particularly when the specifics of past customer orders are absent, is to determine the percentage of total revenue represented by revenue for each of the items being sold. Thus, if steak has been responsible for $80 in sales out of a total of $230, as in the preceding charts, that revenue is equal to 34.78% of total sales. By following this method, it is possible to determine the proportional share of total sales (PSTS) attributable to each item, as shown in Figure 3.9. The individual variable rate of each item may then be multiplied by the proportional share of total sales (PSTS) represented by each item

FIGURE 3.8

Estimated Unit Sales	Item	Unit VC	Unit SP	Total $ VC	Total $ S
10	Steak	5.00	8.00	50	80
10	Scallops	3.00	6.00	30	60
10	Chicken	2.00	5.00	20	50
10	Spaghetti	1.00	4.00	10	40
40				110	230

FIGURE 3.9

	Total Revenue	PSTS
Steak	$ 80	.3478
Scallops	60	.2609
Chicken	50	.2174
Spaghetti	40	.1739
Variable	$230	

and the products may be added together in order to determine the total average VR (see Fig. 3.10).

At this point, it becomes possible to determine the break-even point, as previously illustrated. For example, if the above restaurant had fixed costs of $64,328, then BE would be:

$$BE = \frac{\$64,328}{1 - .478}$$

Therefore, for this establishment BE = $123,233.72. Sales above that dollar level will be profitable; sales below that dollar level will result in a loss.

Once the break-even point has been calculated, it is simple to determine the number of customers required to reach that break-even point. In Figure 3.8 above, there were 40 customers spending a total of $230.00, so the average check was $230.00 divided by 40, or $5.75.

Next, one would divide BE gross of $123,233.72 by the average of $5.75 to determine that 21,432 customers would be required for the establishment to break even. This can be further broken down into the average number of customers required per month or per week to break even. Management can then determine whether or not the potential market exists to reach the necessary sales level.

CHANGING THE BREAK-EVEN POINT

Unquestionably, there are times when analysis indicates that management's expectations cannot be reached—when the potential market is too small, or the

FIGURE 3.10

	VR		PSTS		Weighted VR
Steak	.625	×	.3478	=	.2174
Scallops	.5	×	.2609	=	.1305
Chicken	.4	×	.2174	=	.0870
Spaghetti	.25	×	.1739	=	.0435
				VR Total Average	.4784

required volume level is beyond the capacity of the restaurant. At such times, management must be prepared to make adjustments, any or all of which will result in a change in the sales required to break even. Essentially, there are three possibilities:

1. Increase menu prices.
2. Reduce variable costs.
3. Increase sales volume.

Figure 3.11 illustrates the effect of adjusting menu prices upward using the information from Figure 3.6. Let us assume that the price of the product was raised

FIGURE 3.11
Break-even Analysis at Increased Menu Price

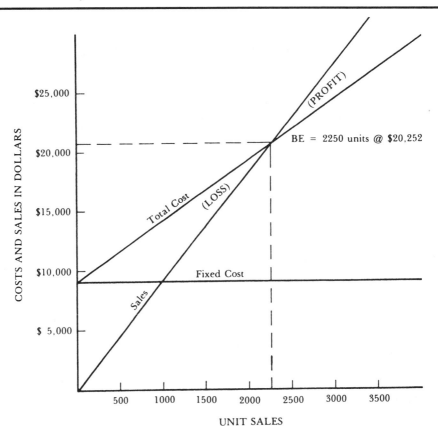

from $8.00 to $9.00. No change is made in fixed costs ($9.000) or in variable cost ($5.00). Break-even is determined as follows:

$$VR = \frac{\$5}{\$9} = .5556$$

$$BE = \frac{\$9,000}{1 - .5556}$$

$$BE = \frac{\$9,000}{.4444}$$

$$BE = \$20,252.03$$

This represents approximately 2,250 customers, a decrease of 750 customers necessary to break even ($20,252.03/$9.00).

Raising prices has the effect of changing the slope of the sales line and shifting the break-even point to the left and downward. If the business is able to maintain its previous unit sales of 3,000 customers, a profit of $3,000 would now be obtained (see Fig. 3.11).

Figure 3.12 illustrates the effect of reducing variable costs. Going back to our original example, if we reduce portion sizes or take other measures to reduce the cost of the portion served by $.50, the new break-even point is calculated as follows:

$$VR = \frac{\$4.50}{\$8} = .5625$$

$$BE = \frac{\$9,000}{1 - .5625}$$

$$BE = \frac{\$9,000}{.4375}$$

$$BE = \$20,571$$

This represents 2,571 customers, a decrease of 429 customers necessary to break even ($20,571/$8,00). Lowering prices has the effect of changing the slope of the total cost line and again shifting the break-even point to the left and downward.

The third alternative, attempting to increase sales volume, is typically accomplished through advertising and other promotional efforts. However, one must note that costs increase as a result of advertising and the break-even point will consequently increase. If the additional volume and profit are not greater than the additional costs, then the restaurant will be in a worse position than it was before advertising.

FIGURE 3.12
Break-even Analysis at Reduced Variable Cost

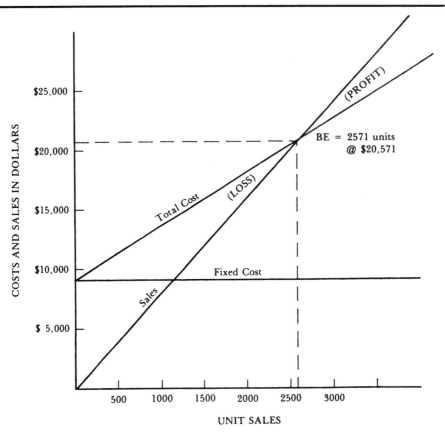

Restaurant managers typically do not attempt just one of these three ways of changing the break-even point. They usually attempt all of them at the same time: raising prices a little, reducing costs somewhat, and undertaking limited advertising, all the while hoping that current customers will not react adversely.

ONE FINAL POINT

A primary objective in any business is to make a profit, not just to break even. Many food and beverage managers treat profit as a fixed cost and include it when determining the break-even point. The amount of profit to be added to fixed costs is a discussion outside the scope of this text and includes such considerations as rate of return on investment capital, desire to build sales volume, and alternative investment opportunities.

CHAPTER ESSENTIALS: PART B

In this portion of the chapter, we have illustrated various dollar calculations, showing how the basic cost/volume/profit equation may be used to solve for any one of several possible unknowns. We have explained several unit calculations, including computation of average sale, average variable cost, and average contribution margin. We have shown how the break-even point may be represented graphically. We have calculated the average variable rate for a restaurant serving a variety of menu items with various costs and sales prices. Finally, we have explained and graphically illustrated three fundamental ways of changing the break-even point to achieve more desirable results.

KEY TERMS: PART B

Average sale or cover

Average variable cost

Average contribution margin

Average variable rate

Unit sales required to break even

Proportional share of total sales (PSTS)

QUESTIONS AND PROBLEMS

1. In your own words, define the following terms:
   a. Break-even point
   b. Contribution margin
   c. Contribution rate
   d. Variable rate
2. Given the following information, find contribution margin:
   a. Average sales price per unit $8.22; average variable cost per unit $3.78.
   b. Average sales price per unit $7.50; average variable rate .36.
   c. Average sales price per unit $6.20; average contribution rate .55.
   d. Average variable cost per unit $4.20; average variable rate .3.
   e. Average variable cost per unit $3.60; average contribution rate .6.

   (From this point on, the use of the term "average" will be eliminated. This will have no effect on the problems or their solutions.
3. Given the following information, find variable rate:
   a. Sales price per unit $9.25; variable cost per unit $3.70.
   b. Total sales $164,328; total variable cost $72,304.32.

    c. Sales price per unit $8.80; contribution margin $5.72.

    d. Sales price per unit $6.37; total fixed costs $62,408; total unit sales 19,364; total profit $12,952.80.

4. Given the following information, find contribution rate:

    a. Sales price per unit $8.50; contribution margin $4.08.

    b. Sales price per unit $7.50; variable cost per unit $4.95.

    c. Total sales $64,726; total variable cost $40,130.12.

    d. Sales price per unit $6.50; profit $13,381.80; total unit sales 18,440; total fixed costs $56,137.

5. Given the following information, find break-even point in dollar sales:

    a. Fixed costs $48,337.80; contribution rate .6.

    b. Variable rate .45; fixed costs $155,410.31.

    c. Variable cost per unit $1.85; sales price per unit $7.40; fixed costs $64,065.60.

6. Given the following information, find break-even point in unit sales:

    a. Fixed costs $113,231.64; contribution margin $2.28.

    b. Sales price per unit $7.22; fixed costs $95,035.68; variable cost per unit $3.98.

    c. Contribution rate .6; sales price per unit $8.20; fixed costs $119,423.16.

7. Given the following information, find dollar sales needed:

    a. Fixed costs $60,000; profit $18,000; sales price per unit $8.00; variable cost per unit $5.

    b. Variable rate .45; profit $21,578.10; fixed costs $58,382.

    c. Sales price per unit $6.60; profit $21,220.00; contribution margin $4.29; fixed costs $56,000.

8. Given the following information, find unit sales needed:

    a. Fixed costs $58,922; profit $9,838; contribution margin $3.82.

    b. Profit $11,603; sales price per unit $7.00; fixed costs $47,197; contribution rate .6.

    c. Variable cost per unit $3.30; profit equal to 18% of $101,000; sales price per unit $6.30; fixed costs $36,609.

    d. Sales price per unit $6.20; fixed cost $59,425.36; variable rate .4; profit $14,000.

9. Given the following information, find fixed costs:

    a. Total sales $104,672; profit $18,000; variable rate .42.

    b. Profit $12,000; unit sales 18.392; variable cost per unit $2,63; sales price per unit $5.34.

    c. Sales price per unit $4.60; profit $24,000; unit sales 26,712; variable rate .35.

    d. Contribution rate .65; sales price per unit $8.40; unit sales 16,549; profit $13,000.

10. Given the following information, find profit:

    a. Fixed costs $82,449.40; total sales $167,543.20; variable cost $55,629.60.

    b. Variable rate .4; unit sales 26,412; fixed costs $93,764.40; sales price per unit $7.60.

    c. Total sales $90,830.66; variable cost per unit $3.64; fixed costs $35,919.70; sales price per unit $6.22.

11. The owner of the Barn Lodge Restaurant estimates that fixed costs for the coming year will be $360,000. Based on his investment in the business, he wants a profit for the year of $120,000. Experience has shown that the average check is $12.00.

    a. If total variable cost is $720,000, what level of dollar sales will be required to earn the target profit?

    b. Given total variable cost and total sales figures above, what variable rate is the owner projecting?

    c. Given the variable rate calculated in (b) above, determine the contribution rate.

    d. Given the contribution rate calculated in (c) above, determine the average contribution margin based on a $12.00 average sale.

    e. At what level of dollar sales will the restaurant break even?

12. The following information is from the records of the Hassle Inn Restaurant:

Sales	$400,000
Cost of sales	140,000
Cost of labor	104,000
Cost of overhead	120,000

Assume that the given cost of labor is apportionable as 30.0% variable and 70.0% fixed.

    a. Calculate profit.

    b. Calculate break-even point in dollar terms.

    c. Calculate required dollar sales level to earn a profit of $50,000.

    d. If variable costs increase by $8,200, what level of dollar sales will be required to earn a profit of $36,000?

    e. If cost of overhead increases by 10%, what level of dollar sales will be required to earn the $36,000 profit?

13. Given the following information, determine break-even point in unit sales volume:

   a. Fixed cost $24,000; contribution margin per unit $3.20.

   b. Fixed cost $37,192; contribution margin per unit $4.91.

   c. Contribution margin per unit $2.27; fixed cost $8,722.48.

14. Given the information below, determine the break-even point in dollar sales volume:

   a. Fixed costs $12,419; variable rate .39.

   b. Average sale $6.25; average variable cost per unit $2.38; fixed cost $26,427.40.

   c. Fixed cost $14,827.

Menu Items	% of Revenue	VR
A	40	.45
B	25	.60
C	35	.50

   d. Fixed cost $21,617.43; contribution rate .443.

15. Determine dollar sales volume needed to achieve each of the following:

   a. Annual profit before taxes of $20,000 in an operation with fixed costs of $35,422 and an average variable rate of .545.

   b. Annual profit before taxes equal to 12% return in invested capital of $200,000 in a restaurant with fixed costs of $47,387 and a contribution rate of .415.

   c. Annual profit before taxes equal to 11% return on invested capital of $250,000 in an operation with fixed costs of $56,725 offering a simple menu of the following items:

Menu Item	% of Return	VR
A	30	.60
B	20	.45
C	35	.35
D	15	.25

16. Determine the unit sales volume needed to achieve each of the following:

   a. Annual profit before taxes of $24,000 in a restaurant with fixed costs of $32,000, an average sale of $7.22, and an average contribution margin of $2.25.

   b. Annual profit before taxes equal to 14% return on invested capital of $300,000 in an establishment with fixed costs of $44,500, an average sale of $8.40, and an average variable rate of .625.

17. In a certain restaurant with fixed costs of $24,000 and a projected average sale of $8, the owner wants to earn profit before taxes equal to a 10% return on $120,000 of invested capital. The owner is projecting 15,000 unit sales for the coming year. What average variable rate should be planned for? At that level, what will be the average contribution margin per sale?

18. a. Given the following information, determine the break-even point in dollar sales volume:

    Fixed cost, $15,000
    Variable cost per unit, $3.00
    Sales price, $5.00

    b. Determine the break-even point for the above establishment if the variable cost per unit is reduced by $1.00.

    c. Determine the break-even point for the establishment in (a) above if the sales price is increased to $9.00 per unit.

19. Following the example provided by Figure 3.6, prepare break-even analysis graphs of the three problems in Question #18 above.

20. The XYZ Restaurant has fixed costs of $36,400 annually. Management operates at an average variable rate of .65. The average check price is $5.00. For the upcoming year, management plans to decrease the variable rate to .6 and at the same time to adjust menu prices upward so that the average check price will be $5.50.

    a. What has the break-even point been in dollar and in unit sales for the year now ending?

    b. What will the break-even point be in the upcoming year in dollar and in unit sales if management makes the changes described above?

    c. Prepare break-even analysis graphs to illustrate both (a) and (b) above.

    d. If management's target profit for the upcoming year is $19,000, how many unit sales will be needed to achieve this goal?

21. A certain restaurant offers a simple menu to the public as follows:

Menu Item	% of Revenue	Variable Rate
A	15	.30
B	20	.35
C	28	.42
D	18	.55
E	19	.48

    Fixed costs total $101,010.

    a. Determine the break-even point in dollar sales.

b. At an average check price of $6.50, determine the break-even point in unit sales.

c. Prepare a break-even analysis graph to illustrate the above.

d. If the management in this operation achieves 17,500 unit sales, how much dollar profit should result?

e. If only 13,000 unit sales are achieved, what will be the amount of the dollar loss?

chapter 4

Electronic Data Processing and Control

Learning Objectives

After reading and studying this chapter, the student should be able to:

1. Outline the development of data processing from its probable beginnings to the present.
2. Define the Key Terms for this chapter.
3. Describe the process by which a computer provides output to management.
4. List the reasons why computers are now just beginning to come into common use in the food service industry
5. List and describe five common categories of programs used in business.
6. List various outputs food service managers require from computers.
7. List the two factors that enable managers to make intelligent selections among alternative systems.

Before proceeding to specific control procedures and techniques, one more important topic must be introduced: electronic data processing (EDP) for control purposes in food and beverage operations. Because various EDP systems—including computer systems, some of which are more sophisticated and complicated than others—are more and more commonly used in hotels and restaurants, it will be increasingly necessary to understand their present and future roles. The authors therefore recommend that any student planning a career in hotels and restaurants take at least some introductory course work in computer operations. This chapter will provide some elementary understanding of control applications of EDP, some historical perspectives, and basic terms, as well as describe computer operations in simple terms and suggest some control applications.

HISTORICAL PERSPECTIVES

Business has used systems and procedures for processing data for several thousand years. Quite possibly the predecessors of today's hoteliers and restaurateurs used early data processing (DP) devices to facilitate bill calculation and help ensure accuracy. Those devices would not have resembled the ones used today, nor could they have performed many of today's sophisticated operations, but technically they were DP equipment. Perhaps the earliest was the abacus of ancient China. The abacus consisted of beads strung on wires within a rectangular frame. A skilled operator could use it to add, subtract, multiply, and divide.

Other devices invented for processing data include the adding machine, invented by Pascal in 1642, and the calculating machine, which Liebnitz developed around 1700. Such devices were operated manually and would be considered quite slow by today's standards. The development of electric motors in the late nineteenth and early twentieth centuries made possible the processing of data with electromechanical devices that worked at considerable speed. Twentieth-century advances in electronics have eliminated the mechanical aspects of data processing. Mechanical equipment for these purposes is now disappearing, and such devices will probably be museum pieces by the end of the twentieth century. (Interestingly, the abacus—the earliest of the devices—was neither mechanized nor electrified, and it is still commonly used in some parts of the world.)

Taking the place of mechanical and electromechanical equipment are electronic devices of varying degrees of complexity. Such devices use electrical impulses transmitted through circuits to perform calculations and otherwise process information, rather than the gears and other moving parts that characterized the earlier equipment. Most people are familiar with the small hand-held calculators commonly used for basic arithmetic as well as for some more complex operations and have seen the various electronic replacements for the mechanical cash registers used in earlier days.

After the Second World War, an entire electronic data processing industry began to develop in the United States. Many of the pioneering organizations in this field were outgrowths of companies that formerly produced electromechanical devices. Soon after the war, business and industry leaders recognized the useful applications of EDP, and company employees at many levels began to work with various EDP systems and devices, many of which were the forerunners of those used today.

COMPUTERS AND THEIR RELATION TO HUMAN WORK

Most people have some basic familiarity with that special class of EDP equipment known as computers. However, computers differ significantly from other classes of EDP equipment in some important technical ways. The development of EDP equipment has enabled information to be processed at speeds billions of times faster than was possible before. The words used to refer to these speeds are nanosecond (the billionth part of a second) and picosecond (the trillionth part of a second). Such speeds enable people to accomplish many complicated tasks that were impractical or even impossible before the advent of this new equipment.

As used today, the term **computer** refers to an EDP device with capabilities far beyond those of any earlier EDP equipment. Computers can store, manipulate, and otherwise process information at incredible speeds without direct human intervention at each step during processing; they can also produce reports based on the stored and processed information. A computer, then, may be defined as a machine that processes data automatically, in a programmable way. For those who have not studied computers formally, some general information about what computers do and the terms used to discuss them will be useful.

Anyone who has been in a restaurant knows that considerable "data" must be processed, particularly by a cashier. A restaurant cashier is a very busy individual who must process guest checks, verify their accuracy, collect money and make change (or process credit card transactions for those who do not pay in cash), and prepare some elementary reports of sales activity. Because the job of cashier is common to most restaurants, an analysis of some aspects of the job can help identify the parts and functions of a computer system.

For purposes of the following discussion, imagine a cashier who is expected to process guest checks accurately and give the manager a daily report of both charge and cash sales. This report is the expected **output** (information retrieved), and is to be produced only with the aid of paper, pencil, adding machine, cash drawer, and credit card imprinter.

To ensure the output's accuracy, the cashier must be certain that the prices charged customers are accurate. Therefore, he must have at his work station information that can be used to check correct menu prices against those recorded by servers. This information could be a small file drawer containing one 3×5 card for each menu item, or a copy of the menu posted on the wall. Either way, the cashier would have some **storage** capability, to retain information that must be available for ready reference.

To produce a report showing total cash and charge sales, the cashier must be provided with information about each individual sale. This is accomplished when each departing guest presents him with a guest check. This information is the **input** used by the cashier.

For the report to be accurate, each individual check must be accurate; the cashier must add up each one to ensure the total is correct and to determine the proper tax to be charged. In other words, he must possess some **arithmetic** ability. Also, he must be able to differentiate between cash and charge sales so that output will be correct. Therefore, he must be able to exercise some **logic** in discriminating the one from the other (see Fig. 4.1).

So far the cashier has been responsible for several capabilities—output, storage, input, arithmetic, and logic. All of these capabilities must be coordinated so

FIGURE 4.1

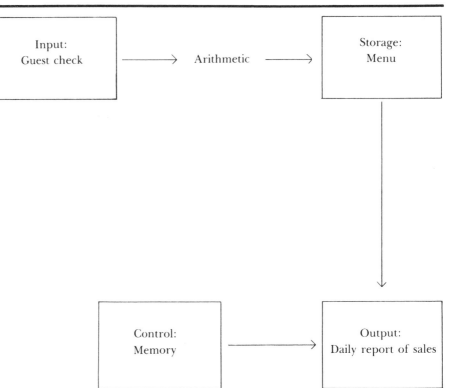

that each is used at the appropriate time. For example, he must know that a guest check must be totaled before the tax is computed, and that these tasks must be completed for all checks before a report can be provided. Somehow these capabilities must be made to work together. Because he understands the job of cashier in this establishment and can efficiently coordinate all the required capabilities, **control** is present.

The manner in which the cashier performs his job provides some insights into the way a computer operates. Just as information must be provided to a cashier, so data must be provided (or input) to the computer. This is usually accomplished by special devices, the most common of which is known as a terminal. **Terminal** is a term used to describe a device for inputting or outputting data. It usually consists of a keyboard and either a printer, a screen, or both. Input data can be stored, manipulated, and retrieved.

The storage, arithmetic, and logic processes for which the cashier is responsible are carried out in a part of the computer commonly referred to as its "brain" but more accurately called a **central processing unit**, or CPU. This highly sophisticated device is composed of several major components that process and otherwise manipulate data, provide storage capacity (or memory), and coordinate and control the computer's internal operation.

If the cashier's job were as simple as described, the development of sophisticated EDP equipment for food service operations would not be necessary. But some aspects of the cashier's work can be very complex. For control purposes, many managers nowadays seek summaries and reports that cashiers can provide in reasonable time only with electronic assistance. Such summaries and reports enable management to monitor operations in a more timely manner than would be possible with manually prepared data, some of which could take hours or even days to calculate.

COMPUTER TERMINOLOGY

The computer field is quite new and is advancing daily. Therefore, not surprisingly there is not always complete agreement on the exact meaning of some terms. This text will attempt to use terms and definitions that have reasonably broad acceptance. These should be sufficient to provide the student with some general understanding of computers.

Several terms have already been used—input, output, storage, logic, arithmetic, control, central processing unit, and terminal. But these alone are not sufficient: some additional terms and concepts must be introduced.

Data Input and Output

Because computers store and process data in the form of electronic signals, an intermediary device is required to translate input data into these signals and to convert output data to human language. Input/output (IO) devices stand between the human user and a computer and assist in performing these functions. A number of I/O terminals are available to the food and beverage industry, including the visual display terminal (VDT), which characteristically consists of a keyboard and some form of visual display screen. As an operator inputs data by means of a keyboard, the data is displayed on the screen so that it can be verified before it is stored. Stored data may subsequently be requested via the keyboard and displayed on this screen. Such output displayed on a screen is called **soft copy**; output produced on paper—more common for management reports—is known as **hard copy**. The output of hard copy requires a special terminal called a line printer. The simultaneous output of hard copy and soft copy is possible in a system that includes both a VDT and a line printer.

Input data must be stored in some way, or it will be lost when a computer is turned off. Data is technically said to be stored on **media**, a general term used to describe such items as magnetic tapes, diskettes, and hard disks, to name the most common. Data so stored can readily be retrieved and thus revised, up-dated, manipulated in a variety of ways, and rendered as a report.

Hardware and Software

Two terms that inevitably come up in any discussion of computers are **hardware** and **software**.

Hardware refers to the visible, tangible elements—processing units, terminals, monitors, disk drives, hard drives, printers, modems, and so on. A computer system is a collection of integrated hardware components, carefully selected to work together to perform some task or tasks. The basic elements of the most common computer systems we see today are the CPU, together with keyboard, monitor, printer, and one or two disk drives.

Software, on the other hand, is a term used broadly to refer to applications programs. An **applications program**, usually referred to simply as a **program**, is a complex set of instructions for a computer, normally written by an expert known as a programmer. A program is designed specifically to direct a computer through an intricate set of steps, the result of which will be the processing of input data in a predictable and productive manner by the individual using the program. At present, computers have no intelligence analagous to human intelligence; they can accomplish nothing without the step-by-step directions contained in programs, all of which have been devised and written by human intelligence. Without appropriate programs, computers are worthless and helpless. Programs tell the system what to do and how to do it. Like data, programs are stored on media.

Computer programs are available from several sources. Some are written by consultants for use by specific companies that choose to avail themselves of the consultants' services, which are usually very expensive. Because of the cost, only the largest organizations can normally take this approach. Another less costly way is to find a software company that has written a package or packages which are industry- or application-specific and buy their product, which many other organizations may also be using. A third approach is to determine one's special needs, then select and purchase off-the-shelf software that may be adapted to the needs of one's organization. The fourth and least expensive method is to purchase so-called generic software and, in effect, to "program" it to accomplish particular goals.

Today, one finds an almost limitless number of specific programs available for computer users in business, and the number seems to grow daily. Many of these fall into particular categories, and these categories are worthy of some discussion.

There are five categories of software commonly used in business: accounting, inventory, word processing, spreadsheets, and data bases.

Accounting

There are numerous and varied accounting programs available to the business user, some quite simple and others so complex that they can meet all the accounting needs of many medium-sized businesses. Some are modular; in other words, one can buy a single module for a small business designed to handle, say, cash receipts journal, cash disbursements journal, payroll journal, and general journal. As the business grows, one might acquire additional modules for specialized journals and ledgers, such as purchase journal, accounts receivable ledger, and accounts payable ledger. Programs such as these are sufficient to meet the accounting needs of most small foodservice establishments.

Inventory

As will become apparent in later chapters, food and beverage operators are well advised to maintain complete, accurate, and up-to-date records of inventory for a number of reasons. There are many basic inventory programs on the market that can readily be adapted for use in food and beverage establishments. Too, there are some now available that have been designed specifically for hotel and restaurant food and beverage inventories. Although more costly than the basic programs, primarily because of the comparatively limited size of the market for such programs, they are well-designed and worthy of examination by operators who can justify their cost.

Word Processing

Perhaps the most common business programs available today, word processing programs can have virtually unlimited use—from handling routine correspondence to producing error-free menus. Word processing programs are software packages designed to enable the user to employ the computer as a typewriter, with additional features to permit visual inspection of written material before it is printed; revision of written material on screen; manipulation of words, sentences and paragraphs; and many, many others, depending on the particular program selected. The writer can save the written material and recall it at will, thus eliminating many laborious hours of repetitive typing.

Spreadsheet

Spreadsheet programs are nearly as common in business today as word processing packages. They have many applications in hotels and restaurants and serve to automate many of the routine business calculations that were formerly done by hand or by calculator. A spreadsheet is a series of numbered vertical columns and numbered horizontal rows, such that each location on the spreadsheet, called a **cell**, can be identified by citing its row number and column number. Figures entered in these cells can be used in various calculations, including addition, subtraction, multiplication, and division, by following instructions provided with the software package. Applications in the hotel and restaurant industries are many and varied. One application, illustrated below in Figure 4.2, is derived from the discussion of budgeting presented in Chapter 2.

The student will note that the spreadsheet is divided into 7 columns and 27 rows, a total of 189 cells. Total sales for the current year, $325,000, appears in the

FIGURE 4.2
The Graduate Restaurant Computer-generated Flexible Budget

	1	2	3	4	5	6	7
			Current Year		%	Forecast (10% increase)	Forecast (12% increase)
1							
2	Sales						
3							
4		Food Sales	$276,250.00			$303,875.00	$309,400.00
5		Beverage Sales	$48,750.00			$53,625.00	$54,600.00
6		Total Sales		$325,000.00	100.0%	$357,500.00	$364,000.00
7							
8							
9	Cost of Sales						
10		Food Cost	$96,687.00		35.0%	$106,355.70	$108,289.44
11		Beverage Cost	$12,188.00		25.0%	$13,406.80	$13,650.56
12		Total Cost		$108,875.00	33.5%	$119,762.50	$121,940.00
13							
14							
15	Gross Profit on Sales			$216,125.00	66.5%	$237,737.50	$242,060.00
16							
17	Controllable Expenses						
18		Fixed Payroll	$39,000.00			$42,120.00	$42,120.00
19		Var Payroll	$26,000.00			$28,600.00	$29,120.00
20		Tx & Benefits	$16,250.00			$17,680.00	$17,810.00
21		Other	$48,750.00			$55,250.00	$55,250.00
22		Total		$130,000.00		$143,650.00	$144,300.00
23	Profit before Occupation Costs			$86,125.00		$94,087.50	$97,760.00
24	Occupation Costs			$32,500.00		$34,500.00	$34,500.00
25	Profit Before Depreciation			$53,625.00		$59,587.50	$63,260.00
26	Depreciation			$16,250.00		$16,250.00	$16,250.00
27	Profit Before Income Taxes			$37,375.00		$43,337.50	$47,010.00

cell identified as row 6, column 4 (r6c4). Similarly, projected gross profit on sales for the coming year, $237,737.50, is to be found in r15c6. Some of the figures in the illustration have been input by the authors—food sales and beverage sales for the current year in cells r4c3 and r5c3, for example. Other figures have been calculated by the computer, such as total sales for the current year in r6c4, using formulas entered by the authors. A list of the formulas used in this spreadsheet appears below in Figure 4.3.

Database

Database programs, although more complex and difficult to use than spreadsheets, are particularly useful for storing, manipulating, up-dating, and retrieving information. In a database, the basic unit for storing data is known as a **file**. Each file is subdivided into smaller units, each of which is known as a **field**. A file contains a finite number of fields, and the length of a field can typically be defined by the user. Each field may be further defined as to type. There are three basic types of fields: **numeric**, containing only numbers, such as Social Security numbers; **date**, containing only records of dates, such as date of birth; and **alpha-numeric**, containing both alphabetical and numeric characters in any combination, such as street addresses.

FIGURE 4.3
Formulas for Worksheet in Figure 4.2

Row	Col	Formula	Row	Col	Formula
4	7	r4c3*1.12	19	6	r6c6*r19c3/r6c4
5	7	r5c3*1.12		7	r6c7*r19c3/r6c4
6	4	sum(r4c3+r5c3)	20	6	sum(r18c6+r19c6)*0.25
	5	r6c4/r6c4		7	r20c3/(r18c3+r19c3)*(r18c7+r19c7)
	6	sum(r4c6+r5c6)	21	6	r21c3+6500
	7	sum(r4c7+r5c7)		7	r21c6
10	5	r10c3/r4c3	22	4	sum(r18c3+r19c3+r20c3+r21c3)
	6	r4c6*r10c5		6	sum(r18:21c6)
	7	r4c7*r10c5		7	sum(r18:21c7)
11	5	r11c3/r5c3	23	4	r15c4-r22c4
	6	r5c6*r11c5		6	r15c6-r22c6
	7	r5c7*r11c5		7	r15c7-r22c7
12	4	sum(r10c3+r11c3)	24	6	r24c4+2000
	5	r12c4/r6c4		7	r24c6
	6	r12c5*r6c6	25	4	r23c4-r24c4
	7	r6c7*r12c5		6	r23c6-r24c6
15	4	r6c4-r12c4		7	r23c7-r24c7
	5	r15c4/r6c4	26	6	r26c4
	6	r15c5*r6c6		7	r26c6
	7	r6c7*r15c5	27	4	r25c4-r26c4
18	6	r18c3*1.08		6	r25c6-r26c6
	7	r18c6		7	r25c7-r26c7

One obvious use of a database would be for the maintenance of personnel records. One would create a file for each employee. Within each file, there would be a number of fields of various types and lengths. One type would be a date field, probably quite short, in which one would keep records of the hire dates of employees. Another would be a numeric field for records of employees' wages or salaries. This, too, would probably be a relatively short field. A third field would be for employees' names. Other possibilities would include addresses, Social Security numbers, and so on. Once all appropriate records had been input, it would be comparatively easy to design a report in which the data was sorted by field. Thus, one could print a list of employees according to seniority, or Zip code, or salary level, among many other possibilities.

AN INDUSTRY EXAMPLE

Our industry has used some EDP devices for a great number of years, but it is generally agreed that hotels and restaurants have not been quick to adopt computers. In fact, except for a handful of the larger firms and properties, only during the 1970s did one began to see any widespread use of computers in hotels and restaurants. These larger organizations initially used them primarily to speed certain specific bookkeeping and accounting functions, and hotels used them for reservations. At first, even in these organizations, control applications were secondary to speedy record-keeping. There were a number of reasons for this:

1. The high cost of computer systems, designed primarily for major corporations, could not be justified by most individual hotel and restaurant units.
2. Systems reliable enough for most industries were simply not reliable enough for hotels and restaurants, which could not tolerate the "down time" resulting from system failure.
3. Early programs for hotels and restaurants required a level of operator sophistication that was uncommon among typical industry employees.

In the last decade the computer industry has made progress in three major areas, and the effect has been to increase the use of computers by our industry. Miniaturization of computer components has made possible the production of comparatively small devices. The cost of systems has been reduced, and simultaneously their storage capacity has increased. Improvements in programming have enabled even those without extensive computer knowledge and training to carry out highly sophisticated operations. Such developments make the use of computers entirely feasible for an ever-growing number of food and beverage operations.

Figure 4.4 shows a comparatively small restaurant that uses a system consisting of the following components:

FIGURE 4.4

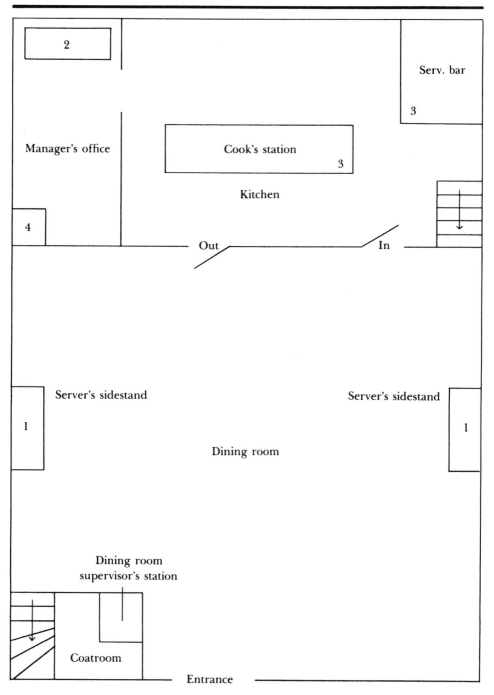

1. Server's terminals   2. Manager's terminal   3. Remote printers   4. CPU

> CPU in manager's office
>
> Two VDTs with printers at servers' stations
>
> One VDT at manager's desk
>
> Remote printers at service bar and cooks' station

Servers arriving for work change into uniforms on a lower level (not shown on the diagram), then proceed to their sidestands in the dining room. On each sidestand is a small VDT that dining room personnel use to log in—in other words, they record their arrival for work much as they would with a time clock. Other personnel log in at the terminal in the manager's office.

Guests enter by the dining room supervisor's station, leave their coats in the coatroom, and are seated by the supervisor, who leaves menus at the table. Servers greet the guests and take their orders for drinks; these are written on ordinary white pads rather than on guest checks. Each server proceeds to a terminal and opens an account equivalent to a guest check in computer memory. This is done by entering server number, table number, and a special code assigned for creating a new account. With the account opened, the server, using a numerical code, enters the customer's orders for drinks. These data, together with the time of the order, is stored in the CPU, which has been programmed with correct prices for each drink. The system is programmed to send the recorded drink orders to the service bar, where they are output on a remote printer. The hard copy provided to the bartender is an order to prepare the drinks, and includes the server number, table number, and order time.

The bartender tears the hard copy of the order from the printer and places it on the tray with the prepared drinks, thus eliminating questions about which drinks are for which server and what time the orders were entered. At the appropriate time, the server follows similar procedures for placing food orders. Different codes are used for foods, and the orders are output on the remote printers at the cooks' station. All ordered items are stored in memory, but the only items output on the remote printer at any preparation station are those appropriate to that station. Thus food orders are not output at the service bar, and orders for coffee, handled by the servers themselves, do not appear on any remote printers.

At the end of the customer's meal, the server obtains a guest check by requesting from the terminal and printer at the sidestand a hard copy of the data stored by table and server number. This hard copy is torn from the printer and given to the diner. In this particular establishment each server acts as a cashier for his or her own checks, and settlement is recorded for each check as the server receives cash or credit card.

At the end of a shift the server reports to the manager's office to settle the receipts. The manager uses her terminal to obtain summary data indicating charge and cash sales attributable to the particular server, and she collects cash and charge vouchers accordingly. Before changing out of uniform and leaving the premises, the server logs out, using the manager's terminal.

At the conclusion of business, a manager seeking a detailed breakdown of the day's business may request a wealth of data stored in the computer. A suitable program will provide such output as total dollar sales categorized into cash sales and charge sales, with the charge sales divided by type of credit card; total dollar sales separated into food sales and beverage sales, with the food sales broken down into dollar sales by menu category or by individual menu items; average dollar sale per customer, per server, per seat, per table, or per hour, or any number of these; seat turnover; number of orders of each food and beverage item sold (a reflection of the sales mix); total dollar sales per hour; sales in any category for the period to date; total payroll cost for the day, for any part of the day, or for the period to date; and a vast amount of food and beverage cost data, including standard costs.

Management can monitor operations at will as the day progresses. Such data as gross sales volume, numbers of customers served, numbers of checks outstanding, sales mix, numbers of portions of particular items sold, and any number of other possibilities may be of special interest at given times through the day.

Conceivably, a clerical staff could produce all of the above information. However, it should be obvious that considerable time would be needed to produce such data, and the consequent cost would be great. In addition, the time required might render the data out-of-date before it is even produced. Finally, the very accuracy of the data might be questionable.

The foregoing illustration shows a small, hypothetical system. However, larger and more sophisticated systems are already being used, particularly by some chain and other multiple-unit operations that require such output as hourly sales analysis, daily inventory data, unit financial reports, labor cost analysis, and customer counts on a unit, district, or systemwide basis. Computers with specialized hardware and complex, individualized software are essential in meeting such requirements.

Regardless of an operation's size or the size of a particular computer system, all have at least two important control applications in common:

1. Monitoring operations in a timely manner so that judgments can be made about such concerns as cost, sales, and employee performance.
2. Increasing control over employees' actions by requiring adherence to established standard procedures. For example, under the system previously described, a server would find it difficult to obtain food or a beverage without recording an item on a guest check.

Changes occur almost daily in EDP. New hardware and software packages continue to be introduced, and increasing numbers will be designed specifically for foodservice operations. Many chefs, stewards, managers, and other foodservice professionals will soon accomplish some of their normal work routines at computer terminals. Managers will soon face the problem of selecting an appropriate system from among an increasing number available from a growing list of vendors. The key to selection will lie in managers' ability to evaluate the capability, reliability, and compatibility of various hardware and software components and their understanding of desired outputs from the system. In the foodservice industry, desired outputs can be determined best through understanding food, beverage, and labor control processes, procedures, and goals.

CHAPTER ESSENTIALS

This chapter briefly traced the development of data processing equipment from early uses through recent advances that have brought electronic data processing equipment and computers within the reach of large numbers of businesses, including foodservice operations. By using the simple analogy of the restaurant cashier, we provided an explanation of the way that computers process data, and introduced a number of terms with which foodservice operators and managers should familiarize themselves as computers become more a part of the everyday life of the foodservice manager. We illustrated and explained the operation of a system resembling some currently used in foodservice, and suggested some applications for larger, centralized systems in organizations more complex than the individually-operated restaurant. Finally, we offered the two keys central to management selection of computer systems for food service establishments.

KEY TERMS IN THIS CHAPTER

Computer	Hard copy
Input	Word processing
Terminal	Cell
Program	Storage
Media	VDT
Database	Software
Field	Soft copy
Output	Spreadsheet
CPU	File
Hardware	Field

QUESTIONS AND PROBLEMS

1. Explain why the abacus and mechanical adding machine can be considered data processing devices.
2. List three advantages of electronic data processing devices over mechanical devices used to process information.

3. List the five basic capabilities of a computer system.

4. Software is encoded on media. List five types of media used with computers.

5. List the three primary reasons for the hospitality industry's delay in adopting computer systems.

6. What knowledge will a food and beverage manager need to make intelligent choices among alternate computer systems?

7. How can computer systems aid in establishing control in foodservice operations?

8. The third step in the control process discussed in Chapter 3 is to "monitor performance and compare actual performance to established standards." What outputs of the system illustrated in this chapter would help a manager do this?

9. Define each of the following terms:

Computer	VDT	Soft copy	Storage
Output	Terminal	Hard copy	Spreadsheet
Storage	Hardware	Media	Database
Input	Software	Word processing	File
CPU	Programs	Cell	Field

10. For each of the terms in Question 9 above, write a sentence relating to the foodservice industry.

For Computer Users

11. Using the income statements in the introductory chapter for data, create a spreadsheet to process the information and prepare a report for the Rush Hour Inn, then use the same spreadsheet to prepare a similar report for the Graduate Restaurant.

12. Refer to Question 16, Chapter 2. Prepare the operating budget for the coming year as a spreadsheet.

13. Refer to Question 17 and 18, Chapter 2. Prepare the operating budget for the coming year and the revised operating budget as spreadsheets.

part two

Food Control

With some understanding of the nature of costs, sales, controls, and computer basics, it is now possible to begin an investigation of the subject rather loosely termed "food control." In the course of our investigation, we will look into various means of controlling food, as well as controlling, measuring, and judging food costs and food sales. Our approach will be to discuss the several accepted steps in the chain of daily events that make up the foodservice business—from initial purchase of raw materials to the sale of the products prepared from those materials. Following these discussions, we will look into several techniques for measuring food costs. Finally, we will investigate ways to judge food costs in relation to food sales and suggest approaches to improve performance from the figures determined.

We will begin with a discussion of the controls needed in purchasing foods.

chapter 5

Purchasing Control

Learning Objectives

After reading and studying this chapter, the student should be able to:

1. Describe the application of the four-step control process to the purchasing function in a foodservice establishment.
2. Distinguish between perishable and nonperishable foods.
3. Describe how quality standards for food purchases are established.
4. Describe how quantity standards for perishable and nonperishable food purchases are established.
5. Write a standard purchase specification.
6. Describe the process used to determine the quantity of perishable foods to be purchased.
7. Compare and contrast the periodic and perpetual methods for purchasing nonperishable foods.
8. Determine order quantities using the periodic and perpetual inventory methods.
9. List the normal sources of supply for restaurant food purchases.
10. Describe the procedures for establishing price standards for the purchase of perishable and nonperishable foods.
11. List five methods for training purchasing employees.
12. Discuss the possible consequences of failing to train purchasing employees.
13. List and explain the advantages and disadvantages of centralized purchasing.
14. List and explain the advantages and disadvantages of standing orders.
15. Explain one application of the computer in purchasing.
16. Define the Key Terms listed at the end of the chapter.

RESPONSIBILITY FOR PURCHASING

Responsibility for purchasing can be delegated to any one of a number of persons in restaurant operations, depending on organizational structure and management policies. It is not uncommon to find the owners or managers taking the responsibility in some establishments, while in others, either the chef or the steward may be assigned the purchasing duties. In some hotel operations, foods may even be ordered by some individual in the office of the purchasing agent.

In order to facilitate discussions, we will arbitrarily fix responsibility for purchasing the necessary foods with the steward. This should not be taken to mean that the authors believe that this responsibility should always be given to the steward; on the contrary, the determination of who should be assigned this responsibility must be based on situations and conditions existing in each individual restaurant operation. The important point to be made here is that for control purposes, the authority to purchase foods, and the responsibility for doing so, should be assigned to one individual. One individual can then be held accountable for operating the system of control procedures established by the food controller.

CONTROL PROCESS AND PURCHASING

In Chapter 2, control was defined as a process by means of which managers attempt to direct, regulate, and restrain the actions of people in order to achieve desired goals. The control process was identified as a four-step process, requiring that standards and standard procedures be established, that employees be trained to follow those standards and standard procedures, that employee output be monitored and compared to established standards, and that remedial action be taken as needed. This is a general process that can be applied to the control of any activity in foodservice or any other business. Our objective in the present chapter will be to apply the control process to the problem of purchasing food.

The types of foods to be purchased for any operation may be divided into two categories: perishables and nonperishables. Because several significant differences exist between the techniques and procedures for purchasing foods in these categories, it will be necessary at this point to differentiate between them.

PERISHABLES AND NONPERISHABLES

Perishables are those items, typically fresh foods, that have a comparatively short useful life after they have been received. Various kinds of lettuce and fresh fish, for example, begin to lose their quality very quickly. Some meats and cheeses will retain their quality for somewhat longer periods, but they too will begin to lose their quality far sooner than, say, a can of tomato puree. Perishables, then, should be purchased for immediate use in order to take advantage of the quality required at the time of purchase. If a steward is always careful to purchase the best quality available for intended use, then it would be wasteful and costly not to make use of that carefully selected quality.

Nonperishables are those food items that have a longer shelf life. Often referred to as groceries or staples, they may be stored in the containers in which they are received, often on shelves and at room temperature, for weeks or even months. They do not deteriorate quickly, at least as long as they are kept in sealed containers. They are typically purchased and stored in jars, bottles, cans, and boxes; the storage area in which they are kept, called a storeroom, would resemble the shelves of a supermarket to the layman.

Because these foods do not deteriorate quickly, it is possible to keep a reasonable supply of each on hand, for use as needed. For example, a restaurant that used an average of four No. 10 cans of whole, peeled tomatoes daily (more than four cases per week) could conceivably keep a supply of eight cases on hand without running any risk of spoilage. Foods that typically fall into this category of staples include salt, sugar, flour, canned fruits and vegetables, spices, and flavorings.

DEVELOPING STANDARDS AND STANDARD PROCEDURES

The primary purpose for establishing control over purchasing is to ensure a continuing supply of sufficient quantities of the necessary foods, each of the quality appropriate to its intended use, purchased at the most favorable price. Therefore, we will discuss purchasing from this point of view, beginning by establishing the essential standards and standard procedures for effective purchasing. Standards must be developed for:

1. The quality of food purchased.
2. The quantity of food purchased.
3. The prices at which food is purchased.

ESTABLISHING QUALITY STANDARDS

Before any intelligent purchasing can be done, someone in management must determine which foods, both perishables and nonperishables, will be required for day-to-day operations. The basis for creating a list of these foods is the menu. However, this is not as easy as it may at first appear. For example, most restaurants use tomatoes and tomato products for a variety of purposes—as salad ingredients, as sauce ingredients, and so on. At the same time, tomatoes and tomato products are available for purchase fresh and processed, and in various grades. Before purchasing, important decisions must be made about brands, sizes, packaging, grades, and degree of freshness, among other things.

Quite clearly, developing a complete list of foods and their characteristics for an operation is a complex and time-consuming enterprise, but one that must be undertaken by those who choose to establish effective control over purchasing. If a restaurant is to produce products of consistent quality, it must use raw materials of consistent quality. Therefore, it is important that the food controller, in cooperation with other members of the management team, draw up the list of all food items to be purchased, including those specific and distinctive characteristics that best describe the desired quality of each. These carefully written descriptions are known as **standard purchase specifications**. These specifications are often based on grading standards established by the federal government, or, in some instances, when federal grading standards are considered too broad, on grading standards common to the appropriate commodities market. However, the restaurant is not restricted to these possibilities. Many knowledgeable individuals write specifications that are far more precise and thus more useful for indicating to purveyors the exact quality desired. Once these standard purchase specifications have been written and agreed upon by the management team, they are often duplicated and distributed to potential purveyors to ensure that each fully understands the restaurant's exact requirements. Figure 5.1 gives five examples of standard purchase specifications.

Standard purchase specifications, if carefully prepared, are useful in several ways:

1. They force the management team to determine exact requirements in advance for any commodity.
2. They are often useful in menu preparation, in that it is possible to use one cut of meat, purchased according to specifications, to prepare several different items on the menu.
3. They eliminate misunderstandings between the steward and purveyors.
4. Circulation of specifications for one commodity to several purveyors makes competitive bidding possible.
5. They eliminate the need for detailed verbal descriptions each time a commodity is ordered.
6. They facilitate checking food as it is received, the importance of which will be discussed in Chapter 6.

Although specifications are written down at one particular time, they need not be considered fixed for all time. If conditions change, they can be rewritten and recirculated.

This critically important step, the determination of quality standards and the consequent writing of standard purchase specifications, helps to ensure that all foods purchased will be of the desired quality for their intended use.

ESTABLISHING QUANTITY STANDARDS

Although purchase specifications can be established at one particular time and merely reviewed and updated on occasion, quantity standards for purchasing are

FIGURE 5.1
Standard Purchase Specifications

Strip Loin	Bone-in 10″ cut. USDA Prime, upper half. Range #2, minimum 14 lbs., maximum 16 lbs. One-half to three-quarters of an inch fat except for seam fat. Moderate marbling, light red in color to slightly dark red. New York cut, chilled upon delivery. Free from objectionable odors, deterioration, and evidence of freezing or defrosting.
Flounder (grey sole)	Whole, dressed, fresh day of delivery. Minimum 2 lbs., maximum 4 lbs. Fish should be twice as long as is broad, with oval body. Flesh should be firm and elastic, meat should be white and slightly translucent, color should be bright and clear. Gills should be free from slime and reddish-pink in color, and scales should adhere tightly to the skin. No stale odors of ammonia. Yield of 40% to the fillet.
Grapefruit	Florida. Medium to large; 3-3/4″ to 4″ in diameter. Light yellow in color; approximately 12 to 14 sections; oval to round. Thin-skinned, tender, delicate flesh. No visible spotting or bruising on skins. Medium acidity and sweetness, faint bitterness. Packed 36 to a crate.
Canned Peaches	Yellow, cling halves—canned. US Grade A (Fancy), heavy syrup. 19–24 Brix, minimum drained weight. 66 ounces per #10 can. Count per #10 can: 30 to 35. Quote by dozen #10 can. Federal Inspector's certification of grade required.
Asparagus tips, frozen	Tips large, all green, frozen. US Grade A (Fancy). Packed in 2-1/2 lb. cartons, 12 cartons per case. Must be delivered at 10°F or below. Quote by pound net. Federal Inspector's certification of grade required.

subject to continual review and revision, often on a daily basis. All foods deteriorate in time, some more quickly than others, and it is the job of the food controller to provide a system that will ensure that only those quantities are purchased that will be needed immediately or in the relatively near future.* In cooperation with the steward, the food controller does this by instituting procedures for determining the

---

* It must be noted that there are exceptions to the rule, as, for example, when the opportunity arises for purchasing a four-month supply of a nonperishable commodity at a substantial discount.

appropriate quantities of each item that should be purchased. These procedures are based principally on the useful life of the commodity.

For purchasing purposes, foods are divided into the two categories previously discussed, perishables and nonperishables. The procedures for determining quantities to purchase vary somewhat and will be discussed separately.

Perishables

The very nature of perishable commodities suggests the importance of always using up those already on hand before purchasing additional quantities. Therefore, the purchasing routine must include determining amounts already on hand. Decisions also must be made as to total quantities needed. Once these have been arrived at, the difference between them is the correct amount to order.

A basic requirement of the purchasing routine is that the steward take a daily inventory of perishables. This daily inventory may be an actual physical inventory in some cases. In others, it may be only an estimate based on physical observation. For example, the steward would probably count the actual number of ribs of beef but might only estimate the quantity of chopped beef. Or the steward might count the avocados but count only the cases of lettuce.

A very important and useful tool for the steward to use in taking this daily inventory is a standard form called the "Steward's Market Quotation List," illustrated in Figure 5.2. This form, generally available from stationers who cater to the hotel and restaurant industry, is a listing of the most common perishables, arranged by types, with several blank lines provided for the special requirements of each restaurant. (Restaurants that offer menus so specialized that this particular form is useless—such as Chinese or Near-Eastern restaurants—are well advised to devise their own and have them duplicated.)

In order to take the daily inventory of perishables, the steward usually goes through the refrigerators and freezers with the form in hand and, next to the appropriate items in each category, fills in the column on the left, marked "on hand." After completing this survey, the steward has a relatively accurate inventory of perishable commodities.

The next step in the routine involves determining anticipated total needs for each item, based on future menus, and often on experience as well. Depending on the restaurant, these figures for total anticipated needs are determined sometimes by the chef, sometimes by the steward, and often by the two working together. Two heads are usually better than one. As in the illustration in Figure 5.2, it is helpful to write this figure for total anticipated needs in the "article" column, just after the name of the item in question.

After making this determination, the steward enters the difference between total anticipated needs and the amount on hand in the "wanted" column at the right. This difference is the amount that should be ordered to bring supply up to the total quantity required.

The use of the Steward's Market Quotation List is illustrated in Figure 5.2. For example, the steward has determined that legs of lamb are on the menu and that a total of seven legs will be required to meet anticipated demand. This number is recorded in the "article" column, just after the name of the item. Since the daily inventory indicates two legs, written in the "on hand" column, the quantity to be purchased is five legs, recorded in the "wanted" column, and found by subtracting the quantity on hand (2 legs) from the total amount required (7 legs).

Nonperishables

While nonperishable foods do not present the problem of rapid deterioration, they do represent considerable amounts of money invested in material in storage. Obviously cash tied up in nonperishables is not available to meet other operating expenses of the business. Therefore, one goal of the purchasing routine for nonperishables should be to avoid having excessive quantities on hand. Additional benefits to be derived from reducing quantities on hand include the elimination of some possibilities for theft, the reduction of storage space requirements, and possibly the reduction in the number of personnel required to maintain the storage area.

Fixing labels on shelves is one important step that should be taken in every storeroom to identify permanently the location of each item maintained in stock. In this way no item will ever be found in more than one location at once. When items appear in several different locations, there is a tendency to order additional quantities in the unwarranted belief that stock is running low. Moreover, when locations are identified, it becomes easier to find things when regular personnel are off duty or when personnel change.

For the convenience of stewards, a form available from stationers lists nonperishables, just as the Steward's Market Quotation List itemizes perishables. It is not widely used, however, since lists of groceries are not as universally applicable as are lists of perishables. A great number of stewards prefer to make up lists of their particular storerooms' contents and to have them inexpensively duplicated. These serve the same purpose: to list amounts to be ordered and competitive prices.

While there are a number of specific systems for maintaining grocery inventories at appropriate levels, most are variations on the following methods.

Periodic Order Method

Perhaps the most common method for maintaining stores' inventories at appropriate levels is the so-called periodic method, which, by contrast with methods for ordering perishables, permits comparatively infrequent ordering. Because nonperishable items have longer shelf life than perishables, it is both possible and desirable to order them less frequently, thus leaving the steward free to attend to perishables, which typically require considerable time. When this method is followed, a steward will normally establish, with the advice of management, periods for ordering

FIGURE 5.2
Steward's Market Quotation List

ON HAND	ARTICLE	WANTED	QUOTATIONS
	BEEF		
	Corned Beef		
	Corned Beef Brisket		
	Corned Beef Rump		
	Corned Beef Hash		
	Beef Chipped		
	Beef Breads		
	Butts		
	Chuck		
4	Filets	10 / 6	
	Hip Short		
	Hip Full		
	Kidneys		
	Livers		
	Loin, Short		
3	Strip	12	
6	Shell Strip		
	Ribs, Beef	11 / 9	
	Shins		
	Suet, Beef		
	Tails, Ox		
	VEAL		
	Breast		
	Brains		
	Feet		
	Fore Quarters		
	Hind Quarters		
	Head		
3	Kidneys	8	
	Legs	7	
	Liver		
1	Loins		
	Racks	3 / 4	
	Saddles		
	Shoulder		
	Sweet Breads		

ON HAND	ARTICLE	WANTED	QUOTATIONS
	Provisions (Cont'd)		
	Pig's Knuckle Fresh		
	Pig's Knuckle Corned		
	Pig, Suckling		
1	Pork, Fresh Loin	6	
	Pork, Landing		
	Pork, Spare Ribs		
	Pork, Salt Strip		
1	Pork, Tenderloin	9	
	Sausages, Country		
	Sausages, Frankfurter		
	Sausages, Meat		
	Shoulders, Fresh		
	Shoulders, Smoked		
	Shoulders, Corned		
	Tongues		
	Tongues, Beef Smoked		
	Tongues, Fresh		
	Tongues, Lambs		
	Tripe		
	POULTRY		
1 / 6	Chickens, Broiler		
	Chickens, Roast		
	Chickens, Broilers		
	Chickens, Broilers		
	Chickens, Supreme		
	Cocks		
	Capons		
	Ducks		
	Ducklings		
	Fowl		
	Geese		
	Goslings		
	Guinea Hens		
	Guinea Squabs		
	Pigeons		
	Poussins		

ON HAND	ARTICLE	WANTED	QUOTATIONS
	FISH (Cont'd)		
	Carp		
	Codfish, Live		
	Codfish, Salt Boneless		
	Codfish, Salt Flake		
	Eels		
	Finnan Haddie		
	Flounders		
	Flounders, Fillet		
	Fluke		
	Haddock		
	Haddock, Fillet		
	Haddock, Smoked		
	Halibut		
	Halibut, Chicken		
	Herring, Smoked		
	Herring, Kippered		
	Kingfish		
	Mackerel, Fresh		
	Mackerel, Salt		
	Mackerel, Spanish		
	Mackerel, Smoked		
	Perch		
	Pickerel		
	Pike		
	Porgies		
	Pompano		
	Redsnapper		
	Salmon, Fresh		
	Salmon, Smoked		
	Salmon, Nova Scotia		
	Scrod		
	Shad		
	Shad Roes		
	Smelts		
	Sole, English		

ON HAND	ARTICLE	WANTED	QUOTATIONS
	Vegetables (Cont'd)		
	Estragon		
	Egg Plant		
	Garlic		
	Horseradish Roots		
	Kale		
	Kohlrabi		
	Lettuce		
	Lettuce, Ice Berg		
	Lettuce, Place		
	Leeks		
	Mint		
	Mushrooms		
	Mushrooms, Fresh		
	Okra		
	Onions		
	Onions, Yellow		
	Onions, Bermuda		
	Onions, Spanish		
	Onions, White		
	Onions, Scallions		
	Oyster Plant		
	Parsley		
	Parsnip		
	Peppermint		
	Peas, Green		
	Peas		
	Peas		
	Peppers, Green		
	Peppers, Red		
	Potatoes		
	Potatoes, Bermuda		
	Potatoes, Idaho		
	Potatoes, Idaho		
	Potatoes, Sweet		
	Potatoes, New		
	Potatoes, Yams		
	Pumpkins		

ON HAND	ARTICLE	WANTED	QUOTATIONS
	FRUIT (Cont'd)		
	Dates		
	Figs		
	Gooseberries		
	Grapes		
	Grapes		
	Grapes, Concord		
	Grapes, Malaga		
	Grapes, Tokay		
	Grapefruit		
	Grapefruit		
	Guavas		
	Lemons		
	Limes		
	Limes, Florida		
	Limes, Persian		
	Muskmelons		
	Oranges		
	Oranges		
	Oranges		
	Peaches		
	Pears		
	Pears		
	Pears, Alligators		
	Pineapples		
	Plums		
	Plums		
	Pomegranates		
	Quinces		
	Raspberries		
	Strawberries		
	Strawberries		
	Tangerines		
	Watermelons		
	Watermelons		

MUTTON

Fore Quarters		
Kidneys		
Legs		
Racks		
Saddles		
Saddles, Hind		
Shoulder		
Suet		

LAMB

Breast		
Fore Quarters		
Feet		
Fries		
Kidneys		
Loins		
Legs	IV	10
Lamb, Spring		
Racks, Double		
Racks, Spring		
Saddles		
Shoulder		

PROVISIONS

Bacon		50
Bologna		
Bologna		
Crepinette		
Salami		
Hams, Corned		
Hams, Fresh		
Hams, Polish		
Hams, Smoked	6	4
Hams, Virginia		
Hams, Westphalia		
Head Cheese		
Lard		
Lyon Sausage		
Phil. Scrapple		
Smoked Butts		
Pig's Feet		
Pig's Head, Corned		

FISH

Bass, Black	
Bass, Sea	
Bass, Striped	
Blackfish	
Bluefish	
Bloaters	
Butterfish	

SHELL FISH

Clams, Chowder		
Clams, Cherrystone		
Clams, Little Neck		
Clams, Soft		
Crabs, Hard		
Crabs, Meat		
Crabs, Oyster		
Crabs, Soft Shell		
Crabs, Soft Shell Prime		
Lobsters, Meat		
Lobsters, Tails	4	3
Lobsters, Chicken		
Lobsters, Medium		
Lobsters, Large		
Oysters, Box		
Oysters, Blue Points		
Oysters		
Scallops		
Shrimps		100
Turtle		60

GAME

Birds	
Partridge	
Pheasant, English	
Rabbits	
Quail	
Venison, Saddle	

Squabs

Turkeys, Roasting	6
Turkeys, Boiling	
Turkeys, Spring	

VEGETABLES

Artichokes	
Asparagus	
Asparagus	
Asparagus, Tips	
Asparagus, Fancy	
Beans	
Beans, Lima	
Beans, String	
Beans, Wax	
Beets	
Beets, Tops	
Broccoli	
Brussels Sprouts	
Cabbage	
Cabbage, Red	
Cabbage, New	
Carrots	
Carrots	
Cauliflower	
Celery	
Celery Knobs	
Chicory	
Chives	
Corn	
Chervil	
Cranberries	
Cucumbers	
Dandelion	
Escarole	
Endive	

Sole, Boston	
Sole, Lemon	
Sturgeon	
Trout, Brook	
Trout, Lake	
Trout, Salmon	
Weakfish	
Whitebait	
Whitefish	
Whitefish, Smoked	

Romaine	
Radishes	
Rhubarb, Fresh	
Rhubarb, Hot House	
Sage	
Shallots	
Sorrel	
Sauerkraut	
Spinach	
Squash Crooked Neck	
Squash Hubbard	
Tarragon	
Thyme	
Tomatoes, New	
Tomatoes, Hot House	
Turnips, White	
Turnips, Yellow	
Turnips, New	
Watercress	

FRUIT

Apples, Cooking	
Apples, Baking	
Apples, Crab	
Apples, Table	
Apricots	
Bananas	
Blackberries	
Blueberries	
Blueberries	
Cantaloupes	
Cantaloupes	
Honey Balls	
Melons, Casaba	
Melons, Honeydew	
Melons, Persian	
Melon, Spanish	
Cherries	
Cherries	
Cherries	
Currants	
Chestnuts	

BUTTER

Print	
Cream, Fresh	
Sweet	

EGGS

White	
Brown	
Mixed Colors	
Pullets	

CHEESE

American, Kraft	
American, Young	
Bel Paese	
Camembert	
Camembert	
Cheddar	
Cottage	
Cream	
Cream, Phila.	
Cream, Phila.	
Edam	
Gorgonzola	
Liederkranz	
Parmesan, Grated	
Roquefort	
Roquefort, Broken	
Stilton	
Stove	
Swiss	
Swiss, Gruyere	
Swiss, Gruyere	

Miscellaneous

purposes. On a regular basis—once every week, or every two weeks, or even once each month, depending on the policies of management as to the amount of money to be tied up in inventory—the steward reviews the entire stock of nonperishable items and determines how much of each to order to ensure a supply sufficient to last until the next regularly scheduled order date. The calculation of the amount of each item to order is comparatively simple:

$$
\begin{array}{r@{\ }l}
& \text{Amount required for the upcoming period} \\
- & \text{Amount presently on hand} \\
+ & \text{Amount wanted on hand at the end of the} \\
& \underline{\text{period to last until the next delivery}} \\
= & \text{Amount to order}
\end{array}
$$

For example, in a certain restaurant ordering once a month, one of the items ordered might be #2½ cans of sliced pineapple, packed twelve cans to a case. The item is used at the rate of ten cans per week, and delivery normally takes five days from the date an order is placed. If the steward in this establishment found fifteen cans on the shelf, anticipated normal use of forty cans during the upcoming period of approximately four weeks, and wanted fifteen cans on hand at the end of the upcoming month, the calculation would be

$$
\begin{array}{r@{\ }l}
& \text{40 cans required} \\
- & \text{15 now on hand} \\
+ & \underline{\text{15 to be left at the end of the month}} \\
= & \text{40 to be ordered on this date}
\end{array}
$$

However, since orders are normally placed for this item in cases rather than in cans, it is likely that the steward would round the order up to the next highest purchase unit and that the order placed would be for four cases, consisting of forty-eight cans. While this rounding procedure may appear to lead to overpurchasing, in fact the steward is subtracting quantities on hand at the beginning of each period before placing the orders, and thus any such small overpurchases are likely to be used up at the beginning of the next period. Additionally, the order for the next period is, in effect, reduced by the amount of the small overpurchase in the current period.

The student might well ask how the steward knows the requirements for the upcoming period. Storerooms have hundreds of items, and it is impossible for a person to know, without records, how much of most items is needed. Fortunately, the steward is aided by the salespersons. In addition, many establishments keep records of amounts used. Smaller establishments typically rely on salespersons to keep track of previous orders. The steward can then look on the storage shelf and make an approximate calculation of the amount used by subtracting what is remaining from what was ordered. While this is probably a better method than having no knowledge of usage, it is unreliable because it fails to take into account the amount on hand at the beginning of any period. Nevertheless, this method is very common in the food and beverage industry. One additional note: if an establishment orders every time a salesperson calls, the order period will vary from item to item, as salespersons do not all call with the same frequency.

A more systematic method of determining usage requires that certain additional steps be taken. A desirable first step is to enhance the utility of shelf labels by including additional information on them. For example, if the label were somewhat larger than standard size, it would be feasible in many establishments to record the quantities added to and taken from shelves right on the label. When used in this form, labels become known as bin cards, an example of which is shown in Figure 5.3. As each delivery is received and placed on the shelf, both the date and number of units so placed are entered on the bin card. As quantities are issued for use, those dates and amounts are recorded as well. More spaces are provided for items issued than for items received, for the obvious reason that purchases are comparatively infrequent, but issues may occur daily. A balance column is provided so that a steward may determine and enter amounts on hand at any desired time, such as when a salesperson calls or when the periodic ordering date arrives.

At such times, it is quite simple to determine approximate usage by looking on the card for the balance on hand on the date the last order was placed, adding to that figure the number of units placed on shelves when the last order was received, and subtracting the balance currently on hand. The result will be approximate usage in the most recent period, regardless of the length of that period. The assumption is made that this quantity was used productively, although this may not always be the case and should be considered in determining the amount to order for the next period. When such a system is followed, it is normally wise to compare the balance on the bin card with the number of units of the item actually on the shelves in order to be sure that all items issued have been suitably recorded. If a discrepancy exists, the balance shown on the bin card will not be entirely reliable in measuring actual usage during the period, and the missing items, presumably issued, must be added to the derived usage figure to achieve a more accurate figure.

If the amount used in the preceding period was the amount ordered for the coming period, the strong possibility exists that the establishment would end the coming period with no units of that item left on the shelf. Since this might make it impossible to produce certain items on the menu, or might make it necessary to

FIGURE 5.3
Bin Card

ITEM Pineapple Slices								DESIRED ENDING INVENTORY	15
DATE	IN	DATE	OUT	DATE	OUT	DATE	OUT		BALANCE
10/1									15
		10/2	2	10/3	2	10/4	2		9
10/6	48	10/5	2						55

secure some emergency supply in order to carry on to the next delivery date, most restaurants that follow this periodic method establish the amount that should be on hand at the end of any period and that should be sufficient to last until the next delivery is received. Once established, this is known as the desired ending inventory, and is entered on the bin card. Both delivery time and daily usage for that time must be used in determining the desired ending figure. Furthermore, it is advisable to add on to this figure some carefully considered amount as a safety factor, in case of delay in delivery. In many cases this safety factor may also include some amount to be kept on hand in the event that business volume in the coming period rises above normal levels.

It is important for anyone planning to enter this business to realized that all of the amounts mentioned in the preceding paragraphs should be continually reevaluated. After all, many changes occur in usage from period to period, and the steward or manager who fails to take changes into account is taking risks needlessly. For example, as the weather and menus change, some foods will be used in greater quantities. If demand for some items increases, usage is likely to increase as well; the converse would also be true. Thus, before ordering, it is normally advisable to compare usage in similar periods in preceding years. If menus and sales volume have changed as well, these too must be taken into account.

Perpetual Inventory Method

While it is better for control purposes than the periodic method, the perpetual inventory method is not as widely used. This is because its successful use requires that specialized personnel maintain complete and accurate records, and also because none but large establishments can normally justify maintaining such personnel. However, because some large operations, particularly those in chain organizations, do employ these methods, students should be aware of their underlying purposes and the procedures necessary for their successful implementation.

The primary purposes of the perpetual inventory system are to ensure that quantities purchased are sufficient to meet anticipated need without being excessive and to provide effective control over those items that are being stored for future use. This method requires the use of perpetual inventory cards, such as that illustrated in Figure 5.4. These cards, while similar to the bin card illustrated in Figure 5.3, include some additional information and are used differently. One very important difference is that the perpetual inventory card is not normally affixed to the shelf on which the covered item is maintained but is kept outside the storeroom and maintained by persons who do not work in the storeroom. The amounts of food purchased are recorded on the appropriate cards, and as items are issued for use, those amounts issued are similarly recorded. If the amounts recorded accurately reflect the movement of items into and out of storage, it is possible at any given time merely to consult the perpetual inventory card to determine how much of an item is in stock at the moment. This system makes it possible to compare

FIGURE 5.4
Perpetual Inventory Card

ITEM	Pineapple Slices	COST	$9.84 per 12 can case
SIZE	#2½ can	PAR STOCK	32
SUPPLIER	ABC Co.	REORDER POINT	15
	18 120th St.	REORDER QUANTITY	24
	N.Y.C.		

DATE	ORDER #	IN	OUT	BALANCE
10/1	#222 - 24		2	15
10/2			2	13
10/3			2	11
10/4			2	9
10/5			2	7
10/6		24		31
10/7				
10/8				

balances on the perpetual inventory cards with actual items on shelves to determine if any items are not accounted for.

The additional information, including the name and address of the supplier, as well as the most recent purchase price for the item, facilitates ordering. Three additional terms used on the card—par stock, reorder point, and reorder quantity —are also of considerable use in facilitating purchase, and require further discussion.

The **reorder point** is, quite simply, the number of units to which the supply on hand should decrease before additional orders are placed. Thus, if the reorder point for a given item is twenty-two cans, then no order for that item should be placed until the supply, as shown in the balance column, has reached that number. To establish a reorder point for any item, it is necessary to know both normal usage and the time needed to obtain delivery. Furthermore, it is advisable to include in the calculations a certain additional amount to allow for delivery delays and for possible increased usage during that period. In effect, the reorder point in the perpetual inventory method is the equivalent of the desired ending inventory in the periodic method and is calculated in the following manner. If normal usage is two cans per day, and it takes five days from date of order to get delivery, then the basic number needed is ten cans. However, because delivery may be delayed, or because usage may increase for unforeseen reasons, or because both of those possibilities may occur at once, it is advisable to increase that amount somewhat, possibly by as much as 50%, thus establishing a reorder point of fifteen cans. Under the periodic method, the desired ending inventory would similarly be calculated as fifteen cans.

The perpetual inventory card also provides for a **par stock** figure for each item in stock. While it is generally acknowledged that par stock is a number of units related to usage and the time needed to get delivery, there is no general agreement on an exact definition of the term. Since the term is used in a variety of ways in the industry, the student should be aware of some of its more common uses. In some places, their term "par stock" is taken to mean a maximum quantity of a given item that should be on hand after the most recent order has been received. In others, it means a normal quantity that should be on hand at all times. Still another possibility is to treat par stock as a range defined by maximum and minimum quantities between which the actual quantities on hand should vary.

For purposes of this discussion, we will take par stock to be the maximum quantity of any item that should be on hand at any given time. That maximum quantity can be determined only after careful weighing of the following considerations:

1. Storage space.
2. Limits of inventory valuation prescribed by management.
3. Desired frequency of ordering.
4. Usage.
5. Purveyors' minimum order requirements.

Because storage space is limited for all but a few most fortunate operators, it is obviously necessary to calculate the maximum amount of space available for all nonperishable storage and then to allocate wisely the use of that space. For example, with those items normally purchased in comparatively large packages, such as bulk flour and sugar, it may be necessary to restrict space to that required for the storage of a one-week supply.

To the extent that management chooses to restrict the amount of cash invested in inventory, it becomes necessary to restrict the amount of any item that one can maintain on hand. If the cash for meeting payroll and for paying outstanding bills is in comparatively short supply, then management will often choose to reduce the size of inventory and direct rather more frequent ordering of smaller quantities. In some cases, it is possible to accomplish this by restricting only the purchase of the more expensive items in the inventory, without effecting any change in purchase procedures for the less costly commodities.

Obviously, management must establish some schedule of desired frequency. In addition, while the foods involved are typically referred to as nonperishables, some are, in fact, more perishable than others, and this should be taken into account.

Determination of par stock should always take into account the relative quantities of an item used, which may change over time. If anticipated consumption of an item is expected to be high in a given period, then the par stock should be higher than at, say, another time or season when consumption is rather low.

Because a considerable number of purveyors prefer to supply items in standard wholesale purchase units, such as cases and fifty-pound bags, the minimum order requirements of purveyors must be taken into account as well. Once all of the foregoing has been considered and a par stock figure has been established for each inventory item, it is entered on the appropriate perpetual inventory card.

The final consideration is the establishment of a reorder quantity—the amount that will be ordered each time the quantity of a particular item diminishes to the reorder point. The quantity ordered should be sufficient to bring the total inventory up to the par stock level. At first glance, that quantity would appear to be the difference between established par stock and reorder point. However, that figure would fail to take into account normal usage between order date and delivery—previously calculated as ten cans for the example in figure 5.4. This quantity must be added. Therefore, the calculation of reorder would be

	Par stock	32
−	Reorder point	15
=	Subtotal	17
+	Normal usage until delivery	10
=	Reorder quantity	27

However, food is normally purchased in case lots of six, twelve, or twenty-four, or some other quantity per case, depending on the item and size of container, and this must be taken into account. If the establishment needs twenty-seven units of something packed twelve to the case, the order placed must be in some multiple of twelve. In this case, the reorder quantity will be two cases, or twenty-four cans, rather than the twenty-seven determined above. Upon delivery, the stock is brought to thirty-one units, or approximately to par.

Many establishments choose not to use either of these systems in precisely the forms described above. There are a number of reasons for this. Some appreciate the value of perpetual inventory records removed from the control of those who receive and issue food but are unwilling or unable to place orders on the daily basis presupposed by pure perpetual method. Others fear the comparative absence of control in the periodic method. For these and other reasons, some have developed what amount to hybrid systems that selectively employ the more desirable features of both systems.

One such system is essentially a perpetual method, but with reorder points and par stocks set sufficiently high so that orders need not be placed at precisely the moment that reorder points are reached. Such establishments might use the reaching of a reorder point merely as a signal that a particular item should be ordered on the next regularly scheduled day for placing orders, and would merely add the item to a list. If the reorder point were set high enough, there would be little danger of consuming the remaining quantity through normal usage prior to next delivery.

The final determination of a routine—whether one of the illustrated procedures or some variation—must be based on the needs of the individual operation and the policies established by management. The important point to be made is that the purchasing procedure must take into account the need for determining, on an ongoing basis, the quantities of each commodity that will be adequate for anticipated demand. It must guard against overpurchasing—the purchasing of unneeded quantities. In the case of perishables, overpurchasing increases the possibilities for both spoilage and theft. In addition, it increases the possibilities for overproduction and consequent waste. In the case of nonperishables, overpurchasing clearly increases the possibilities for theft; it may increase the need for personnel, and it certainly ties up unwarranted amounts of money in inventory. Because these are the very conditions that control systems are established to guard against, it is obviously important to set up procedures for determining appropriate quantities for ordering.

ESTABLISHING STANDARDS FOR PRICE

Once we have established purchase specifications so that we know what quality to buy, and inventory procedures so that we know what quantity to buy, it is time to discuss the question of price. Since it is desirable to buy commodities of the appropriate quality in adequate quantities at the lowest possible price, it is desirable to ensure that the steward will purchase foods on the basis of competitive prices from several possible suppliers.

The availability of sources of supply varies considerably from location to location. Major cities, for example, tend to offer a great number of possibilities, both in terms of different categories of suppliers and number of suppliers in each category. On the other hand, isolated areas offer few possibilities; sometimes establishments in remote areas must be content with what they can get. In general, depending on ownership policy, availability of suppliers, and general market conditions, foodservice operators look to suppliers who fall into the following general categories:

- Wholesalers
- Local producers
- Manufacturers
- Packers
- Local farmers
- Retailers
- Cooperative associations

In most instances, the restaurant operator will deal with several of the sources of supply to obtain the necessary foods. For example, a restaurant might turn to a local producer for dairy and bakery products, a packer for canned meats, a wholesaler for fresh meats, a different wholesaler for canned fruits and vegetables, and a local farmer for eggs. In recent years there has been a trend for wholesalers to diversify their product lines in an attempt to better meet the needs of their restaurant customers. In some instances, they are able to supply virtually all of the food-related needs of a restaurant. In general, one will deal with as many as may be necessary to ensure the supply of foods of appropriate quality at the lowest prices.

To ensure that purchases are made at the lowest favorable price, the steward must secure prices from several competing suppliers for each commodity he or she intends to buy. The procedures differ for perishables and nonperishables.

Perishables

Because prices for perishables often fluctuate daily, it is necessary for the steward to telephone several different suppliers of the same commodity to ascertain current prices each time an order is to be placed. If copies of specifications have previously been sent to each, the steward can be assured that each supplier is quoting on commodities of comparable quality. The Steward's Market Quotation List, shown in Figure 5.2, provides four columns for price quotations on each commodity, with space at the top of each column for the name of the supplier. Ideally, the steward will obtain prices from at least three suppliers for each item and will select the lowest price. In reality, other things also should be taken into account, such as delivery time, the manager's preference for one dealer over another, the reliability of the dealers in meeting specifications, and so forth. Once prices have been obtained, the steward selects the supplier to be used and calls that dealer to place the order. Normally it is placed with the lowest bidder. As the order is placed, the steward circles that particular price quotation next to the item to be supplied. Thus, when all perishables have been ordered, the steward has a complete record of commodities ordered, as well as of prices, quantities, and suppliers. As we shall see in the next chapter, this list will be valuable for checking purposes when the food is delivered.

Nonperishables

Procedures involved in securing competitive prices for nonperishables are somewhat different. Usually the steward will deal with fewer sources of supply in the case of nonperishables. It is often possible to obtain price lists from wholesale supply houses, each of which may be able to supply most of the groceries the steward intends to order. The steward can compare prices and make selections at greater leisure than in the case of perishables. Although the steward will normally select the lowest price consistent with the quality desired, there are exceptions here as well. For example, if dealer A were offering all but one item at a lower price than dealer B, and dealer B's price for that one item were only two cents per can lower, the steward would be likely to place his order for twelve cans with dealer A in spite of the higher price, the difference being only a matter of $.24. The expenditure would be more than justified by the simplification of the ordering. In addition, it is possible that dealer B might not accept an order as small as twenty-four cans of a single item, because the profit might be more than offset by the cost of making the delivery.

TRAINING FOR PURCHASING

As everyone in the foodservice industry knows, formal training programs for food purchasers are not common. General food purchasing courses are taught in many schools, colleges, and universities, and seminars are conducted by such organizations as the National Restaurant Association. These are useful, but they cannot be considered substitutes for training workers to follow the standards and standard procedures established for an individual foodservice operation. The owner or manager is ultimately responsible for the training or lack of training of employees.

As discussed in Chapter 2, the second step in the control process is training employees to follow established standards and standard procedures. Having described such standards for food purchasing, we will turn to applying this second step in the control process.

To train an employee means to teach her to perform a given job in the manner expected by management. Assuming that the employee has the ability and basic knowledge needed to do the work, training her is easier if standards and standard procedures have been carefully and conscientiously developed. If these have not been formulated, training might be impossible. An example will illustrate this: one cannot train a server to wait on tables unless one has determined how the job is to be done: place settings must be standardized; service procedures must be developed; ordering procedures in the kitchen must be formalized, and so on. Unless there are standard procedures for servers to follow, each will perform his job in his own way. Some customers may be served quickly while others wait for long periods; some may find teaspoons in their place settings, while other must request them of the server.

Purchasing personnel must also be trained, and the training is easier when the kinds of standards and standard procedures discussed earlier in this chapter are in place. For example, if management has established the periodic order method as the standard procedure for maintaining supplies of nonperishables, a manager can explain the method to a new steward and, if necessary, work with that steward when he tries for the first time to use the method for determining correct order quantities. If neither the periodic order method nor any other method has been established as the standard, and if each previous steward has done the job his or her own way over the years, it is difficult to imagine how someone in management could begin to explain the details of the job to a new steward.

To the extent that new employees bring specific knowledge of their field to a job, training is far easier. It may be possible to devote minimal time to training under these circumstances, merely acquainting such employees with their surroundings and explaining various general company policies and practices. However, when new employees with specific knowledge are not available and management is forced to hire those with little knowledge and experience, training becomes critical to the proper functioning and even survival of the enterprise. It will be the responsibility of management not only to explain general policies and procedures but also to impart the basic knowledge and skills that a better-qualified employee would have brought to the job.

There are many acceptable methods for training employees, including classroom instruction, on-the-job training, simulation exercises, training manuals, and training films, to name but a few. Proper methods must be determined for each foodservice operation after careful review of the setting, the conditions, various budgetary considerations, and management's willingness to meet its responsibility for training.

MONITORING PURCHASING PERFORMANCE

The third step in the control process is to monitor employee performance and compare it with established standards and standard procedures. If proper control is to be established over the purchasing of foods, this third step is of great importance. Without this critical step, management has no assurance that the standards and standard procedures are being followed. For example, if management has directed that purchases of a given quality of beef be made at the lowest price, there can be no assurance that this policy is being followed unless the steward's purchasing performance is monitored.

Performance can be monitored in a number of ways. Some of these were discussed in general terms in Chapter 2, including observing and correcting employee actions and requiring records and reports. For example, management may require that the Steward's Market Quotation List be turned in daily with selected prices circled for daily verification. Another possibility would be to telephone purveyors from time to time to be sure that the prices written by the steward were accurate. Many other monitoring techniques may be used as well, some daily and some periodically, depending on circumstances and management's perceived need to monitor purchasing performance.

TAKING CORRECTIVE ACTION

The fourth step in the control process was defined in Chapter 2 as taking appropriate action to correct deviations from standards. It represents management's opportunity to do whatever may be necessary to ensure that employees' future performance will more nearly approximate established standards and standard procedures.

This fourth step may be very simple in some cases, and far more difficult in others. For example, a willing and loyal employee may merely have forgotten one or more standards, or may have been momentarily distracted while working. In such cases, a simple reminder may be the only corrective action needed. In other cases—those involving theft or drug abuse—sterner measures are required.

It is important to remember that any deviation from established standards, no matter how slight, means that employee performance is not measuring up to the goals of management. Such deviations will doubtless have long-term negative impact on the overall performance of the enterprise, and many have noticeable short-term consequences, including production of inferior products for sale to customers. In extreme cases, if a steward has neglected to purchase some foods necessary for the production of the day's menu, it could mean no production of certain menu items. Corrective action would be warranted, and mandatory.

CENTRALIZED PURCHASING

No discussion of purchasing procedures would be complete without some mention of the existence of centralized purchasing systems, widely used by chain operations, and occasionally established by small groups of independent operators with similar needs. Under a centralized purchasing system, the requirements of individual units are relayed to a central office, which determines total requirements of all units and then purchases that total, either for delivery to the individual units by the dealer or for centralized delivery. This last method obviously requires that a whole system for distribution be maintained and operated by the organization doing the centralized purchasing. There are both advantages and disadvantages to these centralized systems, and these should be understood by anyone involved in food management.

Advantages

1. Foods and beverages are purchased at a lower price because of volume purchasing.
2. It provides a better opportunity to obtain desired quality, because the purchaser has a greater choice of markets.
3. Goods can be obtained to the purchaser's exact specifications.
4. Larger inventories can be maintained, ensuring a more constant supply to individual units.
5. Greater control over dishonesty of individual unit food purchasers can be maintained.

Disadvantages

1. Each unit must accept the standard item in stock and has little freedom to purchase for its own peculiar needs.
2. Units cannot take advantage of local "specials" at reduced prices.
3. Menus usually must be standardized, thus limiting the individual unit manager's freedom to change a menu.

Finally, it should be noted that decisions about whether or not to become involved in centralized purchasing systems are normally made by top management, not by food controllers. However, there are times when food controllers may be called upon for advice and opinions, and they should understand what is involved in centralized purchasing.

STANDING ORDERS

Although it is desirable for needed quantities to be carefully determined each time orders are placed, stewards commonly make arrangements with certain purveyors for the delivery of goods without specific orders. These arrangements are known as standing orders, and they typically take one of two forms.

One arrangement calls for the delivery of specific numbers of a certain item each day; for example, twelve loaves of bread. The number would remain constant unless specifically changed by the steward. The second arrangement usually calls for the replenishing of stock each day up to a certain predetermined number. For instance, the steward might arrange with a dairy supplier to leave sufficient quantities of bulk milk each morning to bring the total supply up to a predetermined figure, such as twenty gallons. While these arrangements are convenient, they do present a number of possibilities for both waste and excessive cost to develop.

COMPUTER APPLICATIONS

Today, many restaurants are using computers and computer systems for a variety of purposes, and increasing numbers will do so each year. One obvious use of a computer is to maintain information about the food inventory.

Assume that management elects to maintain supplies of nonperishables by the perpetual inventory method, and that all relevant data are recorded in computer memory, including reorder point, reorder quantity, previous purchases and issues, and any other information that would be useful in making purchase decisions. With all such data available through a computer, management could quickly determine the current status of the entire inventory, including a list of those items at or below reorder point. In effect, the perpetual inventory card for each item would be filed in the computer, rather than in a metal or wood file drawer.

Using one of the common database programs, it is comparatively simple to create an inventory file for the nonperishable food inventory. Using some combination of text fields, numeric fields, and other specialized fields that vary from program to program, one could record such information as the items in the inventory, various vendors, purchase units, current prices, quantities purchased, and quantities issued. The purchase and issue field for each item would be used to determine a quantity on hand, which could be compared to the reorder point, and a report could be generated listing those items for which the quantity on hand had reached the reorder point. In the case of an individual restaurant, this report would be used by the steward to place orders. In a chain organization, similar reports from all units might be sent electronically to a home office, where they could be compiled into one complete list of purchases to be made centrally for the entire organization, conceivably at considerable savings.

While there are many advantages to maintaining food inventories with computers, this approach is not without some problems. For example, perpetual inventory files in a computer must be kept current in the same basic manner as perpetual inventory cards in a file drawer: someone must be given responsibility for recording all purchases and issues. Unless this information is recorded with complete accuracy, the records will be useless for the purpose of making purchasing decisions. And recording data in a computer terminal requires as much time and concentration as recording those data on index cards. If management directs that computers be used as aids in record keeping and decision making, it must be prepared to accept an expense for the time one or more employees will spend at the computer terminal keeping the records current. Computer use is presently most common in larger restaurants and in chain organizations, because it may be difficult for small operators to justify the cost by foreseeable benefits.

The foregoing is but one example of the many possibilities offered by computers for more effective management of the purchasing function in food service.

CHAPTER ESSENTIALS

In this chapter, we described the application of the four-step control process to food purchasing. We discussed the need for fixing responsibility for purchasing, the establishment of appropriate quality and quantity standards, and a method for determining optimum purchase prices. Specific procedures for the purchase of perishable and nonperishable foods were outlined, including the two most common methods for purchasing nonperishable foods: the periodic order method and the perpetual inventory method. The most common sources of supply used by foodservice operators were listed, and various considerations that affect selection of particular suppliers were described. We discussed the need for training purchasing personnel, as well as techniques for monitoring their performance and, when necessary, taking corrective action. We described centralized purchasing and discussed its advantages and disadvantages. We defined standing orders and discussed their use by some establishments, pointing out various risks associated with their use. Finally, we discussed the use of computers as aids in record keeping to improve management of the purchasing function and provided an illustration of how the computer can be employed in this way.

KEY TERMS IN THIS CHAPTER

Perishable foods

Nonperishable foods

Standard purchase specifications

Steward's Market Quotation List

Periodic order method

Bin card

Perpetual inventory method

Par stock

Perpetual inventory card

Reorder point

Reorder quantity

Centralized purchasing

Standing orders

QUESTIONS AND PROBLEMS

1. List ten food items you would consider perishable. Do the same for ten nonperishable food items.

2. Write a standard purchase specification for each of the following:

   a. Rack of lamb

   b. Lug of tomatoes

   c. Case of No. 10 cans of string beans

3. Write a one-paragraph explanation of why the standard purchase specifications would differ for eggs depending on whether they were used for the breakfast menu or in the bake shop for bakery items.

4. A restaurant uses the periodic order method. Determine amounts to order for canned peaches if orders are placed every two weeks and

   a. Normal usage is one case of twenty-four cans per week.

   b. Ten cans are presently on hand.

   c. The amount desired as an ending inventory is sixteen cans.

5. Assume a restaurant uses the periodic order method. Determine amounts to order for tomato juice if the steward orders once a month and

   a. Normal usage is one case of twelve cans per week.

   b. Six cans are presently on hand.

    c. The amount desired as an ending inventory is eighteen cans.

    d. The coming month is expected to be very busy, requiring 50% more tomato juice than normal.

6. Assume a restaurant uses the perpetual order method. Determine the reorder point, and at that point the amount of canned pears to order given the following:

    a. Normal usage is twenty-one cans per week.

    b. It takes four days to get delivery of the item.

    c. Par stock is set at forty-two cans.

    d. Cans come packed twelve to a case.

7. Assume a restaurant uses the perpetual order method. Determine the reorder point for canned green beans and the amount of canned green beans to order given the following:

    a. Normal usage is two cans per day.

    b. It takes five days to get delivery of the item.

    c. Par stock is set at twenty-nine cans.

    d. Cans come packed six to a case.

8. Assume you have been hired as the purchasing steward of a new restaurant located in an area that is completely unfamiliar to you. How would you obtain information on sources of supply for perishable and nonperishable foods?

9. How can the computer help management establish control over the purchasing function?

10. Define each of the Key Terms listed at the end of the chapter.

For Computer Users

11. Using any database program you choose, create a simple inventory file to incorporate the data provided in Figure 5.4.

12. Using the file initiated in question 10 above, substitute the information provided below for a second item in the inventory—whole, peeled tomatoes:

Item:	Tomatoes, whole, peeled
Size:	#10 can
Supplier:	EZ Foods
	41027 Fountain Avenue
	Chicago, IL
Cost:	$11.85 per case
Par Stock:	108
Reorder Point:	18
Reorder Quantity:	102

Record the following data in the proper fields, then determine from the file the proper date for reordering:

10/1—Balance in inventory: 37
10/1—Issued 7 cans
10/2—Issued 6 cans
10/3—Issued 6 cans
10/4—Issued 5 cans

chapter 6

Receiving Control

Learning Objectives

After reading and studying this chapter, the student should be able to:

1. List and explain the three standards of receiving control.
2. List and explain the six components of standard receiving procedure.
3. Describe the duties of a receiving clerk.
4. List the essential equipment and supplies needed for proper receiving.
5. Define an invoice, and explain its use.
6. Explain the significance of the invoice stamp and list five reasons for its use.
7. Identify the receiving clerk's daily report, list the information found in it, and explain how and why it is used.
8. Distinguish between Directs and Stores.
9. Describe a meat tag, list the information found on it, and explain how it is used.
10. Discuss the importance of training receiving personnel.
11. Explain the need for monitoring the performance of receiving personnel.
12. Describe one productive use of the computer in the receiving process.

If great care is taken to establish effective controls for purchasing but no attention is given to receiving controls, all earlier efforts may be wasted. After all, ordering specific quantities and qualities at optimum prices constitutes no guarantee that the commodities ordered will actually be delivered. Either by accident or by design, purveyors may deliver foods in incorrect quantities, of higher or lower qualities, not at the prices quoted, or all three. Receiving controls, therefore, have as a primary purpose verifying that quantities, qualities, and prices conform to orders placed.

In our discussion, we will assume the existence of a receiving clerk to whom management assigns the full responsibility for receiving food deliveries and carrying out the control procedures set up by the food controller. In larger operations, particularly those with complete food control systems, this is often the case. In smaller operations that deem the payroll expense of a receiving clerk unwarranted, food deliveries may be received by any one of several individuals, including the owner, the manager, the chef, or the steward. Although we use the title of receiving clerk here to facilitate discussion, we are aware that others do receive deliveries. The point to be made here does not involve the title of the person doing the receiving; what is important is the development of a set of standard procedures for receiving food deliveries and the verification that these deliveries conform to orders in *every* respect.

As was illustrated in the preceding chapter, controlling any aspect of foodservice operations is dependent upon applying the four-step control process. In attempting to establish control over the receiving function, therefore, it is important to begin with the first step—establishing standards and standard procedures.

ESTABLISHING STANDARDS FOR RECEIVING

The primary purpose of receiving control is to verify that the quantity, quality, and price of each item delivered conforms to the orders placed. To ensure that this is the case, it is necessary to establish standards to govern the receiving process, as follows:

1. The quantity of any item delivered should be the same as the quantity listed on the Steward's Market Quotation List or the Steward's Staple List, and this should be identical to the quantity listed on the invoice, or bill, that accompanies the delivery.
2. The quality of any item delivered should conform to the establishment's standard purchase specification for that item.
3. The price for any item on the invoice should be the same as that circled on the Steward's Market Quotation List or on the Steward's Staple List.

THE INVOICE

All food deliveries should be accompanied by an **invoice**, which is another word for a bill. A typical invoice form is illustrated in Figure 6.1. This is usually presented to the receiving clerk in duplicate by the person making the delivery, who will expect the receiving clerk to sign and return the second copy, thus acknowledging to the purveyor that the establishment has received the commodities listed. The original is, in effect, a bill that must be routed to the bookkeeper or other individual responsible for paying bills. This routing procedure will be dealt with later in this chapter.

Invoices not listing prices should be discouraged. Prices should be checked on receipt of the goods. Otherwise, the purveyor might bill at the wrong prices, either by accident or by design.

FIGURE 6.1
Invoice

| | | Invoice
Market Price Meat Co.
300 Market St.
New York, N.Y. | | |
|---|---|---|---|---|

Date June 11

To   The Graduates Restaurant

Quantity	Unit	Description	Unit Price	Amount
30	lbs.	Strip Steak	7.95	238.50
10	lbs.	Breast of Veal	4.65	46.50
				$285.00

ESTABLISHING STANDARD PROCEDURES FOR RECEIVING

Although the authors recognize that exact procedures and techniques for receiving will vary from one establishment to another, it will be useful to examine the following standard procedures that many managers would find appropriate for use in their establishments.

1. Verify that the quantity, quality, and price for each item delivered conforms exactly to the order placed.
2. Acknowledge that quantity, quality, and price have been checked by stamping the invoice with the rubber stamp provided for that purpose.

3. List all invoices for foods delivered on a given day on the Receiving Clerk's Daily Report for that day, and complete the report as required.
4. Fill out meat tags for all appropriate items.
5. Forward completed paperwork to proper personnel.
6. Move all delivered food to appropriate storage areas.

Each of the elements in this standard procedure will be discussed below.

Verifying Quantity, Quality, and Price

In order for the receiving clerk to carry out the verification procedure, he must have certain supplies and equipment available, including

1. A permanent copy of the standard purchase specifications.
2. Appropriate equipment for determining weight, including such items as a hanging scale and a platform scale.
3. Certain paper forms, tags, rubber stamps, and related office supplies.

Quantity verification entails weighing, counting, or otherwise enumerating the quantity of a particular food delivered by the vendor, then checking to see that the same quantity appears on both the invoice and on the order (the Steward's Market Quotation List or the Steward's Staple List). In some larger establishments, a purchase order might be used in place of the Steward's Staple List.

Quality verification requires knowledgeable inspection of delivered foods and careful comparison of perceived quality with the quality established in the standard purchase specifications. For example, the individual receiving strip loins of beef should be able to determine that the beef he is inspecting conforms to the restaurant's standard purchase specifications. Given the specification for strip loin illustrated in Figure 5.1 in the previous chapter, inspection should reveal prime beef, bone in, with weight ranging from 14 to 16 pounds, with fat limited to one-half to three-quarters of an inch except for seam fat, with moderate marbling, and with light red to slightly dark red color to the meat. Each item delivered should conform to the standard purchase specification written for it.

Price verification requires comparing the unit price appearing on the invoice with the price quote circled on the Steward's Market Quotation List, the Steward's Staple List, or on the purchase orders. Obviously, the price on the invoice should be the same as the listed purchase price used by the steward.

In the event that quantity, quality, or price of foods delivered does not conform to the orders placed, appropriate steps should be taken. Sometimes this will involve returning inferior foods with the delivery driver. Sometime it may involve changing the quantities listed on the invoice and having the delivery driver initial the change. For purposes of this discussion, it is important only to note that each discrepancy should be noted and attended to at the time of delivery.

One difficulty frequently presents itself: delivery drivers do not have the time to wait for verification to be completed. Therefore, it is important to maintain good working relationships with vendors so that any discrepancy found after the driver has left can be readily resolved by such means as credit memos or telephone calls. From time to time, some foodservice operators have found it necessary to put aside unacceptable food for return to the vendor at the earliest opportunity.

Stamping the Invoice

It is generally good practice to provide the receiving clerk with a rubber stamp to be used on all invoices. This invoice stamp, a suggested form for which is illustrated in Figure 6.2, is used for a number of reasons. It provides for:

1. Verification of the date on which food has been received.
2. The signature of the clerk who has received the food and vouches for the accuracy of quantities, qualities, and prices.
3. The steward's signature, thus acknowledging that she is aware that the food has been delivered.
4. The food controller's verification of the arithmetical accuracy of the bill.
5. Signatory approval of the bill for payment by an authorized individual before a check is drawn.

Listing Invoices on Receiving Clerk's Daily Report

The Receiving Clerk's Daily Report is an important accounting document, particularly in large establishments that maintain complex management information systems. In these operations, managers divide all food into at least two different

FIGURE 6.2
Invoice Stamp

Invoice Stamp

Received J. Wilson ______ Date 6/11/XX

Steward ______

Prices and
Extensions
Verified ______

OK for
Payment ______

categories, because some foods are purchased for immediate use, while others are purchased to be kept in inventory until needed. The former become part of cost immediately, while the latter are not included in cost until they are issued from the inventory. In food control, all foods that are charged to cost immediately are called Directs, and all foods that are charged to cost when issued from an inventory are called Stores. An understanding of the differences between the two, as well as working definitions for both, will be increasingly important in future chapters.

Directs are those foods that, because of their extremely perishable nature, are purchased on a more or less daily basis for immediate use. The quality of these foods tends to diminish quickly, and if they are not used very soon after the time of purchase they become unusable for their intended purposes. Foods that typically fall into this category are fresh fruits and vegetables, fresh baked goods, and most dairy products. Ideally, the quantities of each purchased on any given day should be sufficient for that day alone. Therefore, since they are purchased for immediate use, they are issued as they are received and included in food cost figures on the day of delivery. The *working definition* will be that Directs are those items that will be issued and charged to food cost as received.

Stores, on the other hand, are those foods that, while ultimately perishable, will not significantly diminish in quality if they are not used immediately. They can be held in storage and carried in inventory for a day or so, or in some instances for considerable periods of time. Meats, for example, if stored under proper conditions, can be maintained for reasonable periods of time. So too can those grocery items that are purchased in cans, bottles, and boxes. All these items are purchased on the basis of anticipated needs, not necessarily immediate, and are kept in inventory until they are needed. When the need arises, they are released from inventory and *issued* to the kitchen. Since we have seen that cost occurs when food is used, these items will be included in the food cost figures when they are issued for use. The *working definition* will be that Stores are those items that will be charged to food cost as issued.

It is possible to have long, elaborate discussions—even arguments—about the category into which any given item should be placed. Unquestionably, there are differences from restaurant to restaurant. In some establishments, for example, fresh fish is included with Directs, because it is purchased for use on the day of delivery. Other places may buy whole fish, which are cleaned and otherwise prepared for use the following day, and thus include fresh fish with Stores. Such discussion serves no useful purpose within this context. It is sufficient to say that the food controller in each establishment must make those decisions individually on the basis of use and then must consistently include each item in the preselected category.

The Receiving Clerk's Daily Report, illustrated in Figure 6.3, is a summary of invoices for all foods received on a given day. It is prepared by a receiving clerk, who merely copies data from each invoice to appropriate columns on the report, then enters the total for each invoice into one of the three columns under the general heading "Purchase Journal Distribution"—Food Direct, Food Stores, or

FIGURE 6.3
Receiving Clerk's Daily Report

Quant	Unit	Description	✔	Unit Price	Amount	Total Amount	Food Direct	Food Stores	Sundries
							Purchase Journal Distribution		
		Market Price Meats							
30	lbs.	Strip Steak	✔	7.95	238.50				
10	lbs.	Breast of Veal	✔	4.65	46.50				
						285.00		285.00	
		Ottman Meats							
15	lbs.	Pork Tenderloin	✔	2.50	37.50	37.50		37.50	
		Jones Produce & Fruit							
1	Crate	Lettuce	✔	12.50	12.50				
1	Bag	Onions		6.75	6.75				
1	Box	Grapefruit	✔	9.50	9.50				
1	Crate	Peaches	✔	12.00	12.00				
						40.75	40.75		
					363.25	363.25	40.75	322.50	

No. 1
Date June 11, 19XX

Receiving Clerk's Daily Report

Sundries. In the illustration, the invoice previously described in Figure 6.2 has been entered as the first invoice of the day, with the individual items and the totals copied. The total dollar value of food listed on that invoice, $285.00, has been recorded in the Food Stores column. This is because these items have been purchased for future use and will be held in inventory until needed, at which time they will be charged to cost. By contrast, the third invoice on the report, from Jones Produce and Fruit, totaling $40.75, is found in the Food Direct column because the listed items have been purchased for immediate use and will thus be charged to cost on the day they are received.

Filling Out Meat Tags

In the majority of restaurants, meats, poultry, fish, and shellfish constitute the most costly group of foods on the menu. Because of this comparatively high cost,

FIGURE 6.4
Meat Tag

No. 20624	
	Date Rec'd. 6/11
Item Strip Steak	Grade U.S. Prime
Weight 15	Lbs. @7.95
Dealer M P M	Extension 119.25
Date Issued _____	
William Allen & Co., N.Y. Stock Form 9247	

No. 20624
Date Rec'd. 6/11
Item Strip Steak
Wt. 15   Lbs. @7.95
Ext. 119.25
Dealer M P M
Date Issued _____

establishments with complete food control systems set up special controls for these items. Each package or piece received is tagged by the receiving clerk before it is placed in storage. In general, the rule followed is that items typically purchased to be sent to the kitchen for immediate use are not tagged; those that are typically held in inventory for one or more days before use are tagged.

A meat tag (Fig. 6.4) is usually printed on heavy card stock for durability and is perforated for convenient division into two parts. The tags can be purchased from any number of stationers catering to the industry and are numbered sequentially, with the number appearing on both parts. They are used in numerical order. The receiving clerk fills in all information except the date of issue, which cannot be filled in until the meat is issued to the kitchen for preparation. After filling out the tag, the receiving clerk detaches the smaller part and sends it to the food controller. The receiving clerk will dispose of the larger part by either (a) attaching it securely to the piece or package of meat, or (b) sending it to the steward. Because both approaches have advantages and disadvantages, there is no general agreement about which is preferable, and decisions about which procedure to follow are often made by the food controller on the basis of practicability.

The further use of meat tags and their importance to the operation with a complex control system will be discussed in Chapter 11.

Forwarding Completed Paperwork

By the time all deliveries for the day are in, preferably as early in the day as possible, the receiving clerk will have stamped and signed all invoices and entered each on the Receiving Clerk's Daily Report, often referred to simply as the receiving sheet. The sheet with the invoices attached should then be sent to the steward, who signs the invoices and routes them to the food controller, who checks the arithmetical accuracy of each invoice.* When the checking has been completed, the controller sends the receiving sheet and the invoices on to the accounting department, where the figures will be entered in the purchase journal.

---

* In some establishments the food controller will not be concerned with arithmetical accuracy, because the accounting department will verify all bills prior to payment.

However, while the food controller still has the receiving sheet, one very important total figure is recorded: the total cost of Directs. Because Directs are charged to the food cost as received, the food controller will need this figure in order to compute the daily cost of food sold. When we reach the chapter concerned with computing daily food cost, it will be important to keep in mind that the daily cost of Directs comes from the receiving sheet.

Moving All Delivered Food

Once deliveries have been received in the manner described above, it is recommended that foods be moved to appropriate storage areas as quickly as possible, with those that will most quickly deteriorate at room temperature being put away first. The spoilage and theft that may occur between receiving and storing foods can be a major cause of excessive cost. Therefore, the food controller should check from time to time to be sure that foods are being moved to storage areas at optimum times.

The purpose of establishing control procedures for receiving is to ensure that the establishment receives food in the quantities ordered, in the qualities specified, and at the prices quoted. These steps are basic and should be common to all foodservice operations, regardless of size. More complex systems of control, operated as they are with greater number of personnel and more equipment and procedures for checking, obviously offer greater measures of protection but do so at greater cost. However, even the small owner-operated restaurant should take these basic steps to guard against excessive costs that may develop from the receiving of improper quantities or qualities or the charging of improper prices.

In smaller establishments that do not have elaborate food control systems, some of the foregoing steps will be skipped, and the invoices are merely given to a bookkeeper by the person receiving the deliveries. However, this precludes a number of important possibilities for effective control. For example, such simplification makes it virtually impossible to compute a daily food cost. We will see that operating without knowledge of the daily food cost may be somewhat risky, and possibly a great disadvantage.

TRAINING FOR RECEIVING

Establishing standards and standard procedures for receiving is merely the first step. This must be followed by employee training, or there is no reasonable way for management to expect that the established standards and standard procedures will be observed.

At first glance, training for receiving does not appear to be difficult. After all, the routines for counting, weighing, and copying data from one paper to another can all be taught to an employee of reasonable intelligence. But there is more to receiving than routine clerical work.

The great problem faced by those who attempt to employ or train skilled receiving personnel lies with the vast amount of knowledge of foods these workers should have. They should be able to recognize whether or not particular items meet the established standard purchase specifications. They should be able to examine meats, for example, to determine grade, degree of freshness, and extent of trimming, among other considerations. With produce, they should be able to determine variety, degree of ripeness, and grade, at the very least. In other words, receiving personnel really need extensive knowledge if they are to do the proper job of checking quality. Anyone at all can be taught to weigh and count, but only a very few can make the necessary judgments as foods are received.

This may explain in part why so many restaurateurs do not require that receiving clerks check for quality as foods are delivered. They know that their receiving clerks do not have the knowledge. Instead, they rely on some other employee to check the quality after the receiving process has been completed. Some rely on a knowledgeable steward to do this. If the steward is unable, the chef may be required to do it. If the chef does not have the knowledge, the owner or manager may be forced to make the judgments personally. And if the owner or manager does not make them, the judgments about food quality will finally be made in the dining room by the customers, probably with devastating results.

MONITORING RECEIVING PERFORMANCE AND TAKING CORRECTIVE ACTION

Even though counting, weighing, and transferring data from one form to another are comparatively simple routines, management must never assume that they are being done and done correctly. Monitoring is required.

While the techniques used for monitoring vary from one establishment to another, there are some common points. Managers should occasionally be present when foods are received to be sure the clerk is following established standard procedures. Since employees are more likely to do so when a manager is present, some prefer to wait until after the process has been completed, then quietly count or weigh one or two items and compare the results to the invoice. Managers do not do this every day with every delivery unless they find that employees are becoming lax. In that case, more frequent monitoring and appropriate corrective action will be required until receiving employees have improved their performance to the desired extent.

COMPUTER APPLICATIONS

If a restaurant or chain of restaurants is to make purchase decisions on the basis of data stored in computer memory, then it will be important to input data reflecting all items purchased as received. All of these data are listed on the invoices checked by the receiving clerk. Management might designate some individual to input data for all foods received and thus keep stored data current, both for quantity and price. In effect, this replaces the work presently done manually in those operations that keep data on perpetual inventory cards. Moreover, depending on the individuals involved and on the decisions of particular managers, it is possible to eliminate the receiving clerk's daily report, because the essential information about purchase journal distribution and accounts payable may be input as the invoices are input to update quantities.

Another possibility might be to require that the steward placing orders record in a terminal the items and quantities ordered and to provide the receiving clerk with a terminal for outputting these data as deliveries are received. This would provide a means for comparing items and quantities ordered with items and quantities received. Depending on management policy, prices could also be compared by this means.

CHAPTER ESSENTIALS

In this chapter, we described the application of the control process to the receiving function in a restaurant, explaining why foods received should conform to orders placed in respect to quantity, quality, and price. We listed and explained common standards and standard procedures for receiving, then described various forms and pieces of equipment required for proper receiving, including the invoice, invoice stamp, Receiving Clerk's Daily Report, and meat tags. We distinguished between Directs and Stores and established useful working definitions for each. We described the procedure for tagging meats and other high-cost stores and pointed out the importance of effective receiving control in preventing excessive costs. We discussed training receiving personnel and pointed out their need for considerable knowledge of foods if they are to be effective. We indicated the importance of monitoring the performance of those who receive food and suggested several techniques that managers can employ for monitoring. Finally, we showed how the computer can be an effective tool for a receiving clerk to use for inputting data that can be of use in both purchasing and accounting.

KEY TERMS IN THIS CHAPTER

Invoice	Stores
Invoice stamp	Purchase journal distribution
Receiving Clerk's Daily Report	Meat tag
Directs	

QUESTIONS AND PROBLEMS

1. In your own words, explain several significant effects of improper receiving controls.
2. Why are the following pieces of equipment necessary for effective receiving control?
   a. Platform scale
   b. Hanging scale
3. Assume that fifty pounds of strip steak were ordered and received but the invoice showed an incorrect quantity and price. How would you rectify the errors?
4. Why is it necessary for the receiving clerk to have a complete set of the establishment's standard purchase specifications?
5. What possible cost effects might there be if food deliveries all arrived at the same time?
6. Distinguish between Directs and Stores.
7. Is it possible for proper receiving to take place in the absence of standard purchase specifications? Explain your answer.
8. The text stated that some establishments do not use a receiving clerk's daily report form but check each item against the invoice. What are the possible advantages and disadvantages of this alternative procedure?
9. A certain restaurant does not use meat tags but treats meats as Directs. What are the immediate effects of this procedure on food cost? What are the possible ultimate effects?
10. The receiving clerk in a certain restaurant is also the dishwasher and has had no previous education or training in foods or in the food and beverage business. Discuss the possible effects on restaurant operations of having such an employee in this position.
11. In many restaurant operations, the steward who purchases food also functions as the receiving clerk. What are some of the possible positive and negative effects of this procedure?
12. How can the computer aid management in establishing control over the receiving function?

For Computer Users

13. Using Figure 6.3 as a model, create a spreadsheet that could be used in place of the Receiving Clerk's Daily Report.

chapter 7

Storing and Issuing Control

Learning Objectives

After reading and studying this chapter, the student should be able to:

1. List and explain the three causes of unplanned costs that can develop while food is in storage.
2. List and explain the five principal concerns that standards for storing food should address.
3. List optimum storage temperatures for the five classifications of perishable foods.
4. Explain the importance of establishing standards for each of the following:

   storage temperatures for foods.

   storage containers for foods.

   shelving.

   cleanliness of storage facilities.

   assigned fixed locations for the storage of each particular food.

5. Explain the principle of stock rotation as applied to foodservice.
6. Distinguish between issuing procedures for Directs and those for Stores.
7. Price and extend a food requisition.
8. Discuss the need for training personnel who store and issue food.
9. Describe the primary technique for monitoring the performance of those who store and issue food.
10. Distinguish between interunit and intraunit transfers, and give two examples of each.
11. Explain the significance of transfers in determining accurate food costs.
12. Explain how computers can assist in establishing control over the storing, issuing, and transfer of foods.

The two previous chapters were devoted to explaining the need for establishing control over purchasing and receiving and to describing the application of a control process to ensure that the proper foods are purchased at optimum prices, and that items purchased are received precisely as specified. When a foodservice operator selects particular qualities and quantities of food and places orders at particular prices, she is, in effect, creating and accepting the costs for food that will be served in the establishment. Eventually these costs will be reflected in the income statement. Having accepted a particular level of cost, it is clearly in the operator's best financial interest to take all necessary steps to prevent the development of additional, unplanned costs before the foods are sold to customers. These unacceptable costs normally develop from spoilage, waste, or pilferage (the industry's term for theft). In this chapter, we will describe how the four-step control process can be applied to storing and issuing to reduce or eliminate the development of unplanned, unwarranted costs.

STORING CONTROL: ESTABLISHING STANDARDS AND STANDARD PROCEDURES FOR STORING

In general, the standards established for storing food should address five principal concerns:

1. Condition of facilities and equipment.
2. Arrangement of foods.
3. Location of facilities.
4. Security of storage areas.
5. Dating and pricing of stored foods.

Each of these will be discussed separately.

Conditions of Facilities and Equipment

The factors involved in maintaining proper internal conditions include temperature, storage containers, shelving, and cleanliness. Any or all of these may lead to spoilage and waste.

Temperature

One of the key factors in the storing of foods, particularly perishables is temperature. Food life can be maximized when food is stored at the correct temperature and humidity. The food controller should occasionally check the temperature gauges on the refrigerated storage facilities to see that the appropriate temperatures are being maintained. The temperatures that follow are generally accepted as optimum for storing the foods indicated.*

- Fresh meats: 34 to 36°F.
- Fresh produce: 34 to 36°F.
- Fresh dairy products: 34 to 36°F.
- Fresh fish: 30 to 34°F.
- Frozen foods: −10 to 0°F.

If temperatures are permitted to rise above these levels, shelf life is shortened, and the risk of food spoilage is increased for perishables.

Temperature can also be important in keeping nonperishables. Storage facilities for staple commodities should usually be room temperature, approximately 70 to 72°F. Sometimes, particularly in older establishments, staples are kept in facilities that are either too warm because of their proximity to hot stoves or steam pipes running through the ceiling, or too cold because they are located in an unheated part of the building. While the degree of risk is not as great with staples, it should be remembered that all foods are ultimately perishable, and that food life is increased by storage at proper temperatures.

Storage Containers

In addition to maintaining foods at proper temperatures, care must be given to storing them in appropriate containers. In the case of staples, most, but not all, are purchased in airtight containers. Some, however, are purchased in unsealed containers, often paper bags, boxes, and sacks, which are susceptible to attack by insects and vermin. Whenever practicable, such commodities should be transferred to tight, insect-proof containers. In the case of perishables, both raw or cooked, care should be given to storing them in whatever manner will best maintain their original quality. Many raw foods such as apples or potatoes may be stored as purchased for reasonable periods; others, such as fresh fish, should be packed in shaved ice. In general, cooked foods and opened canned foods should be stored in stainless steel containers, either wrapped or appropriately covered.

Shelving

For perishable foods, shelving should be slatted to permit maximum circulation of air in refrigerated facilities. For nonperishables, solid steel shelving is usually

---

* While these temperatures are acceptable in very general terms, there are numerous exceptions. Bananas and potatoes, for example, should be stored at higher temperatures. For specific temperature for storage of any particular commodity, consult such authorities as Kotschevar, *Quantity Foods Purchasing,* or various publications of the United States Department of Agriculture.

preferred. At no time should anything be stored on the floor. Appropriate shelving raised a few inches above the floor level should be provided for large and heavy containers that must occasionally be used in storerooms or refrigerators.

Cleanliness

Conditions of cleanliness should be enforced in all storage facilities at all times. In refrigerated facilities, this will prevent the accumulation of small amounts of spoiling food, which will give off odors and may affect other foods. In storeroom facilities, it will discourage infestation by insects and vermin. Storerooms should be swept and cleaned daily, and no clutter should be allowed to accumulate. Extermination should be accomplished on a regular basis to prevent rodents and vermin from reaching population levels large enough to cause damage and disease.

Arrangement of Foods

The factors involved in maintaining appropriate internal arrangement include rotating stock, fixing definite locations for each item, and keeping the most-used items readily available.

Fixing Definite Location

Each particular item should always be found in the same location, and attention should be given to ensuring that new deliveries of the item are stored in the same location. All too often, one commodity is stored in several locations at once—for example, six cans on a shelf, and two partially used cases in two other areas. This increases the chances for overpurchasing, spoilage, and theft. In addition, it makes difficult the monthly process of taking a physical inventory, which will be discussed in the next chapter. Incidentally, separate facilities for storage of different classes of foods should be maintained whenever practicable and possible. Eggs, for example, should not be stored with fish, cheese or other foods that give off odors, because their shells are quite porous and they will absorb flavors from other foods. Fish should always be stored in separate facilities.

Rotation of Stocks

The food controller must ensure that older quantities of any item are used before any new deliveries. This is known as the **first-in, first-out** method of stock rotation, commonly called FIFO in the industry. The steward and his staff must be held responsible for storing new deliveries of an item *behind* the quantities already on hand, thus ensuring that older items will be used first. This reduces the possibilities for spoilage. If this procedure is not followed, if those who store foods are permitted to put new food in front of old food on shelves, the chances are increased that the older items will spoil before they are used. This is particularly important with perishables, but it should not be neglected with nonperishables.

Availability According to Use

It is usually helpful to arrange storage facilities so that the most frequently used items are kept closest to the entrance. Although it has no effect on spoilage and theft, it does tend to reduce the time required to move needed foods from storage to production, and thus tends to reduce labor costs.

Location of Storage Facilities

Whenever possible, the storage facilities for both perishable and nonperishable commodities should be located between receiving areas and preparation areas, preferably close to both. Such locations facilitate the moving of foods from the receiving areas to storage and from storage to the preparation areas. A good storage facility will have the effect of

1. Speeding the process of storage and issue.
2. Maximizing security.
3. Reducing labor requirements.

All too often, storage facilities are located in areas that are unusable for other purposes. Often that policy is penny wise and pound foolish, because temperature, security, and sanitary conditions are inadequate.

Dry storage areas should be sealed to reduce the risk of infestation. Obviously, it is impossible to seal an area if its location is susceptible to rodents.

Security

Food should never be stored in a manner that permits pilferage. This is another reason for moving foods from the receiving area to storage as quickly as possible. Once in storage, appropriate security must be maintained at all times. A storeroom for staple commodities should never be left unattended. Employees should not be permitted to remove items at will. Typically, a storeroom is kept open at specified times for specified periods well-known to the staff, and is otherwise closed to enable the attendant to perform other duties. When the storeroom is closed, it is locked, and the one key is in the storeroom clerk's possession. In such cases, one additional "emergency" key is usually kept by the manager or in the office safe.

Security is also an important consideration in storing perishables, particularly in the case of high-cost items such as meat and fish. The importance of security obviously increases with the value of the items stored. It is sometimes advisable to establish separate control procedures for steaks, liquor, and other high-cost items.

Dating and Pricing

It is desirable to date items as they are put away on shelves, so that the storeroom clerk can be certain of the age of each item and make provisions for use before spoilage sets in. Of particular concern are items that are used infrequently. The storeroom clerk should visually check the stock frequently to ascertain which items are beginning to get old and then inform the chef, so that items can be put on the menu before they spoil.

In addition, all items should be priced as goods are put away, with the cost of each container clearly marked. Following this procedure will greatly facilitate issuing, because the storeroom clerk will be able to price requisitions with little difficulty. If items are not priced as they are put away, the storeroom clerk will waste considerable time looking up prices when goods are sent to the kitchen.

ISSUING CONTROL: ESTABLISHING STANDARDS AND STANDARD PROCEDURES FOR ISSUING

In Chapter 6, a distinction was made between Directs and Stores. Directs were defined as those foods charged to cost as received, and Stores as those carried in inventory and charged to cost as issued. From a food controller's point of view, that distinction becomes particularly important in a discussion of issuing.

There are two elements to the issuing process: the physical movement of foods from storage facilities to food preparation areas, and the record keeping associated with determining the cost of the food issued.

Physical Movement of Foods from Storage Facilities

As described in the discussion of standards and standard procedures for storing, foods should be stored in fixed locations and under secure conditions in order to ensure that they will be available readily and in the purchased quantities when needed. When a cook needs a particular item, it must be removed from a storage facility and transported to the preparation area. Practices vary from one establishment to another. In some, all facilities are locked and cooks must list all their needs on requisitions, which are turned over to a steward who sees to the delivery of the various items. In others, storage facilities are unlocked and any cook who needs an item simply goes to get it. In many, some of the storage facilities are locked—the storeroom and the walk-in refrigerators for meat, for example—while others are left unlocked—refrigerators containing produce or leftovers.

There is no universal practice, but it should be obvious that establishments that take greater precautions tend to have greater control over unauthorized issuing. At the same time, it must be noted that these establishments tend to make issuing more time-consuming and thus costly by requiring written requisitions that must be filled by additional personnel. In general, small establishments tend to follow more informal practices, while large organizations are more likely to employ specific procedures requiring paper records and specialized staff. Standards and standard procedures for the physical movement of foods must be determined specifically for a given establishment, often on the basis of cost–benefit ratio.

Record Keeping for Issued Foods

Directs

Directs are charged to food cost as they are received, on the assumption that these perishable items are for immediate use. Theoretically, these foods will be moved to appropriate facilities in or near the kitchen and will be entirely used in the course of the day's food preparation. In practice, this is not normally the case. Some of the Directs received on a given day are likely to be left over and used the following day; in fact, most establishments purposely purchase more than one day's supply of many Directs. While this greatly simplifies the record keeping associated with determining the cost of Directs, it does introduce some inaccuracy in the records maintained.

As we will see, establishments that determine daily food costs use the total dollar figure in the Directs column on the Receiving Clerk's Daily Report as one component of the daily cost of food. This is based on the presumption that all Directs received on a given day have been consumed, and should thus be included in costs for the day. Since this is not strictly true, these daily costs tend to be artificially high on days when all Directs received have not been consumed and artificially low on days when Directs included in costs for previous days are actually being consumed.

For record keeping purposes, then, Directs are treated as issued the moment they are received, and no further record is kept of particular items. The alternative would be to follow an issuing procedure similar to that described below for Stores, which would require significant additional time and labor. Finally, it should be noted that waste, pilferage, or spoilage of Directs will result in unwarranted additions to food cost figures.

Stores

The food category known as Stores was previously described as one consisting of (a) staples and (b) tagged items, primarily meats. When purchased, these foods are considered part of inventory until issued for use and are not included in cost figures until they are issued. Therefore, it follows that records must be kept of issues in order to determine the cost of Stores. For control purposes, some system must be established to ensure that no Stores are issued unless the kitchen personnel submit lists of the items and quantities needed.

The Requisition   A **requisition,** illustrated in Figure 7.1, is a form prepared by a member of the kitchen staff listing the items and quantities needed from Stores. Each requisition should be reviewed by the chef, who should check to see that each item appearing is genuinely required in the amount listed. The requisition is then approved and signed by the chef. It is next given to the storekeeper, who fills the order.

FIGURE 7.1
Requisition

Quantity	Description	Unit Cost	Total Cost
	Date 9/8, 19XX		
	Supply __Main Kitchen__ Dept.		
6	#10 Cans Green Peas		
50	Lbs. Sugar		
40	Lbs. Ground Beef		
6	Loins Pork		
	Charge to __Food__ Dept.		
	__J. Lemon__		
	Chef		

Whenever practical, it is advisable to require that requisitions be submitted in advance to enable the storekeeper to prepare the order without haste. In some places, it has been found practical to insist on requisitions being submitted the day before food is needed. This has the desirable effect of forcing kitchen personnel to anticipate needs and plan for the following day's production.

It is also desirable, in many instances, to set definite times for the issuing of food by the storekeeper, who, after all, has a number of other duties to perform, including keeping the storerooms and refrigerators clean, maintaining stocks of staples on shelves, rotating stock, and doing considerable paperwork. Some operations have achieved good results by restricting the times for issuing food to two hours in the morning and two in the afternoon. Naturally, such decisions must be left to management in any particular operation.

Pricing the Requisition   After Stores have been issued from the appropriate stockroom, refrigerator, or freezer, it is the storekeeper's responsibility to list on each requisition the cost of listed items and to determine the total dollar value of the foods issued. As will be discussed in Chapter 11, this information is necessary for a daily determination of food costs.

Meats and Tagged Items   As meats are issued, the tag is detached from each piece and the dollar value recorded on the requisition. If one requisition requires the issuing of several pieces of meat, the tag values are totaled before entering. When meat tag values are entered, the tags are attached to the requisitions.

Staples   The unit cost of each listed item must be entered and multiplied by the number of units issued in each case. This is called **extending the requisition.** The unit cost will come from one of the following, depending on the system in use:

1. The unit cost of each item is marked on each container as it is stored, making it readily available to the storekeeper.
2. A book or card file is maintained for all staple items, one page or card per item. As prices change, the most recent purchase price is always entered.
3. The most recent purchase price is listed on a perpetual inventory card for each item.
4. The storekeeper keeps a mental index card for each item and usually has the purchase price of each in mind from constant use.

   While the first method is generally preferred, it unquestionably involves considerable labor and consequently is costly to maintain. Therefore, though preferred, it is not the method in general use. More often than not, prices come from the storekeeper's head. Although the accuracy of this "system" leaves much to be desired, it is the method requiring the least time and labor. Many operations have found that the resulting inaccuracies have no significant effect over the long run.

   Once the values of tagged items have been entered and the unit costs of staples entered and extended, each requisition is totaled, as illustrated in Figure 7.2. At the end of the day, all requisitions are sent to the food controller with meat tags attached.

   Thus on the following morning the food controller will have figures available for the principal components of a daily food cost:

1. Cost of Directs from the receiving sheet.
2. Cost of Stores from the requisitions, with meat tags attached.

As has been previously illustrated, the first step in the control process—establishing standards and standard procedures—is the proper beginning, which must be followed by three additional steps. We will now direct our attention to the application of those steps—training employees, monitoring their performance, and taking corrective action as required—in storing and issuing control.

FIGURE 7.2
Requisition

			Date 9/8,	19XX	

Supply ___Main Kitchen___ Dept.

Quantity	Description	Unit Cost	Total Cost
6	#10 Cans Green Peas	$2.79	$16.74
50	Lbs. Sugar	.39	19.50
40	Lbs. Ground Beef	2.59	103.60
6	Loins Pork (108 lbs per tags)	2.39	258.12
			$397.96

Charge to ___Food___ Dept.

___JJ Lemon___
Chef

TRAINING FOR STORING AND ISSUING

The importance of training may best be illustrated by negative example. Let us suppose that the owner of a particular establishment hires inexperienced personnel to store and issue foods, pays them low wages, and restricts training to the barest minimum, merely telling people what their duties are in the most general way. Consider some of the possible problems that could arise: foods could be stored in inappropriate containers, or at improper temperatures, and quality could deteriorate very quickly; one single item might be stored in several locations, with quantities in one area spoiling because no one knew they were there; new deliveries might be stored in front of old, with the old spoiling while the new were being used; pilferage could increase significantly if storage areas were not secured; the dollar value of issues might not be identifiable because those issuing foods had neglected to record item prices on the requisitions. These are but a few examples; a list of the many such problems occurring in foodservice establishments that fail to train adequately would be considerably longer.

Fortunately, training for storing and issuing is not as difficult as training for purchasing. Purchasing personnel, after all, require considerable prior knowledge of food and the distinctions between food qualities. Storing and issuing personnel, on the other hand, can be taught the proper methods and procedures by a qualified trainer, one who knows the correct techniques for storing and issuing and can explain them clearly to the new employee.

There are two elements at work here. First, correct storing and issuing techniques are not universally known. Frequently there are a few correct ways and an infinite number of wrong ways to store a given item. For issuing, it is important that older items be issued before newer ones. At best, the new employee will learn the methods and procedures he is taught. If the trainer is not qualified to teach correct methods, stored foods are not likely to be maintained for their maximum useful life, with obvious implications for cost. Second, those employed to store and issue foods are not normally hired specifically for their ability to train others, and they may not be able to explain the necessary information clearly to those they are expected to train. Misunderstandings resulting from inability to convey knowledge clearly can also have negative impact on cost.

In the area of training, large organizations often have an advantage over their smaller counterparts. The large organization frequently has a sufficient number of new employees needing training to justify the expense of a training department staffed by professionals, while the small establishment must rely on the questionable training skills of regular employees to prepare new workers for their jobs.

Training employees to store and issue each food item properly is important to the successful operation of all foodservice establishments, large and small, and it is important that those who manage small operations recognize the training obstacles they face and seek to overcome them.

MONITORING STORING AND ISSUING PERFORMANCE, AND TAKING CORRECTIVE ACTION

While properly trained employees are probably more reliable performers than they would be otherwise, it is not advisable for management merely to assume that each is correctly following the routines and procedures in which she was trained. Efforts must be made to compare the actual performance of each employee to the expected performance, a process by now familiar to the reader as monitoring.

Perhaps the primary technique for monitoring the performance of those who store and issue food is to observe the results of their work. To monitor storing procedures, management must inspect the storage facilities on a regular basis to determine that facilities are kept clean and well-organized, that refrigerators and freezers are operating at proper temperatures, that each food item is being stored in its assigned location, that stocks are being rotated, and that established security precautions are being maintained. To monitor issuing procedures, management must examine paperwork to verify that requisitions are being properly prepared, priced, and extended. From time to time, management must check to see that food is not being issued without requisitions.

To the extent that observation reveals that employees are not adhering to the standards and standard procedures they have been trained to follow, some corrective action will be required. In some instances, simple reminders will suffice; in others, more vigorous steps may be required. Finally, management must take the required corrective action as quickly as possible, or risk continuing failure to meet established standards in the affected areas.

FOOD AND BEVERAGE TRANSFERS

So far in our discussions we have assumed that a restaurant purchases, receives, stores, and issues food for use in one kitchen in which all production is accomplished. By doing so, we have quite purposely ignored the existence of a number of possible complications, which it will be useful to consider at this point. For example, even in small restaurants, food production in the kitchen may require the use of certain beverage items, such as wines and liquors, not purchased specifically for kitchen use. Conversely, many establishments purchase some food items knowing that they will be used at the bar for drink production. Whole oranges and lemons, as well as heavy cream, are good examples. In addition, in some large hotel and motel operations more than one kitchen is in operation, and it may be necessary or desirable from time to time or even regularly to transfer food from one to another. Transfers may occur in chain operations, where one unit may produce such items as baked goods for other units, or where one unit in the organization, running short of needed items, may be encouraged to secure them from another unit.

Since the goals of food control include determining food cost as accurately as possible and matching food cost with food sales, it is often necessary to maintain records of the cost of the food transferred. When the amounts involved are relatively insignificant and have little appreciable effect on cost and on the cost-to-sales ratio, they may be, and usually are, disregarded. But when the amounts become somewhat larger and have more significant effects, records of some type must be developed.

Intraunit Transfers

Between Bar and Kitchen

Food and beverage transfers between the bar and the kitchen occur frequently in operations of all sizes. Many kitchens use such beverage items as wine, cordials, brandy, and even ale for the production of sauces, parfaits, certain baked items, and rarebits. Occasionally, these items are purchased by the food department for use in the kitchen, kept in a storeroom until needed, and then issued on requisitions directly to the kitchen. In such cases additional records are not required; the quantities and values listed on the requisition are sufficient to permit accurate calculations of cost. However, in most instances when these beverage items are needed in the kitchen, appropriate amounts are secured from the bar. After all, if sufficient supplies are already being maintained at the bar, it makes little sense to keep additional quantities for specific use in food production.

The same may be said of certain food items in the Directs category used by bartenders in drink production: if supplies of oranges, lemons, limes, heavy cream, and eggs are already available in the kitchen, it makes little sense in most operations to purchase specific supplies of these items for exclusive use at the bar. It is far simpler merely to secure the needed items from the kitchen. When it becomes necessary or desirable to achieve a high degree of accuracy in determining costs to match with sales, records of these transfers between the food and beverage departments must be maintained. The form used to maintain these records is the Food/Beverage Transfer Memo, illustrated in Figure 7.3. As transfers are made, items and amounts are recorded on such memos by authorized individuals. When these memos have been completed, they may be sent to the food controller, who can use them to adjust food cost figures to achieve greater accuracy, and then routed to an accounting office, where the appropriate entries can be made in the financial records.

FIGURE 7.3
Food/Beverage Transfer Memo

<table>
<tr><td colspan="4" align="center">**Food/Beverage Transfer Memo**
Date   9/8,   19XX</td></tr>
<tr><td colspan="4">From   Bar</td></tr>
<tr><td colspan="4">To   Main Kitchen</td></tr>
<tr><td>Quantity</td><td>Description</td><td>Unit Price</td><td>Amount</td></tr>
<tr><td>1</td><td>750 ml Sneed's Sherry</td><td>$3.95</td><td>$3.95</td></tr>
<tr><td>1</td><td>750 ml Red Wine</td><td>2.65</td><td>2.65</td></tr>
<tr><td></td><td></td><td></td><td></td></tr>
<tr><td></td><td></td><td>Total</td><td>$6.60</td></tr>
<tr><td colspan="4">Sent by   Joe - bartender
Received by   Paul - Chef</td></tr>
</table>

Between Kitchen and Kitchen

In some hotel and motel operations with more than one kitchen and dining room, it is common practice to determine food costs for each separately and to match the costs for each operating unit with the sales generated by that unit. Where some food items are transferred from one kitchen to another, higher degrees of accuracy in determining food costs may be achieved by keeping records of items and amounts so transferred. In cases where, for example, one unit closes earlier than another, and cooked foods may be conveniently transferred from a closing unit to one remaining open until a later hour, it would be possible to achieve a higher degree of accuracy in determining costs for each unit by crediting cost the early closing unit for the value of the items transferred and by adding the amount to the cost for the later closing unit.

Even in cases where items are not so transferred but are merely returned to a central kitchen or commissary for reissue to the same or to other units on succeeding days, recording the value of the items returned on transfer memos or on other similar forms makes possible more accurate determination of food costs, and consequently of cost-to-sales ratios for operating periods.

Interunit Transfers

The two examples that follow illustrate the problem of interunit transfers and the effect of such transfers on food costs.

In a number of instances small chains produce some items—baked goods, for example—in only one unit and then distribute those items to other units in the chain. If the ingredients for the baked goods come from that particular unit's regular supplies, then some record must be made of the cost of the ingredients used. Failure to do so would result in overstating the food cost of the producing unit by the value of the ingredients used, and in understanding the food costs of the receiving units by the value of the foods they receive. In addition, if the matching principle is to be followed, and if food sales are reported separately for each unit, then food cost figures that do not include the cost of all those foods sold, including the baked goods from another unit, cannot be said to be truly matched with sales. Under such conditions, if one of management's goals is to match costs and sales with a reasonably high degree of accuracy, it is necessary to use the transfer memo or some similar form to record the value of ingredients used in the production of finished products for transfer to other units.

With such records available, it is possible to credit cost of the producing unit. Appropriately increasing the food cost figures of the receiving units may pose more of a problem. If each unit receives an equal share of the goods produced, then one could simply divide the cost of the goods produced and credited to the producing unit by the number of units to which items had been transferred and increase the food cost of each by one equal share. However, if the total produced for distribution to the various units is not divided among them equally, then some more equitable means for apportioning cost must be found. One possible solution is to record the values of transferred items at standard costs. The question of calculating standard costs of production for this and for other purposes will be deferred to the next chapter.

Another problem involving the value of foods transferred from one unit to another may be found in those chain organizations that permit or encourage unit managers to use foods from other units when their own supplies run low and when additional purchases are precluded by time. When units are comparatively close to one another and offer identical menus, occasions may arise when one of the units nearly exhausts the supply of some important item and does not discover this shortage until it is clearly too late to purchase an additional amount. In some organizations, items are borrowed and returned within a day or so as a matter of course, and no complications arise as long as all borrowed items are appropriately returned. However, not all cases are quite so simple, as, for example, when a perishable item borrowed by one unit does not appear on the menu again for some considerable period of time. Rather than maintain records over long periods in order to ensure the return of borrowed items, it is often simpler to record such transfers of foods on transfer memos and to use the information so recorded to increase the cost of the unit that has borrowed, and correspondingly to decrease the cost of the supplying unit.

An interesting problem that may arise in connection with this procedure is the extent to which it influences some managers purposely to maintain short supplies of some high-cost and perishable items. If the organization permits one to secure needed supplies from other units at the same prices one would pay in the market, some managers will be encouraged to reduce the possibilities for excessive costs due to spoilage and pilferage in their units simply by maintaining inadequate supplies. Under such conditions, discouraging managers from taking advantage might entail establishing a price for transfer purposes somewhat higher than the current market price.

It is quite probable that there are in this industry a reasonably large number of transfers of the various types discussed above, but it is equally probable that a large number involve comparatively small amounts of food of relatively insignificant value. Consequently, because the amounts involved are usually negligible in most places, records are often not used. However, if and when the amounts become significant, provision must be made for maintaining adequate records to ensure that good cost figures include the cost of beverages used in food preparation and exclude the cost of food items sent to the bar for beverage preparation, and that food cost figures for one unit of a large organization include the cost of food items sold in that unit. In every case, to the extent feasible, the cost of items sold in a department, division, or unit should include all items reflected in sales figures.

COMPUTER APPLICATIONS

From the previous chapter, the student will recall that computers can store information about quantities purchased and received as well as purchase prices. It would also be possible to establish a computer code for all storage locations, so that each particular item in storage would be assigned a particular location. Before any food purchases were stored, one could determine from computer memory the correct storage location for each item, in order to help ensure that all available quantities of a given food item were consolidated in one particular location.

Issuing control offers many possibilities for computer assistance. For example, rather than require the chef to write out a requisition and present it to the steward, management might ask that the chef enter the needed items in a terminal. The chef would thus help update stored information on inventory levels, for the items would be treated as issued when entered by the chef. If a local area network (LAN) were installed, there would be a printer in the storeroom, and the chef's clearly legible order would be available to those who would fill it. The requisition could be printed instantly or at a later time, and the handwritten requisition so commonly used now could be eliminated. Another desirable feature of this procedure would be that the chef could output inventory data to learn the quantities of particular items on hand. This would have obvious benefits for menu planning.

Transfers may be processed in much the same way as requisitions. If a bartender needed fruit or other Directs for making drinks, these needs would be entered in a terminal at the bar and printed out in the storeroom so that delivery to the bar might be made. Beverages required for food production would be entered by the chef and printed out at the bar. Any transferred items would be stored in memory until needed for accurate food cost determination.

CHAPTER ESSENTIALS

In this chapter, we described the application of the control process to the storing and issuing functions in a restaurant. We explained that unwanted costs can develop from spoilage, waste, and pilferage, and listed the five principal concerns that standards for storing must address: conditions of facilities and equipment, arrangement of foods, location of facilities, security of storage areas, and dating and pricing of stored foods. Included were discussions of temperature, storage containers, shelving, cleanliness, food locations, and rotation of stock. We distinguished between issuing procedures for directs and stores and indicated the importance of the requisition and the meat tag in issuing stores. We discussed training, pointing out again the importance of proper training if standards and standard procedures are to be maintained, and we described some of the negative consequences of failing to train storing and issuing personnel adequately. We described the primary technique for monitoring the performance of those who store and issue foods. We defined food and beverage transfers and illustrated several types, pointing out the possible effects on food costs that such transfers may have. We described the means for maintaining records of transfers for the purpose of introducing greater accuracy into food and beverage cost determination. Finally, we indicated several ways in which computers can be used to help management establish control over the storing, issuing, and transfer of items in inventory.

KEY TERMS IN THIS CHAPTER

Unplanned costs

Unacceptable costs

Rotation of stock

Requisition

Extending a requisition

Food and beverage transfers

Intraunit transfers

Interunit transfers

QUESTIONS AND PROBLEMS

1. What are some of the possible problems implicit in allowing the chef, receiving clerk, or dining room manager to have keys to the storeroom?

2. Even with restricted access to storeroom keys, it is sometimes desirable to change locks. Under what specific conditions would you as a food controller advise the manager to change locks?

3. In your own words, explain how excessive food costs may be reduced through proper rotation of stock.

4. List and explain the disadvantages in locating a storage area at some distance from the receiving and preparation areas. Are there any advantages?

5. If a new storeroom clerk discovered an item on his shelves still in good condition, but six months old, what, if anything, should she do about it? Why?

6. Referring to the price list below, calculate the total value of the following requisitions.

Item	Purchase Unit	Unit Price
Applesauce	#10 can	$2.10
Beets, sliced	#10 can	1.62
Carrots, diced	#10 can	2.63
Clams, minced	#10 can	4.29
Cocktail sauce	gallon	5.75
Coffee	pound	1.15
Corn, whole kernel	#10 can	2.13

Item	Purchase Unit	Unit Price
Cranberry sauce	#10 can	1.89
Flour, all purpose	pound	.23
Fruit cocktail	#10 can	2.05
Garlic powder	pound	3.48
Ketchup	12 oz.	.48
Linguine, #18	pound	.32
Mushrooms, whole	#10 can	3.21
Mustard	8 oz.	.25
Olive oil	gallon	3.72
Peaches, halves	#10 can	2.45
Pepper, black	pound	2.54
Pepper, white	pound	2.98
Pineapple, crushed	#10 can	1.89
Rice	pound	.18
Salt	pound	.10
Sauerkraut	#10 can	2.23
Sugar, granulated	pound	.39
Tomato puree	#10 can	1.98
Tomatoes, whole peeled	#10 can	1.49
Vinegar	gallon	2.58

a. July 6

Quantity	Item	Unit Price	Extension
24—8 oz.	Mustard		
24—12 oz.	Ketchup		
20 lb.	Salt		
2 lb.	Black pepper		
5 gal.	Olive Oil		
5 gal.	Vinegar		
10 lb.	Sugar		

Total: _____

Authorized by: H. Sneed, Maitre D'

b. July 6

Quantity	Item	Unit Price	Extension
12—#10	Tomatoes, whole		
12—#10	Tomatoe puree		
10 lb.	Coffee		
2 lb.	White pepper		
50 lb.	Salt		
50 lb.	Flour, all purpose		
2—#10	Sauerkraut		
3—#10	Carrots, diced		
1—#10	Fruit cocktail		

Authorized by: P. Noir, Sous Chef   Total: _____

c. July 7

Quantity	Item	Unit Price	Extension
3—#10	Corn, whole kernel		
6—#10	Beets, sliced		
3—#10	Peaches, halves		
2—#10	Applesauce		
25 lb.	Rice		
3—#10	Cranberry sauce		
1 gal.	Cocktail sauce		
2—#10	Mushrooms, whole		

Authorized by: G. Chambertin, Chef   Total: _____

d. July 8			
Quantity	Item	Unit Price	Extension
2—#10	Clams, minced		
5 lb.	Linguine #18		
1 lb.	Garlic powder		
6—#10	Pineapple, crushed		

Authorized by: P. Chardonnay, Relief Chef   Total: _____

7. The Somerset Restaurant Company owns and operates three small units in one community. Gross food sales and food costs as recorded on the books of each unit are as follows:

	Unit A	Unit B	Unit C
Sales	$155,400	$98,300	$228,000
Food Cost	80,808	30,473	77,520

The above figures do not include the values of food transferred from Unit A to the other two units, including all baked goods used in the chain, which are produced in one bake shop located in Unit A. During the period, transfers from Unit A to the other two units totaled $20,000, of which $8,000 was sent to Unit B and the remainder to Unit C.

   a. Calculate food cost percents before transfers are taken into account.

   b. Adjust food cost figures by the amounts of the transfers to determine more accurate food costs.

   c. Calculate food cost percents based on the costs determined in (**b**).

8. Food cost percent is often one of the elements used to judge a manager's ability to control food costs. Explain how failure to take the value of transferred foods into account before calculating food cost percents can affect the performance ratings of managers who send food items to other units and of managers who receive food from other units.

9. A certain small chain operates four units in one city. Each unit purchases for its own needs and produces for its own sales on premises. Each produces its own rolls, cakes, and pies. However, when one unit underproduces, the manager is encouraged to secure needed quantities from another unit in the chain before purchasing from outside. One item, apple pie, costs $1.35 to produce in-house and is available outside for $2.75 from nearby bakeries. What would be an appropriate transfer price for apple pies sent from one unit

to another? What effect would the transfer price you decide on have on the volume of transfers between units?

10. Why should food not be stored on the floor at any time? What may happen to food so stored?

11. Explain how computers may be of assistance to management in each of the following areas:

    a. Storing control.

    b. Issuing control.

    c. Control of transfers.

For Computer Users

12. Create a simple spreadsheet to be used in place of the requisition illustrated in Figure 7.2.

13. Use the model spreadsheet developed in Question 12 above to solve Question 6 above.

chapter 8

Production Control I: Controlling Portion Production

Learning Objectives

After reading and studying this chapter, the student should be able to:

1. Define each of the following:

    Standard portion size.

    Standard recipe.

    Standard portion cost.

    Cost factor.

    Yield factor.

2. Explain the importance of standard portion sizes, standard recipes, and standard portion costs to foodservice operations.

3. List four methods for determining standard portion costs, and describe the type of food product for which each is used.

4. Calculate standard portion costs using each of the four methods.

5. Use cost factors derived from butcher tests and cooking loss tests to determine new costs in the face of changing market prices.

6. Use yield factors derived from butcher tests and cooking loss tests to determine correct purchase quantities.

7. Discuss the levels of knowledge and skill needed by food production employees, and explain some of the resulting managerial approaches to the problem of training in the production area.

8. Describe several ways that managers can use computers as aids in the control of production.

As was pointed out earlier in the text, a foodservice operation must be viewed as a complex array of interrelated systems, each of which has special goals. The purchasing system, for example, is designed to ensure the availability of an adequate supply of the ingredients required for production, each of a carefully selected quality, acquired at an optimum price. The best means for ensuring that the purchasing system will achieve its aims—that purchasing events will conform to plans—is to apply a control process. This is true not only for the purchasing system but also for the systems designed for receiving, storing, and issuing foods. As we will see, it is equally true for the production system.

Following the pattern established previously, in this chapter we will describe the application of the four-step process of control to the production phase of foodservice operation.

ESTABLISHING STANDARDS AND STANDARD PROCEDURES

The standards and standard procedures for production control are designed to ensure that all portions of any given item conform to management's plans and are identical to one another in ingredients, proportions, production method, and size. In order to accomplish this, it is necessary to develop the following controls for each item produced:

> Standard portion size
> Standard recipe
> Standard portion cost

Standard Portion Size

One of the most important standards that a restaurant must set is the portion size, the quantity of any item that is to be served each time that item is ordered. In effect, the **standard portion size** for any item is the fixed quantity that management intends to give each customer in return for a fixed selling price. It is possible and desirable for management to establish these fixed quantities in very clear terms. Every item on a menu can be quantified in one of three ways: by weight, by volume, or by count.

Weight, normally expressed in ounces (or grams, if the metric system is used), is frequently used to measure portion sizes for meat. Steak is served in portions of varying sizes, typically ranging from eight to sixteen ounces, with the particular size for a particular restaurant being set by management. The same is often true of roasts, often served in four- or five-ounce portions. Vegetables, particularly those purchased frozen, are commonly portioned by weight as well.

Volume is used as the measure for portions of many menu items. Liquids—soups, juices, coffee, and milk, to name but a few—are commonly portioned by volume expressed as liquid ounces (milliliters in the metric system). A cup of soup may contain five ounces, while a bowl of soup might contain eight; a portion of orange juice may be three or four ounces; coffee may be served in a five-ounce portion; a glass of milk may contain eight ounces.

Count is also used by food service operators to state portion size. Such items as bacon, link sausage, eggs, chops, shrimp, and asparagus are all portioned by count. Some foods are purchased by count, and this plays a major role in establishing portion size. Shrimp, for example, are purchased by number per pound—sixteen to twenty per pound is a common purchase size—and then portioned by number per shrimp cocktail—four or five to one order. Potatoes and grapefruit are purchased by count per purchase unit, which clearly serves as a determinant of portion size. Potatoes for baking, for example, can be purchased in fifty-pound boxes with a particular number per box specified. The higher the count per box—120 rather than 90—the smaller the portion size served the customer. Count is important even with some dessert items, such as pie, with the portion size expressed in terms of the number of slices of equal size to be cut from one pie.

An interesting variation occurs with those items portioned by such implements as scoops or slotted spoons. A portion size is stipulated to be one or more such measures, but the measuring device selected holds a particular quantity of the item to be portioned. In one sense, the item in question is portioned by count, while in another, it is portioned by volume.

There are many devices available to help the foodservice operator standardize portion sizes. Among the more common are the scoops and slotted spoons mentioned above, but there are many others, including ladles, portion scales, and measuring cups. Even the number scale or dial on a slicing machine, designed to regulate the thickness of slices, can aid in standardizing portion size: a manager may stipulate a particular number of slices of some item on a sandwich and then direct that the item be sliced with the dial at a particular setting.

Standard portion sizes help reduce customer discontent, which leads to lost sales. No customer can compare his or her portion unfavorably with that of another customer and feel dissatisfied or cheated. In addition, repeat customers will be more inclined to feel they receive fair measure for their money on each visit.

Standard portion sizes help eliminate animosity between kitchen help and dining room personnel, which can lead to delays in serving and make personnel antagonistic to patrons. When portion sizes are left to the whims of the kitchen help, arguments can develop concerning whether or not some server is receiving larger portions for his customers, thus ensuring larger tips.

Standard sizes help eliminate excessive costs. Cost for any given item varies with the quantity served, so the cost for any item will be proportional to the quantity served to the customer. It stands to reason that an eight-ounce portion of anything costs twice as much as a four-ounce portion of the same item—if four ounces cost $.40, eight ounces will cost $.80.

Except in rare instances, selling prices do not vary with portion sizes. Prices are typically printed in a menu and usually are not changed until the menu is reprinted. Even when not printed, prices cannot be changed from customer to customer. If an item is listed at $2 on a certain day, then each and every portion of that item will be sold for $2. If one customer receives a four-ounce portion costing $.40, and a second customer receives an eight-ounce portion of the same item costing $.80, it is apparent that costs are not under control, and it is probable that customers and servers are dissatisfied.

Such situations often have a number of unpleasant consequences. Customers complain, never return, or both. Servers argue and sometimes quit. From a food controller's point of view, perhaps the most important undesirable consequence is that costs are not under control and excessive costs develop. In addition, under such conditions, gross profits vary on sales of the same item. The gross profit is $1.60 on the sale to the first customer, and $1.20 on the sale to the second customer. As we shall see in a later chapter, such conditions make it impossible to determine the relative profitability of one menu item over another.

Once standard portion sizes have been set, it is obviously important to ensure that each person who produces an item knows what size portion to prepare. Methods of accomplishing this vary. One effective way is to post charts conspicuously on kitchen walls for ready reference. This approach is particularly effective in large establishments with high rates of employee turnover.

Standard Recipes

Another important production standard is the recipe. A **standard recipe** lists ingredients and quantities to be used and a procedure to be followed each time a particular item is produced. The use of standard recipes helps ensure that the quality of any item will be the same each time the item is produced. Consequently, the standard recipe (see Fig. 8.1) also helps to guarantee consistency of taste,

FIGURE 8.1
Standard Recipe

Seafood Newburg (10 4-oz. portions)

1 lb. lobster meat	1 cup butter
1/2 lb. shrimps, raw, out of shell	salt and pepper to taste
1/2 lb. scallops	1 T. paprika
1/2 lb. filet of sole	1 cup sherry wine
1 cup heavy cream	6 egg yolks
3 cups cream sauce	extra sherry wine
	10 slices of toast

a. Sauté all seafood in the melted butter well.
b. Add a little sherry and simmer until wine is absorbed.
c. Add paprika and cream sauce; combine well and simmer for a while.
d. Beat egg yolks and cream and add slowly to pan; combine well.
e. Check for seasoning; pour into serving dishes and add toast points and sherry.

appearance, and customer acceptance; if the same ingredients are used in the correct proportions, and the same procedure is followed, identical products should be produced each time the standard recipe is used, even in the face of rapid employee turnover. Moreover, each repeat customer will likely be served an item of identical quality each time she orders.

The term "standard recipe" does not necessarily imply a recipe developed by some outside agency for use in numerous restaurants. It means a recipe that will produce an item of acceptable quality for a particular operation. These recipes can be, and often are, developed in individual kitchens and tested and modified until an acceptable recipe that produces the intended product is agreed on. That recipe then becomes the standard—the recipe that will be used each time a certain item is made.

In many operations, these standard recipes are recorded on cards that are made readily available to those responsible for production. They are clearly and legibly written so that the standard recipes can be easily followed. At times, they are printed on special cards that are then plastic-coated for durability. In some establishments, these cards include either drawings or photographs of the finished products to illustrate for the production staff exactly how the final product should look when served to the customer. In addition to providing uniform appearance, these cards are particularly important to restaurants that illustrate menus with photographs.

Standard recipes are very important to the food controller. If they are not in use, costs cannot be controlled effectively. If any item is produced by different methods, with different ingredients, and in different proportions each time it is made, costs will be different each time any given quantity is produced.

Once standard recipes and standard portion sizes are established, and steps are taken to ensure that personnel follow necessary preparation and portioning procedures, standard costs for portions can be developed.

Standard Portion Cost

A cost can be calculated for every item on every menu, provided the ingredients, proportions, production method, and portion size have been standardized in the manner discussed above. In general, this merely requires that one calculate the cost of each ingredient in the portion and add the ingredient costs to determine the total. The techniques for doing this will be described in detail below.

Before explaining the several means for determining portion costs, it is very important for the student to understand that the portion costs determined by these techniques will only be calculated, or planned, costs—indicating to management what portion costs should be. True portion costs may be quite different. There are many possible reasons for this. For example, if employees give customers 3 or 7 shrimp in the shrimp cocktail, rather than the 5 established by management as the standard, the true cost of the portion will vary from the calculated or planned costs. The true cost may be either higher or lower, depending on whether customers have been given too many or too few shrimp, but it will clearly be different from the planned cost. The same will be true if employees fail to use portion scales, or use improper portioning devices, or fail to follow standard recipes, or purchase ingredients other than those stipulated. If the seafood newberg recipe illustrated in figure 8.1 were prepared with pollock being substituted for the lobster, it is quite clear that true portion cost would be lower than planned.

These calculated or planned portion costs are best known by the term **standard portion cost.** Standard portion cost is defined as the dollar amount that a standard portion should cost, given the standards and standard procedures for its production. There are several reasons for determining standard portion costs. The most obvious is that one should have a reasonably clear idea of what a product's cost is before establishing a sales price for the product. For control purposes, there are additional reasons, including making future judgments about how closely true costs match these standard costs and the extent to which operating efficiency can be improved, topics which will be discussed in later chapters.

Calculating Standard Portion Costs

There are several commonly used methods for calculating standard portion costs in the foodservice industry:

1. Formula.
2. Recipe detail and cost card.
3. Butcher test.
4. Cooking loss test.

Managers should be familiar with and able to use all of these methods, each of which is discussed below.

Formula   For many, perhaps even for a majority, of the items served in restaurants, determining standard portion cost is simple. For a large number of foods, one may determine portion cost by means of the formula

$$\text{Standard Portion Cost} = \frac{\text{Purchase Price per Unit}}{\text{Number of Portions per Unit}}$$

For example, in an establishment serving eggs on a breakfast menu, where two eggs are the standard portion, one could determine the standard cost of the portion by dividing the cost of a thirty-dozen case of eggs—say, $27—by the number of two-egg portions it contained—180—to find standard portion cost to be $.15.

$$\frac{\$27 \text{ purchase price per case}}{180 \text{ standard portions per case}} = \$.15$$

This simple formula could also be used to find the standard cost of each of the additional items served in a typical standard breakfast, including the juice, bacon, toast, butter, and coffee. The sum of the standard costs of the individual items would thus be the standard cost of the whole breakfast, possibly offered in some particular restaurant as Breakfast Special #3, at $4.95 menu price.

In many restaurants today, large amounts of food are purchased already portioned by the vendor. Determining the cost of one portion of any of these items is comparatively simple—divide the purchase price by the number of portions bought. Frankfurters purchased twelve to the pound for $2.40 cost $.20 each. Frozen heat-and-serve entrees are often purchased in individual units, in which case the purchase price is the portion cost. Most preportioned foods come in containers showing the exact number of portions inside.

So, determining the portion cost of many menu items may be done rather simply, merely by applying the formula given above. However, not all foods may be so simply portioned after purchase, and other techniques must be developed to determine the standard portion costs of more complex items, such as those prepared from standard recipes.

Recipe Detail and Cost Card　When standard recipes are used, it is possible to determine the standard cost of each item prepared with those recipes.

A standard recipe yields a predetermined number of standard portions. Thus it is possible to determine the cost of preparing one portion by dividing the number of portions produced into the total cost of preparing the recipe. To find the total cost, it is necessary only to list each item and quantity from the recipe on a form, such as that in Figure 8.2, and multiply each by its unit cost. In the example given, the second ingredient is one-half pound of shrimp. If one pound of shrimp costs $7.50, then one-half pound of shrimp costs $3.75; that figure is entered on the right in the column headed "Ext," the abbreviation for extension.

Determining the cost of an ingredient can sometimes be rather complex. If, for example, a recipe called for three diced onions, it would be necessary to determine the number of average-size onions in the sack and then determine the price of one onion by dividing the total number into the price of the sack of onions. Multiplying the price of one onion times three gives the price for the onions in the standard recipe. If chicken stock were an ingredient, it would be necessary to refer to a separate recipe detail and cost card to determine the cost of one measure of stock prepared according to standard recipe.

In the case of an ingredient such as "a pinch of salt," it is not worthwhile to calculate the value. In such cases the figure entered is some token amount, usually more than enough to cover the cost.

When fresh meat, poultry, or fish are used, it is necessary first to follow certain procedures involving butcher tests, cooking loss tests, or both, These will be discussed later in this chapter.

Once the cost of each ingredient has been established, the total cost of preparing the recipe is determined by adding the costs of the individual ingredients.

FIGURE 8.2
Recipe Detail and Cost Card

Recipe Detail & Cost Card

Item: Seafood Newburg   Menu: Dinner

S.P. $8.50
Cost $2.48
F.C.% $29.2

Yield: 10 portions   Portion Size: 4 oz of Seafood, + sauce   Date 6/22/XX

Ingredients	Quantity	Unit	Cost	Ext.	Procedure
lobster meat	1 lb.	lb.	11.25	11.25	Sauté all seafood well in melted
shrimps	1/2 lb.	lb.	7.50	3.75	butter. Add sherry & simmer
scallops	1/2 lb.		6.00	3.00	until wine is absorbed. Add
filet of sole	1/2 lb.	lb.	4.50	2.25	paprika and cream sauce, then
heavy cream	1 cup	qt.	2.40	.60	combine and simmer. Beat egg
cream sauce	3 cups	–		.75	yolks and cream, add slowly to
butter	1 cup	lb.	2.00	1.00	pan, and combine well. Check for
salt & pepper				.05	seasoning, pour into serving
paprika	1 T			.10	dishes, and add sherry. Add
sherry wine	8 oz.	750 ml	3.20	1.01	toast points.
egg yolks	6 ea.			.42	
sherry wine	1 oz.			.13	
toast	10 slices			.50	
Total				24.81	

This total, divided by the number of portions produced (called the yield), gives the cost of one standard portion. As long as ingredients of standard quality are purchased at stable prices, this should be the cost of producing one standard portion, provided there is no waste. Measuring waste and other inefficiency in terms of the dollars involved will be covered in later chapters.

It must be recognized that standard costs of standard portions must be recalculated occasionally as the market prices of the ingredients vary. The frequency of the recalculations will depend largely on conditions in the market as well as the availability of personnel to do the arithmetic. If market conditions and prices remain fairly constant, it should not be necessary to recalculate more frequently than every three or four months.

For some items—steaks portioned in the restaurant from wholesale cuts of beef, or portions of roast lamb, for example—the simple formula is not useful for determining standard portion cost. For these items, and for many like them, portion costs cannot be determined until after some processing has taken place. The processing may be trimming, butchering, cooking, or some combination of these. During this processing, fat, bone, and other inedible or unnecessary parts will be removed. In some cases, this is accomplished by cutting them away. In others— roasts, for example—fat is removed by melting during the cooking process. Any such processing results in weight loss: the quantity available for portioning weighs less than the quantity originally purchased. It should be apparent, then, that the true quantity available for portioning is not known until after the processing is complete. The item to be portioned cannot be weighed to determine the quantity available for portioning until after processing.

There are two special techniques used to determine standard portion costs for those items requiring the kinds of processing described above. They are known as the butcher test and the cooking loss test, each of which is discussed in detail below. In general, the butcher test is used to determine standard portion costs for those items portioned before cooking, while the cooking loss test is used for those items portioned after cooking. In some instances, both tests may be required to determine standard portion costs.

Butcher Test   When meat, fish, and poultry are purchased as wholesale cuts, the purchaser pays the same price for each and every pound of the item purchased, even though, after butchering, the resulting parts may have entirely different values. If, for example, a particular cut of beef is approximately half fat and half usable meat, the two parts clearly have different uses and different values, although they were purchased at the same price per pound because both were part of one wholesale cut. Among other purposes, the butcher test is designed to establish the value of the primary part of the wholesale piece.

A butcher test is usually performed under the supervision of a food controller, who presents a particular cut of meat to the butcher. The butcher then breaks it down into its respective parts, keeping the parts separate so they can be weighed. As the work begins, the food controller detaches the meat tag from the piece and records information from the meat tag on the top of the butcher test card (Figure 8.3).

Figure 8.3 describes the results of a butcher test performed on a beef tenderloin purchased as a wholesale cut at $6.11 per pound. As purchased from the XYZ Meat Company on March 21, it weighed exactly nine pounds. The purchase price for the piece was $54.99.

The butcher keeps the parts separated to determine their individual weights after the butchering. The names of the parts are recorded in the column at the left, marked "Breakdown," and the weights of the parts go into the next column to the right. Ideally, the total weight of the individual parts equals the total original weight. However, some small measure of weight is usually lost during the butchering, and it is common to find an entry in the breakdown and weight columns for "loss in cutting."

In Figure 8.3, the entries made in the Breakdown column are Fat, Loss in Cutting, and Usable Meat. The weights for each have been written in the Weight column: 4 pounds 8 ounces for fat, and 4 pounds 4 ounces for usable meat. The weight for Loss in Cutting, 4 ounces, is determined by adding the weights for all other parts, then subtracting that total from the purchased weight.

Fat	4 lbs.	8 oz.	Purchased Weight	9 lbs.	0 oz.
+ Usable Meat	4 lbs.	4 oz.	− Total of Parts	8 lbs.	12 oz.
= TOTAL	8 lbs.	12 oz.	= Loss in Cutting		4 oz.

FIGURE 8.3
Butcher Test Card

Butcher Test Card

Item **Beef Tenderloin**

Pieces **One**

Total Cost $ **54.99**

Grade **U.S. Choice**

Weighing **9** Lbs. **0** Oz.

At $ **6.11** Per **Lb.**

Date **3/21/XX**

Average Weight ——

Supplier **XYZ Meat Co.**

Breakdown	No	Weight		Ratio to Total Weight	Value Per Lb.	Total Value	Cost of Each Usable		Portion		Cost Factor Per	
		Lb.	Oz.				Lb.	Oz.	Size	Cost	Lb.	Portion
Fat		4	8	50.0%	.13	.59						
Loss in Cutting			4	2.8%	-0-	-0-						
Usable Meat		4	4	47.2%		54.40	12.80	.80	8 oz.	6.40	2.0949	1.0475
Total		9	0	100.0%		54.99						

The next column, labeled "Ratio to Total Weight," represents the percentage of each part in relation to the whole. The ratio of each weight to the whole is calculated by following the formula:

$$\frac{\text{Weight of Part}}{\text{Weight of Whole}} = \text{Ratio to Total Weight}$$

$$\frac{\text{4 lbs. 8 oz. (4.5 lbs)}}{\text{9 lbs. 0 oz. (9.0 lbs.)}} = .5, \text{ or 50.0\% Fat}$$

$$\frac{\text{0 lbs. 4 oz. (.25 lb.)}}{\text{9 lbs. 0 oz. (9.0 lbs.)}} = .02777 = .028, \text{ or 2.8\% Loss}$$

$$\frac{\text{4 lbs. 4 oz. (4.25 lbs.)}}{\text{9 lbs. 0 oz. (0.0 lbs.)}} = .47222 = .472, \text{ or 47.2\% Usable}$$

This ratio is of particular interest to a food controller when comparing similar cuts of meat supplied by two or more dealers. Comparisons of ratios of usable parts may help determine which dealer offers better value. In addition, food controllers often compare meats of different quality to determine which is more economical to serve. This ratio is also known as a **yield percentage,** or a **yield factor.** Specific calculations using this percentage or factor will be discussed later in the chapter.

The "Value per LB." column appears mysterious but is possibly the simplest to complete. The values per pound for all parts except the principal part—the desire for which occasioned the original purchase—are merely the current prices that each of the parts would cost if purchased separately in the open market. In most instances, these figures are obtained from one of the regular suppliers of meat to the restaurant. The values per pound are determined in this manner on the theory that one would pay this price to buy each of the parts separately, and thus each price entered is its reasonable value. No value per pound for the principal part is entered. It will be determined after the total values for all the other parts have been calculated in the next column, marked "Total Value."

The total value for each of the secondary parts is obtained by multiplying the value per pound by the weight. The total value of the primary part is determined by

1. Adding the total values of the secondary parts, and
2. Subtracting that figure from the Total Cost indicated at the top of the form.

In Figure 8.3, the following calculations have been performed:

a. 4.5 lbs. of Fat × $.13 per lb. = $.585 = $.59

b. Total cost $54.99
    − Value of Other Parts   .59
    = Value of Primary Part $54.40
        (Usable Meat)

Thus the sum of all total values will equal the total original cost.

With both the weight and total value of the principle part known, the cost of each usable pound and ounce—the next two columns to the right—can be determined by division.

$$\frac{\text{Total Value of Usable Meat}}{\text{Weight of Usable Meat}} = \text{Cost per Usable Lb.}$$

$$\frac{\$54.40}{4.25 \text{ lbs.}} = \$12.80 \text{ (Cost per Usable Lb.)}$$

$$\frac{\text{Cost per Usable Lb.}}{16 \text{ oz. per lb.}} = \text{Cost per Usable Oz.}$$

$$\frac{\$12.80}{16} = \$.80 \text{ (Cost per Usable Oz.)}$$

Management determines standard portion sizes. This figure, typically in ounces, is entered in the next column, Portion Size. The portion cost is calculated by multiplying the portion size in ounces by the cost of each usable ounce.

$$\text{Portion Size} \times \text{Cost per Usable Oz.} = \text{Portion Cost}$$

$$8 \text{ oz.} \times \$.80 = \$6.40$$

The remaining two columns are used for recording the cost factors per pound and per portion, both of which will require explanation.

Cost Factors   The price of meat is seldom if ever stable. Meat prices change monthly, weekly, and sometimes even daily. As market prices change, the usable pound costs and portion costs change as well. Therefore it is desirable to find some means to calculate both the new usable pound costs and portion costs without having to complete a new butcher test with each change in market price. The cost factors serve this purpose and are calculated in the following manner:

$$\frac{\text{Cost per Usable Lb.}}{\substack{\text{Dealer Price per Lb. of} \\ \text{Original Wholesale Piece}}} = \text{Cost Factor per Lb.}$$

$$\frac{\$12.80}{\$6.11} = 2.0949$$

$$\frac{\text{Portion Cost}}{\substack{\text{Dealer Price per Lb. of} \\ \text{Original Wholesale Piece}}} = \text{Cost Factor per Portion}$$

$$\frac{\$6.40}{6.11} = 1.0475$$

These factors are extremely useful. Suppose one were to learn that the dealer price per pound for beef tenderloin was expected to increase from the present $6.11 to $6.37. It is clear that this would increase portion cost, but those in foodservice management must know more than this obvious truth: they must know the standard portion cost at the new, higher dealer price. One could, of course, proceed to complete a new set of butcher test calculations. While that could be done, it would take some time. The simpler, faster method is to use the cost factors determined previously. These can be used as follows:

$$\text{Cost Factor per Lb.} \times \text{New Dealer Price per Lb.} = \text{Cost of a Usable Lb. at New Dealer Price}$$

$$2.0949 \times \$6.37 = \$13.3445 = \$13.34$$

$$\text{Cost Factor per Portion} \times \text{New Dealer Price per Lb.} = \text{Cost of a Portion of Same Size at New Dealer Price}$$

$$1.0475 \times \$6.37 = \$6.672575 = \$6.67$$

By this means, one can determine quite specifically that the $.26 increase in the dealer price per pound will lead to an increase of $.54 in the cost of a usable pound and $.27 in the portion cost. Moreover, one can make all these determinations much more quickly than one could complete all the calculations required on the butcher test form.

There is one potentially serious problem associated with the portion cost factor: it can be used only if the size of the portion for which one is determining cost is identical to that of the portion used to establish the cost factor. If the cost factor is based on a six-ounce portion and one is attempting to determine the cost of a five-ounce portion at a new market price, the portion cost factor cannot be used. It would be necessary to use the cost factor per pound to determine the cost of a usable pound at the new market price, divide that by 16 ounces to determine the new cost of one ounce, and then multiply that ounce cost by the number of ounces in the portion—a cumbersome business.

In order to make it easier to determine costs using factors, the authors recommend the derived formula given below, which can be used to determine the cost of a portion of any given size at any given market price, provided that one has determined a cost factor per pound.

$$\text{Cost Factor per pound} \times \text{Portion Size (expressed as a decimal)}$$
$$\times \text{Dealer Price} = \text{Portion Cost}$$

The decimal equivalent of a given number of ounces is determined as follows:

$$\frac{\text{Number of Ounces}}{16 \text{ (ounces in a pound)}}$$

Therefore

$$\frac{8 \text{ oz.}}{16 \text{ oz.}} = .5$$

The following is an example of the use of the cost factor per pound calculated in the butcher test in Figure 8.3. This new formula may be used to find the cost of the eight-ounce portion at the $6.37 dealer price, as follows:

2.0949 × .5 (8 oz. as a decimal) × $6.37 = $6.6722565 = $6.67.

While one can find the cost of the eight-ounce portion using the portion cost factor alone, it cannot be used directly to determine the cost of a seven-ounce portion. The new formula can be so used:

2.0949 × .4375 (7 oz. as a decimal) × $6.37 = $5.8382241 = $5.84

In fact, for all practical purposes, this single formula can be used to replace both formulas illustrated previously in the chapter to use cost factor to determine cost of a usable pound at the new dealer price, and cost of a portion at a new dealer price.

These formulas provide the food controller with a technique for determining new food costs as market prices change, and enable her to suggest changes in selling prices when necessary to maintain a relatively stable cost-to-sales ratio.

In order to increase the accuracy in the figures derived by this method, it is necessary to perform these tests periodically on a reasonable number of pieces. The test on one piece alone is not reliable, because it may not be a typical piece, even though it was purchased according to specifications. It is better to have test results on a number of different pieces in order to arrive at averages.

Establishments that do butcher tests find several other important uses for the results.

1. Butcher tests on pieces purchased according to specifications from two or more dealers give results that are useful in determining from which dealer to buy.
2. Butcher tests conducted on a periodic basis allow the manager to appraise the extent to which any one dealer is adhering to specifications.
3. Menu prices can be more intelligently planned, because exact costs are known.

The student should note that the butcher test is conducted far less frequently today than it was formerly. A primary reason for this is the availability of preportioned meats—steaks, chops, and other items portioned before cooking—from meat vendors. However, the butcher test can be extremely valuable to the manager who wants to compare the portion cost of a preportioned item purchased from a vendor with the cost of an identical item portioned in the restaurant.

FIGURE 8.4
Cooking Loss Test Card

Cooked One _____ Hours Ten _____ Hours _____

Cooking Loss
Minutes at 385 _____ Degrees
Minutes at _____ Degrees

Breakdown	No	Weight Lb.	Weight Oz.	Ratio to Total Weight	Value Per Lb.	Total Value	Cost of Each Usable Lb.	Cost of Each Usable Oz.	Portion Size	Portion Cost	Cost Factor Per Lb.	Cost Factor Per Portion
Original Weight		8	8	100.0%	3.19	27.12						
Trimmed Weight		6	8	76.5%		27.12						
Loss in Trimming		2	0	23.5%		-0-						
Cooked Weight		5	8	64.7%		27.12						
Loss in Cooking		1	0	11.8%		-0-						
Bones and Trim		1	8	17.6%		-0-						
Salable Weight		4	0	47.1%		27.12	6.78	.42	4 oz.	1.68	2.1254	.5266

Remarks:

Portion Size: 4 oz.   Portion Cost Factor: .5266

Item: Leg of Lamb

Typically, one would expect to find standard portion cost lower for the item portioned in the restaurant but this figure would take into account only food cost for the item, not labor cost. On the other hand, the portion cost for the preportioned item purchased from a vendor would include the vendor's labor cost. Therefore, to make a valid comparison, management would have to determine labor cost per portion for items portioned in the restaurant.

Although the butcher test enables the food controller to determine portion costs for entree items portioned before cooking—steaks, chops, and filets—many other items cannot be portioned until after cooking. Consequently, portion costs for these items—typically roasts of beef, pork, lamb, and other meats—cannot be determined until after the cooking process is complete. A different procedure, known as the cooking loss test, is required.

Cooking Loss Test   The primary purpose for the cooking loss test is the same as that for the butcher test: determination of standard portion cost. The cooking loss test is used for those items that cannot be portioned until after cooking is complete, because for these items weight loss occurs during cooking. Therefore one cannot determine the quantity remaining to be portioned until cooking is completed. Cooking loss varies with cooking time and temperature, and it must be taken into account in determining standard portion costs. Moreover, while the availability of preportioned meats has rendered the butcher test less common in recent years, the cooking loss test is as important and useful as ever.

Before beginning a detailed explanation of the cooking loss test, it will be useful to point out that the butcher test form and the cooking loss form have many similarities (see Figure 8.4). A quick examination of the form shows that all the column headings are the same. The major difference between the forms lies in the "Breakdown" column: on the butcher test form (Fig. 8.3), terms are written in this column as the butcher test progresses; on the cooking loss test form, they are preprinted—Original Weight, Trimmed Weight, and so on. It will be important, then, to learn the meanings of these terms if one is to understand the cooking loss test.

The cooking loss test is perhaps best explained by illustration. Referring to Figure 8.4, one will see a completed set of test results for one leg of lamb. As purchased, the lamb weighed 8 pounds 8 ounces. At a dealer price per pound of $3.19, the purchase price for the leg was $27.12. All this information is recorded on the first line of test form, "Original Weight."

The leg of lamb required some butchering before it could be cooked. Presumably, it was given to a butcher who cut away unnecessary parts—probably fat and shank—to prepare the leg for roasting. After the butcher was finished, the leg was found to weigh 6 pounds 8 ounces. This weight is recorded on the line marked "Trimmed Weight."

Next, Trimmed Weight (6 lbs. 8 oz.) is subtracted from Original Weight (8 lbs. 8 oz.), and the difference (2 lbs. 0 oz.) is recorded on the line marked "Loss in Trimming." Original Weight, then, represents the piece as purchased; Trimmed

Weight represents the piece after in-house butchering, if any; Loss in Trimming represents that difference between the two.

At this point, the trimmed leg of lamb ("Trimmed Weight") is put into an oven to cook. After cooking for one hour and ten minutes at 385°, it is removed from the oven and weighed. The weight is 5 pounds 8 ounces, found recorded on the line marked "Cooked Weight." Next, Cooked Weight (5 lbs. 8 oz.) is subtracted from Trimmed Weight (6 lbs. 8 oz.) to determine the entry for the following line, "Loss in Cooking:" 1 pound 0 ounces.

Because the cooked piece includes bone and considerable cooked fat, all 5 pounds 8 ounces cannot be portioned. Usable meat must be removed from the bone and weighed to determine the quantity available for portioning. The weight of the portionable meat is recorded on the line marked "Salable Weight"—4 pounds 0 ounces, in this instance. This is subtracted from the Cooked Weight (5 lbs. 8 oz.) to determine the amount of unportionable waste, noted on the line marked "Bones & Trim"—1 pound 8 ounces.

Having completed the entries in the Weight column, one can proceed to fill in the "Ratio to Total Weight" column. The percentage recorded on each line is the ratio of the weight of that part to the original weight of the piece as purchased. These ratios are calculated in exactly the same manner as was previously described in the discussion of the butcher test.

This is a most important step. These ratios may be used by the food controller to compare similar pieces of meat. Comparisons may be made, for example, to determine which of several available grades of meat would yield the maximum quantity of salable meat of a desired quality. In addition, important comparisons may be made between pieces cooked at different temperatures or for different lengths of time, or both, to determine the optimum cooking times and temperatures.

The Value per Lb. column is used only once in cooking loss tests. The only value recorded is that on the first line, Original Weight. This is actually the dealer price per pound for the original piece as purchased.

The Total Value column is most interesting. Note that the total value of the original purchase was $27.12, and that there was no change in the total value of the piece from time of purchase to time of portioning. The weight changed, of course—reducing from the 8 pound 8 ounce purchase, to the raw, trimmed 6 pound 8 ounce roast, to the cooked 5 pound 8 ounce roast, to the 4 pounds of portionable meat—but the total value did not change. With each step in processing, the decreased weight assumes a greater value per unit of weight, so that the costs of all nonportionable pounds are transferred to the salable weight. This clearly underscores the need for the cooking loss test. It is impossible to determine portion costs until cooking loss has been calculated and accounted for.

Once the weight and value of the salable meat are recorded and the portion size is entered from the restaurant's chart of standard portion sizes, the remaining calculations are performed in the same manner as in the butcher test.

The foregoing discussion has been based on a piece of meat not requiring extensive butchering before cooking. However, in many instances meats require considerable butchering—for example, in cases where the parts trimmed away have usefulness and value to the establishment. In these instances, the original and trimmed weights on the cooking loss test will appear as very different figures. This is because a butcher test has first been performed and values have been assigned to the secondary usable parts. The weight and value of the primary usable part becomes the weight and value entered on the cooking loss test as trimmed weight. The original weight and value remain that of the piece of meat as purchased.

Depending on the nature of the menu item, using one or more of the foregoing techniques can help one determine with reasonable accuracy the standard cost of one portion of any item on a menu. Once the standard cost of one portion is known, it is possible to set or adjust the selling price.

Using Yield Percentages

The **yield percentage** (or yield factor) is the percentage of a total piece of meat available for portioning. This percentage is calculated by dividing the weight of portionable meat by the weight of the piece originally purchased. These calculations are included in the butcher test and cooking loss test calculations. On the butcher test, the yield percentage is found in the Ratio to Total Weight column on the line reserved for the usable meat. For example, in Figure 8.3, the Ratio to Total Weight for the usable meat is 47.2%. On the cooking loss test, the yield percentage is found in the Ratio to Total Weight column on the line labeled Salable Weight. On the cooking loss test illustrated in Figure 8.4, the Ratio to Total Weight for the Salable Weight is 47.1%.

Once determined, yield percentages—also called yield factors—can be used in a number of quantity calculations. The general formula for these is:

$$\text{Quantity} = \frac{\text{Number of Portions} \times \text{Portion Size (as a decimal)}}{\text{Yield Percentage (or Yield Factor)}}$$

As with any such formula, it is possible to solve for any one of the terms, provided the other three are known. Thus given quantity, portion size, and yield factor, one could determine the number of standard portions that should be produced from the given quantity. Or, given quantity, number of portions, and yield factor, one could determine the portion size that should be served to feed a given number of people with a given quantity of meat. While there are many very practical uses for this formula, one illustration will suffice—determination of the quantity of a given item that must be purchased to serve portions of a given size to a particular number of people.

Let us refer to the leg of lamb in the cooking loss test (Fig. 8.4). Intuitively one can see that each leg of lamb would produce sixteen portions, because each portion weighs one-quarter of a pound and there are four pounds of usable meat.

Thus one can also see that if thirty-two portions were desired, one would purchase two legs of lamb, each yielding sixteen portions, or seventeen pounds of raw lamb. However, for more difficult calculations one would have to use the mathematical formula above. It would be calculated as follows:

$$\text{Amount to purchase} = \frac{32 \times .25}{.471}$$

$$\text{Amount to purchase} = 16.985 \text{ pounds}$$

The minor discrepancy between the intuitive calculation and the mathematical calculation is due to the rounding of the yield percentage figure.

It is important to note that the above formula assumes that future purchases of lamb will yield the same proportional amount as the tested leg. This means that the meat would contain the same relative amount of bone, fat, and lean and that it would be cooked at the same temperature for the same period of time so that shrinkage would be relatively the same as in the tested lamb.

TRAINING FOR PRODUCTION

Having established standards and standard procedures to control production, the next logical step, as illustrated in previous chapters, is to train staff members to follow the standards as they perform their jobs. All job performance requires some combination of knowledge, skill, and experience. This is particularly true for food production jobs. The problems for the foodservice operator are, first, to determine the level of knowledge, skill, and experience required for the performance of a particular job and, second, to determine how much time and money he is willing to spend to help employees acquire the necessary knowledge and skill on the job and in the process gain the experience.

There are a number of levels of knowledge and skill needed in food production. At the lowest, an employee removes a preportioned item from a freezer, unwraps it if necessary, places it in a heating device, sets a timer, turns the unit on, and waits for a signal to indicates that the item is ready for serving. This describes the work of a substantial number of employees in the fast-food segment of the industry and of some of those in industrial and institutional foodservice. The knowledge and skill required are minimal and are easily learned in a job setting by most people. The experience required is also minimal.

At the highest levels of knowledge and skill, an employee may be expected to prepare a number of grand sauces to accompany the exquisite, classical dishes prepared and served by some of the world's finest hotels and restaurants. Extensive knowledge, high levels of skill, and some considerable experience are required to do this kind of work. At the extreme, a highly talented chef may be expected to create original recipes and present original dishes.

Between these extremes fall the majority of jobs in the foodservice industry, each of which has a definable knowledge and skill quotient inherent in it. It is clearly the responsibility of a manager to define this requirement for each job.

Having thus defined jobs in this special way, management must address the question of whether to institute comprehensive training for employees or to hire only those whose backgrounds include the knowledge, skill, and experience required for particular jobs. In general, managers tend to prefer selecting knowledgeable, highly skilled personnel for those positions requiring extensive knowledge and skill, thus keeping training time and cost to a minimum. For example, few managers would willingly attempt to train a newcomer to the industry as a pastry chef. Most would prefer to fill such a position with someone who had already acquired the necessary knowledge and skill, such that training would consist largely of acquainting her with the equipment, recipes, portion sizes, and routines of the particular establishment. On the other hand, managers often prefer to select inexperienced personnel for positions at the opposite end of the job spectrum. Fast-food operations abound with examples. Managers who purposely hire the inexperienced must commit themselves to spending the time and money necessary for training. Employees working at these lower levels can normally be hired at comparatively low wages, and managers often find that employee training can begin without having to break bad work habits or inappropriate work routines learned elsewhere. At the same time, many managers have found that hiring and training inexperienced workers is often the best means of ensuring that certain jobs will be done well, conforming to the standards established for the work. Sometimes inexperienced workers are the only ones available to take such jobs, and managers may have no choice but to hire and train them.

Regardless of the level of knowledge and skill that workers bring to their jobs, some amount of training is required for all production workers in foodservice if the standards and standard procedures established to control production are to be met. If management has met its responsibility of establishing the necessary standards and standard procedures for production, employees must be made keenly aware of these standards. If portion sizes have been carefully set, employees must have instant access to the standard portion size for each menu item. It is normally insufficient simply to inform new employees of these standards; over time, employees may forget or distort the standards. An important aspect of training may be to prepare a list of standard portion sizes—as part of a manual, or as a wall chart for the kitchen—so no production worker need ever rely on his memory alone to produce portions of the proper size. Failure to do this may result in the production of portions of varying sizes, with results as described early in the chapter. A similar problem could develop if employees were not given adequate access to established standard recipes, leaving them little choice but to prepare menu items as they saw fit, possibly by using their own recipes. At the minimum, the products prepared would be different from those defined by the standard recipes; they might be either better or worse than the standard products, but they would clearly differ in cost with the established standards.

MONITORING PRODUCTION PERFORMANCE AND TAKING CORRECTIVE ACTION

Adherence to production standards can be monitored in a number of ways. Most commonly, the person in charge of production—the chef or sous chef—routinely observes production in progress, tasting as required, to be sure that resulting products conform to planned products as described by the standards. Sometimes managers monitor production—tasting various items, including finished products, weighing uncooked portions of some entree items, observing plated products as they are taken to the dining room, and so on.

In addition to these direct monitoring techniques, several indirect means are employed. Customers' reactions to products may indicate that one or more production standards are not being followed. If, for example, a customer complains about a product, the complaint should be investigated. If a number of guests complain about the same item during one meal, it is almost certain that something is seriously wrong with the item, and it may be necessary to halt all sales of it for the duration of the meal. Because many guests do not make formal complaints about products they find inferior, some managers make it a practice to observe plates being cleared from tables and sent to the dishwasher. If the customers are not eating a particular item, the cause may lie in improper production, and the manager who notices this is doing an excellent job of monitoring production performance.

If production performance does not adhere to the standards established, it is clearly important that some corrective action be taken. The first approach would normally be to call the attention of the chef to the problem so that she could investigate and correct it. If the chef could not or did not correct the problem satisfactorily, additional action would be required, and the course of that action would depend on an assessment of the underlying problem.

COMPUTER APPLICATIONS

Production control is another area in which computers can provide invaluable aid. One very simple method of providing lists of standard portion sizes to production workers is to store the data in a word processing file from which it can be printed at will. Stored in this way, the file can be updated or changed quickly and easily as the menu is changed and as changes are made in standard portion sizes. This eliminates the problems inherent in costly commercial printing of lists that quickly become obsolete.

In much the same way, computers are particularly useful in storing standard recipes. Management could, for example, store each recipe as an individual file, all on one diskette. This would work reasonably well in a small establishment with one microcomputer of limited capacity and a simple word processing program. The files could be readily updated, edited, deleted, or printed, with new files being created for new recipes as needed. A more sophisticated approach would be to store the recipes as individual worksheets by using a spreadsheet program. This would enable management to use the special features offered by spreadsheet programs to calculate recipe costs and portion costs.

Spreadsheets are particularly useful tools for butcher test and cooking loss test calculations. Templates can be set up to enable one to input test results and obtain instant information about ratios, values, costs, and factor from the appropriate spreadsheet cells. A next logical step would be to set up spreadsheet formulas to do any or all of the calculations possible with pound cost factors, portion cost factors, or yield factors.

For those not interested in tailoring generic applications programs to their own particular purposes, there are increasing numbers of commercially developed programs designed to accomplish many tasks related directly or indirectly to production control, including those suggested above. Many of these are advertised regularly in the trade journals catering to the foodservice industry.

CHAPTER ESSENTIALS

In this chapter, we explained the application of the control process to the production phase of foodservice operations. We listed and discussed the standards and standard procedures required for control, including standardization of ingredients, proportions, production method, and portion sizes. We described the importance of the standard recipe in maintaining standards and suggested a number of possible consequences of failure to maintain production standards. Having established basic production standards, we listed and explained in detail four methods for determining standard portion costs, including formula, recipe detail and cost card, butcher test, and cooking loss test. We described the procedures for calculating the cost factor per pound, the portion cost factor, and the yield factor and explained and illustrated their use in foodservice operations for calculating portion costs as market prices change and for solving specific quantity problems faced by those who purchase food. We described management's need to determine the particular knowledge and skill levels required by employees in specific jobs and pointed out the common tendency of managers to provide extensive training for those whose jobs require the least knowledge and skill, while expecting those requiring the highest levels of knowledge and skills to have been trained before hiring. We explained several techniques used to monitor the performance of employees engaged in production and indicated the importance of the role customers play in the process. We discussed the primary method used to take corrective action and suggested an alternative approach when that method is not successful. Finally, we described a variety of ways in which computers can help the manager who applies the control process to the production phase of foodservice operations.

KEY TERMS IN THIS CHAPTER

Standard portion size	Butcher test
Standard recipe	Cooking loss test
Standard portion cost	Cost factor per pound
Recipe detail and cost card	Portion cost factor
Yield	Yield factor (yield percentage)

QUESTIONS AND PROBLEMS

1. In each of the following cases determine selling price for one portion of a recipe yielding thirty portions, when the standard recipe cost and desired cost-to-sales ratio are as indicated below.

	Recipe Cost	Desired Cost Percentage for One Portion
a.	$ 55.25	30.0%
b.	22.58	18.0%
c.	124.50	45.0%
d.	105.00	21.0%
e.	12.60	40.0%

2. Define each of the following:

    a. Standard portion size.

    b. Standard portion cost.

    c. Standard recipe.

3a. Using the form illustrated in Figure 8.3, complete the butcher test calculations on a beef tenderloin, U.S. prime, from the information given below:

> Weight as purchased: 8 lbs. 8 oz.
> Dealer price: $4.19 per pound
> Portion size for filet mignon: 8 oz.

Breakdown:

Fat 4 lbs. 12 oz.	Value per lb.: $ .10
Tidbits 12 oz.	Value per lb. 2.49
Filet Mignon 3 lbs. 0 oz.	

3b. Using the cost factors developed determine:

1. Cost of the eight-ounce portion if the dealer increases his price for beef tenderloin to $4.49 per pound.
2. Cost of each usable pound at the increased dealer price of $4.49.

3. Cost of a six-ounce portion at the increased dealer price of $4.49.
4. The maximum number of ounces that can be served for a $5.55 portion cost after the dealer has raised his price to $4.49 per pound.

4. Using the forms for butcher test and cooking loss test illustrated in Figures 8.3 and 8.4, complete the calculations for the butcher test and cooking loss test on a rib of beef, U.S. choice, weighing 38 lbs. 12 oz. and purchased from a dealer at $3.19 per pound.

Breakdown:

Fat	6 lbs. 8 oz.	Value per lb. $ .10
Bones	4 lbs. 4 oz.	Value per lb. .32
Short ribs	3 lbs. 4 oz.	Value per lb. 1.49
Chopped beef	2 lbs. 8 oz.	Value per lb. 1.59
Loss in cutting	0 lbs. 4 oz.	
Oven-ready rib	22 lbs. 0 oz.	
Cooked weight	20 lbs. 4 oz.	
Bones and trim	1 lb. 4 oz.	

Portion size for roast beef: 10 oz.

5. A cooking loss test on a leg of lamb shows a yield percentage of 42.5%.

a. Determine how many pounds of uncooked oven-ready leg of lamb to purchase if forty-eight portions are needed and each portion weighs four ounces.

b. Determine how many pounds of uncooked oven-ready leg of lamb to purchase if fifty-five portions are needed and each portion weighs five ounces.

c. Given a cost factor per pound of 2.1387, determine the cost of the portions in (a) and (b) above if the dealer price per pound for leg of lamb is $3.19.

6. The data below have been collected from butcher tests on ten legs of veal, U.S. choice, purchased over the last several weeks from the Shifty Meat Company. The legs are purchased to produce five-ounce portions of veal cutlet. The restaurant paid $814.28 for the ten legs, which weighed 247 pounds 8 ounces as purchased.

Fat	41 lbs.	8 oz.	Value $.10 per lb.
Bone	56 lbs.	8 oz.	Value $.38 per lb.
Shanks	19 lbs.	12 oz.	Value $1.49 per lb.
Trimmings	47 lbs.	4 oz.	Value $1.89 per lb.
Loss in cutting	2 lbs.	8 oz.	
Veal cutlets	80 lbs.	0 oz.	

a. Given these data, complete butcher test calculations to determine standard cost of the five-ounce portion, as well as yield factor, portion cost factor, and cost factor.

b. Find the cost of the standard five-ounce portion at each of the following dealer prices:

    1. $3.19 per pound.
    2. $3.39 per pound.
    3. $3.49 per pound.
    4. $3.89 per pound.

c. Find the cost of each of the following:

    1. A six-ounce portion, if dealer price is $3.19 per pound.
    2. A four-ounce portion, if dealer price is $3.59 per pound.
    3. A four-ounce portion, if dealer price is $3.69 per pound.

d. The manager of the restaurant wants portion cost to be $2.65 regardless of variations in dealer price. Determine proper portion size if:

    1. Dealer price is $3.69 per pound.
    2. Dealer price is $3.03 per pound.

e. Develop a chart showing the costs of four-ounce, five-ounce, and six-ounce portions at dealer prices of $3.00 per pound, $3.05 per pound, and so on in $.05 increments up to $4.00 per lb.

f. How many pound of veal leg (as purchased) will be needed to prepare and serve five-ounce portions to 235 people?

g. Given the weight of the average leg of veal as determined in the butcher test, how many legs should the steward order to serve the 235 people?

h. Records show that the restaurant used forty-eight legs of veal last month. How many standard five-ounce portions should have been produced from these forty-eight legs?

i. The restaurant has a banquet for 500 people scheduled for tonight, and veal cutlet is the listed entree. The steward neglected to order veal legs for this specific party, but there are twenty-four legs of veal in the house and veal cutlet is not on the regular dining room menu for tonight. Using these twenty-four legs of veal for the party, what size portion should be prepared so that all 500 people can be served?

7. The steward of a restaurant purchases oven-ready legs of lamb, U.S. choice, according to specifications. They are used to produce seven-ounce portions of roast lamb. Over a period of several weeks, the food controller has kept

records of the original weights, cooked weights, and salable weights of fifteen legs selected from the total number purchased. The information is summarized below:

Original weight (15 pieces):   135 lbs. Purchased @ $2.10 per lb. = $283.50
Cooked weight: 120 lbs.
Salable weight: 75 lbs.

a. Using the data above, complete cooking loss test calculations for the fifteen legs of lamb, finding the yield factor, the standard cost of the seven-ounce portion, and the cost factors.

b. Find the cost of the standard seven-ounce portion at each of the following dealer prices:

    1. $2.25 per pound.
    2. $2.49 per pound.
    3. $1.89 per pound.

c. Find the cost of each of the following:

    1. A six-ounce portion, if dealer price is $2.19 per pound.
    2. A five-ounce portion, if dealer price is $2.29 per pound.

d. Assume that dealer price increases to $2.25 per lb. and management wants portion cost to be $1.65. What size portion should be served (in ounces)?

e. How many average-sized legs of lamb should be purchased to serve six-ounce portions to 270 people?

f. Last month, this restaurant used eighty-two legs of lamb. How many standard seven-ounce portions should have been produced from these eighty-two legs?

g. If the standard portion size had been six-ounces, how many portions could have been produced from the eighty-two legs of lamb used last month?

h. The restaurant has only thirty legs of lamb on hand today, and these must be used for a banquet function tonight for 350 people. What size portion should be served?

8. List and discuss three possible customer reactions to nonstandard portion sizes.

9. How can failure to follow standard recipes affect the portion cost and the quality of a particular item?

10. A restaurant has not established standard cooking times and temperatures for the production of one of the principal items on the menu, roast prime ribs of

beef. On one particular day, two full standing ribs have been roasted. One is well done and the other is rare. Assume that standard portion size is ten ounces. Will ten-ounce portions cut from each roast have identical costs? Why?

11. Select a recipe that could be used as a standard recipe in a foodservice establishment. Following the form illustrated in Figure 8.2, use current market prices to determine the standard cost of one standard portion of the item. Determine an appropriate menu sales price for the item if the desired food cost percent is 35.0%.

For Computer Users

12. Following the form illustrated in Figure 8.2, create a spreadsheet to accomplish the same purposes: determination of standard portion cost and calculation of food cost percent per portion given a sales price.

13. Select one simple recipe of the type indicated in Question 11 above, then calculate standard portion cost for the item produced by that recipe using the spreadsheet created in Problem 12 above.

14. Using a word processing program of your choice, create a collection of ten standard recipes, one to a file, and print them as individual documents, one to a page.

15. Using a spreadsheet program of your choice, and following the forms illustrated in figures 8.3 and 8.4, create worksheets to complete the necessary calculations for butcher test and cooking loss test. Save the templates and use them to do Question 4 above.

16. Use the spreadsheet templates created in Question 15 above to complete the test calculations required in questions 6a and 7a above.

17. Using a spreadsheet program of your choice, create worksheets to complete the calculations required for the solution of questions 6b through 6i and 7b through 7h above.

chapter 9

Production Control II: Controlling Production Quantities

Learning Objectives

After reading and studying this chapter, the student should be able to:

1. Define the standard for controlling production volume and explain its importance.
2. List and describe three standard procedures required for achieving control over production volume.
3. Define sales history and describe two methods for gathering the data that make up the sales history.
4. List three basic patterns for arranging data in a sales history.
5. Define popularity index.
6. Calculate the popularity index for menu items.
7. Use the popularity index in forecasting portion sales.
8. Describe the production sheet and calculate needed production for menu items.
9. Describe a void sheet and explain its use.
10. Complete a portion inventory and reconciliation.
11. Describe a procedure used for controlling high-cost, preportioned entrees.
12. Describe the use of computers in forecasting sales and controlling production quantities.

In the preceding chapter, the focus of our attention was the portion—controlling the ingredients that constitute a portion, the proportions of the various ingredients to one another, and the size of each portion. The purpose for controlling these three factors was shown to be the control of a fourth item: portion cost.

In the present chapter, we will assume that control has been established over individual portions and shift our focus to the question of number of portions produced for each item on a menu for a given day or meal. After all, if the cost of a portion of some item is controlled at, say, $2.50 per serving, and the establishment produces 100 portions but sells only 40, there will be 60 portions left over unsold, which may or may not be salable at another time. If they are salable, these portions are likely to be sold at lesser quality than they had when first produced. It is also possible that they cannot be sold in their original form but must be made into something different from it that may be sold at a lower sales price. Sometimes, none of these possiblities is feasible, and it is necessary to throw the food away. In any event, there is excessive cost, either for the cost of the food or, arguably, the cost of additional labor that would not have been required if the establishment had produced 40 portions rather than 100.

The excessive costs suggested above can be reduced or eliminated by applying the four-step control process to the problem of quantity production.

ESTABLISHING STANDARDS AND STANDARD PROCEDURES

The standard for controlling production volume is to produce, for any menu item, the number of portions that is likely to be sold on any given day or date. It is essential that foodservice establishments know this with some reasonable degree of accuracy so that intelligent plans can be made for purchasing and production. If, for example, one establishes that forty portions of an item are likely to be sold, one need purchase the ingredients for producing that number of portions. Failure to establish this standard can lead to excessive purchasing, with its obvious implications for cost.

In order to achieve any standard, it is necessary to establish appropriate standard procedures. To control production volume, several standard procedures are required. These include

Maintaining sales history.

Forecasting portion sales.

Determining production quantities.

Maintaining Sales History

A **sales history** is a written record of the number of portions of each item sold every time that item appeared on the menu. It is a summary of portion sales. In some establishments, sales histories are maintained for every item on the menu, from appetizers to desserts. In others, information is developed only for entree items. In many instances, the extent and complexity of the sales history is related to the length and scope of the menu itself. In all instances, the best decisions on the nature of the sales history are based on the need for information that can be put to use in improving operations. Unless the information maintained is useful in leading to better control over costs, it cannot be justified.

Because the sales history records customers' selections, the basic data are developed by those who record these selections: the serving personnel of a restaurant. To determine how the data is developed for the sales history, it is necessary to examine the two methods for recording customer selections: manual and electronic.

Manual Method

Establishments that record customer selections manually are those that use the traditional guest checks. Essentially, there are two kinds of guest checks: single checks and checks that come in pads of 25, or 50, or some other number. Servers commonly record customer selections on these checks manually, using pen or pencil, and the check is ultimately given to the customer as a bill to be paid. Payment is made to a cashier or to the server, and the check is retained by the establishment. Assuming that all selections have been recorded completely and legibly on the check, it is clearly a source document for the development of the sales history. The key is to set up a routine for abstracting the data from the check.

Abstracting of the information on the guest checks may be accomplished in any one of a number of ways. The simplest and perhaps most widely used method involves maintaining a running count of portion sales as they occur. This is most often done by a cashier, who records information from the checks as they are presented by customers. The information is recorded either on a copy of the menu, on a special score sheet (Fig. 9.1), or on one of several types of mechanical counting devices widely available to the industry. At the conclusion of a meal or at some other appropriate time, such as the end of the day, the information is sent to the food controller so that it can be added to the records developed from previous days. This method has the advantage of adding little or no cost to operations.

FIGURE 9.1
Portion Sales Breakdown

Day Tuesday	Date 2/2/XX	Meal Dinner
Item	Number of Portions	Total
A	H̶H̶t̶ H̶H̶t̶ H̶H̶t̶ H̶H̶t̶ 111	23
B	H̶H̶t̶ H̶H̶t̶ H̶H̶t̶ H̶H̶t̶ H̶H̶t̶ H̶H̶t̶ H̶H̶t̶ H̶H̶t̶ H̶H̶t̶ H̶H̶t̶ H̶H̶t̶ H̶H̶t̶	60
C	H̶H̶t̶ H̶H̶t̶ H̶H̶t̶ H̶H̶t̶ H̶H̶t̶ H̶H̶t̶ 1111	34
D	H̶H̶t̶ H̶H̶t̶ H̶H̶t̶ H̶H̶t̶ H̶H̶t̶ H̶H̶t̶ H̶H̶t̶ H̶H̶t̶ H̶H̶t̶	45
Total		162

In some operations, where the cashier is too busy for this extra work, the food controller takes the guest checks after the meal, or at the close of business, and breaks down the sales, usually on a score sheet. While this method is time-consuming, it does present some advantages, which will be discussed in the chapter on sales control. A variation involves the cashier giving the checks to someone in the accounting department, who records the necessary information and forwards it to the food controller.

Electronic Method

Increasingly, electronic terminals are being used in foodservice establishments. Some interface with complex systems, while others are little more than electronic versions of the old mechanical cash registers. Virtually all have the capacity to maintain cumulative totals of the numbers of portions of menu items sold. Essentially, there are two methods for inputting data: by depressing a key marked with the name of the menu item selected, or by depressing a two- or three-digit code for each menu item selected in a ten-key numeric keypad. In the first instance, if the customer ordered a cheeseburger, the server would depress a terminal key marked "cheeseburger." In the second, the server would translate "cheeseburger" into the code set up for that item—the three-digit number 472, for example—then enter the code number in a terminal keypad. At the end of a day or a meal period, the food controller could obtain a report from the terminal listing all menu items available and the number of portions of each that were sold.

This portion sales data is added to the cumulative records developed to date. If the establishment used manual techniques, the data would be added to master records kept on file cards or in an analysis book. If electronic means were employed, the data might be transcribed manually on cards or in a book or added to a computer database or spreadsheet designed for this special purpose. Regardless of whether the data are stored manually or electronically, the arrangement of the data is likely to be in one of the following patterns.

1. By operating period, such as one week, so that sales for each day of one week were all recorded on the same page or card. (see Fig. 9.2.)
2. By day of week, so that sales for Tuesdays, for example, might be compared for a period of several weeks.
3. By entree item, so the popularity of an item might be determined on a particular series of days.

Many operators have found it desirable to combine two of these systems in order to provide an overall picture of sales for the entire week at one glance, in addition to providing some clues as to the relative popularity of items when they appear on the menu with other varying items. An illustration of the technique appears in Figure 9.3.

FIGURE 9.2
Sales History

Sales History—Portions Sold—Month of February 19XX

Weather	Fair	Snow	Cold	Fair	Fair	Fair	Cold	Cold										
Day	M	T	W	H	F	S	S	M	T	W	H	F	S	S	M	T	W	H
Date	1	2	3	4	5	6	7	8	9	10	11	12	13	14	15	16	17	18
Item																		
A	75	23	60	63	70	82	73	72										
B	60	60	55	65	62	58	61	65										
C	6	34	22	18	15	12	16	20										
D	159	45	140	149	150	161	154	155										
Total	300	162	277	295	297	313	304	312										

FIGURE 9.3
Sales History

Sales History—Month of February 19XX

Item	Monday			Tuesday			Wednesday			Thursday			Friday			Saturday			Sunday	
	1	8	15	2	9	16	3	10	17	4	11	18	5	12	19	6	13	20	7	14
A	75	72		23			60			63			70			82			73	
B	60	65		60			55			65			62			58			61	
C	6	20		34			22			18			15			12			16	
D	159	155		45			140			149			150			161			154	
Total	300	312		162			277			295			297			313			304	

Other Information in Sales Histories

It should be noted that sales histories often include provision for recording additional information—relevant internal and external conditions that may shed light on sales data. One of the most common pieces of information included in sales histories is weather. Most foodservice operators find that weather conditions have definite impact on sales volume. In many establishments, bad weather keeps sales volume low, and including some information about the weather each day will often help explain why sales were high or low on that day. Interestingly, hotels in large metropolitan centers often find the impact of weather on sales to be the opposite of that experienced by others: bad weather seems to increase food and beverage sales in these properties, probably because bad weather keeps guests from going out to try other restaurants.

Special events can considerably influence sales and are often included in sales histories. The occurrence of a national holiday on a particular day, or the presence of a particular convention group in a hotel, can affect sales considerably. So can such varied conditions as faulty kitchen equipment, or a torn-up street in front of the restaurant, or a major sale at a neighboring department store, In general, an effort should be made to include in the sales history any information about events that may have affected sales and that should be considered in forecasting volume of sales at some particular time in the future. In hotel restaurants, the house count, or the number of people registered in the hotel on a particular day, is often included so that a determination can be made of the percentage of registered guests who are using the dining room, and judgments made in the future as to numbers of portions to prepare for any given date or rate of occupancy.

Popularity Index

In addition to maintaining histories of portions sold, many food controllers use the figures to determine the percentage of total portion sales represented by each item, as shown in Figure 9.4, often referred to a popularity index.

The popularity index is calculated by dividing the number of portions of a given item sold by the total number of portions of all menu items sold on the same

FIGURE 9.4
Popularity Index

Item	*Portions Sold*	*Percent of Total Sales (Popularity Index)*
A	23	14.2
B	60	37.0
C	34	21.0
D	45	27.8
Total	162	100.0%

day or in the same time period. For example, the popularity index for item A in Figure 9.4 is calculated as follows:

$$\text{Popularity Index} = \frac{\text{Portions of Item A Sold}}{\text{Total Number of Portions of All Menu Items Sold}}$$

$$= \frac{23}{162}$$

$$= .1419 = .142, \text{ or } 14.2\%$$

These ratios are of far greater use in determining an item's popularity than are raw figures that simply indicate number of portions sold. For example, the sales history might show portion sales of item B from a low of twelve portions to a high of seventy-eight. This knowledge would not be as useful as information indicating that the twelve portions had represented 35% of total sales that day, and the seventy-eight portions had represented 39%. Given this information, as well as the information that item B represented 37% of total sales on another recent day, we might conclude that this particular item accounted for approximately 37% of sales each time it appeared on the menu. If this has been the trend for some time, the information should be useful for predicting the future.

Such ratios to total sales can be useful in determining whether to continue offering a certain item on the menu. If an item consistently represented only 2% of total sales whenever it appeared, serious consideration should be given to removing it from the menu or substituting a more popular item. In some operations, particularly those with relatively stable menus, these sales ratios can be developed for particular time periods and used effectively in forecasting.

Forecasting Portion Sales

Forecasting is a procedure in which data are used to predict what is likely to occur in the future. It amounts to intelligent, educated guesswork about future events. If the future can be predicted with reasonable accuracy, appropriate plans can be made in advance for likely happenings. In the food industry, which deals with highly perishable products, this advance planning can be a large factor in operating profitably.

Forecasting is a principle element in cost control. If sales volume can be predicted accurately, then plans can be made for purchasing appropriate quantities of food to prepare for anticipated sales. Purchasing unneeded quantities can be avoided, thus reducing some of the possibilities for waste, spoilage, and pilferage. In addition, plans can be made for producing particular numbers of portions for sale on particular dates, thus reducing possibilities for excessive costs to develop. Moreover, such planned control over purchasing can lead automatically to control over production; it is impossible to prepare a greater number of portions than necessary if the raw materials for overproduction do not exist.

A usual first step in forecasting is to predict total anticipated volume: anticipated numbers of customers for particular days or particular meals. To arrive at a figure, reference is made to the sales history to find the total number of sales that occurred on each of a number of comparable dates in the recent past. When wide differences are apparent, every effort must be made to determine the reasons for the differences. The causes are often revealed by the information in the history relating to weather and other conditions that existed at the time of the sales. The effect of each of these conditions must be judged—some increase sales, others decrease them.

When the effects of surrounding conditions have been evaluated, it is important next to judge the extent to which these conditions will exist on a particular date in the future. This usually involves checking the local calendar of coming events, weather forecasts, and any other pertinent sources of information.

After these steps have been taken, it is possible to guess the total business volume that may be anticipated for a particular date. If, for example, recent history reflected 275 to 300 sales for dinner on Tuesdays in pleasant weather, one could reasonably anticipate that the next Tuesday would bring approximately the same volume of business if good weather were expected. In this case, it would probably be safe to predict 300 sales.

The next step is to forecast the anticipated number of sales of each item on the menu. This is simpler to do if the menu is identical to those that have appeared on Tuesdays in the past. However, it can also be done for changing menus if the sales history is set up to reflect relative popularity of certain items when they have appeared with other items in the past. This type of forecasting is more difficult, but by no means impossible.

When the sales history shows the sales ratio for an item over a period of time, this may be taken as the popularity index and used for predicting. For example, if item M usually represents 20% of total sales on Tuesday evenings, it would be fairly safe to predict that next Tuesday, item M would also represent 20% of the anticipated 300 sales, or 60 portions.

This procedure is followed for every item that will appear on the menu, and thus a forecast is made of anticipated sales for a particular date. However, it should be recognized that this forecast must be somewhat flexible, subject to change as conditions may change. A change in the weather forecast, for example, might necessitate changing the sales forecast sometime before the date in question.

Once the forecast is completed, usually by a food controller, it should be reviewed by someone else, often the manager. Forecasting is educated guesswork, and two heads are usually better than one.

The completed forecast represents management's best judgment of the sales volume anticipated, and the information should be shared with appropriate personnel in the operation. One member of the staff who can make valuable use of this information is the person in charge of staffing the dining room. With accurate forecast, She can better make plans to hire sufficient personnel yet keep the total to the minimum necessary, thus maintaining control over labor costs.

Perhaps the most important person with whom to share the information is the chef, who must be aware of anticipated volume, partly in order to anticipate labor requirements. In addition, with information about anticipated portion sales for each menu item, the chef is better equipped to advise the steward on the appropriate quantities of food to have on hand. If sales of sixty portions of item M are forecasted for next Tuesday, the steward need not purchase a greater quantity of the perishable ingredients than is necessary. The consequent control of purchasing can be one of the most important factors in limiting excessive costs. When needed quantities are known, only those quantities should be purchased.

Determining Production Quantities

The Production Sheet

Production sheets such as that illustrated in figure 9.5 are often prepared to reflect the forecast determined by the food controller. A production sheet lists each menu item and, by listing the number of portions of each that are expected to be sold, sets production goals for the chef and his staff. These sheets should be viewed as an effort by management to control production and eliminate waste.

Production sheets vary in form and complexity from kitchen to kitchen. One very simple form appears in Figure 9.5. It should be completed by a manager or food controller as many days in advance as possible and forwarded to the chef immediately. Upon receiving it, the chef would know both total anticipated volume for a particular meal and the anticipated number of portion sales of each item on the menu. With this information in hand, he would be better equipped to determine needs for perishable foods, for which the steward would place orders, and for nonperishable foods, which would be requisitioned from the storeroom. Provision is made for adjusting the forecasted figures upward or downward on the basis of weather or other changes.

FIGURE 9.5
Production Sheet

	Production Sheet	
Day Tues.	Date 6/9/XX	Meal Dinner
	Volume Forecast 305	

Menu Item	Forecast	Adjusted Forecast
L	75	80
M	60	65
N	20	20
O	150	165
Total	305	330

Ideally, the changes will be minor. In any case, adjustments can be made immediately before the forecasted date, often the night before, sometimes on the morning of the date in question. The final figures in the Adjusted Forecast column are production goals for the chef, who should be responsible for seeing to it that leftover foods are used in meeting those goals whenever possible, provided that their use does not violate the establishment's quality standards.

In some operations, this very simple version of the production sheet is not sufficient. Where additional control over production is desirable, a more elaborate form, such as that pictured in Figure 9.6, might be used. This form establishes greater control in several ways. It restates the portion size for each item, thus continually reemphasizing management's concern that the size of each portion served be carefully controlled. This may be particularly important in those places that offer portions of different sizes for luncheon, for dinner, and for banquets. It also directs the kitchen staff in the production method to be employed, which might be of considerable importance when several recipes exist for the same item and management has particular preferences or wants to try a different one. The purpose of the Portions on Hand column is to force the chef, before beginning the production, to take an inventory of leftovers from the previous day or meal. While this is not desirable in some places because of the quality standards established, it is perfectly permissible in others.

In such instances, the figure in the Total Available column equals that in the Adjusted Forecast column, and at the same time is the sum of the leftover portions and additional portions produced. As a further control, there is a column for portions left over. Whenever possible, this figure should be carried over to the production sheet for the next day or meal, in order to ensure that these leftovers will be sold. If portions of uncooked meats have been left over, and the number recorded cannot be located for a following day or meal, immediate steps can be taken to eliminate future possibilities for pilferage.

FIGURE 9.6
Production Sheet

Production Sheet

Day Tues.   Date 6/9/XX   Meal Dinner

Volume Forecast 305

Menu Item	Forecast	Adjusted Forecast	Portion Size	Production Method	Portions on Hand	Needed Production	Total Available	Left Over
L	75	80	6 oz.	Recipe #62	—	80	80	0
M	60	65	8 oz.	Recipe #4	5	60	65	5
N	20	20	4 oz.	Recipe #19	—	20	20	0
O	150	165	12 oz.	Broil	20	145	165	6
Total	305	330						

Regardless of the degree of complexity involved, the purpose of any production sheet is to establish control by setting goals for production in order to eliminate a major cause of excessive cost. Unsold portions appear in cost figures but are not reflected in sales figures for the day. Therefore, to keep costs in line, controlling food production is necessary and desirable. Under ideal conditions, no unsold portions would ever be left over after a meal. Everyone recognizes that this is impossible, but it is a desirable goal nevertheless. To the extent to which unsold portions can be eliminated, food costs can be better controlled and excessive costs eliminated. With this goal in mind, production sheets are established and used.

In most operations, the cost of entree items represents the greatest part of food cost. Meats and fish, after all, usually constitute the largest portion of food cost per customer served, and thus additional control procedures to isolate instances of waste and inefficiency are often concerned with entree items.

TRAINING FOR PRODUCTION

To establish control over the number of portions produced, it is clearly important that complete and accurate information be obtained each day about the number of portions of each menu item sold. That information must be recorded accurately and reliably in a sales history, then used carefully to forecast future sales. A key element in all this is the completeness and accuracy of the data recorded.

Management must take great care to train employees to record complete and accurate data. If manual techniques are used, then servers must be made aware of the need for legibility on all guest checks and of the special importance of recording all necessary data on each check. Someone other than the server will be reading these checks to abstract the data, and the data must therefore be complete and accessible. Poor handwriting and items remembered by the server but never recorded on the checks are clear impediments to developing the sales history. Although using electronic techniques does eliminate the problem of legibility, one must train servers to record all information and to do so accurately, or the data will be less than useful.

Many operators find it desirable to explain the goals of production control techniques to their employees, finding that the servers who understand the aims of the system are more likely to comply with management's directives concerning accuracy of imput. The educated employee who understands her role in the collection of these important data can be among the most useful and reliable of employees—one who may be singled out for special managerial training over the long term.

Training personnel for forecasting requires selection of those with experience and judgment, both qualities essential to effective forecasting. It is unlikely that more than one or two persons on the staff will be trained and able to forecast sales and prepare production sheets. After all, these are special tasks clearly tied to the central functions of management; thus they are usually reserved for the food controller, the chef, or, more commonly, the manager.

MONITORING QUANTITY PRODUCTION AND TAKING CORRECTIVE ACTION

There are two purposes for monitoring quantity production:

1. To determine whether the sales forecast has been reasonably accurate concerning both the total number of customers and their individual preferences for particular menu items.
2. To judge how closely the chef has followed the production standards established on the production sheet.

These will be discussed separately.

Monitoring Accuracy of Forecasting

To make judgments about the accuracy of the forecast, one must have detailed information about both the forecast and the actual sales on the day for which the forecast was prepared. For the former, one need have only a copy of the forecast itself; for the latter, full details should be available in the sales history. Information from both sources can be recorded on a form such as that illustrated in Figure 9.7, which shows that the adjusted forecast for total sales was with six of the actual—98.2% accuracy, a degree of accuracy that most food service operators would find acceptable. However, examination of the figures for particular items suggests several points.

1. Item L was underforecasted. Five portions above the forecast were sold, and one would question where these portions came from. It is possible that they were produced by reducing the size of other portions, so that a number of customers ordering item L received less than the standard portion size. On the other hand, these five additional portions might have been produced from

FIGURE 9.7
Comparison: Sales Forecast and Actual Sales

Day Wednesday	Date 6/9/XX	Meal Dinner	
Item	Sales Forecast	Actual Sales	Difference
L	80	85	+5
M	65	60	−5
N	20	20	-0-
O	165	159	−6
Total	330	324	−6

inventory, which might reduce inventory on hand for the following day to unacceptable levels.

2. Item N appears to have been perfectly forecasted. However, it is possible that the kitchen ran out of this item before the end of the meal period and customers who had selected item N were forced to make alternative selections. If this has been the case, then actual sales of items L, M, and O may be higher than they would have been otherwise. It is important, therefore, that the food controller make an appropriate notation in the sales history about the time any item runs out so that this information may be taken into account as other forecasts are made in the future. In many restaurants, the host makes note of this in a log book kept in the dining room.

3. Items M and O, both of which sold fewer portions than were forecast, may indicate both inefficient forecasting and excessive cost, depending on how and whether these items can be reused.

Judging Whether Production Standards Were Followed

It is important to keep in mind that the numbers in Figure 9.7 are not related to actual kitchen production in any way. Figure 9.7 merely compares numbers forecast to numbers sold. The next step, then, is to monitor the performance of the kitchen staff to judge how closely the chef has followed the production quantity standards described on the production sheet for the day. In order to do this, it will first be necessary to describe a procedure for keeping records of portions rejected by customers and returned from the Dining Room. Records of these may be kept on a so-called void sheet.

The Void Sheet

Every restaurant offering steaks, chops, and other similar a la carte entrees has probably had some experience with items being returned from the dining room for one reason or another. Often portions are returned because a customer is difficult or impossible to please. However, on many occasions portions are returned because some member of the staff was not listening carefully to the customer, who consequently did not receive what she ordered. Sometimes this is because of a careless server, sometimes because of a careless or overworked cook. In any instance, these returned portions represent cost and should be accounted for. Therefore, many restaurants use a void sheet similar to that illustrated in Figure 9.8. Whenever a portion is returned, an authorized individual, such as a kitchen supervisor or chef, must make note of it, indicating the name of the item, the number of the check on which it appeared, and the reason for its return.

The entries on such sheets can be most revealing to an alert food controller. For example, if one particular server appears on the list with greater than usual regularity, he is possibly not paying careful attention to customer orders. Such negligence can be costly and should be attended to quickly. On the other hand, it

FIGURE 9.8
Void Sheet

Void sheet				Day Tues.	Date 6/9/XX
Check #	Waiter #	Item	Reason for Return	Authorization	Sales Value
11031	6	O	Too well done	SJC.	7.95
11034	6	M	Dropped on floor	SJC.	6.95
11206	4	O	Too well done	SJC.	7.95
11227	3	O	Too well done	SJC.	7.95

might be noted that the number of broiler items returned is far greater when one particular employee is working. This might suggest the need for the chef to observe this employee's job performance and perhaps attempt to get her to improve. If the number of returns is consistently great, investigation might suggest the need for additional personnel to better satisfy customer demand.

There are other important uses of the void sheet, particularly when efforts are being made to control portions by some method such as that described below as the par stock control of portions. If portions are not accounted for, kitchen personnel can easily claim that they were returned by a difficult customer and thrown away. If all such portions must be recorded on the void sheet and attested to by some member of the management team, it is more difficult for kitchen personnel to be careless with food. In addition, the recording of returned portions, taken with other techniques previously described, makes possible the reconciliation of kitchen records of portions produced and records of portions sold.

Portion Inventory and Reconciliation

One useful means of determining how closely the chef has followed quantity production standards established for the day involves the use of a form similar to that illustrated in Figure 9.9. The procedure used follows logically from the production sheet illustrated in Figure 9.6. In fact, Figure 9.9 may be viewed as an elaboration on the earlier figure.

FIGURE 9.9
Portion Inventory and Reconciliation

Portion Inventory and Reconciliation

Day __Wed.__   Date __10/8/XX__

Portion Production:

Item	Opening Inventory	Portions Prepared	Additional Preparation	Total Available	Closing Inventory	Portions Consumed
AB	—	180		180	15	165
BH	5	60		65	5	60
CJ	—	110	10	120	14	106
DZ	20	145		165	8	157

Sales Reconciliation:

Item	Portions Sold	Portions Void	Total	Consumed (From Above)	Difference	Comment
AB	165	—	165	165		
BH	58	2	60	60		
CJ	103	1	104	106	2	2 missing checks
DZ	156	1	157	157		

Prepared by: _____
      Food Controller

Reviewed by: _____
      Manager

To use the technique effectively, one lists each menu item on the form before kitchen production begins. Next, an inventory is taken of any portions left over from previous meals that may be used again. Reusing leftovers in this way is common in some establishments but unacceptable in others.

If leftovers are to be used, the number of portions on hand is deducted from the quantity scheduled for production, and only the difference is prepared. That number is written in the Portions Prepared column. Additional quantities prepared, if any, are indicated in the next column. At the conclusion of the serving hours, an inventory of the portions on hand (Closing Inventory) is made. When these columns are completed, the form is sent to the food controller.

On receiving the form, the food controller determines the total available by adding and then subtracting the closing inventory to find the number of portions consumed. Following this determination of the number of portions consumed according to kitchen records, the food controller obtains from the cashier (or other source) the records of portions sold that have been prepared for entry into the sales history. Because this figure may not include records of small parties or banquets served in private rooms, provision is made for entering the number of portions of banquet items sold. The number of portions voided, or returned to the kitchen, is subtracted from the total of these two, and the result is entered in the Total column.

The next step is to determine the difference, if any, between the kitchen records and the portion sales records. That difference is written in the appropriate column. In the example given, kitchen records show the production of 106 cooked portions of CJ, while sales records indicate only 104 portions sold. The difference (2 portions) is entered and should be investigated immediately while events are still fresh in the minds of the personnel involved. Once the causes of the discrepancy are known, steps can be taken to eliminate the problem in the future. After all, two portions unaccounted for represent 1.9% of portions produced. These portions will appear in the cost figures and, by not being reflected in sales figures, will raise the cost-to-sales ratio excessively.

While this technique is most useful in restaurants serving foods cooked to order, it can be helpful in other establishments as well. Its use requires that someone be able to estimate with some degree of accuracy the number of portions contained in, say, a steam table pan of beef goulash. The records resulting from the use of this reconciliation procedure will not be as precise in this type of foodservice establishment, but they can be helpful in attempting to isolate problems.

If portion sizes are carefully controlled and standard portion costs known, the number of portions unaccounted for can be translated into dollars quite simply. In the previous example, if the missing portions of CJ have a standard cost of $3.35 each, then simple multiplication determines that the loss of these portions has increased costs by $6.70 on that particular day. Such a figure might not seem large, but if equal losses occur seven days a week throughout the year, it amounts to a weekly loss of $46.90 and an annual loss of $2,438.80, a substantial amount. The cost is excessive in every sense and should be eliminated. If the loss can be eliminated without increasing other costs, profits will be increased by the amount saved.

While the foregoing procedure for reconciling portion production and sales is useful, it does, after all, address itself only to entree items, and in most instances extending it to cover other items on the menu as well would be unwieldy. Although it is true that entree items usually represent the greatest proportion of cost, this does not mean that the cost of other items can be neglected. Also, this reconciliation does not take into account the waste, if any, that occurred in the preparation of the number of portions that were finally listed on the form. It is possible, for example, that several steaks were improperly cut and discarded, never having been listed on the reconciliation form.

For these and other reasons, some large establishments, with the personnel and time necessary to complete the work, prepare various daily reports to determine the dollar difference between standard costs and actual costs. These topics will be discussed in chapter 12.

Par Stock Control of Preportioned Entrees

Another useful technique for controlling the preparation of quantities of some specialized items is illustrated in Figure 9.10 and discussed below. Expensive cuts of meat, such as steaks and chops, are either purchased already portioned or portioned in the restaurant before cooking. These items are usually cooked to order and are typically held in a refrigerator close to the broiler or range. Under such circumstances, the cook will usually be responsible for putting the items on the fire when they are ordered.

Therefore, many managers and food controllers find it useful to make the cook fully responsible for these expensive items by requiring her to sign a sheet such as that illustrated in Figure 9.10. By signing, the cook acknowledges receipt of the number of portions of each item indicated.

The number of portions that the steward issues should be equal to the number of sales forecasted for each item. In case the forecasted number is incorrect, provision is made for additional issues, for which the cook also will sign. At the conclusion of serving hours, the number issued can be totaled in the next column. The number of portions returned, if any, will be entered in the Returned to Steward column, and the steward will sign for the returns. Total Issues minus Returns equals the number of portions consumed, and the steward fills in this figure before sending the form on to the food controller.

One advantage of this procedure is that it makes the cook accountable for a particular number of portions. Knowing the certainty of being questioned about missing portions, the cook will be less likely to give any away to staff members.

The use of the form illustrated in Figure 9.9 will typically bring to light any discrepancies between management's plan for production—the forecast—and the actual production—the total of portions sold, returned, and left over. It is of obvious importance to determine the cause of any such discrepancies and to take action to reduce their number and extent in the future. In the foodservice industry, some degree of inefficiency is normally tolerated in day-to-day operations, and management in a given operation must determine the level considered acceptable.

FIGURE 9.10
Control Sheet for Preportioned Entrees

Item	Portions Issued	Additional Issues	Total Issues	Returned to Steward	Portions Consumed
D	165	—	165	6	159

Day Tues.

Date 2/9/XX

Issues received _J. Jones_

Additional Issues ____

Returned portions received _Paul Smith_

steward

COMPUTER APPLICATIONS

Given the many electronic sales terminals available today, developing sales history data has become simpler and faster than it was in the past. With stand-alone sales terminals, it is necessary at the end of a day or a meal period to print out a report of portion sales during that period for inclusion in a manually maintained history. With sales terminals integrated into a system, portion sales data may merely be stored in computer memory for future reference. The problem would be to create a suitable program for rendering the data in a form useful for forecasting.

With historical records of portion sales stored in memory, forecasting might take the following form. The manager or food controller would enter in a terminal the projected menu. The items would be displayed in a column on the left side of the CRT. In columns to the right of each item, the manager would see numbers of previous sales from specific dates, or the popularity index for each, depending on the program employed. The cursor would appear on the top line at the right of the screen opposite the first menu item and would flash in that position until an entry had been made reflecting forecasted portion sales. Before making such an entry, the manager or food controller would obviously consider carefully all displayed records and make the necessary judgment about future sales.

As the manager entered his forecast, the cursor would move from line to line until sales had been forecasted for each menu item. At that point, it would be possible to obtain a printout of the complete forecast, either as a simple forecast or in the form of one of the production sheets described in the chapter. As many copies as necessary could be obtained, so that various key individuals in the establishment could be informed of anticipated future sales forecasts.

CHAPTER ESSENTIALS

In this chapter, we explained the application of the control process to the quantity production phase of foodservice operations. We described the standard for quantity production as that number of portions of a given item likely to be sold on a given date and discussed techniques for establishing that standard. We defined sales history and described the two means of collecting the data included in a sales history. We illustrated several possible patterns for maintaining sales histories. We defined the popularity index and illustrated the formula for its calculation. We explained how the sales history and popularity index are used to prepare a forecast of portion sales. We defined and illustrated two forms of production sheet and explained their use. We described several techniques for monitoring performance: comparing the sales forecast to actual sales in order to make judgments about the accuracy of the forecast, and comparing production records to sales records to determine the extent to which kitchen production has approximated that called for on the production sheet. We illustrated a technique for controlling and accounting for such preportioned items as steaks and chops. Finally, we discussed the use of computers in developing records for a sales history, for maintaining sales history, and for forecasting.

KEY TERMS IN THIS CHAPTER

Sales history   Popularity index

Sales forecast   Production sheet

Void sheet   Portion reconciliation

Par stock control

QUESTIONS AND PROBLEMS

1. Compute the popularity index for the following sales. Round percentages to the nearest .1%.

    a. | Item | Portions Sold | % of Total Sales |
        |------|---------------|------------------|
        | A | 60 | |
        | B | 20 | |
        | C | 80 | |
        | D | 40 | |

    b. | Item | Portions Sold | % of Total Sales |
        |------|---------------|------------------|
        | A | 30 | |
        | B | 42 | |
        | C | 73 | |
        | D | 115 | |

    c. | Item | Portions Sold | % of Total Sales |
        |------|---------------|------------------|
        | A | 86 | |
        | B | 113 | |
        | C | 55 | |
        | D | 44 | |
        | E | 25 | |

2. In Question 1a above, predict the sales for each item if sales for all items are expected to be 300.

3. In 1b above, predict the sales for each item if sales for all items are expected to be 150.

4. In 1c above, predict the sales of each item if sales for all items are expected to be 450.

5. In Question 2 above, assume that the adjusted forecast is 20% less than the original forecast and prepare a production sheet, using Figure 9.5 as a guide.

6. In Question 3 above, assume that the adjusted forecast is 10% greater than the original forecast and prepare a production sheet, using Figure 9.5 as a guide.

7. List and discuss four possible causes of discrepancies between figures listed in the Portions Consumed and Portions Sold columns on the form illustrated in Figure 9.9.

8. Define sales history and list two ways information for a sales history is gathered.

9. What advantages and disadvantages do you see in each of the ways described for maintaining sales history information?

10. Describe a procedure used in controlling high-cost precut entrees.

11. If a food controller were looking for ways to reduce excessive food costs, would she find void sheets of any use? Why?

12. Of what use is an electronic sales terminal in developing a sales history?

For Computer Users

13. Using any spreadsheet program of your choice,

    a. Reproduce the sales history illustrated in Figure 9.2.

    b. Insert columns as required and calculate popularity index for each item on each date.

    c. Calculate popularity index for each item based on total sales for the eight days recorded in the sales history.

14. Using the popularity index for each item in Question 13c, create a spreadsheet to generate a production sheet for the same menu items, given fair weather conditions and an expected total of 375 sales.

chapter 10

Monitoring Operations I: Monthly Inventory and Food Cost Determinations

Learning Objectives

After reading and studying this chapter, the student should be able to:

1. Explain the importance of monitoring the overall performance of a foodservice operation on a monthly basis.

2. Describe the procedure for taking physical inventory at the end of the month.

3. List and explain five ways to assign costs to units of food in inventory.

4. State the formula for calculating cost of food consumed.

5. Explain the difference between cost of each of five acceptable methods of assigning cost to the closing inventory.

6. List and explain the adjustments needed to translate cost of food consumed into cost of food sold.

7. Define the terms *opening* (or *beginning*) *inventory* and *closing* (or *ending*) *inventory.*

8. Explain the relationship between the monthly calculation of cost of food sold and the monthly income statement.

9. Devise a simple monthly food cost report to management, given the necessary figures.

10. Calculate cost of food consumed, cost of food sold, food cost percent, and cost per dollar sale, given appropriate figures.

11. Explain the possible shortcomings of a system that calculates cost of food sold only once a month.

12. Explain how computers may assist management in determining both inventory values and employee adherence to standard procedures for food issue.

In the preceding chapters, we have examined methods used to implement the control process through various phases of foodservice operation, including purchasing, receiving, storing, issuing, and production. In each chapter, we described techniques for monitoring the operations under discussion. Now, having established control over many critical phases of the foodservice enterprise, we will turn to an examination of the techniques and procedures used by managers to monitor the totality of a food production operation, rather than individual aspects. For purposes of academic discussion, it is both useful and productive to examine individual parts of the operation closely. However, although a foodservice manager should be able to do that, she must also be able to look at the whole operation and monitor its overall performance. It should be obvious that the success of a foodservice operation is measured in terms of the whole, not one or more of its parts. Too, it is quite possible that the operation may be successful even though one or more aspects of it could be improved through better control.

The examination of techniques and procedures for monitoring overall operations will be the subjects of the next three chapters. The most common approach to monitoring is one requiring that various procedures and calculations be completed once a month. The month is a basic unit of time in the accounting process, and most of the procedures described in this chapter are actually accounting procedures designed to provide managers with monthly reports on the progress of a business and its financial status. Arguably, these procedures enable management to monitor the effectiveness of the control processes established for the operation. While they will not pinpoint specific problems in an enterprise, they will provide some reasonable estimate of its overall financial health. For example, a restaurant that has food costs of 55% and labor costs of 45% is certain to be less financially healthy than another establishment with food costs of 30% and labor costs of 35%, assuming other costs to be equal. The former has difficulty, obviously, but one cannot tell with any degree of precision which specific aspects of operation are responsible. However, unless these basic monthly determinations are made, management will have no idea of the existence or the extent of difficulty until it is too late to attempt improvement.

The purpose of the present chapter, then, is to determine on a monthly basis whether or not the control mechanisms established are effective in enabling the business to meet desired goals. To make these determinations, it is necessary to take a number of steps designed to measure performance. The first of these is monthly inventory.

MONTHLY INVENTORY

Taking Physical Inventory

In most business establishments, including food and beverage operations, a universally accepted practice is the taking of a physical inventory. This is done at the close of an accounting period, typically after the close of business on the last day of a calendar month. In our discussion here we will be concerned only with those dealing in food and beverage items purchased primarily for making and selling food and beverage products.

The process of taking a physical inventory requires that one physically count the actual number of units on hand of each item in stock and record that number in the appropriate place in an inventory book, such as that illustrated in Figure 10.1, or in some other similar place. It is normally considered good practice to list the items in stock in a book specifically for that purpose, in the same order in which they are maintained in stock. This facilitates a procedure that can be long and tedious, depending on the number of commodities in the inventory.

Taking a physical inventory in a storeroom, for example, commonly requires two people, one to count the units on the shelves and the other to record the amounts in the inventory book. If the storeroom is arranged as suggested in Chapter 7, it is possible for the two to begin in one logical spot and work their way around in order, finding items on shelves in the same order as that listed in the inventory book.

Once quantities are determined for each item, total values can be calculated for each. To do this, one records the unit cost of each commodity and multiplies it by the number of units of each in the physical inventory. Once the total value of

FIGURE 10.1
Storeroom Inventory

Month of	September, 19XX			October, 19XX			Novem	
Articles	Quantity	Price	Amount	Quantity	Price	Amount	Quantity	Price
Brought forward	—	—	$743.82					
Tomato Paste #2½	16	1.24	19.84					
Tomato Paste #10	6	3.49	20.94					
Tomato Puree #10	8	3.29	26.32					
Tomato Juice, 46 oz.	24	.99	23.76					
Tomato Juice, 6 oz.	60	.29	17.40					
Tomato Sauce, #10	18	2.99	53.82					
Tomatoes, whole, peeled #10	15	2.89	43.35					

each commodity has been determined, the totals can be added to determine the total dollar value of the inventory. This dollar figure, known as the **closing inventory valuation** for the period, automatically becomes the opening inventory vaulation for the next period.

One of the principal difficulties with the above procedure is determining unit costs or values for each item, since all purchases are not made at the same price. It is not uncommon for prices to change several times during the course of the month. Determining what value to assign to units remaining in inventory at the end of the month raises the question of which, if any, of the various prices should be assigned for purposes of inventory valuation.

Valuing the Physical Inventory

There are at least five possible ways of assigning values to units of commodities in inventory, each of which will be explained. Because each provides a different answer to the question of inventory value at the end of any given period, the student is advised to become familiar with these approaches, any one of which management might select as appropriate for use in a particular establishment given a particular set of circumstances.

Because it would be unwieldy and possibly confusing to illustrate each of the five by attempting to treat a complete set of inventory figures, we will restrict ourselves to only one item in the stores inventory of a particular restaurant, #10 cans of fruit cocktail. Records from the restaurant for a certain month reveal the following:

Opening inventory on the 1st of the month:	10 cans @ $2.35 = $23.50
Purchased on the 7th of the month:	24 cans @ $2.50 = $60.00
Purchased on the 15th of the month:	24 cans @ $2.60 = $62.40
Purchased on the 26th of the month:	12 cans @ $2.30 = $27.60

A physical inventory on the thirty-first of the month showed that twenty cans remained in stock. From this we may deduce that fifty cans were consumed in the course on the month in this manner:

Opening Inventory	10 cans
+ Purchases during the Month	60 "
= Total Available for Use	70 "
-- Closing Inventory (number of units still available)	30 "
= Amount Consumed (number of units no longer available)	40 cans

Because both the value of the opening inventory ($23.50) and the purchases of this item ($150.00) are known, it is also possible to add both values together to determine the value of the total number of units available, or $173.50. It should be obvious that it is possible to determine the value of the amount consumed only if one can somehow determine the value of the number of units in the closing inventory and then subtract it from the value of the total available. The following are five accepted methods of assigning these unit values.

Actual Purchase Price Method

Perhaps the most reasonable approach would be to value the remaining items— those in the closing inventory—at actual purchase price. However, this can be done only if those prices are marked on the units. If the cans are marked with actual purchase prices, totaling their value is obviously a simple clerical job requiring no more complex procedure than addition. Hence, it is possible to determine the value of the 20 cans as:

$$
\begin{array}{rl}
4 @ \$2.35 &= \$9.40 \\
12 @ \ \ 2.30 &= 10.40 \\
4 @ \ \ 2.60 &= 10.40 \\
\hline
20 \ \ \ \ \ \ \ \ \ \ &= 47.40
\end{array}
$$

If the cans were not marked, an alternative procedure would be not necessary.

First-In, First-Out Method (Latest Prices)

If actual purchase prices are not marked on the cans, an alternative procedure is to assume that stock has been rotated during the period and that the units consumed were the first to be placed on the shelf, so that those remaining on the shelf are those most recently purchased. In many cases, these are not valid assumptions, but we will make them for purposes of discussion.

In order to establish a value for the closing inventory under this method, it would be necessary to know that the latest purchase on the twenty-sixth of the month was for twelve cans and that the next previous purchase on the fifteenth was for twenty-four cans. With that information available, it is possible to determine the value of the twenty cans as:

$$
\begin{array}{rl}
12 @ \$2.30 &= \$27.60 \\
8 @ \ \ 2.60 &= \ \ 20.80 \\
20 \ \ \ \ \ \ \ \ \ \ &= \ \ 48.40
\end{array}
$$

However, if there were no particular assurances that the stock on the shelves had been properly rotated during the month, this would not be the safest course, since it rests largely on the assumption of rotation.

Weighted Average Purchase Price Method

Where no certainty exists that stock had been rotated, and where large quantities of goods are involved, it is possible to determine a weighted average purchase price by multiplying the number of units in the opening inventory and in each purchase by their individual purchase prices, adding these values to determine a total value for all units together, and then dividing by the number of units involved. By following this procedure, the weighted average value of one unit could be determined by dividing seventy units into their $173.50 total value, which yields $2.48. Therefore, the value of the closing inventory would be:

$$20 \text{ @ } \$2.48 = \$49.60$$

It should be apparent that, while this procedure makes logical sense on paper, it requires access to extensive documentation. In fact, it is rather cumbersome and far too time-consuming to be used in most food and beverage operations.

Latest Purchase Price Method (Most Recent Price)

A simpler, faster, and more widely employed approach is to use the latest price in valuing the closing inventory. One justification for this approach is that if it were necessary to replace the remaining cans, the cost of replacement at the present moment would likely be the latest price at which the items were purchased. If this method were followed, as it frequently is in the food and beverage business, the value of the closing inventory of this item would be:

$$20 \text{ @ } \$2.30 = \$46.00$$

Last-In, First Out Method (Earliest Prices)

In certain specialized circumstances, particularly in periods of high inflation and when management chooses to minimize profits on financial statements in order to decrease income taxes, it is possible to maximize cost by minimizing the value of closing inventory. This can be achieved in times of rising prices by valuing the units remaining in inventory at the close of a period at the earliest purchase price. By following this procedure with the current example, the value of the twenty cans would be:

$$
\begin{aligned}
10 \text{ @ } \$2.35 &= \$23.50 \\
\underline{10 \text{ @ } \quad 2.50} &= \underline{\quad 25.00} \\
20 \quad\quad\quad &= \quad 48.50
\end{aligned}
$$

It should be borne in mind that a food controller does not normally determine the method to be used in valuing inventories. Although he may contribute to discussion of the question, the decision probably lies with the firm's accountant. Additionally, once the decision is made, it cannot be changed capriciously; various accounting conventions and Internal Revenue Service regulations preclude simple change.

Comparison of Methods

If the prices of goods purchased were fixed, the selection of method for valuing a closing inventory would be of no importance; all methods would yield the same figure. However, in a period of fluctuating prices—which, after all, describes most periods in our business—the selection of one method over another may bring a significantly different result. A comparison of the values of the twenty cans in closing inventory described above illustrate the point:

1. Value based on actual purchase price method: $47.40
2. Value based on first-in, first-out method: 48.40
3. Value based on weighted average method: 49.60
4. Value based on latest purchase price method: 46.00
5. Value based on last-in, first-out method: 48.50

Using the lowest established value, $46.00, as a base, a difference of 7.8% exists between the highest value and the lowest value in this particular case. And while the dollar differences for this one example do not appear particularly great, the difference would be significant if one were dealing with an entire inventory.

With the information available from our discussions in this and previous chapters, it is now possible to calculate the cost, cost-to-sales ratio, or actual cost percentage of operation for any establishment, regardless of the size and the nature and complexity of the control procedures in effect.

MONTHLY FOOD COST DETERMINATION

Cost of food sold for the month is determined by means of the following formula:

Opening Inventory	(food on hand the first day of the month)
+ Purchases	(both Directs and Stores)
Total Available	(total value of all food available for sale)
− Closing Inventory	(food on hand the last day of the month)
= Cost of Food	(includes waste and pilferage)

Opening inventory for any accounting period is by definition identical to the closing inventory for the previous period and is available from accounting records. Purchases include all Directs and Stores purchased during the period as listed on invoices and summarized on the receiving clerk's daily reports throughout the period. Total available thus reflects the total dollar value of all foods, both Directs and Stores, available for the production of menu items for sale during the period. From this total, one subtracts the value of closing inventory as established by means previously described. The resulting figure represents cost of food for the period and includes the cost of all food whether used productively or not.

It should be noted that the closing inventory figure does not include the value of any Directs that have been purchased but not consumed. This results in a food cost figure somewhat higher than it should be. In practice, this is often ignored on the theory that any error in this procedure in one month will be offset the following month. In other words, some Directs that will be used at the beginning of each month will have been included in cost for the previous month, and since Directs are purchased in small quantities for nearly immediate use, the value of these should be fairly constant from month to month. In some large organizations, these Directs are in a category termed Foods in Process, which is subtracted from total available along with the closing inventory of Stores.

At this point it will be useful to illustrate the effect of the various methods of establishing value of closing inventory on the cost of food for a period, using the figures determined earlier in this chapter #10 cans of fruit cocktail (per Fig. 10.2). While the illustration shows only one item out of an inventory, it should be apparent that these effects would be cumulative over an entire inventory. Thus, although owners and accountants should jointly decide which method to use, a knowledgeable food controller should be aware of the effects of the various inventory valuation methods on food cost.

Once food cost for a given period has been determined, food cost percent

FIGURE 10.2
Comparison of Food Costs

	Actual Purchase Price Method	First-In, First-Out Method	Weighted Average Method	Latest Purchase Price Method	Last-In, First-Out Method
Opening Inventory	$ 23.50	$ 23.50	$ 23.50	$ 23.50	$ 23.50
Purchases	150.00	150.00	150.00	150.00	150.00
Total Available	173.50	173.50	173.50	173.50	173.50
Closing Inventory	47.40	48.40	49.60	46.00	48.50
Cost of Food	126.10	125.10	123.90	127.50	125.00

may be calculated. For purposes of the following illustrations, let us hypothesize a small restaurant. Assume that the records reveal the following figures for the month of March:

Opening Inventory	$ 2,000
Food Purchases	6,000
Closing Inventory	3,000
Food Sales	15,000

Given these figures, we may now determine the cost of food for March by means of the previously stated formula:

Opening Inventory	$2000
+ Purchases	6,000
Total Available	8,000
− Closing Inventory	3,000
= Cost of Food	$5,000

Once the cost of food is known, the cost percentage can be calculated by using the formula discussed in Chapter 1:

$$\frac{\text{Cost}}{\text{Sales}} = \text{Cost}\%$$

$$\frac{5,000.}{15,000.} = 33.3\%$$

This is the same as saying that the cost of food has been $.333 per dollar of sales.

However, it must be emphasized that while the $5,000 figure represents the cost of food, it is really the cost of food issued, not necessarily the same as the cost of food consumed. Determining the cost of food consumed may require that the cost of food issued be adjusted to account for a number of possible alternative uses of the food issued.

Adjustments to Cost of Food Issued

If there have been transfers between the kitchen and the bar, adjustments must be made to take the value of the transfers into account. Similarly, if there have been transfers from units in a chain to other units in that same chain, these must be totaled and used to adjust the cost figures of all concerned. In some hotel operations, where separate cost records are kept for the several food outlets in one hotel, certain similar adjustments must be made for food items transferred from one operation to another. And transfers, including the intraunit transfers of cooking liquor and food to bar (Directs), and the interunit transfers of such items as baked goods, are not the only possible adjustments to food cost figures. In order to achieve more accurate food costs, many operations make one or more of the following adjustments.

Grease Sales

In many establishments, particularly those that butcher meats on premises, raw fat is one of the byproducts of kitchen operation. Many of these places save the raw fat and sell it to rendering companies, which convert it to industrial fats and oils. The sale of this fat at so much per pound results in income to the establishment, which is generally treated as a credit to cost.

Steward Sales

In some hotels, and occasionally in restaurants, employees are permitted to purchase food at cost for their own use. Employees will sometimes take advantage of this possibility for special family occasions when, for example, a particular cut and grade of meat was not available in local supermarkets. When steward sales are permitted, the resulting income is considered a credit to cost, reducing periodic cost by the value of the raw foods sold to employees. Were this procedure not followed, the cost of these foods would be included wrongfully in cost figures.

Gratis to Bars

In many establishments, the kitchen is expected to produce various hot and cold hors d'oeuvres that are given away at the bar. Since the purpose of this is to promote beverage sales, it seems logical to reflect the cost of the hors d'oeuvres in the cost of operating the beverage department and to credit food cost for their value.

Promotion Expense

In cases where the owner or manager of the operation entertains persons who may bring in business, food is consumed but sales revenue is not increased because no one pays the check. If management seeks food cost figures that are as accurate as possible, it becomes necessary to credit food cost for the value of foods so consumed and to charge their cost to another account, such as promotion expense.

Determining Cost of Food Consumed

When the above are taken into account, the monthly determination of cost of food consumed takes the following form:

$$
\begin{array}{l}
\text{Opening Inventory} \\
+\ \text{Purchases} \\
\hline
=\ \text{Total Available for Sale} \\
-\ \text{Closing Inventory} \\
\hline
=\ \text{Cost of Food Issued} \\
+\ \text{Cooking Liquor} \\
+\ \text{Transfers from Other Units} \\
-\ \text{Food to Bar (Directs)} \\
-\ \text{Transfers to Other Units} \\
-\ \text{Grease Sales} \\
-\ \text{Steward Sales} \\
-\ \text{Gratis to Bars} \\
-\ \text{Promotion Expense} \\
\hline
=\ \text{Cost of Food Consumed}
\end{array}
$$

While use of the above expanded formula will yield the cost of food consumed, it must be noted that not all of the food consumed results in sales revenue. In most establishments, employees eat on premises as a matter of course and are not charged for the food they consume. Therefore, to determine the cost of food sold, it is necessary to subtract the cost of employee meals from the cost of food consumed.

Cost of Employee Meals

While there are numerous ways of dealing with the cost of employee meals, the four techniques that follow illustrate those that foodservice operators most commonly employ.

One approach involves separate-issue requisitions; this requires that employees be given food other than that which is prepared for customers. All food used in the preparation of employee meals must be issued separately and listed on requisitions, which are kept separately from all other requisitions used by the establishment. When the food issued is so listed, the requisitions may be costed in the normal way, thus determining the cost of food for employee meals. This approach is perhaps best suited to establishments that are large enough to maintain a separate preparation area and separate dining room for employees. Thus it is used in some of the largest hotels but in few restaurants.

A somewhat more common approach is for the manager to direct the chef to prepare specific meals that will cost no more than a certain amount per employee. This amount will be credited to food cost for each employee, and it is then necessary only to keep some reasonable record of the number of employees who are fed each day. This number, multiplied by the preestablished cost per meal, will give the cost of employee meals for the day.

Because it is difficult in some establishments to keep a record of the number of employees who are fed each day, management sometimes takes the simple course of telling the chef that food cost will be credited for a specific number of dollars per day to cover the cost of all employee meals, regardless of the number who actually eat. It is then up to the chef to estimate the number who may eat, and either prepare food that will not exceed the cost guideline or offer employees food prepared for customers that does not exceed the permissible cost.

Another technique requires that all employees who eat record their selections on checks that resemble guest checks used in the dining room. The menu price is recorded next to each selection. These checks are totaled for the month, although employees are not asked to pay them. The total is then multiplied by the average food cost percent in recent periods to arrive at a reasonable cost figure for employee meals for that period.

By means of one of these techniques, or some other alternative, it is possible to determine the cost of employee meals. When this has been determined, it is deducted from the cost of food consumed to determine the cost of food sold, the figure that should be used for establishing the cost-to-sales ratio, or cost percent. To the extent that some operators fail to take employee meals into account when calculating food cost, they are overstating cost and distorting the food cost percent.

DETERMINING COST OF FOOD SOLD

Using all of the above adjustments, the calculation of cost of food sold in the month of March for the restaurant previously described is as follows:

Opening Inventory		$2,000
+ Purchases		6,000
= Total Available for Sale		8,000
− Closing Inventory		3,000
= Cost of Food Issued		5,000
+ Cooking Liquor	$200	
+ Transfers from Other Units	$250	450
Subtotal		5,450
− Food to Bar (Directs)	$ 68	
− Transfers to other units	$349	
− Grease Sales	27	
− Steward Sales	12	
− Gratis to Bar	72	
− Promotion Expense	22	550
= Cost of Food Consumed		4,900
− Cost of Employee Meals		300
= Net Cost of Food Sold		4,600, or $.307 per dollar of sale

Using the sales figure of $15,000 previously given, food cost percent is 30.7%, 2.6% lower than it appeared to be before the adjustments were made.

Although this information is interesting, it becomes more relevant when it is compared with figures for similar periods. Such comparisons are facilitated when current and past figures are recorded side by side on reports to management.

REPORTS TO MANAGEMENT

Once food costs and cost percentages have been determined, they can be reported to management. The nature of the report must be determined separately for each individual establishment or chain, based on management's need for information as well as the food controller's ability to supply it. When the food control system is somewhat complex, more detailed information can be furnished. In such instances, management is better informed and thus better equipped to make decisions.

Although management reports differ from place to place, a reasonable number have some points in common. For this reason, it will be worthwhile to generalize these points of commonality and to illustrate several types of reports that some establishments might find useful, from the comparatively simple to the more complex.

In some small establishments, where there are few formal control procedures and no specific control personnel, it is often impossible to prepare formal reports more frequently than once a month. These monthly reports are based on information furnished by an accountant, who often prepares them between the first and tenth days of a month for the preceding month. The figures are taken solely from the accounting records of the business and indicate the food cost and food cost percentage based on purchases and inventory, as illustrated previously. Simple report forms are available from stationers. However, reports to management should always be based on management's need for information, not on the availability of a particular form. If no appropriate form exists, it is not difficult to devise one that will meet a particular operation's needs.

The form illustrated in Figure 10.3 is one of the simplest that might be devised for reporting to management.

Current figures are in the first column, and the figures for the previous year are in the second. When both are available, side by side, it is possible to compare them and to make a judgment about the relative effectiveness of current operations. Thus, if the 31.0% cost-to-sales ratio for the same period last year was

FIGURE 10.3
Food Cost Report

	July 19X1	July 19X2
Food Sales	$15,000	$14,000
Net Cost of Food Sold	$ 4,600	$ 4,340
Food Cost Percent	30.7%	31.0%

acceptable to management, it is likely that the 30.7% figure this year will also be acceptable, provided there have been no significant changes in menu or operating procedure and no significant drop in sales.

In some instances, particularly when figures for previous periods have been unacceptable, it is possible to judge the effectiveness of changes made with the goal of improving performance. If, for example, comparisons were made between two consecutive months, as in Figure 10.4, it would be possible to tell whether changes instituted because of unacceptable results for one month had the desired effect in the following month.

If management had considered the cost-to-sales ratio of 38.0% in June unacceptable and instituted changes to bring about a reduction in the figure for July, it would be possible to make some judgments about the effectiveness of the changes. In the instance cited, it is possible that the reduction in the cost percentage from 38.0% to 30.7% would be considered acceptable and the procedural change judged effective, so that it would become a permanent part of the procedures used daily in the future.

The cost percentage may be a measure of the effectiveness of the business. It will be useful to compare it to similar measures of effectiveness for other months. If the cost percentage for this month is approximately what it was in other months, and if the cost percentage had been considered satisfactory in other months, then it might well be considered satisfactory now, providing there has been no significant change in menu or purchase prices. However, if there has been some major change, if the cost percentage is considerably higher or lower this month, management will probably want to find the reasons for the change. Once the reasons are known, steps may be taken to ensure that the occurrence will or will not happen again.

Operating figures and comparisons between them are a little like sightings taken by mariners. No one sailing a ship across several thousand miles of ocean would dream of setting a course on leaving port and not taking various kinds of readings during the voyage. Anyone who did that would probably find himself some considerable distance from his destination at the end of the voyage. During the voyage, readings are frequently taken to determine the ship's location. Then comparisons are made with a chart of the course to determine how far the ship is off course, and corrections are made to bring the ship back to the course set for it. The more frequently this is done, the closer the ship will stay on its original course. If readings are taken infrequently, the ship will have strayed considerably off course,

FIGURE 10.4
Food Cost Report

	July 19XX	June 19XX
Food Sales	$15,000	$12,000
Net Cost of Food Sold	$ 4,600	$ 4,560
Food Cost Percent	30.7%	38.0%

and considerable time and money may be lost in coming back on course. In the food business, monthly readings on the course of the business are usually too infrequent. The business can stray quite far off course during the month and can be brought back into line only at considerable difficulty and expense.

The difficulty with relying on the cost percentage calculation is that it is often impossible to determine why changes occur from month to month. One cannot always look back over a period of three or four weeks with any degree of accuracy, unless significant records are available. It is hard to recollect what happened two or three days ago, let alone what happened weeks ago. When causes cannot be determined, it is almost impossible to effect changes.

In addition, it is too late for any changes in methods and procedures to have any beneficial effects on what happened during the period that has passed. If the cost percentage for March was a disaster, we must still live with the results of March forever. The best we can hope for is that changes we make will effect significant improvements in April.

In recognition of this, many establishments operate with daily or weekly reports, with varying degrees of complexity. In general, the more frequent the reports and the more detailed the information rendered, the better will be the oportunities for management to control events and to ensure that the events conform to objectives.

For those reasons, many large restaurants prefer to have cost percentages and other operating figures calculated more frequently, often on a daily basis. The manager who can find out what happened yesterday has a better opportunity to get at the causes and direct necessary changes immediately, because the causes of problems can be better located when no great time span exists between the problem and the considerations of its causes.

Daily costing procedures and daily reports to management will be discussed in Chapter 11.

INVENTORY TURNOVER

Sound food management demands that sufficient supplies of food be available for use when needed. However, excessive amounts on hand leads to (1) spoilage, because food must be held too long before being used; (2) excessive capital tied up in inventory; (3) higher than necessary labor cost to handle the greater amount of food; (4) greater than necessary space allocated to storage; and (5) unwarranted opportunities for theft.

Large establishments need greater storage space and more food in storage than smaller ones. All foodservice establishments have slow periods during the year when less food than normal is needed on the premises. Thus, it is impossible to establish a set number of food items that should be in the storeroom or a set dollar valuation for food in inventory. However, management must in some way determine that appropriate—but not excess—levels of food are kept in inventory.

One commonly accepted method is to calculate how often the inventory of food on hand has been ordered and used during a period of time. For example, if one were to order sufficient food to last one full year, most reasonable people would agree that the amount was excessive and would lead to waste, inefficiency, and greater than necessary costs. On the other hand, if one were to order enough food to last only one day, reasonable people would agree that greater amounts should be ordered and that savings could result by purchasing in larger quantities. Somewhere between the two extremes is an idealized amount of food to have on hand for a specific period. This amount will vary from place to place and will be determined by many factors, including the amount of cash available for such purposes, the space available for storage, and the time necessary to receive food once it is ordered. For most restaurants an amount to last one or two weeks is considered normal, and we will use that range as our guide.

To measure how often food has been ordered and used, food operators have historically calculated the frequency of turnover of the food in the inventory. For example, if a restaurant orders and uses an inventory two times each month, an inventory turnover of twenty-four times each year would result, and this is in approximate agreement with our guideline. One should note that all food is not turned over during the prescribed period of time. Perishables will turn over daily, and some nonperishables, canned items, for example, will turn over much less frequently.

Calculations are typically made when physical inventories are taken—once each month. The formula for this calculation is as follows:

$$\frac{\text{Average Inventory}}{\text{for the Month}} = \frac{\text{Opening Inventory} + \text{Closing Inventory}}{2}$$

$$\frac{\text{Inventory Turnover}}{\text{for the Month}} = \frac{\text{Food Cost for the Month}}{\text{Average Food Inventory}}$$

Putting actual figures to the equation, the inventory turnover for Restaurant A might look like this:

$$\text{Opening Inventory} = \$5,650$$

$$\text{Closing Inventory} = \$5,350$$

$$\text{Food Cost} = \$9,900$$

$$\frac{\$5,650 + \$5,350}{2} = \$5,500 \text{ (average inventory)}$$

$$\frac{\$9,900}{\$5,500} = 1.8 \text{ (inventory turnover for month)}$$

If each month's results were the same, the total for the year would be 21.6 times each year, or once every 2.4 weeks, slightly greater than our guide of once every one or two weeks.

The astute student will question the accuracy of the average inventory figure calculated above, for there is an assumption, perhaps an invalid one, that the opening and closing inventory figures used truly represent levels of inventory during the month, and that is not always and perhaps might not typically be the case. It is possible for inventories to be at a much higher figure during the month, no ordering taking place the last week of the month, and the ending figure a result of a planned usage of food to bring inventory to a desired level. This does happen frequently. But the only alternative would be to take a physical inventory more frequently, a procedure that in itself is costly.

COMPUTER APPLICATIONS

If all quantities received and issued have been stored in computer memory, then it is possible for the computer to provide a report of the quantity of each item in inventory at any given time. The most appropriate time for this report would be at the end of a month, the time when physical inventory is taken. Use of the computer does not eliminate the need for physical inventory, because the computor does not have data concerning actual quantities in inventory. Instead, it has data concerning the quantities that *should* be found in inventory. This is an important distinction. If, for example, food has been used or stolen without being recorded in a terminal, then such usage or pilferage will not be reflected in computer output. However, if physical inventory is taken and compared item by item with computer output, management can determine the extent of unauthorized use of food. This would be considered some measure of the extent to which employees were following the standard procedures established for operation.

The physical inventory will provide information that can be used to update the data in computer memory. With this data updated and current at the end of the accounting period, it will be possible to obtain a report showing the value of inventory by one of the methods previously discussed. It will be readily apparent that the calculation of the closing inventory value can be completed much faster by computer than by manual means.

With the above data available in computer memory, it is very simple to determine cost of food issued. It is also possible to determine cost of food consumed and cost of food sold, but only if additional data were input.

The computer would be extremely useful for generating reports to management for the current period and for such previous periods as required, provided, of course, that the data for periods were retained in memory for future use. These reports could be either of the relatively simple variety illustrated in this chapter or of the more extensive and detailed types to be seen in the following chapter.

CHAPTER ESSENTIALS

In this chapter, we have examined the simplest means of monitoring overall performance in a foodservice operation. We have described a series of monthly procedures used in a majority of restaurants for this purpose. We have described the procedure for taking monthly physical inventory of food and discussed five methods of assigning cost values to the foods in this inventory. After illustrating each of these methods, we showed the calculations necessary to determine food costs. We defined and differentiated among cost of food issued, cost of food consumed, and cost of food sold, and described the way in which each of these is calculated, taking into consideration transfers, grease sales, steward sales, promotion expense, and employees' meals. We illustrated the calculation of food cost percent and cost per dollar sale and showed how these figures are commonly reported to management for the purposes of making comparisons with other operating periods and judging operational performance. We described and illustrated the calculation of inventory turnover rate and discussed its significance to foodservice managers. Finally, we described how computers can be used to determine employee adherence to standard procedures for issuing food, as well as inventory valuations and for preparing management reports.

KEY TERMS IN THIS CHAPTER

Physical inventory	Grease sales
Opening inventory	Steward sales
Closing inventory	Gratis to bar
Total available	Cost of employee meals
Actual purchase price method	Cost of food issued
First-in, first-out method	Cost of food consumed
Weighted average purchase price method	(Net) cost of food sold
Latest purchase price method	Inventory turnover
Last-in, first-out method	Average inventory
Monthly food cost	

QUESTIONS AND PROBLEMS

1. In each of several restaurants, the following total values were recorded during the month of November. Calculate issues for each.

    a. Opening inventory $1,500.00
        Purchases 4,600.00
        Closing inventory 1,722.00

b. Closing inventory $12,083.00
   Opening inventory 10,371.00
   Purchases 28,468.00

c. Purchases $65,851.08
   Closing inventory 18,335.10
   Opening inventory 19,874.77

2. Given the following information for each of several restaurants, calculate both cost of food issued and cost of food consumed for each.

   a. Purchases $8,300.00
      Opening inventory 2,688.00
      Closing inventory 2,540.00
      Grease sales 76.00
      Cooking liquor 94.00
      Gratis to bar 119.00

   b. Food to bar (Directs) $189.00
      Closing inventory 6,647.00
      Transfers to other units 339.00
      Purchases 19,472.00
      Steward sales 53.00
      Transfers from other units 223.00
      Opening inventory 6,531.00

   c. Opening inventory $6,622.40
      Transfers from other units 47.35
      Cooking liquor 253.65
      Purchases 24,182.55
      Closing inventory 6,719.30
      Transfers to other units 347.60
      Food to bar (Directs) 337.40
      Grease sales 91.85
      Gratis to bar 177.35

3. In each of the following cases, determine the cost of employee meals for the month.

   a. In March, 337 employees were given lunch and 381 were given dinner. Management credits food cost figures of $.70 per employee for lunch and $1.10 for dinner.

   b. In September, employees were required to record their food selections on checks and to enter next to each selection its menu selling price. The sales value of the food employees consumed was found to total $7,826.95. In recent months the food cost percent has been approximately 35%.

   c. In the ABC Restaurant in February 19XX, the chef has been directed to prepare food for the employees at a cost not to exceed $25 per day, regardless of the number of employees fed. This particular establishment is closed on Mondays and open the other six days of the week.

4. Given the following information for each of several restaurants, calculate the cost of food sold for the month.

a. | | |
|---|---:|
| Cooking liquor | $210.50 |
| Steward sales | 27.58 |
| Purchases | 12,339.42 |
| Food to bar (Directs) | 201.38 |
| Gratis to bar | 267.50 |
| Grease sales | 95.60 |
| Closing inventory | 4,278.37 |
| Opening inventory | 4,031.19 |

Employee meals:
328 lunch @ $.65
449 dinner @ $.95

b. | | |
|---|---:|
| Closing inventory | $3,427.30 |
| Grease sales | 92.60 |
| Purchases | 11,230.45 |
| Opening inventory | 3,012.80 |
| Transfers from other units | 128.65 |
| Cooking liquor | 298.40 |
| Gratis to bar | 427.80 |
| Food to bar (Directs) | 312.45 |
| Transfers to other units | 155.75 |

Employee meals:
$2,576.45 sales value; recent average food cost percent; 34.0%

c. | | |
|---|---:|
| Purchases | $68,543.36 |
| Promotion expense | 81.17 |
| Grease sales | 167.42 |
| Closing inventory | 20,963.71 |
| Gratis to bar | 58.73 |
| Transfers from other units | 637.38 |
| Food to bar (Directs) | 296.35 |
| Opening inventory | 22,687.40 |
| Transfers to other units | 784.29 |
| Cooking liquor | 543.18 |

Employee meals:
Executives: $1,833.75 sales value; recent average food cost percent: 31.0%
Other staff: 1422 Breakfasts @ $.55
1208 Lunches @ $.80
1012 Dinners @ $1.05

5. Use the food cost figures determined in Question 4 to determine food cost percent and cost per dollar sale figures for each of the restaurants, given the sales figures below:

   a. $26,173.55

   b. $25,819.45

   c. $191,405.95

6. The inventory records of the Yellow Dog Restaurant reveal the following information about one of the items carried in the food inventory for the month of January:

1/1 Opening Inventory	12 units valued at $1.05 per unit
1/5 Purchased	18 units @ $1.15 per unit
1/12 Purchased	18 units @ $1.20 per unit
1/19 Purchased	12 units @ $1.30 per unit
1/26 Purchased	6 units @ $1.40 per unit

   On January 31, the physical inventory shows nine units left in stock. Determine the value of the closing inventory of the item, as well as the cost of the units issued, using each of the five possible methods illustrated and discussed in this chapter.

7. Given the following information, taken from the records of several restaurants for the month of May 19XX determine the rate of inventory turnover for each.

a. Opening inventory	$3,287.40
Closing inventory	3,322.60
Food cost	13,220.00
b. Food cost	$18,448.30
Opening inventory	6,327.65
Closing inventory	6,581.75
c. Closing inventory	$21,971.38
Food cost	67,346.93
Opening inventory	23,168.49

8. Define each of the following terms: opening inventory, closing inventory, average inventory, and rate of inventory turnover.

9. Explain and compare the following: cost of food issued, cost of food consumed, and cost of food sold.

10. List as many possible causes as you can for each of the following:

    a. Food cost percent increase from one month to the next.

    b. Food cost percent decrease from one month to the next.

    c. Increase in inventory turnover rate from one period to the next.

    d. Decrease in inventory turnover rate from one period to the next.

For Computer Users

11. Using any spreadsheet package of your choice, create a suitable template for Questions 4a, b, and c. Then use the template to calculate cost of food sold for the month for each of the three problems.

12. Use your spreadsheet package to solve Questions 7a, b, and c.

chapter 11

Monitoring Operations II: Daily Food Cost Determination

Learning Objectives

After reading and studying this chapter, the student should be able to:

1. Compute the daily cost of food sold.
2. Compute the daily food cost percentage and cumulative cost percent.
3. Prepare and interpret a daily report of food sold and food cost.
4. Establish the value of the book inventory
5. Explain the relationship between book and actual inventory.
6. Outline various causes for differences in book and actual inventory.
7. Discuss the use of computers for generating daily reports of food costs and food sales for management.

The difficulty with the monthly review of operating figures is the length of time between reports. When the figures for one month reveal that problems have developed, and steps are taken to eliminate the problems, it is necessary to wait a full month to determine the effectiveness of the steps. If management makes erroneous judgments about causes of excessive cost and the measures taken are based on those erroneous judgments, it is a full month before the next report reveals that the steps have not had the desired effect. This delay can be very costly. To avoid this delay and to avail management of more timely figures for making day-to-day operating decisions, a number of the large, well-organized restaurant operations employ daily food cost calculations.

It is possible to determine the daily cost for any operation if certain procedures and forms discussed in previous chapters are used. Since all foods are categorized as either Directs or Stores in food control, the total costs for these two will be the two basic components of the daily food cost.

All Directs are charged to food cost as received. Therefore, it is necessary to determine the total of Directs received on any given day. This figure is readily available if the receiving clerk's daily report is completed each day. The total figure in the Directs column on the report for any day is the figure a food controller will use in the daily calculations.

On the other hand, Stores are charged to the food cost as issued, so the food controller must determine the value of Stores issued each day. Since all issues must be listed on requisitions, the determination is not difficult. To determine the value of the issues, the food controller merely totals the values of all requisitions for any day.

In operations where transfers are made between the food and beverage departments or between units in a chain organization or other types of transactions, such as grease sales, steward sales, and promotion expense, are common, other figures must be taken into account. For example, any Directs charged to food cost as received but subsequently transferred to the beverage department would be subtracted from food cost figures. These items, typically oranges, lemons, and the like, would be listed on a transfer memo. In this case, it would be necessary to determine their value and subtract it from cost figures. By the same token, the value of any alcoholic beverages transferred from the beverage department to the food department for use in food preparation would be added to food cost. In addition, a reasonable number of establishments even take the cost of employee meals into account on a daily basis.

Thus, the daily cost of food can be determined in the following way:

	Cost of Directs (from the receiving clerk's daily report)
+	Cost of Stores (from requisitions, or from requisitions and meat tags, depending on the procedure followed)
+	Adjustments for transfers from the beverage department to the food department, or for transfers in from other units
−	Adjustments for transfers from the kitchen to the bar (including food to bar—Directs), Gratis to Bar, steward sales, grease sales, and promotion expense
=	Cost of Food Consumed
−	Cost of Employee Meals
=	Daily Cost of Food Sold

Once the daily food cost has been determined, the daily sales figure must be obtained, usually from accounting records. When both food cost and food sales figures are known, the daily cost-to-sales ratio can be determined.

However, by itself this daily food cost percentage may not be a very meaningful figure. Direct may be purchased every other day, and this will affect the daily food cost, making it artificially higher on the days when Directs are purchased and correspondingly lower on the other days. In addition, some foods may be issued before the days when they will be used. Salt, for example, may be issued to the kitchen once a week to avoid the need for daily requisitioning. In other cases, wholesale cuts of meat may be issued a day in advance for butchering. Both cases will have the effect of raising the food cost percentage on the day of issue, because the food is not reflected in sales until one or more days later.

To partially overcome the problem of an artificially high food cost percentage one day and a low food cost percentage another, many establishments also calculate the food cost percentage to date, which is the cumulative food cost percentage for a period. The food cost percentage to date takes into account the costs for all the days so far in the period, as well as all of the sales so far. In order to arrive at a cumulative cost percentage to date, the cost to date is divided by the sales to date.

A simple form (see Fig. 11.1) can be devised and inexpensively reproduced to give the procedure order and continuity. In order to maintain simplicity for purposes of discussion, we have limited the number of adjustment columns to two—one for additions to cost and the other for subtractions from cost. However, in practice there is no barrier to increasing the number of columns to whatever number would be necessary for achieving the desired degree of accuracy in any particular operation. The procedure may be followed on a daily cumulative basis for any number of days, depending on the information needs of management. In many cases, the figures are maintained on a weekly basis, and in others they are maintained over a month.

An alternative form (see Fig. 11.2) is useful for establishments that use meat tags and wish to have separate figures for meats and staples. Inasmuch as meats represent the largest single element of food cost, the form gives a clearer picture of where the money is being spent. Since meat tags are attached to requisitions, the food controller can simply total the values of the meat tags attached to requisitions and subtract that total value from the requisition total in order to arrive at figures for both categories.

The form illustrated in Figure 11.2 includes three additional columns on the right for purchases, issues, and inventory. These columns are used to maintain a daily balance of Stores inventory, and are discussed in detail later in this chapter (see Fig. 11.8).

In some very large establishments, where there is a need for detailed information and there are personnel to compile the figures, costs are sometimes divided into even greater numbers of categories. Directs might be broken down into

FIGURE 11.1
Daily Cumulative Cost Record

Date	Directs	Stores	Adjustments		Cost today	Cost to date	Sales today	Sales to date	Cost % today	Cost % to date
			Beverage to Food	Food to Beverage						
3/1	50	100	—	—	150		500		30%	
3/2	25	75			100	250	250	750	40%	33.3%

FIGURE 11.2
Daily Cumulative Cost Record, Using Meat Tags

| Date | Directs | Meat | Stores | Adjustments | | Total Cost | | Total Sales | | Food Cost% | | Food Inventory | | |
				Beverage to Food	Food to Beverage	Today	To Date	Today	To Date	Today	To Date	Purchases	Issue	Balance
10/15	500	275	100	20	10	885	885	2,000	2,000	44.3%	44.3%			
10/16	325	275	100	20	20	700	1,585	2,100	4,100	33.3%	38.7%			
10/17	400	300	125	25	20	830	2,415	2,200	6,300	37.7%	38.3%			
10/18	375	290	115	30	25	785	3,200	2,450	8,750	32.0%	36.6%			
10/19	490	450	105	30	30	1,045	4,245	3,400	12,150	30.7%	34.9%			
10/20	80	525	140	40	40	745	4,990	3,600	15,750	20.7%	31.7%			

the costs of vegetables, fruits, dairy products, and so on. Meats might be divided into figures for beef, veal, and lamb. Figure 11.3 illustrates a form on which such a breakdown is accomplished.

DAILY REPORTS

Given the tools developed in the preceding chapter, it is possible to construct a report that reflects the position of the operation for that day and for all the days to date for the period and that at the same time compares these figures to those for a similar period. A simple report that accomplishes this is illustrated in Figure 11.4.

When the position is set forth daily in this manner and compared to one or more recent periods, and determinations are made about the effectiveness of current operations, the causes of undesirable results can be investigated while the events are relatively fresh in the minds of those concerned. Thus, in effect, the course of operations can be reset daily. If, for example, investigation reveals that a high cost percentage is the result of overpurchasing of Directs, plans can be made to use up the quantities on hand before more purchases are made. This will keep the cost of Directs down for a day or so and will have immediate impact on the cost-to-sales ratio. Another instance, the requisitioning of too many items from Stores, might cause a high food cost. In such a case, plans might be made for using up the quantities issued to the kitchen before additional quantities are requisitioned, thus keeping down the cost of issues. When daily food costs are determined, the effect of these kinds of measures can be assessed daily, with the expected effect that by the end of the operating period, costs will be in line with management's goals. This is not always the case, but it is always more in the realm of possibility when food costs are determined daily.

Making intelligent plans to eliminate undesirable effects is never possible until causes are known. Occasionally, the determination of causes is simple. More frequently, the causes are several and are not readily determined from the figures on the reports previously illustrated. In some small operations, it is possible to go into the kitchen and make a complete first-hand investigation of all possible causes. In larger operations, this is not usually the case. To reduce the amount of time and effort involved in finding the causes of higher-than-necessary costs, some food controllers develop more complex figures and reports. Figure 11.5 gives an example of one possible set of figures to help accomplish this end.

A variation on this technique involves using the same form of report but shows the cost breakdown in terms of ratios rather than raw-dollar figures. This is particularly useful in operations that offer a relatively fixed menu. Ratios are established between direct costs and sales, both today and to date, and the same is done for other costs as well. In the example given in Figure 11.6, it will be seen that while sales figures have varied somewhat, the ratio of cost components to sales have not, suggesting that no significant changes have taken place in operating procedures. If one or more of the ratios change considerably from what it should

FIGURE 11.3
Food Cost Analysis / October, 19XX

1	2	3	4	5	6	7 Total Directs	8	9	10	11
Date	Day	Vegetables	Fruits	Dairy	Bakery	Directs	Beef	Poultry	Provisions	Other
10/1	Mon.	150.00	100.00	75.00	75.00	400.00	200.00	100.00	50.00	25.00
2	Tues.	100.00	50.00	25.00	25.00	200.00	100.00	50.00	40.00	10.00
3	Wed.	175.00	125.00	25.00	25.00	350.00	225.00	125.00	20.00	20.00
4	Thurs.	100.00	50.00	50.00	25.00	225.00	100.00	75.00	15.00	30.00
5	Fri.	175.00	100.00	75.00	75.00	425.00	250.00	125.00	25.00	50.00
6	Sat.	—	—	50.00	25.00	75.00	70.00	10.00	—	10.00
		700.00	425.00	300.00	250.00	1,675.00	945.00	485.00	150.00	145.00
10/8	Mon.	175.00	125.00	100.00	50.00	450.00	225.00	100.00	75.00	20.00
9	Tues.	100.00	75.00	25.00	25.00	225.00	100.00	75.00	—	10.00
10	Wed.	125.00	100.00	25.00	50.00	300.00	200.00	100.00	50.00	15.00
11	Thurs.	75.00	50.00	25.00	25.00		75.00	25.00	40.00	20.00
12	Fri.	200.00	100.00	100.00	25.00	425.00	250.00	150.00	40.00	—
13	Sat.	—	—	50.00	40.00	90.00	75.00	15.00	—	15.00
		675.00	450.00	325.00	215.00	1,665.00	925.00	465.00	245.00	80.00
10/15	Mon.	225.00	125.00	100.00	50.00	500.00	200.00	50.00	25.00	—
16	Tues.	100.00	100.00	75.00	50.00	325.00	100.00	125.00	25.00	25.00
17	Wed.	150.00	100.00	100.00	50.00	400.00	150.00	100.00	30.00	20.00
18	Thurs.	175.00	100.00	75.00	25.00	375.00	125.00	115.00	25.00	25.00
19	Fri.	200.00	150.00	115.00	25.00	490.00	225.00	150.00	75.00	—
20	Sat.	—	—	40.00	40.00	80.00	300.00	150.00	50.00	25.00
		850.00	575.00	505.00	240.00	2,170.00	1,100.00	690.00	230.00	95.00

be, causes can be investigated and changes made. If, for example, the cost-to-sales ratio had gone up, and the ratio of meat cost to total sales jumped drastically while other ratios remained approximately the same, the cause of the increase would be effectively localized. The food controller could disregard Directs and groceries when searching for a cause for the increase and instead look into possible problems in the category of meats.

Where time and personnel exist to do the job, it is possible to extend this approach and develop ratios of costs to sales for individual categories of foods, as illustrated in Figure 11.7. This technique is even more effective in localizing problems and in permitting more intensive investigation than might otherwise be possible.

FIGURE 11.4
Report to Management / 10/20/XX

	Today	To Date This Week	To Date Last Week
Food Cost	$ 745	$ 4,990	$ 4,200
Food Sales	$3,600	$15,750	$12,600
Cost Percentage	20.7%	31.7%	33.3%

FIGURE 11.3
(continued)

12 Total Meat	13 Total Storeroom	14 Bar → Food Cooking Liquor	15 Food → Bar Directs	16 Total Costs Today	17 Total Costs to Date	18 Total Sales Today	19 Total Sales to Date	20 Food Cost % Today	21 Food Cost % to Date
375.00	135.00	—	10.00	900.00	900.00	2,000.00	2,000.00	45.0%	45.0%
200.00	150.00	—	—	550.00	1,450.00	1,500.00	3,500.00	36.7%	41.4%
395.00	145.00	20.00	10.00	900.00	2,350.00	2,700.00	6,200.00	33.3%	37.9%
220.00	120.00	5.00	20.00	550.00	2,900.00	1,800.00	8,000.00	30.6%	36.3%
450.00	240.00	20.00	10.00	1,125.00	4,025.00	3,600.00	11,600.00	31.3%	34.7%
90.00	135.00	25.00	25.00	300.00	4,325.00	1,300.00	12,900.00	23.1%	33.5%
1,730.00	925.00								
420.00	160.00	30.00	10.00	1,050.00	1,050.00	2,000.00	2,000.00	54.5%	52.5%
185.00	135.00	10.00	5.00	550.00	1,600.00	1,600.00	3,600.00	34.4%	44.4%
365.00	115.00	—	5.00	775.00	2,375.00	2,200.00	5,800.00	35.2%	40.9%
160.00	90.00	—	—	425.00	2,800.00	1,400.00	7,200.00	30.4%	38.9%
440.00	215.00	30.00	10.00	1,100.00	3,900.00	3,400.00	10,600.00	32.4%	36.8%
105.00	105.00	25.00	25.00	300.00	4,200.00	2,000.00	12,600.00	15.0%	33.3%
1,675.00	820.00								
275.00	100.00	20.00	10.00	885.00	885.00	2,000.00	2,000.00	44.3%	44.3%
275.00	100.00	20.00	20.00	700.00	1,585.00	2,100.00	4,100.00	33.3%	38.7%
300.00	125.00	25.00	20.00	830.00	2,415.00	2,200.00	6,300.00	37.7%	38.3%
290.00	115.00	30.00	25.00	785.00	3,200.00	2,450.00	8,750.00	32.0%	36.6%
450.00	105.00	30.00	30.00	1,045.00	4,245.00	3,400.00	12,150.00	30.7%	34.9%
525.00	140.00	40.00	40.00	745.00	4,990.00	3,600.00	15,750.00	20.7%	31.7%
2,115.00	685.00								

In many instances, changes in these ratios may be caused by changes in customer ordering habits. However, in cases where demand has remained constant and market prices relatively so, increases in these ratios will be caused by problems existing in kitchen operation. When problems are thus localized, they may be more easily uncovered.

FIGURE 11.5
Report to Management / 10/20/XX

	Today	Same Day Last Week	To Date This Week	To Date Last Week
Food Sales	$3,600	$2,000	$15,750	$12,600
Food Cost	$ 745	$ 300	$ 4,990	$ 4,200
Food Cost Percentage	20.7%	15.0%	31.7%	33.3%
Cost Breakdown:				
Directs	$ 80	$ 90	$ 2,170	$ 1,665
Stores	$ 665	$ 210	$ 2,800	$ 2,495
Meats	$ 525	$ 105	$ 2,115	$ 1,675
Groceries	$ 140	$ 105	$ 685	$ 820

FIGURE 11.6
Daily Food Cost Report

Day Saturday   Date 10/20/XX   W/E 10/20

		To Date		
Description	Today	This Week	Last Week	Same Wk, Last Mo.
Food Sales	3,600	15,750	12,600	
Food Cost	745	4,990	4,200	
Food Cost %	20.7%	31.7%	33.3%	

Item		Vegetables	Fruits	Dairy	Bakery	Total Directs	
This Week		850	575	505	240	2,170	13.8%
Last Week		675	450	325	215	1,665	13.2%

Item	Beef	Poultry	Provisions	Other	Total Meat		Total Stores	
This Week	1,100	690	230	95	2,115	13.4%	685	4.3%
Last Week	925	465	245	80	1,675	13.3%	820	6.5%

Item	Cooking Liquor	Food to Bar (Directs)
This Week	165	145
Last Week	95	45

BOOK VERSUS ACTUAL INVENTORY COMPARISON

In Chapter 10 we discussed the reasons and procedures for determining the value of closing inventory at the end of each monthly period. Once completed, the closing inventory valuation is considered a real or actual inventory valuation and is so recorded in the business's financial records and statements. This figure includes the value of all items counted in the inventory—those that were physically present and could be found, counted, and valued.

Some foodservice operators next determine what the value of the closing inventory should be and compare that figure, known as book inventory, to the actual inventory figure established through taking a physical inventory at the close of the period. One method of establishing the value of the book inventory is readily available to those who maintain daily food cost figures in the manner illustrated in Figure 11.2. Such a form provides the means for maintaining cumulative book inventory figures for any period, as shown in Figure 11.8.

The closing inventory for September becomes the opening inventory for October. To this figure of $6,305 must be added any Stores purchases received on October 1 as recorded on the receiving clerk's daily report (see Chapter 6). From

FIGURE 11.7
Daily Food Cost Report

| Day Saturday | | Date 10/20/XX | | W/E 10/20 | | |

| | | | To Date | | | |
Description	Today	This Week		Last Week		Same Wk, Last Mo.
Food Sales	3,600	15,750		12,600		
Food Cost	745	4,990		4,200		
Food Cost %	20.7%	31.7%		33.3%		

Item		Vegetables	Fruits	Dairy	Bakery	Total Directs
This Week		5.4%	3.7%	3.2%	1.5%	13.8%
Last Week		5.4%	3.6%	2.6%	1.7%	13.2%

Item	Beef	Poultry	Provisions	Other	Total Meat	Total Stores
This Week	7.0%	4.4%	1.5%	.6%	13.4%	4.3%
Last Week	7.3%	3.7%	1.9%	.6%	13.3%	6.5%

		Cooking Liquor		Food to Bar (Directs)		
This Week		1.0%		.9%		
Last Week		.8%		.6%		

those two must be subtracted the value of any Stores issued on that same day as found recorded on requisitions, or on a combination of requisitions and meat tags. Since the cost of meats and other issues from Stores has normally been recorded in appropriate columns on figure 11.2 one must really only transfer the total of those two to the Issues column. So to find the closing book inventory valuation for any day, one merely starts from the closing inventory valuation for the preceding day, adds any Stores purchases, and subtracts any Stores issues. This procedure may be

FIGURE 11.8
Daily Book Inventory Balance

Date	Purchases	Issues	Inventory (Balance)
9/30			$6,305
10/1	273	510	6,068
10/2	946	350	6,664
10/3	498	540	6,622
10/4	734	340	7,016

followed daily throughout any period. If it is followed daily for a calendar month, the final figure represents the closing book value of the Stores inventory for that period.

It is possible to determine the closing book value of the Stores inventory in establishments that do not determine daily food cost figures, but only if some form of receiving report and daily issue requisitions is used. If such is the case, the calculation is as follows:

> Opening Inventory (Closing Inventory for the preceding month)
> + Purchases (total value of Stores purchased for the period, as listed on the receiving clerk's daily reports)
> _
> = Total Available (total value of the Stores available for sale during the period)
> − Issues   (total value of foods listed on issue requisitions for the period)
> _
> = Closing Book Value of the Stores Inventory

Under ideal conditions, the values of the book inventory and the physical inventory should be the same. However, for a number of reasons, some usually acceptable and others never acceptable, this is seldom true. Some of the acceptable reasons include an occasional human error in costing out requisitions, the use of the most recent purchase price rather than actual purchase price in valuing the physical inventory, and the mismarking of actual purchase prices on items when that method is used. Reasons that are never acceptable include the issuing of Stores without requisitions, the disposing of meats that have been allowed to spoil, and the theft of food.

Depending on the volume involved, discrepancies of some small percentage between book inventory and physical inventory can often be attributed to acceptable causes and are of no further concern, except that discrepancies should be pointed out to the employees whose errors have caused them. However, when discrepancies reach an unacceptable level, the food controller has a responsibility to investigate the causes and take appropriate steps to ensure that the variance will be significantly reduced in future periods. This may involve reviewing control procedures for purchasing, receiving, storing, and issuing food and revising those procedures where necessary. It also may involve reviewing the practices of employees responsible for carrying out the control procedures and taking appropriate steps to ensure that established procedures will be followed more closely in the future. In extreme cases, the food controller may have to review all procedures and all employee practices in order to find causes. Once discovered, the causes can be reported to management for necessary action.

Taking an ending inventory is a vital part of the control procedure. In addition to being necessary for accurately determining inventory values at the end of each month so that proper financial statements can be prepared, the determination of a closing inventory value permits the food controller to measure the effectiveness of receiving, storing, and issuing procedures. Significant differences between actual and book inventory figures signal the food controller that control procedures need investigating.

COMPUTER APPLICATIONS

In previous chapters, we discussed the possibility of using a computer to store information about the food purchases and issues. The entry of this data would be simpler if numerical codes were assigned to all food items. For example, assume that each item were assigned a four-digit code. The first digit might differentiate between Directs and Stores; the second digit could be used to distinguish other food groups within either category (such as fruits, vegetables, baked goods, and dairy products within the general category of Directs); the third and fourth digits might identify the particular item (such as apples, bananas, grapefruit, and oranges). With a suitable applications program that records all Direct purchases as issues and thus as charges to food cost, and all Stores issues as charges to cost, obtaining a report of daily food cost would be simple. This could be further refined by recording any adjustments to cost, for transfers and other items, as the transactions occurred, thus making possible a daily food cost report of whatever degree of refinement were considered appropriate.

With the simple addition of one or more sales terminals of the type described in Chapter 4, management could ensure that all sales data were recorded in computer memory as well. These data, summarized by the computer into a daily sales figure and used together with a daily cost figure determined by the computer as described above, would enable management to obtain a daily food cost report of the type described earlier in the chapter. It is afterall, merely a spreadsheet.

By encoding greater detail about food categories, possibly by the use of five- rather than four-digit codes, generating a more detailed report along the lines of that pictured in Figure 11.3 would be entirely feasible. The form of such a report could also be structured like those in figures 11.6 and 11.7. Many managers would consider the summarized data included in such reports to be of great value for day-to-day management decision making.

CHAPTER ESSENTIALS

In this chapter we showed how some establishments compute cost of food sold and food cost percent on both a daily and a cumulative basis, an elementary management information system designed to provide management with more timely data on operations than is available from the monthly calculations described in the previous chapter. We illustrated and discussed various types of reports used to detail and compare information from the current operating period to that from previous periods. We demonstrated how book inventory may be calculated and how book and actual inventory figures may be compared for judging the effectiveness of various control and reporting procedures.

Finally, we described how using computers to obtain timely reports can enable management to make decisions more quickly and easily than is possible with manual reports.

KEY TERMS IN THIS CHAPTER

Inventory book value	Grease sales
Actual inventory value	Promotion expense
Directs	Food Cost today/food cost to date
Stores	Food sales today/food sales to date
Transfers from kitchen to Bar	Food cost percent today/food cost percent to
Transfers from Bar to Kitchen	Daily food inventory balance
Gratis to bar	
Steward sales	

QUESTIONS AND PROBLEMS

1. Compute daily food costs, cumulative food cost to date, and the corresponding cost percentages from the following data.

			Adjustments		
Date	Directs	Stores	Beverage to Food	Food to Beverage	Daily Sales
5/1	$350	$350	-0-	-0-	$1,400
5/2	$250	$175	$25	-0-	$1,000
5/3	$135	$125	-0-	$10	$1,000
5/4	$ 75	$135	$10	$20	$ 500

2. Following the alternative form illustrated in Figure 11.2, compute the daily cost and cost percentage figures, as well as the cumulative cost, sales, and cost percentage figures, for the period shown below from the figures given.

				Adjustments		
Date	Directs	Meats	Stores	Beverage to Food	Food to Beverage	Daily Sales
9/4	$400	$350	$150	-0-	$50	$2,550
9/5	$150	$200	$125	-0-	-0-	$1,500
9/6	$350	$450	$100	$60	-0-	$2,850
9/7	$200	$250	$150	-0-	-0-	$2,850
9/8	$450	$300	$150	-0-	$40	$3,325
9/9	$ 50	$170	$120	-0-	$10	$1,300

3. Use the information given below to prepare a daily and cumulative analysis of food costs, food sales, food cost percents, and inventory balances on a form such as that illustrated in Figure 11.2. The opening inventory figure for November 1 is $9,330.

November 1: From the Receiving Sheet: Directs, $403; Stores, $736. Meat Tags: $320. Requisitions: $271. Sales: $2,241.

November 2: From the Receiving Sheet: Directs, $261; Stores, $108. Meat Tags: $282. Requisitions: $183. Sales: $2,121.

November 3: From the Receiving Sheet: Directs, $273; Stores, $1,463.
Meat Tags: $491. Requisitions: $330. Cooking Liquor: $33.
Food to Bar (Directs): $24. Sales: $2,740.

November 4: From the Receiving Sheet: Directs $521; Stores, $281. Meat Tags: $392. Requisitions: $552. Sales: $4,063.

November 5: From the Receiving Sheet: Directs, $334; Stores, $372. Meat Tags: $751. Requisitions: $470. Cooking Liquor: $19.
Food to Bar (Directs): $29. Sales: $4,682.

4. Use the information given below to determine the book value of the Stores inventory on the morning of May 6.

Closing Inventory for April $11,353.40

5/1—Stores purchases:	$742.38	Stores issues:	$621.80
5/2—Stores purchases:	397.49	Stores issues:	516.76
5/3—Stores purchases:	619.66	Stores issues:	472.51
5/4—Stores purchases:	273.16	Stores issues:	845.26
5/5—Stores purchases:	824.93	Stores issues:	725.77

5. In each of the following cases, determine the book value of the closing inventory for the month of October.

a.	Opening Inventory:	$ 3,748.00
	Purchases:	22,162.00
	Issues:	21,477.00
b.	Issues:	$44,227.60
	Purchases:	42,191.40
	Opening Inventory:	15,308.70
c.	Purchases:	$10,601.58
	Opening Inventory:	4,219.66
	Issues:	9,862.43

6. Given the information below, find book value of the closing inventory as well as the dollar difference between book and actual inventory for the month of January.

a.	Opening inventory:	$ 400
	Purchases:	1,200
	Issues:	900
	Actual value of closing inventory:	$600
b.	Purchases:	$ 6,327
	Issues:	6,498
	Opening inventory:	2,184
	Actual value of closing inventory:	$1,912
c.	Issues:	$12,395.62
	Opening inventory:	4,129.88
	Purchases:	11,623.71
	Actual value of the closing inventory:	$2,673.47

7. In each of the instances in Question 6, calculate the difference between book and actual closing inventory figures as a percentage of issues.

8. Based on the dollar differences determined in Question 6 and on the percentages calculated in Question 7, which, if any, of the three cases in question 6 bears closer examination by a food controller? Justify your answer.

9. Assuming that one or more of the above cases need close examination, how would a food controller go about such an examination? What steps might you, as a food controller, recommend be taken?

10. What are some of the potential advantages of computing daily and cumulative food cost and food cost percents, rather than relying exclusively on end-of-month calculations?

11. Discuss the possible advantages and disadvantages of providing reports to management of the complexity made possible by computers.

For Computer Users

12. Using a spreadsheet package of your choice, create a template to complete the calculations for daily food cost illustrated in Figure 11.1. Then use your spreadsheet to solve Question 2 above.

13. Amend the spreadsheet used for Question 12 to include the three additional columns for inventory illustrated in Figure 11.2. Then use this spreadsheet to solve Question 3 above.

chapter 12

Monitoring Operations III: Actual and Standard Cost Comparisons

Learning Objectives

After reading and studying this chapter, the student should be able to:

1. Define and calculate standard cost.
2. Describe how a Menu Pre-Cost and Abstract form is used.
3. List several ways an undesirable forecasted food cost percentage can be changed.
4. Define and calculate potential savings.
5. Distinguish between daily and periodic calculation of standard cost and potential savings.
6. Explain the role of the computer in determining potential savings.

In previous chapters, considerable attention has been devoted to establishing control over the purchasing, receiving, storing, issuing, and production phases of foodservice operation. Discussion was focused on the establishment of standards and standard procedures for operation, including standard purchase specifications, standard receiving and issuing procedures, standard portion sizes, and standard production methods, among many others. Establishment of these various standards make it possible to establish one additional and very important standard: the standard cost. Standard cost was defined in Chapter 2 as the agreed-upon cost of goods or services used to measure other costs. In Chapter 8, standard portion cost was defined as the dollar amount that a standard portion should cost, given the standards and standard procedures for its production. For example, one portion of filet mignon should cost $4.00 in a given restaurant, provided that the staff has followed all standards and standard procedures established for purchasing, receiving, storing, issuing, and producing the item. To the extent that these standards have not been followed precisely, the actual cost of the portion will be some amount other than what it should be—some dollar figure different from the standard cost.

By using standard portion costs in ways that we will illustrate in this chapter, management can measure operating efficiency with a greater degree of accuracy than would otherwise be possible. Actual costs can be compared to standard costs, and the difference between them will be a useful measure of the extent to which standards are being followed. This difference will indicate the degree of inefficiency in day-to-day operations and will suggest the extent to which costs could be reduced without compromising or reducing standards.

Generally speaking, there are two methods for comparing standard and actual costs. The first involves daily calculation of standard costs and actual costs and the development of cumulative figures over an operating period, such as one month. Daily reports of the results to date are common and lead typically to a final summary report at the end of a period. The second method does not involve daily calculation but relies on periodic determination of standard costs from actual portion sales records for the period. The choice of one method over the other is left to management in any given operation and should be based on the type of menu in effect, management's need for information, and the availability of personnel to prepare the needed information.

While the first method offers the advantage of immediate information and all the attendant benefits of such immediacy, it does require considerable staff time for calculation. The second, although requiring less in the way of daily staff time, does not offer the advantage of immediacy, nor is it able to account for fluctuations in market prices and their effect on standard costs. Because there are considerable differences in procedures, both methods will be discussed here.

DAILY COMPARISON

Once standard costs and selling prices for standard portions are known and forecasts have been made, it is possible to determine in advance what the cost percentage of operation should be. Of course, this figure will be accurate and reliable only if the forecast is accurate and personnel adhere to all established standards.

At the end of the day or after the meal, when the forecasted sales have been made, the figures developed for the sales history can be substituted for the portions forecasted, and the standard cost percentage can be calculated. This will show what the cost percentage should have been, based on actual sales.

Both of these procedures are accomplished on a form known as the Menu Pre-Cost and Abstract, illustrated in Figure 12.1.

FIGURE 12.1
Menu Pre-Cost and Abstract

Date ___Mon. 11/1/XX___

Menu Item	Number Forecast	Forecast					Number Sold	Actual				
		Cost	S.P.	F.C.%	Total Cost	Total Sales		Cost	S.P.	F.C.%	Total Cost	Total Sales
A	80	2.05	5.95	34.5%	164.00	476.00	75	2.05	5.95	34.5%	153.75	446.25
B	65	2.45	6.95	35.3%	159.25	451.75	60	2.45	6.95	35.3%	147.00	417.00
C	10	4.30	12.95	33.2%	43.00	129.50	6	4.30	12.95	33.2%	25.80	77.70
D	165	2.60	7.95	32.7%	429.00	1,311.75	159	2.60	7.95	32.7%	413.40	1,264.05
				33.6%	795.25	2,369.00				33.6%	739.95	2,205.00

The Menu Pre-Cost and Abstract

This form is divided into two sections. The part on the left is used in conjunction with the forecast, at some time before a day or meal. The part on the right is completed later, after the sales have taken place.

The Forecast

After sales have been forecasted, as described earlier, the food controller can enter both the items forecasted and the number of portions of each in the first two columns on the form. The next entries are the standard portion costs for each item, taken from recipe detail and cost cards, butcher test cards, or cooking loss test cards, depending on the nature of the item. In the sales column, the figures entered are taken from the menu. These are the prices for which each item will sell. In the cost percentage column, the figure will be the cost-to-sales ratio for one portion of each item.

When all of these entries have been made, the total standard cost of producing the forecasted number of portions is determined by multipying the portion cost by the number of portions forecasted. Thus, in the example given, eighty portions forecasted multiplied by a single portion cost of $2.05 gives the total standard cost of $164 for producing the needed quantity of item A. This is a standard cost figure. It presupposes that each portion will be produced in the exact standard size specified and according to the exact production method established by the standard recipe. This procedure is followed for each item listed, and the standard cost of producing the required number of portions of each item is determined. The total cost column is then added to determine the total standard cost for producing all items on the menu.

The same procedure is employed for determining the total sales that ideally will result from the production of the numbers of portions forecasted. The selling price for one portion of each item is multiplied by the number of portions forecasted to find the total dollar volume of sales that will result from the production of the portions specified for each item. Once total sales for each have been calculated, the Total Sales column is added to determine the total dollar income that will be generated by the portion sales forecasted.

In this manner, total anticipated costs and sales can be determined, provided, of course, that the forecast reflects all items that will appear on the menu and that the costs and selling prices of each are included. If, for example, the $12.95 selling price for item C includes such side dishes as potato, vegetable, and salad, the cost of each of these items must be included in the portion cost figures.

Once total costs and sales have been forecasted, a cost percentage can be predicted by simply dividing sales into cost and multiplying the result by 100. In the example cited, the total cost of $795.25 divided by the total sales of $2,369.00 is .33569, which multiplied by 100 shows a predicted cost-to-sales ratio of 33.6%. Again, it must be emphasized that this standard cost percentage will correspond to the actual cost percentage only under ideal conditions. However, the differences between the standard cost percentage and the actual cost percentage will give some indication of opportunities for improving operations.

The foregoing has presupposed the existence of a menu scheduled for production for a particular day in the near future, and the desirability of predicting cost and sales figures in connection with that existing menu. However, these techniques for forecasting costs and sales are also useful to the operator who is considering rewriting the menu. If accurate assessment can be made of public demand for the items on a proposed menu, the total costs and sales that should result can be predicted in advance. A manager can often avoid costly mistakes by obtaining from the food controller a forecast such as that above. Public demand for each item must be assessed and translated into the number of portion sales forecasted for each item. This number is multiplied by carefully determined standard costs and selling prices for each item. Total costs and sales are predicted for the proposed menu by adding the totals for each of the items, and the gross profit and cost percentage are forecasted. If the forecast is satisfactory, the manager can send the menu to a printer. If it is not, various changes can be made and their anticipated results should be assessed before the printing. Cost and sales figures may be raised or lowered, depending on which is desirable, by one of the following means:

1. Selling prices may be changed.
2. Costs can be reduced by changing portion sizes, standard recipes, or both.
3. Items may be eliminated.
4. Substitutions may be made.

Conceivably, all of these means might be employed, and the final version of the new menu might bear little or no resemblance to that originally proposed. However, while the original proposal might have led to undesirable results, the new menu should not, provided that good judgment and careful calculations have gone into its preparation.

The Abstract

The abstract, or right-hand portion of the form under discussion, is prepared after sales have taken place. The person preparing the abstract, usually the food controller, refers to the figures developed for inclusion in the sales history, enters them in the Number Sold column, and multiplies each by the standard portion cost and selling price, copied from the forecast section, in order to determine the total standard cost for preparing the portions sold. This is a precalculated cost, based on precalculated standard costs for each portion. The total precalculated cost and the total sales are determined by adding each column. The standard cost percentage for actual sales is determined by dividing total costs by total sales.

The next step is to compare the forecasted cost percentage developed from the abstract. Differences will invariably exist. The differences occur because the total volume forecasted usually differs in some measure from actual volume, and because some items did not sell as well as was anticipated. In addition, some of the items might have sold in greater quantities than were forecasted, which sometimes raises questions about the extent to which the kitchen staff is following production schedules. This is worth noting, because although the additional sales may have brought in additional income, failure to follow production goals established by management indicates that one of the control procedures is not operating effectively. In addition, it is possible that an appropriate quantity of an item was produced but that all portions were undersized. This is undesirable and may lead to loss of business, because it really means that customers have been cheated.

For these reasons, among others, sales in excess of the number forecasted should always be investigated. One important reason for comparing the forecasted cost percentage with the percentage developed from the abstract is that the difference between the two measures not only the extent to which forecasting techniques can be improved but also the extent to which the forecast was wrong, in terms of incorrect total volume, incorrect forecasted sales of particular items, or both. Such a comparison suggests possibilities for improving forecasting performance in order to bring the cost percentage from the abstract more nearly in line with that from the forecast. After all, this forecasted cost percentage has received some measure of approval as an acceptable goal and therefore should not be ignored.

The forecasted cost percentage should reflect the cost acceptable to management to achieve a certain dollar volume of sales. In addition, it should be thought of as reflecting plans for meeting those goals, with the plans translated to established standards and standard procedures. So to the extent that forecasted cost percentages are not in line with those calculated after sales, overall performance, including forecasting, is not all that it should be.

After a cost percentage has been calculated on the basis of the figures on the abstract side of the form, it may be taken as indicating what the cost percentage *should have been* if everything had gone according to plan. If the exact number of portions needed have been prepared according to the standards and procedures set by the management, this is what the cost percentage should be, and as such it reflects the dollar cost that should have been incurred to produce a certain dollar volume of sales.

If developed one meal at a time, or even one day at a time, and then put aside, these figures are not being used as effectively as they might be. It is possible and desirable to develop abstracts of standard costs and sales over a period of some weeks or months. Taken as a test period, the results offer a good indication of what the cost percentage of operation should be over a longer period of time. Figure 12.2 illustrates the results of such figures developed over a seven-day test period. In this case, the restaurant under consideration should generally operate with a

FIGURE 12.2
Summary of Daily Abstracts

Date	Standard Cost	Sales	Standard Cost %
		Week of ____ November 1–7, 19XX ____	
1	$739.95	$2,205.00	33.6%
2	601.50	1,800.95	33.4%
3	782.97	2.316.50	33.8%
4	771.15	2,288.25	33.7%
5	735.50	2,195.55	33.5%
6	825.66	2,435.60	33.9%
7	747.80	2,225.55	33.6%

Total Standard Cost	$ 5,204.53
Total Sales	$15,467.40
Standard Cost %	33.6%

cost-to-sales ratio of 33.6%. Such figures can be useful in judging effectiveness of operations from week to week or month to month.

When standards are in effect for every item served, standard costs are known, and the Menu Pre-Cost and Abstract prepared daily reflects the total menu, it is possible to reconcile standard and actual costs on a daily basis and, thus, to date throughout the period. Actual costs are determined from direct purchases and storeroom issues, as discussed in Chapter 11. The standard or potential cost of preparing all the items sold is taken from the Menu Pre-Cost and Abstract. Sales are taken from accounting department records. All figures are recorded on a form similar to that in Figure 12.3. Actual cost percentage and standard cost percentage are calculated from the figures entered. Typically, the actual cost will be greater than the standard cost. The difference can be regarded either as waste or as excessive cost that can be reduced or eliminated if staff performance is improved. The raw dollar figures indicating that excessive costs have developed are not particularly useful in isolating the roots of inefficiency or other operating difficulties. In many instances, it is helpful to devise techniques for detecting the areas in which the waste has occurred.

Potential Savings

Potential savings are the difference between actual and standard costs and may be recorded as dollars, as percentages of sales, or as both. Potential savings reflect the differences between conditions that exist and those that management would like to see if all plans were carried out to perfection. No kitchen will ever achieve that perfection, of course, but it is usually possible to find ways to improve operations so that the future results will be somewhat closer to perfection.

FIGURE 12.3
Summary of Actual and Standard Food Costs, Food Sales, and Potential Savings

Week of _____ November 1–7, 19XX

Date	Actual Cost		Standard Cost		Sales		Actual Cost %		Standard Cost %		Potential Savings			
	Today	To Date	Today	To Date	Today	To Date	Today	To Date	Today	To Date	Today $	Today %	To Date $	To Date %
1	786.00	786.00	739.95	739.95	2,205.00	2,205.00	35.6%	35.6%	33.6%	33.6%	46.05	2.1%	46.05	2.1%
2	612.33	1,398.33	601.50	1,341.45	1,800.95	4,005.95	34.0%	34.9%	33.4%	33.5%	10.83	.6%	56.88	1.4%
3	806.45	2,204.78	782.97	2,124.42	2,316.50	6,322.45	34.8%	34.9%	33.8%	33.6%	23.48	1.0%	80.36	1.3%
4	795.05	2,999.83	771.15	2,895.57	2,288.25	8,610.70	34.7%	34.8%	33.7%	33.6%	23.90	1.0%	104.26	1.2%
5	761.25	3,761.08	735.50	3,631.07	2,195.55	10,806.25	34.7%	34.8%	33.5%	33.6%	25.75	1.2%	130.01	1.2%
6	842.17	4,603.25	825.66	4,456.73	2,435.60	13,241.85	34.6%	34.8%	33.9%	33.7%	16.51	.7%	146.52	1.1%
7	759.05	5,362.30	747.80	5,204.53	2,225.55	15,467.40	34.1%	34.7%	33.6%	33.6%	11.25	.5%	157.77	1.0%

The conditions that lead to differences between standard and actual costs include overpurchasing, overproduction, pilferage, spoilage, improper portioning, and failure to follow standard recipes, among others. To the extent to which improvements are made and problems existing in these areas are eliminated, actual costs become more equal to standard costs and potential savings are reduced. In general, potential savings and waste are synonymous. The reduction in potential savings means the reduction of waste and of excessive cost.

When these figures are available daily and cumulatively for a period, it is possible to make daily investigations of the causes of the variance between standard and actual cost figures. It will probably never be completely possible to eliminate the discrepancy between standard and actual costs. Management in any given situation must determine the extent to which reduction is possible and must be content to live with a discrepancy of some small percentage between the actual and the standard. No industrywide figure exists for guidance. However, once management has determined on a reasonable figure for the acceptable variance, exceptions can be noted at once and investigation can begin immediately. Such immediate investigation is more likely to uncover causes than will investigation undertaken days or weeks later. When causes are immediately known, one can take remedial action in the hope of correcting problems before their effects become pronounced. Immediate consultation with the chef, steward, and other interested personnel will usually reveal causes and make corrective measures possible.

PERIODIC CALCULATION

In establishments in which daily calculations are impractical or impossible, one can still apply the principles of standard costing techniques periodically to determine the extent of waste under existing conditions. Like the daily techniques, the periodic approach presupposes that standards exist in all the areas previously discussed, that sales histories are maintained, and that standard portion costs are known. Under such circumstances a food controller can calculate standard costs for a test period of one week and compare the findings to the actual costs for that same period to determine the extent of potential savings. This might be done once every three months, or more frequently if time and need exist.

Using a worksheet such as that illustrated in Figure 12.4, the food controller enters from sales history records the items and the number of portions of each sold during the test period. Standard portion costs for each item are recorded from appropriate recipe detail and cost cards, butcher tests, or cooking loss tests. The total standard cost for producing the number of items sold is found be extending the items individually and then adding.

Actual costs for the period are determined from direct purchases, storeroom issues, and sales figures obtained from the accounting office. When daily cost figures are being developed, as discussed in Chapter 11, the figures are already available. The variance between actual and standard costs for the test period can

FIGURE 12.4
Periodic Potential Savings Worksheet

For Test Period ___7/8___ to ___7/22___, 19XX

Item	# Sold	Portion Cost	Total Standard Cost
A	520	$2.25	$1,170.00
B	731	3.85	2,814.35
C	322	4.10	1,320.20
D	903	1.85	1,670.55
E	611	2.45	1,496.95
			$8,472.05

Sales for Test Period:	$25,416.15
Actual Cost	8,877.45
Standard Cost	8,472.05
Potential Savings	$ 405.40
Actual Cost%	34.9%
Standard Cost %	33.3%
Potential Savings as a % of Sales	1.6%

then be determined, both in terms of dollars and as percentages of total sales. To the extent to which the test period is truly representative of day-to-day operations, operational efficiency can be measured and, where necessary, corrective action can be taken to improve results by the next test period. It is usually advisable to select test periods at random, after the fact. The figures developed are then more truly representative than if the employees knew in advance that a certain week was being taken as a test period. In such cases, employees would be likely to pay stricter attention to the standards set by management. While the results of their efforts might be wholly desirable, the measure of actual against standard cost for the period would give a distorted view of day-to-day wastefulness and potential savings.

Once determined, this standard cost percentage may be compared with actual cost percentage during the period between test periods. Thus one can effectively judge the efficiency of operations during the intervening period. Where cost percentages are developed on a weekly basis, it is usually more desirable to compare the figures with a recently calculated standard cost percentage than with a cost percentage from the previous week. Of course, the menu should not have changed drastically in terms of content or price, and the cost of items should be pretty much the same as during the test period. If either or both assumptions are invalid, the concept of comparing the actual cost percentage with the standard would also be invalid. The important point to remember is that a comparison of the cost percentage with a previous period in no way by itself tells the manager if waste is occurring. That determination can be made only by comparison with a standard.

One final word about potential savings is in order. To the extent that savings can be made without incurring other costs, they will increase profits. If, for example, part of the potential savings figure is the result of overproduction and consequent spoiling of food, then by eliminating the overproduction, profits should theoretically be increased by the amount of the total savings. This is illustrated by the following figures.

	Actual	Standard
Sales	$10,000	$10,000
Food Cost	$ 3,800	$ 3,400
Gross Profit	$ 6,200	$ 6,600

It is immediately apparent that reduction in excessive costs brings about an identical increase in gross profit. If this reduction can be brought about without increasing any other costs—for example, the cost of labor—then literally every dollar saved will be an additional dollar in profit. This fact, perhaps more than any other, points up the importance of judging actual cost in comparison to standard costs and of making every practical effort to eliminate the difference.

COMPUTER APPLICATIONS

As we have seen, given appropriate programs, computers can provide standard portion costs and assist in forecasting. Preparing the Menu Pre-Cost and Abstract manually is difficult and time-consuming. However, with the aid of computers, it is a comparatively simple worksheet to prepare, and one that could become much more widely used than it is presently. Provided that standard sales prices were stored in memory, which would be quite likely with modern sales terminals that feature price look-up, the Pre-Cost portion could be displayed or printed before the forecasted date so that any necessary adjustments could be made. The Abstract portion, printed after sales had taken place, would provide total standard cost for those items sold.

Once known, the standard cost for an operation period can readily be compared with the actual cost for the same period, determined by the computer in the manner suggested in Chapter 11. With both actual and standard costs for a period available, a worksheet could be prepared comparing the two; subtracting standard from actual costs can show potential savings for a period of any length. If collected on a daily basis, the data could be filed and reported both daily and cumulatively for a period. Alternatively, the data might be input daily but reported only periodically, possibly once a month, timed to coincide with the accounting cycle.

CHAPTER ESSENTIALS

This chapter presented two methods for determing total standard cost for a given operating period. We showed how a comparison of standard and actual cost for a period reveals a variety of inefficiencies in day-to-day operation, including poor forecasting, overproduction, failure to follow standard recipes, and some instances of overpurchasing. Four means of changing undesirable cost and sales were listed. Potential savings were defined as the difference between actual and standard cost. We illustrated how reductions in excessive cost will result in increases in gross profits and may result in increases in net profits as well. Finally, we described the means for determining potential savings with a computer.

KEY TERMS IN THIS CHAPTER

Standards
Standard procedures
Standard cost
Standard portion cost
Actual cost
Potential savings

Menu Pre-Cost and Abstract
Forecasted sales
Actual cost percent
Standard cost percent
Periodic potential savings

QUESTIONS AND PROBLEMS

1. List and discuss five possible conditions that can lead to differences between actual and standard costs, pointing out how each increases potential saving.

2. It has been said that potential savings, taken as a percentage of sales, may be used as one possible measure of operating efficiency. Do you agree or disagree? Why?

3. Discuss the advantages and disadvantages of using the daily method for determining potential savings over periodic calculations.

4. Using the figures given in each of the cases below, determine actual cost percent, standard cost percent, and potential savings both as a dollar figure and as a percentage of sales.

	Sales	Actual	Standard Cost
a.	$ 400.00	$ 120.00	$ 100.00
b.	860.00	318.20	301.00
c.	3,486.00	1,394.40	1,324.68
d.	11,198.00	3,919.30	3,695.34

5. Using the form illustrated in Figure 12.3, complete the calculation for a four-day period given the following figures.

	Actual Cost Today	Standard Cost Today	Sales Today
Monday	$110	$100	$300
Tuesday	160	145	450
Wednesday	175	160	505
Thursday	185	175	520

6. Given the following information, prepare a complete Menu Pre-Cost and Abstract form. After completing the calculations, determine the forecasted cost percentage and the standard cost percentage.

Item	Portions Forecasted	Portion Cost	Selling Price	Number Sold
A	60	$2.50	$6.00	55
B	20	3.25	8.50	18
C	80	2.25	5.00	80
D	40	2.70	6.50	38

7. Given the following information, prepare a complete Menu Pre-Cost and Abstract form. After completing the calculations, determine the forecasted cost percentage and the standard cost percentage.

Item	Portions Forecasted	Portion Cost	Selling Price	Number Sold
A	30	$3.70	$8.50	28
B	42	3.00	6.80	42
C	73	2.75	6.00	70
D	115	2.50	5.50	106

8. Write a 300-word essay contrasting the approach to controlling costs using the Menu Pre-Cost and Abstract and the portion inventory and reconciliation (Chapter 9).

9. Explain the use of the computer in calculating potential savings.

10. Why might the increased use of computers in foodservice establishments make the Menu Pre-Cost and Abstract a more widely used control document?

11. The owner of the Red Fox Inn has developed a menu for use in her establishment. Each menu item represents a complete meal. She has determined standard cost for each listed item and has kept careful records of sales for the month of March. The data appear below:

Item	Number Sold	Standard Cost
A	310	$5.50
B	270	7.80
C	540	3.80
D	425	5.25
E	175	8.70

Item	Number Sold	Standard Cost
F	340	6.50
G	510	5.70
H	480	4.20

Food sales for March totaled $50,028.50. Using the information provided, calculate total standard cost for the period.

12. The following figures are from the accounting records of the Red Fox Inn cited in Question 11 (above):

Openings inventory	$7414.80
Closing inventory	6327.35
Food purchases	17642.80
Transfers: beverage to food	443.00
Transfers: food to beverage	226.00
Employees' meals	837.00

a. Calculate cost of food sold for the month of March.

b. Select approriate information from Question 11 (above) and calculate the following:

1. Actual cost percent.
2. Standard cost percent.
3. Potential savings in dollars.
4. Potential savings as a percentage of sales.

For Computer Users

13. Using a spreadsheet program of your choice, prepare complete Menu Pre-Costs and Abstracts for Questions 6 and 7 above.

14. Prepare the necessary worksheets to complete Questions 11 and 12 above.

chapter 13

Sales Control

Learning Objectives

After reading and studying this chapter, the student should be able to:

1. List and explain the three goals of sales control.
2. List and discuss the eight determinants of customer restaurant selection.
3. Describe the two principal means of maximizing profits
4. Explain the three most common methods of establishing menu prices.
5. Describe the two principal means of selling products effectively in a restaurant.
6. List and explain the five most important elements of menu preparation.
7. Explain how managers attempt to maximize profits by establishing sales techniques for use by the sales force.
8. Explain the importance of menu engineering as an analytical tool.
9. Complete a menu engineering worksheet, interpret the results, and suggest various possible changes to improve profit.
10. Explain the importance of revenue control.
11. List and explain the three standards established to achieve the goals of revenue control.
12. List and describe five standard procedures for controlling revenue.
13. Describe two ways in which computers are being used in revenue control.
14. Define each of the Key Terms in this chapter.

For many, the term **sales control** is merely a synonym for revenue control—a collection of activities designed to ensure that each customer order results in appropriate revenue for the business. Revenue control is, of course, critically important to the financial health of an enterprise, and we will treat it in suitable detail in this chapter. However, we consider revenue control only one part of sales control.

In our view, a broader interpretation of sales control is required. In Chapter 2, control was defined as a process by means of which managers attempt to direct, regulate, and restrain the actions of people in order to achieve desired goals. Revenue control is clearly an important goal of management, but it is not the only sales-related goal. There are at least two others.

A second goal of sales control is to optimize number of sales—to engage in those activities that will increase the number of customers to the desired level. To some, this number may be almost limitless: twenty-four hours a day, seven days a week, with waiting lines as often and as long as possible. To others, the desired level may be dramatically lower: no lines, leisurely and unobtrusive service so that the staff may prepare and serve each menu item perfectly and each diner will consider his meal a memorable occasion.

A third goal of sales control is to maximize profit. Profit maximization requires two essential activities: pricing products properly, and selling those products effectively. Selling products effectively is done through two essential means: carefully crafted menus and the sales techniques used by the restaurant staff.

In this broad sense, there are three goals to sales control:

1. Optimizing number of sales.
2. Maximizing profit.
3. Controlling revenue.

Each of these will be discussed separately and in some detail.

OPTIMIZING NUMBER OF SALES

There are probably no restaurants that operate at desired sales levels at all times. Most experience both high- and low-volume periods. Sometimes both are evident on the same day; at other times, entire weeks of high volume may be followed by long periods of comparatively low volume. Sometimes the high- and low-volume periods follow seasons of the year; sometimes sales volume is high or low for an entire year.

At one time or another, most owner and managers are faced with the problem of sales volume that is higher or lower than the desired level. Consequently, most are engaged at one time or another in attempting to regulate sales volume—to increase or decrease volume to the desired level. Productive efforts to do either are best made by those who understand the determinants of customer selection of a restaurant. The following are the most important for most people:

Location
Menu Item Differentiation
Price Acceptability
Decor

Portion Size
Product Quality
Service Standards
Menu Diversity

Purposely, these are not listed in any particular order. Every customer has her own important reason for patronizing a restaurant, and these change under varying circumstances. To some, food quality is the single most important reason for patronizing a particular restaurant. However, when time is short a convenient location might be the determining factor. To be successful, a restaurant must meet a sufficient number of the above needs to appeal to a large enough market and hence to cover costs.

Location

If one were to take a given population center and draw concentric circles around it, then place a restaurant at every mile on each of the circles as shown in Figure 13.1, one could judge the effect of location in relation to the population center. Other things being equal, customers will normally choose the most convenient restaurant, and there is a maximum time any customer will travel to go to any particular restaurant.

FIGURE 13.1

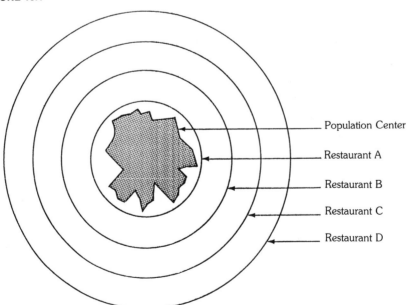

Population Center

Restaurant A

Restaurant B

Restaurant C

Restaurant D

One would expect restaurant A to have more customers at any given time than restaurant B, and the numbers should decrease as one gets farther from the population center. At one extreme, it should be obvious that a restaurant located in the center of Death Valley in California would attract very few customers from Los Angeles, because of the distance from that population center. Most people would be unwilling to travel that far for a restaurant, no matter how fine its reputation. On the other hand, the only Italian restaurant in a city of 100,000 can expect to do well, even if the quality of its product or its prices are not particularly attractive to potential clientele. In actuality the authors have noted that restaurants located in the financial district of New York City do an excellent luncheon business on weekdays, but many of them close for the evening meal and on weekends for lack of business. In midtown Manhattan, however, most restaurants do an excellent dinner business. A good location will not guarantee customers but is usually necessary for volume business. Fast-food operators recognize the importance of location. The national fast-food chains know precisely how many customers they can expect in a given population center, and that is one reason why one seldom hears of a business failure for the 'McDonald's' or 'Burger King' type of establishment.

Menu Item Differentiation

Economists characterize products and services as homogeneous or differentiated. This distinction is based on how similar or different products or services are from one another. A **homogeneous** product or service is one that is so similar to another that customers do not have a preference and will purchase whichever costs less. This means that a general 'market price' exists for these products and services and the individual manager cannot raise prices without losing all or a number of customers. In the grain market, for example, a farmer can sell his entire grain supply for the 'market price' but cannot sell any of it at a price one penny higher. This is because his grain is a homogeneous product and no buyer will pay higher than market price.

A **differentiated** product or service, on the other hand, is sufficiently unique so that customers develop a preference for it. The uniqueness can be real or imagined. As long as customers prefer one product or service over another, whatever their reasons for preference, that product or service is differentiated.

There are comparatively few products and services that can truly be labeled homogeneous. Most are differentiated, some more so than others. Differentiation is a matter of degree for most products and services, and the greater the degree of differentiation, the greater the degree of customer loyalty for those seeking the type of product or service.

The terms homogeneous and differentiated are useful for classifying menu items. To the extent that the foodservice operator can develop and include in his menu products that are differentiated, potential customers desiring those products are likely to be willing to travel greater distances and pay higher prices to obtain them. If Restaurant D in Figure 13.1 offers menu items that customers in the population center find unique and desirable, the operator of the establishment will be able to increase sales volume.

Unique menu items created for this purpose are called **signature items**. Signature items are often specially named for a restaurant, a chef, or a locality. Waldorf salad, for example, was originally a signature item, created and served in New York's famous hotel. Many restaurants create signature items in order to attract greater numbers of customers.

Price Acceptability

One of the most important factors in customer selection of one restaurant over another is price. Given three foodservice establishments exactly alike in every respect except menu prices, the one with the lowest prices will have the greatest sales volume. Of the restaurants in Figure 13.1, Restaurant A would have greatest sales volume unless one of the others, possibly Restaurant C, lowered menu prices significantly. With the lower prices, one would expect Restaurant C to increase volume by drawing customers from Restaurant A and B.

Restaurant menu items tend to be **price-sensitive**, meaning that there is a relationship between sales price and sales volume. The higher the price of a menu item, the lower the number of sales of that item will be. In the food and beverage business, the more homogeneous a menu item is, the more price-sensitive it is. By the same token, the more differentiated the item is, the less price sensitive it is. This helps to explain why so many of the well-known national chains charge approximately the same prices for inherently similar or homogeneous menu items.

In order for a menu item to sell, the menu price must be acceptable to the customer. The customer must judge that the value received, including the food and all the other items that go to make up the product of the restaurant, is sufficient to justify her acceptance of the stipulated menu price. Obviously, every person has a different perception of price acceptability, and the task of the foodservice operator is to establish prices that will be considered acceptable by those who constitute the market segment to which his establishment is targeted.

Decor

There is an old saying that "beauty is in the eye of the beholder." This is particularly true with restaurant decor. Decor helps differentiate one restaurant from another, with each individual establishment attracting customers who accept its decor. However, decor that one individual may find pleasing is likely to be less than pleasing to another. Family groups, for example, tend to prefer informal, light, bright, and cheerful interiors; those patronizing restaurants offering gourmet cuisine expect a more formal setting. A restaurant's decor helps determine not just the type of customer but the number of customers as well. One key to restaurant success, then, is to select decor that will appeal to a sufficiently large segment of the targeted market and thus will help maximize number of customers.

Portion Size

Portion sizes must be appropriate to the clientele that a food and beverage operator wishes to attract. Young, active persons are often want large portions and sometimes patronize the restaurants that are the most generous with servings. Older persons, on the other hand, often eat smaller amounts and sometimes stay away from restaurants with large portion sizes because they feel they will waste food or have to pay for food not consumed. Therefore, it is not true that large portions always attract great numbers of customers. Most customers want value for their money, and portion size is only one element in determining whether or not value is received. Of significance is the principle that portion sizes must satisfy the needs of the clientele the food operator wishes to attract. If they are smaller than desired, business will be lost. If they are larger than desired, unnecessary cost will result, possibly causing reduced profit and certainly leading to wasted food.

Product Quality

Quality, like decor, means something different to each customer. Those with particularly refined tastes—sometimes referred to as gourmets—will often accept nothing but perfection in food, which for them means that all ingredients must be fresh rather than canned or frozen, that soups must be prepared from freshly made stocks, and that vegetables must be cooked only until just tender. Unless the products of a particular restaurant meet these exacting standards, such individuals will not patronize it. On the other hand, most people do not have such demanding standards and are perfectly willing to consume and enjoy food products that might be rejected by the ultra-demanding connoisseur. At the same time, there are those who appear to be completely indifferent to what most people would consider appropriate standards of quality for foodservice products. For them, food of almost any degree of quality, however poor to us, is acceptable. Their reasons for patronizing restaurants are not related to product quality as most people would define it.

In a given population, various segments demand products of various levels of quality, and it is management's responsibility to assess the market and offer products of such quality as will appeal to a large enough segment of the market to ensure sufficient volume for profitability.

Service Standards

Anyone who has ever eaten out realizes the wide range and quality of service available. Fast-food establishments and cafeterias tend to offer as little service as possible, while some older hotel dining rooms and many fine restaurants seem to have extraordinary numbers of attendants for each patron. Where greater service is offered the diner, it is occasionally of the highest quality—swift, unobtrusive, and nearly approximating an art form—but more often it is somewhat indifferent, rather slow, sometimes sloppy and intrusive, and quite obviously untrained.

At the same time, each individual diner or party consciously or unconsciously considers what constitutes appropriate quantity and quality of service for each particular dining occasion. Often time is a factor, and the diner will select the establishment that he feels will allow him to eat within the time frame available. On the other hand, there are customers, often those who are celebrating a special occasion, for whom time is of no particular concern. For them, the pleasure of the dining occasion, consisting of the finest quality in both food and service, is of paramount importance. The former may select one of the nationally known fast-food chains or a popular local cafeteria, while the latter may prefer to travel some distance to seek out a well-known and widely respected restaurant that is renowned for offering service in the time-honored Old World tradition.

Additionally, there are those who are well aware that service means tipping serving personnel, which they prefer not to do. Many people on low or fixed incomes fall into this category. They prefer to use their limited means for food purchase, rather than for tipping serving personnel.

Managers who seek to optimize restaurant sales should be aware of the extent and quality of service that their customers want. With that awareness in mind, certain aspects of the business can be adjusted to suit the patrons. For example, a full-service restaurant may reduce the amount of service by instituting a salad bar and instructing serving personnel to direct diners there between the appetizer and entree courses. This might facilitate a reduction in the number of serving personnel, and at the same time possibly speed up the dining process to suit the aims of both hurried diners and the restaurant manager, who wants to increase customer turnover during the peak dining hours.

Menu Diversity

With the exception of those restaurants that offer homogeneous products—commonly accepted and even sought out by the public, consumed in vast amounts because of their comparatively low prices as well as their staple nature in the diet of the dining public—most establishments need a wide range of items on the menu. A menu that includes only two or three entree choices is obviously of more limited appeal than one that offers twelve or fifteen. Any given diner would be more likely to find an item of his choice on the latter menu. In establishments whose success depends heavily on repeat business, the more limited menu could substantially reduce the number of times in a given period a particular customer would return.

However, the extent of the offerings on any menu must be governed by certain considerations, including the equipment available in the kitchen, the culinary abilities of the kitchen staff, and the cost considerations that arise when a large number of items are being offered and much leftover food results. As a general rule, the greater the scope of the menu consistent with these other considerations, the larger will be the segment of the market to which the menu appeals, and the more likely will be success.

It is probably not possible to find an ideal restaurant, in terms of all of the above considerations. After all, no location is perfect, and it is impossible to assess a market so perfectly that differentiated products can be provided at a price acceptable to all diners in a setting pleasing to all. However, for a restaurant to succeed, management must keep these considerations in mind and offer as great a portion of each as possible to the largest possible segment of the market. Failure to recognize these factors carries with it the risk of failing to attract a sufficient share of the foodservice market to cover costs and establish a successful and profitable enterprise.

MAXIMIZING PROFIT

Profit maximization is achieved by two principal means: pricing products properly, and selling those products effectively. These will be discussed separately.

Pricing Products Properly

Because restaurants establish standard sales prices for their menu items, and because the sum of the prices paid by customers is the total food revenue for a restaurant, it should be evident that the standard prices established are critically important in determining the degree of profitability for the establishment. The menu price of a product is normally set by an owner or manager and is made known to customers by printing it in a menu, or by posting it on signs appearing conspicuously in the restaurant.

The sales price should be determined by cost. A higher-cost item will have a higher sales price than a lower-cost item. Steak usually sells for a higher price than spaghetti because the cost of the ingredients in the meal is usually higher. However, cost is not the only determinant of price.

Other considerations enter into price determination. Of primary concern is the desire to maximize sales. Restaurants with highly differentiated products have more flexibility to raise or lower prices than those with homogeneous products. If McDonald's raises its prices substantially and Burger King does not, McDonald's would most likely suffer a substantial loss of customers. In all probability, the increase in prices would result in less total revenue for McDonald's and lower profit. On the other hand, an exclusive French restaurant with a highly differentiated product might raise its prices with very little adverse reaction from its customers. Thus it is important that each restaurateur have some understanding of price sensitivity as it relates to product and service, so that sales and profits may be maximized. This price sensitivity will vary among restaurants and locations. Typically, locations with low-income residents will have more price-sensitive customers than those with higher-income residents.

Sometimes restaurateurs set prices deliberately to exclude certain customers or to cater to a specific clientele; sometimes changing conditions force concomitant change in pricing policies. For example, a certain restaurant in New England had an excellent location on a major highway and catered primarily to interstate traffic. Prices were quite low, and the restaurant did volume trade in excess of 1,000 customers per day. A new interstate highway was built a short distance from the restaurant, and interstate traffic no longer traveled its their front door. Customer count dropped off to about one-quarter of what it had been, and the restaurant could not profitably operate with low prices. They decided to cater to the local population and increased quality and prices. Profit margins were considerably higher, and once again they were profitable, although with fewer customers than before.

Many methods exist for establishing menu prices.* Most, however complex they may appear, are variations on one or more of the following:

1. Competitors' prices.
2. Cost-to-sales ratios.
3. Contribution margins.

Perhaps the most widely used approach to menu pricing is that termed the "follow the leader" technique: pricing to meet the competition. It is commonly employed by those who have little or no idea of the costs of the items they sell, including those who feel that if a nearby competitor is managing to stay in business by selling hamburgers for $1.25, then they too will find hamburger sales profitable at that price. When such operators find themselves bankrupt, they can never quite understand why. But the use of this imitative approach is not restricted to the unknowledgeable; it is also employed by a substantial number of seasoned and successful operators.

Restaurateurs often feel that if their prices are higher than those of nearby competitors they will lose business to the competition. Tacitly, they are defining their products as homogeneous rather than differentiated, and in many cases they are correct in doing so. Restaurants featuring such common items as steak, roast beef, or hamburgers are often quite similar in product, service, and price. Decor is often the only feature that makes one essentially different from another. In such cases, the restaurant's accessibility to the market it serves is the primary determinant of the number of customers and sales. In many such instances, any increase in price over that charged by the competition may effectively eliminate the small advantage offered by location and lead to an unacceptable loss in sales.

While the policy of pricing to meet the competition can be successful for some operators in some markets, it may lead to disastrous results for others. If selling prices are low, large numbers of customers are necessary to cover fixed costs and show an operating profit. Typically, all restaurants in a given area cannot maintain the necessary volume to survive when selling prices are low, and only the most able

---

* For a detailed treatment of this topic see Jack E. Miller, *Menu Pricing and Strategy,* 2nd Edition (New York: Van Nostand Reinhold Company, 1987).

operators survive. Under such conditions, the failure rate for restaurants in a given area is normally very high.

The second approach to menu pricing, via cost-to-sales ratios, has two variations. In either case, portion costs must be carefully determined by means of the techniques discussed in Chapter 8.

Once portion costs are known, selling prices can be set for each item so that portion cost represents some fixed percentage of the selling price. If, for example, a restaurateur wanted food cost-to-sales ratio to be 40%, she could set a selling price for each item merely by dividing .4 into the portion cost and adjusting the resulting answer to some suitable amount to print in a menu. Thus, $1.24 would be adjusted to $1.25, a more suitable menu price. If this approach were followed with literally every menu item, the cost percent for operation for any period would be 40%, provided that the staff followed all established procedures for purchasing, receiving, storing, issuing, and producing food. Also, if the 40% figure were a reasonable one, it would be determined by subtracting profit, fixed cost, and labor cost as percentages of sales from 1, or 100%.

A second variation based on cost-to-sales ratios requires not only that the manager have complete information about portion costs but also that he establish some tentative selling prices and then forecast sales volume for an upcoming period. The calculations of potential food cost percent based on the forecast, the portion costs, and portion selling prices may be accomplished on the Menu Pre-Cost and Abstract form illustrated and discussed in Chapter 12. If the resulting cost percent is unsatisfactory, then costs, selling prices, and the forecast can be adjusted until a realistic and satisfactory potential result is obtained. If the forecast for the period has been reasonably accurate, and if the staff has observed all standard procedures for all phases of operation, the resulting cost percent for operation should conform to management's expectations.

The third approach, dealing with specific contribution margins for each item on the menu, is becoming more accepted in the industry but is still not widely used. This approach requires that the foodservice operator, knowing the portion costs for each item sold, determine the average contribution margin for menu items needed to cover overhead and yield a desired profit at an expected level of sales volume. For example, a simplified income statement for food might appear as follows:

	Gross Food Sales	$100,000
−	Cost of Food Sold	40,000
=	Gross Profit	
	(total contribution margins)	$ 60,000
−	Overhead Costs	50,000
=	Profit	10,000

Number of customers served during the period: 30,000.

Each customer in this example spent an average of $3.33 and contributed an average of $2 to overhead and profit.

This method would suggest that each menu item be priced at $2 above costs, regardless of the item. A steak with portion cost of $4 would be priced at $6, and a pasta item with cost of $.50 would be priced at $2.50. If this approach were followed and if sales volume matched or exceeded forecasts, the minimum acceptable dollar profit would be assured, provided that costs were kept strictly under control in all areas.

In addition, many might consider this a more equitable method of setting prices. Assuming that no significant difference exists in the cost of producing menu items, each customer is bearing only his or her fair share of the overhead costs and profit, and no more.

Selling Products Effectively

There are two principal means for selling products effectively in a restaurant—the menu, and the sales techniques used by the staff. These will be discussed separately.

The Menu

The menu is the primary selling tool in most restaurants. As such it is largely responsible for which items are sold in the greatest and in the smallest quantities. Those items that are presented most favorably—those featured on the menu—typically outsell other items. Conversely, those items that are least favorably presented will not sell in as large numbers as they might. Since menu items frequently have different costs, contributions margins, and cost percents, the foodservice operator has an opportunity to control the cost percent and gross margin by preparing menus that achieve maximum sales volume, especially for those items deemed the most desirable and most profitable to sell.

Menu preparation is a complete subject in itself, full treatment of which is beyond the scope of a text in food, beverage, and labor control. However, because a good menu is such a key factor in efforts to maximize profits, anyone planning a career in foodservice should have some general knowledge of the most important elements in menu preparation, which are:

1. Layout and design.
2. Variety.
3. Item arrangement and location.
4. Descriptive language.
5. Kitchen personnel and equipment.

Layout and Design

It should be apparent that the entire physical menu—the paper, the color, the printing, and so on—should suit the character and style of the restaurant. One would not, after all, expect an elaborate menu printed in raised type on parchment stock in a common roadside diner, nor should one expect to see the menu of a high-priced and exclusive Continental restaurant printed poorly on the cheapest paper available. Appropriate menu design and layout for each kind of restaurant is essential to satisfy the clientele and achieve maximum revenue.

Anyone unfamiliar with the principles of advertising layout and design would be well advised to consult one or more of the several excellent books on these topics*—as well as reviewing first efforts with a specialist in the field—before having a menu printed.

Variety

For a menu to have maximum public appeal, a suitable variety of foods, preparation methods, and prices is necessary. Variety will satisfy the needs of a broad market and will help the restaurant operator capture the largest possible number of customers. Even in specialty and ethnic restaurants, variety is important. After all, even the chains of hamburger restaurants give the customers a choice of several types and styles of hamburgers.

Several authors and restaurant specialists have suggested that a good general menu should include among the entrees several different types of meat, fish, poultry, and egg dishes. One highly respected consultant has suggested that five is the minimum number of entrees acceptable for a restaurant menu and that the number should include at least one of each of the general types of dishes mentioned above.

In general, menus should also include various kinds of cooking methods. Some items should be sautéed, others roasted, some boiled, and so on. This not only ensures acceptance by customers with various preferences but also adds variety in the appearance of foods reaching the customers' tables.

Appearance of foods is of great importance. The number of combinations of foods that may appear together on plates is vast, and some are more interesting and attractive than others. The possibilities for providing pleasant and appropriate contrasts in color, contour, and texture are always in the mind of the able menu writer. It may sound trite to say that people eat first with their eyes, but it is nevertheless true and should be kept in mind by anyone writing a menu.

---

* Lothar A. Kreck, *Menus: Analysis and Planning, 2nd Edition,* (New York: Van Nostrand Reinhold Company, 1984); Jack E. Miller, *Menu Pricing and Strategy,* 2nd Edition (New York: Van Nostrand Reinhold Company, 1987); Albin G. Seaberg, *Menu Design, Merchandising and Marketing, 3rd Edition,* (New York: Van Nostrand Reinhold Company, 1983).

It is also desirable to include a reasonable variety of entree prices. Not all potential customers desire to purchase the most expensive items, and most restaurants risk losing customers if prices do not appeal to a broad market. This is particularly true when family trade forms a substantial segment of the market and when repeat business is necessary for profitable survival.

Item Arrangement and Location

Perhaps the most significant menu-making principle to a food controller is the physical arrangement of items on the menu. Unless their attention is otherwise directed, American customers read a menu in the same way they would read a book—from beginning to end, from top to bottom, and from left to right. Items listed first and at the top of a list are seen first and make the greatest impression. It stands to reason that those items will sell in the greatest quantities, or at least will sell in greater quantities than if they were placed at the bottom of the list.

Another way of bringing customers' attention to a particular menu item is to feature it in larger type than the items surrounding it. Sometimes a different typeface can have the same effect. In some cases, not only is the type different, but the item is given its own featured spot on the menu. In addition, many restaurants use colored pictures or photographs of some menu items to capture customer attention and to build sales volume for the pictured items.

The significant point is that the items the food controller wishes to sell in the greatest quantities should be the featured items. These may be the items in greatest supply in the kitchen on a particular day, or those with the most favorable cost-to-sales ratios, or those that provide the greatest contribution margins. In some instances, the featured items might be those whose sale would most greatly enhance the restaurant's reputation and thus help build sales volume. Many operators place items with greatest contribution margins in the most prominent places on the menu and relegate those with lesser contribution margins to less conspicuous spots. On such menus, high-cost, high-price items will be more prominent, often appearing first on a list of entrees. Other operators may feature items that require extensive preparation and cannot be used up as leftovers. On such menus, less perishable a la carte items, such as steaks cut and cooked to order, will be far less prominent.

On a well-prepared menu, foods will appear in just those physical locations and with just those degrees of prominence that will induce customers to order what management wants most to sell.

Descriptive Language

The dining experience begins well before customers taste the food they have ordered. It begins with the first impression of the food operation, when the restaurant is first described by a friend, when potential customers read a review or an advertisement, or when they first enter the premises. The physical appearance of the establishment and its staff, and the attitude of the staff toward the diners, will make or reinforce an initial impression or change it.

The menu itself and the language used in it to describe food offerings, may make a good impression and induce customer orders. The descriptions of foods may make the customer hungry and may help to build higher sales than might otherwise have been possible. On the other hand, a menu that describes available items poorly may actually decrease sales. A food and beverage operator can often greatly influence the average check revenue by using descriptions that make menu items sound interesting. Customers tend to react positively to foods that are appealingly described and negatively to those that are not.

Appropriate adjectives tend to increase customer satisfaction because they lead to higher levels of expectation. As long as food lives up to its billing, customers receive greater enjoyment from eating foods that verbal description has suggested will be good. The successful operator knows that a menu item simply labeled "Broiled Steak" has considerably less appeal to the customer than one described as "U.S. Choice Sirloin Steak Prepared To Your Taste, Garnished With The Chef's Special . . ." And after all, "Deep-Fried Maryland Chicken, Southern Style" does conjure up different feelings for the diner than does "Fried Chicken."

Kitchen Personnel and Equipment

There have been all too many horrible examples of zealous foodservice operators writing into their menus various items that are beyond the culinary skill of their kitchen staffs. In fact, the authors know of instances when foodservice consultants have set up menus that included items that could not properly be produced by the kitchen personnel commonly available in the labor market. Too, there have been cases when certain menu items were perfect delights to customers until one or more kitchen employees quit or were fired, and new employees simply were not able to prepare the items satisfactorily. Anyone writing a menu should have clearly in mind the performance abilities of present staff and should be realistic about the possibilities of replacing any staff member with another of equal skill.

At the same time, someone writing a menu should be aware both of the type an quantity of equipment needed to prepare the items being included and of the condition of the available equipment. Before including some dish whose preparation requires precise oven temperature, one should be sure that oven thermostats are in proper working order. And before deciding to include french-fried potatoes with every order, one should be sure that sufficient equipment and staff are available in the kitchen to meet projected demand.

In addition, many kitchens, particular large ones, are organized into stations, and the menu writer must be sure that the menu produced will lead to a reasonable amount of work for each station, with none being either overloaded or under-worked. If analysis of an existing menu suggests that the amount of work in the kitchen is not suitably balanced among the workers or the stations, it may be wise to consider rewriting the menu, adjusting the number of persons working at each station, providing additional equipment, or all of these. If such situations are permitted to develop or continue, the kitchen labor turnover rate may increase significantly.

Failure to take these potential problems into account before writing the menu raises the possibilities of increasing customer discontent over bad food, poorly prepared, served late, and served cold.

Sales Techniques

The second means for selling products effectively is to establish sales techniques to be used by the sales force—the servers in a restaurant. Servers can greatly assist management in selling certain menu items, or for that matter, cause other menu items not to sell. Many successful foodservice operators use the following techniques to exercise some additional control over sales:

1. Meeting daily with sales personnel.
2. Establishing standard selling techniques for personnel.
3. Periodically assessing the performance of sales personnel.

Many establishments hold daily meetings with sales personnel to review and discuss menu items that management wishes to emphasize and to provide the personnel with all necessary information about the preparation and contents of the dishes on the menu. This procedure offers a number of advantages to both management and the customers. For management, it ensures that the sales force will be thoroughly knowledgeable about product, a prime requirement in sales personnel in all businesses. Additionally, management has a fine opportunity to make sales personnel aware of the exceptional items that appear on the menu for that day, including some that would not have been available had not prime ingredients been available in the markets. Obviously, these are the items that management has most interest in selling to the public, since prices have been structured to provide appropriate contribution margins and, because of the seasonality and freshness of such items, it is important that all orders be sold.

The customer, on the other hand, has the distinct advantage of being able to learn from a knowledgeable salesperson whatever he needs or wants to know about the product before it is purchased. Customers then make realistic decisions about what to order or not to order. This helps reduce the number of orders rejected by customers who make incorrect assumptions about food items.

The adoption of certain standard selling techniques can be of great assistance in maximizing sales. These techniques, if properly handled by the sales personnel, not only help build volume sales but also provide each customer with a greater measure of personal attention that she might otherwise receive.

A useful selling technique that many successful operators have their personnel employ is to suggest items to customers that they might not otherwise think of ordering. One common example is the cocktail before dinner, or the wine with the meal. In the case of the cocktail, the operator not only builds sales but also gives customers something with which to occupy their time until their meal is ready. This technique may be expanded to suggesting courses that the customer might not otherwise have considered—appetizers, salads, and desserts.

Another adaptation is to ask the sales personnel to make specific suggestions for particular courses. For example, if the restaurant particularly wishes to sell one item rather than another, the waiters and waitresses may be asked to suggest that item to all diners for a particular meal. If done properly, it can add a pleasant, personal touch to the meal for the customer, while at the same time building sales.

It is normally not difficult to secure employee cooperation in making suggestions to customers, particularly if the personnel are aware that customer tips are typically a percentage of the gross amount of the check and that higher dollar sales lead to higher tips. When daily meetings with sales personnel are held and standard selling techniques are adopted, management is well advised to review, at least periodically, the performance of the sales force. Performance can be assessed in a number of ways, including determining gross sales per employee or average sale per employee for a certain period, such as a week. Those whose performance is significantly below that of the majority may need reminding or coaching or, ultimately, replacing.

If the above sales techniques are established and the menu is prepared according to the principles discussed above, the food controller is better able to maximize sales volume and sell those items that result in the highest profit.

MENU ANALYSIS

A useful topic to introduce at this stage of our discussion is menu analysis. Although it is not technically part of the discussion of sales control as defined earlier in the chapter, it does offer a means of monitoring the effectiveness of efforts to maximize profits. In addition, it offers some general rules that can be used to improve the profitability of a menu.

The technique for menu analysis described below was developed some years ago by Michael Kasavana and Donald Smith. Originally published as *Menu Engineering,* the technique is now widely known and has occasioned numerous papers and articles in the academic community. While some do not agree entirely with the conclusions drawn by Kasavana and Smith, their method for analyzing a menu is both interesting and revealing.

Space does not permit complete discussion and analysis of the method. Within the confines of this chapter, we will limit our presentation to a brief exposition of Kasavana and Smith's techniques and then relate menu engineering to the problem of profit maximization as discussed earlier in this chapter. The student interested in further information should refer to a current edition of the work.

We will begin by presenting an example of the menu engineering worksheet, illustrated in Figure 13.2. The student will note the many similarities to the Menu Pre-Cost and Abstract discussed and illustrated in the previous chapter, including columns for Menu Item, Number Sold, Item Food Cost, Item Sales Price, Menu Cost, and Menu Revenue. Although the terms differ slightly, these are same items used in the Menu Pre-Cost and Abstract. Specifically, the menu engineering sheet closely corresponds to the right, or Abstract, side of the form in Chapter 12. The sources of the data and the required computations are exactly the same.

There are several additional columns that distinguish the menu engineering worksheet: (C) Menu Mix %; (F) Item CM; (L) Menu CM; (P) CM Category; (R) MM Category; and (S) Menu Item Classification. At the foot of the worksheet, there are several additional computations. Both the additional columns and the computations require some explanation.

Column C: Menu Mix Percent

The menu mix percent for each item is calculated by dividing the number of units sold by the total number of units sold for all items together. For example, broiled chicken sold 375 portions out of a total of 2,000 portions of all items sold. The menu mix percent for this item is calculated as:

$$\frac{375}{2000} = .1875, \text{ or } 18.8\%$$

The menu mix percent for each of the other items is calculated in the same way.

Column F: Item CM

The student will recall from discussion in previous chapters that contribution margin (CM) is defined as sales price minus variable cost per unit. For simplicity and for purposes of this analysis, food cost is treated as the only variable cost. Therefore, the CM for broiled chicken is determined by subtracting the food cost for the item from its sales price, as follows:

	Sales Price	$6.50
−	Food Cost	3.00
=	CM	3.50

The CM, of course, is the amount available from each sale to contribute toward meeting all other costs of operation and, when those costs have been met, to providing profit for the owner.

FIGURE 13.2
Menu Engineering Worksheet

Restaurant: Sturnley's   **Period:** March 3–9, 19XX

Date 3/12/XX

A Menu Item Name	B No. Sold (MM)	C Menu Mix %	D Item Food Cost	E Item Sales Price	F Item CM (E-D)	G Menu Costs (D*B)	H Menu Revenues (E*B)	L Menu CM (F*B)	P CM Category	R MM Category	S Menu Item Classification
Broiled Chicken	375	18.8%	$3.00	$6.50	$3.50	$1125.00	$2437.50	$1312.50	L	H	Plowhorse
Strip Steak 12 oz	330	16.5%	$5.50	$13.00	$7.50	$1815.00	$4290.00	$2475.00	H	H	Star
Strip Steak 16 oz	125	6.3%	$6.50	$15.00	$8.50	$812.50	$1875.00	$1062.50	H	L	Puzzle
Stuffed Shrimp	160	8.0%	$5.00	$12.50	$7.50	$800.00	$2000.00	$1200.00	H	H	Star
Scrod	90	4.5%	$3.50	$7.00	$3.50	$315.00	$630.00	$315.00	L	L	Dog
Lobster 1.25 lb.	130	6.5%	$7.50	$16.00	$8.50	$975.00	$2080.00	$1105.00	H	L	Puzzle
Veal Piccata	135	6.8%	$5.50	$14.00	$8.50	$742.50	$1890.00	$1147.50	H	L	Puzzle
Roast Prime Ribs	405	20.3%	$6.00	$13.00	$7.00	$2430.00	$5265.00	$2835.00	H	H	Star
Pork Chops	170	8.5%	$4.00	$9.00	$5.00	$680.00	$1530.00	$850.00	L	H	Plowhorse
Salisbury Steak	80	4.0%	$3.50	$7.00	$3.50	$280.00	$560.00	$280.00	L	L	Dog
COLUMN TOTALS	N 2000	100.0%				I $9975.00	J $22557.50	M $12582.50			

ADDITIONAL COMPUTATIONS

$$K = I/J$$

$$\frac{\$9975.00}{\$22557.50} = 44.2\%$$

$$O = M/N$$

$$\frac{\$12582.50}{2000} = \$6.29$$

$$Q = (1/\text{no. of items} \times 70\%)$$

$$\frac{1}{10} \times .7 = 7.0\%$$

Column L: Menu CM

The menu contribution margin is found by multiplying the number of units sold for each menu item by its contribution margin. Thus for broiled chicken,

$$375 \text{ Units Sold} \times \$3.50 \text{ CM} = \$1,312.50$$

This is the total of contribution margins provided by each item, and the sum of all the individual totals is found in box M.

Box O

The figure in Box O is the average contribution margin, calculated by dividing the total in Box M by the total number of units sold, found in Box N. For the illustrated worksheet, the calculation is

$$\frac{\$12,582.50 \text{ Total CM (Box M)}}{2,000 \text{ Units Sold (Box N)}} = \$6.29$$

This is merely a variation on the calculation of average contribution margin described in Chapter 3.

Box Q

The figure in Box Q requires careful consideration. It is the percentage of an entire menu represented by each item on that menu, multiplied by 70%.* If there are ten items on a menu, each would be one-tenth, or 10%, or the menu. Similarly, if there were 5 items on a menu, each would be one-fifth, or 20% of the total. The figure in Box Q is calculated by dividing one menu item by the total number of items, then multiplying by .7 (70%). Thus

$$\frac{1}{10 \text{ items}} \times .7 = .07, \text{ or } 7.0\%$$

This figure will be used when making entries in column R, which is discussed below.

Column P: CM Category

The entries in this column, L for "low" and H for "high," are made by comparing the contribution margin for each menu item (Column F) with the average contribution margin for the menu (Box O). If the contribution margin for a given

---

* This is a figure established by the developers of menu engineering, based wholly on their own personal experiences in the industry. They state that 70% produces the most useful analysis.

menu item is lower than the average contribution margin, the entry in Column P for that item is L for "low." If the contribution margin is higher than average, the entry is H for "high." For example, the contribution margin for broiled chicken in $3.50, considerably lower than the average contribution margin for the menu, $6.29, so an L has been entered.

Column R: MM Category

The entries in the column—L and H for "high" and "low"—are determined by comparing the menu mix percentages in Column C with the figure in Box Q. For example, the menu mix percentage for broiled chicken is 18.8%. This is high, compared to the 7.0% figure in Box Q, so the letter H has been entered. For salisbury steak, the menu mix percentage is 4.0%, and because this is lower than the 7.0% in Box Q, the letter L has been entered.

Because all entries in Column P and Column R are one of two letters, there are four possible letter combinations used to describe each of the menu items: H/H, L/L, H/L, and L/H. In the language of menu engineering, each of these possible combinations has been given a name:

> H/H is a **Star**: a menu item that produces both high contribution margin and high volume. These are the items that foodservice operators prefer to sell when they can.
>
> L/L is a **Dog**: an item that produces a comparatively low contribution margin and accounts for relatively low volume. In the eyes of many owners, these may be the least desirable items to have on a menu.
>
> L/H is a **Plowhorse**: a menu item that produces a low contribution margin but accounts for relatively high volume. These have broad appeal to customers but contribute relatively little profit per unit sold.
>
> H/L is a **Puzzle**: an item producing a high contribution margin, but which accounts for comparatively low volume of sales.

Because it provides a graphic demonstration of the extent to which each menu item contributes to profitability, the menu engineering worksheet is a tool that can aid the operator in maximizing profit. Having completed the worksheet as described above, the restaurateur can analyze a list of menu offerings, determine whether changes would be wise, and, if so, apply the following general rules to each of the classifications.

1. Dogs: because a dog is both unprofitable and unpopular, it should be removed from the menu and replaced with a more profitable item unless, (a) there is a valid reason for continuing to sell it (as with an item that promotes other sales), or (b) its profitability can be increased to an acceptable level through change. One example of the latter would be changing an item from Dog to Puzzle by

increasing contribution margin per unit, which might be done by increasing sales price.

2. Plowhorses: a Plowhorse is popular but relatively unprofitable. Keep the Plowhorse on the menu, but attempt to increase its contribution margin without decreasing volume. One possibility would be to decrease standard portion size slightly and at the same time improve the appearance of the product.

3. Puzzles: a Puzzle is comparatively profitable but relatively unpopular. Keep the Puzzle on the menu, but attempt to increase its popularity without decreasing its profitability substantially. There are any number of ways to do this, including repositioning the item to a more favorable location on the menu, featuring the item as a special to be suggested to diners by servers, and changing the appearance or the menu description of the item to increase its appeal.

4. Stars: a Star is both profitable and popular, and should probably be left unchanged, unless there is a valid reason for attempting change. Because of the popularity of a Star, it is sometimes possible to increase its menu price without affecting volume, thus increasing profitability.

Some examples of the application of these general rules are useful. For purposes of illustration, we will refer to Figure 13.3, which reflects changes made by management to the menu represented in Figure 13.2. The changes were made in accordance with the general rules listed above. These changes and their effects are as follows:

1. Scrod, a Dog, was replaced with broiled trout, an item with a higher contribution margin. While sales volume did not change, the higher contribution margin changed the classification of the item from Dog to Puzzle. In addition, total revenues, total contribution margin, and average contribution margin were all increased.

2. Broiled chicken, a Plowhorse, was increased in price by $.50. Volume was not affected because of the popularity of the item, its relatively low sales price, and the minimal price increase. While the item remains a Plowhorse, total revenues, total contribution margin, and average contribution margin were all increased.

3. Veal piccata, a Puzzle, was repositioned on the menu and suggested to diners by the servers. This resulted in an increase in sales volume, reclassifying the item from Puzzle to Star. This change had negative impact on the sales of stuffed shrimp, although this item remains a Star. However, the higher contribution margin and higher sales price for veal piccata, compared to stuffed shrimp, produced an overall increase in total revenue, total contribution margin, and average contribution margin. Thus, the net effect was desirable.

FIGURE 13.3
Menu Engineering Worksheet After Changes

Restaurant: Sturnley's   **Period:** March 17–23, 19XX   **Date** 3/26/XX

A Menu Item Name	B No. Sold (MM)	C Menu Mix %	D Item Food Cost	E Item Sales Price	F Item CM (E-D)	G Menu Costs (D*B)	H Menu Revenues (E*B)	L Menu CM (F*B)	P CM Category	R MM Category	S Menu Item Classification
Broiled Chicken	375	18.8%	$3.00	$7.00	$4.00	$1125.00	$2625.00	$1500.00	L	H	Plowhorse
Strip Steak 12 oz	330	16.5%	$5.50	$13.00	$7.50	$1815.00	$4290.00	$2475.00	H	H	Star
Strip Steak 16 oz	125	6.3%	$6.50	$15.00	$8.50	$812.50	$1875.00	$1062.50	H	L	Puzzle
Stuffed Shrimp	145	7.3%	$5.00	$13.00	$8.00	$725.00	$1885.00	$1160.00	H	H	Star
Broiled Trout	90	4.5%	$4.00	$11.50	$7.50	$360.00	$1035.00	$675.00	H	L	Puzzle
Lobster 1.25 lb.	130	6.5%	$7.50	$16.00	$8.50	$975.00	$2080.00	$1105.00	H	L	Puzzle
Veal Piccata	150	7.5%	$5.50	$14.00	$8.50	$825.00	$2100.00	$1275.00	H	H	Star
Roast Prime Ribs	405	20.3%	$6.00	$13.00	$7.00	$2430.00	$5265.00	$2835.00	H	H	Star
Pork Chops	170	8.5%	$4.00	$9.00	$5.00	$680.00	$1530.00	$850.00	L	H	Plowhorse
Salisbury Steak	80	4.0%	$3.50	$7.00	$3.50	$280.00	$560.00	$280.00	L	L	Dog
COLUMN TOTALS	N 2000	100.0%				I $10027.50	J $23245.00	M $13217.50			

ADDITIONAL COMPUTATIONS

$$K = I/J = \frac{\$10027.50}{\$23245.00} = 43.1\%$$

$$O = M/N = \frac{\$13217.50}{2000} = \$6.61$$

$$Q = (1/\text{no. of items} \times 70\%) = \frac{1}{10} \times .7 = 7.0\%$$

The effects illustrated above show clearly the value of menu engineering as an analytical tool which can be used for many purposes. In terms of the present chapter, the most significant of these is profit maximization.

CONTROLLING REVENUE

Throughout the discussion of food control in previous chapters, numerous references have been made to food sales. Each reference has carried with it an unstated assumption that all food sales have been accurately recorded and have resulted in appropriate revenue to the establishment. While accurate recording of sales and inflows of appropriate revenue are both desirable and necessary to the successful operation of a restaurant, neither can be assumed.

There are many possibilities for errors to occur in the recording of sales, both accidentally and purposely. Sales may be incorrectly recorded; incorrect prices may be charged; checks may be lost, stolen, or simply not used at all; correctly recorded sales may not always bring revenue to the establishment because of the actions of dishonest employees or customers. These are but a few of the many possibilities, but they point out the need for establishing some control over revenue.

By this point in the text, the student should be keenly aware of the proper method for establishing control over any phase of operations: instituting the four-step control process first discussed in Chapter 2. To control sales or revenues, then, one must apply the process, beginning with the establishment of standards and standard procedures.

Standards and standard procedures for control can best be established when one has a clear goal in mind. The goal of revenue control is reasonably clear and simple: to ensure that all food served yields the correct revenue to the business. If the food is served to a customer, correct revenue for the food order is the sales price stipulated in the menu; if the food is served to an employee at the discretion of management, the correct sales price may or may not be the menu price, depending on management's policies. In either event, all food served must be accounted for in some appropriate manner. Failure to account for all food served to customers and employees will result in distortions in the cost-to-sales ratio that may lead management erroneously to believe that cost control procedures are not working. In addition, if sales or revenues are not under control, the establishment may be financially unsuccessful even with excellent cost control.

For example, imagine that the costs in a certain establishment are controlled to such an extent that the actual food cost of $350 approximates the standard cost. This food costing $350 should produce sales of $1,000 and result in a cost-to-sales ratio of 35%. If procedures are not established to control sales, it is conceivable that the sales might be recorded as $900, resulting in a cost-to-sales ratio of 38.9%. Gross profit on sales is reduced by $100, and the food cost is 3.9% higher than it would have been if all sales had been recorded.

In such a case, additional controls over cost and additional efforts to improve kitchen performance will not be effective. Steps must be taken to control the recording of sales. While these steps are often under the jurisdiction of an accountant rather than food controller, it is important that everyone in food management understand them and be able to put them into effect if called on to do so.

Establishing Standards and Standard Procedures for Revenue Control

In order to achieve the goals stated above, three standards are required:

1. All food served must be recorded.
2. All food served must be priced appropriately.
3. Foodservice revenues must be accounted for daily.

There are innumerable standard procedures used in foodservice establishments to control revenue. The larger the organization, the more complex the procedures are likely to be. Sometimes standard procedures used in one restaurant appear at first glance to differ markedly from those used by another but on close inspection can be seen as mere variations. Because it is not feasible in a text of this size to describe the many possibilities, we will confine our discussion to common standard procedures the student is likely to find in daily use in our industry.

Using Guest Checks

One of the simplest steps to take in attempting to establish sales control procedures is to require that each item ordered and its selling price be recorded legibly on a guest check. This procedure, followed by the majority of restaurants with the exception of some small owner-operated establishments, serves a number of useful functions. It:

1. Reminds the waiter what has been ordered.
2. Shows the customer an itemized list of charges.
3. Provides a written record of portion sales that can be abstracted and recorded in a sales history.
4. Facilitates verification of the cashier's accuracy.
5. Permits checking back to see that accurate prices have been charged for each item ordered.
6. Provides tax records, where applicable.

Although the use of guest checks provides a certain measure of control over sales, most establishments take the additional precaution of using numbered checks.

Numbering Guest Checks

Most places that use guest checks purchase them in serially numbered quantities. In some instances, the checks are on pads in numerical order. In others, the checks are individual units but are numbered nevertheless. Not all establishments make use of the various possibilities offered by the numerically ordered checks, but those that do so find a number of benefits.

For example, when numbered checks are used, it is possible at the end of any serving period to reassemble them in order to determine if any are missing. Checks may be missing because a waiter or a cashier is dishonest, or because a customer has taken the check with him and has not paid for the food consumed. Immediate investigation should be made when any check is missing, and steps should be taken to end the problem.

Numbered checks make possible the assigning of responsibility for particular numbers to particular employees who can be held accountable for incorrect entries and, to some extent, for missing numbers. In many cases, this responsibility is assigned by requiring that personnel sign for checks by the pad or book. Where this is the practice, it is typical to require that servers sign a book out before a serving period and turn it back in at the end, recording the numbers of used checks as they do so. Figure 13.4 illustrates a typical servers signature book set up for this purpose. In other instances, particularly in expensive reataurants serving haute cuisine from an a la carte menu, personnel sign for individual checks as needed. Figure 13.5 shows an example of a signature book used in this kind of operation.

While the numbering of checks is an important first step in establishing sales control procedures, the control established is not complete. A busy server can still make errors, either purposely or by accident. Incorrect prices may be charged for food recorded on the check, and wrong items may be recorded. A charge of $9.95

FIGURE 13.4
Servers' Signature Book

			Checks			
Date	Waiter No.	Book No.	From	To	Closing No.	Signature
10/1	1	7	700	799		J.J. Jones
10/1	2	8	800	899		S.S. Smith

Date   10/1/XX

FIGURE 13.5
Cashier's Record of Checks Distributed to Servers

H. Martin	Cashier			Sept. 3, 19XX
Check No.	Waiter No.	No. Served	Table No.	Waiter's Signature
100	1	4	2	D. Smith
101	2	2	3	P. Jones
102				
103				
104				
105				
106				
107				
108				
109				
110	3	2	7	J. Crawley
111	4	3	8	B. Miller
112				
113				
114				
115				
116				
117				
118				
119				

might be made, for example, for a sirloin steak that should be sold for $14.95. Or the $14.95 steak might be recorded on the check as a chopped steak selling for $8.95.

Employing a Food Checker

In an effort to eliminate some of these possibilities, many restaurants hired personnel who were known as food checkers. The job of food checker was to remain at a station in the kitchen, close by the exit door to the dining room, and to verify that each food item leaving the kitchen was recorded on a guest check. In many instances, the job of recording selling prices was taken from the waiters and given to the food checker. Often these prices were recorded on the checks mechanically with a register similar to a cashier's register. This technique provided an extra measure of control, because at the end of a serving period the readings in the checker's register should equal the total of cash and charge sales recorded by the cashier, with allowance made for taxes and tips. When the food checker's figure exceeded the cashier's figure, investigation could be made into the causes of the discrepancy. When numbered checks were in use, the numbers of the missing checks could be determined and the waiter involved questioned. Another advantage of this system was that the independent pricing of checks by a food checker afforded some measure of protection against service personnel giving away food or underpricing items purposely in a misguided effort to get larger tips.

However, there are so many disadvantages to using food checkers that this system of sales control has all but disappeared today. One serious disadvantage is that lines tend to form at the food checker's station during busy periods. Service to customers slows down, turnover decreases, cold food is served, and customers are dissatisfied. In addition, particularly in inflationary wage periods, food checkers are considered to be too much of a burden on the payroll. In some instances, attempts have been made to combine the jobs of the food checker and the cashier, often with unsatisfactory results.

Recording Revenues

In most establishments, one employee is usually hired as cashier and given the responsibility of recording cash sales and charge sales as customers leave the premises. The cashier is usually stationed near the exit. Whenever possible, it is desirable to require that sales be recorded in a register and that the registration of the sale be endorsed on each check, whether it is cash or charge. Some restaurants wisely require that all guest checks for cash be stamped "Paid" as the cash is received. Some even require the cashier to deposit all paid guest checks in a locked box as soon as the cash has been collected. The purpose of both these procedures is to prevent the reuse of paid guest checks, which sometimes occurs when serving personnel and cashiers form unhealthy alliances.

It is a frequent practice to require cashiers to record the number of persons served, as well as the breakdown of checks into food sales, taxes, and tips, and also to differentiate between cash and charge sales. While this is frequently done by cash register, it is best illustrated by the typical control sheet shown in Figure 13.6. In this illustration, it should be noted that the total of sales, taxes, and tips equals the total of cash and charge sales. Thus, $46.50 + $3.88 + $6.00 = $56.38; also, $25.54 + $30.84 = $56.38. Where such a form is used, cashiers are typically required to list the checks in numerical order so that missing numbers will be readily apparent. Investigation can then be made to determine if any sales are unrecorded. In establishments that require that printed receipts be attached to duplicate guest checks before food is released, the total food sales recorded by the cashier should agree with the reading taken on the machine that dispenses the printed receipts. The same principle may be applied in restaurants that employ food checkers to record selling prices on guest checks by machine. Moreover, the preceding systems are used in establishments that rely on cash registers rather than the control form illustrated. These registers normally provide for the separate recording of food sales, taxes, and tips on the one hand, and cash and charge sales on the other.

FIGURE 13.6
Restaurant Sales Control Sheet

Check #	Waiter #	# Covers	Food Sales	Tax	Tips	Cash	Charge	Detail
101	6	2	4.00	.48		4.48		
102	3	5	20.00	1.60	5.00		26.60	Diners'
103	2	1	3.00	.24	1.00		4.24	Amex
104	2	2	7.00	.56		7.56		
105	6	4	12.50	1.00		13.50		
Totals		14	46.50	3.88	6.00	25.54	30.84	

Using the Dupe System

One way of maintaining some of the desirable qualities of the food checker system while eliminating some of the attendant problems is to set up what is usually called a "dupe" system. **Dupe** is an abbreviation of the word "duplicate," and with this system, a duplicate copy is made of each order. There are several means of doing this. One is to use pads on which each check is followed by a carbon copy, usually on a paper of a different color and texture. There are variations on this procedure. The important point is that the dupe must be given to personnel in the kitchen before any food is issued, and management instructs kitchen personnel to issue only the food items recorded on the dupes in the quantities indicated. When food has been picked up by servers, the dupes are left behind in the kitchen and, in many places, deposited in a locked box through a slot in the top. At the end of a serving period, dupes bearing the same numbers as the original checks may be matched against the checks to locate any discrepancies.

Although it is conceivable that dupes could be used for all food orders in some kitchens, it is not usually the case. In most instances, dupes are used only for entree items and certain other high-cost items, such as shrimp cocktails, over which management wants to exercise control.

When dupes are used, many establishments match the duplicate to the original check to verify that nothing was given out from the kitchen without an original and that the cashier received all original checks. However, that is a time-consuming job, so some restaurants have taken additional measures to simplify the verification procedure. One such method requires that sales personnel write food orders, but no prices, on checks and dupes as the orders are taken. Then, on the way to ordering the food from the kitchen, each server records prices on the checks with a register similar to that used by a food checker. The register dispenses a printed receipt, which must be attached to the dupe before kitchen personnel will issue any food. When this procedure is followed, it is possible at the end of a meal to compare the readings from the kitchen register with the cashier's register and to locate missing amounts.

In addition to requiring that checks be verified against dupes each day, some establishments take the additional step of requiring that checks be analyzed periodically. Where this is required, the food controller periodically examines the checks for one day, noting the nature and extent of each error as well as the name or number of the person responsible. Pricing errors and errors in addition and in calculation of taxes can be called to the attention of the person in charge of service personnel. In some instances, the list of errors is posted on an employee bulletin board, often with the desirable psychological effect. Few persons like seeing their errors posted for all to see, and often employees make considerable effort to improve.

As well as providing an accounting department with accurate sales information for inclusion in the financial records, these summary forms enable the food controller to determine the average sale per customer for each meal. This average is determined as follows:

$$\text{Average Sale} = \frac{\text{Total Dollar Sales}}{\text{Total Number of Covers}}$$

From the totals in Figure 13.6, it is apparent that each customer has spent an average of $3.32. This is of considerable interest to the food controller and the manager, both of whom are interested in following business trends. If the average sale decreases over a period of time, investigation can be made into the reasons for the changes in customer spending habits. Some possibilities might include a deterioration in service standards, customer dissatisfaction with food quality, inadequate sales promotion, and changes in portion sizes.

These are but a few of the methods and procedures knowledgeable food controllers and managers employ in their efforts to establish effective revenue control procedures. The net effect of these efforts should be an accurate accounting of all sales so that undesirable food cost percentages will not be attributed to improperly recorded sales.

COMPUTER APPLICATIONS

Computers can be of great assistance to managers in their efforts to control revenue. For example, the sales history developed with the aid of a sales terminal can provide management with a valuable body of information indicating customer preferences from among menu offerings. Properly used, this information can lead to the development of menus that include no items unpopular with the clientele of a particular restaurant. This, of course, is only one simple and obvious use.

Another possible use involves a sales terminal capable of generating sales reports quickly while sales are in progress—half-way through the dinner hour, for example. It would obviously benefit a manager to know during the dinner hour how portion sales of the various menu items compared to the forecast of sales, the basis for many purchasing and production decisions. If sales for some item were far less than had been forecast, the manager might want to make some judicious efforts to increase sales (as opposed to orders taken) for the item, possibly by offering some inducement for the waiters and waitresses to "sell" the item. If successful, this type of mini-campaign could have many beneficial outcomes, including a decrease in leftover food, lower costs, and possibly an increase in dollar sales.

Perhaps the most important use of the computer as a sales control device may be illustrated by its ability to eliminate the traditional need for the guest check and dupe. In at least one system currently available for restaurant use, the server records guests' selections on a simple pad of white paper. He signs into the terminal using his individually assigned code and is then led through a program in the course of which the computer records the table number, the number of diners, and their food in computer memory indicating that a selections. All this information is entered by means of preassigned codes, including the menu selections. At this time, a "check" with a particular serial number is opened in computer memory, where it will remain until a printed copy is requested, typically when the diners have completed their meal. As the menu selections are entered, they are transmitted to the various stations of the kitchen, where they are displayed on printers. By this means, various stations are advised of orders placed, including correct number of portions, server placing the order, and the time the order was placed. Servers pick up orders at suitable times for delivery to diners. Additional menu selections for other courses are similarly recorded in the terminal, until finally the diners have finished their meal and requested their check. At that time, the waiter requests a copy of the check at the terminal, and it appears on the attached printer. The data on the check remain in memory where they are stored until the check is settled by payment or charge card. If the check is not settled by the close of business, management will be so informed by printed report, which will show table number, number of guests, name or number of the server, and the outstanding amount. If required, a duplicate copy of the check can be printed.

This particular system offers a number of advantages to managers in their efforts to control sales. First, it helps speed service in the dining room and increase turnover by eliminating the need for each waiter to walk to the kitchen to place each order. Next, it completely eliminates the need to maintain traditional guest checks, to verify the accuracy of each, and to ascertain that none are missing at the end of a meal period. Finally, by means of the printers at various kitchen stations, it becomes possible to ensure that each food item ordered and picked up has actually been ordered by a guest in the dining room. The system offers many advantages for the control of both sales and costs.

CHAPTER ESSENTIALS

In this chapter, we have explained the scope of sales control and listed its three goals—optimizing the number of sales, maximizing profit, and controlling revenue.

We listed eight determinants of customer restaurant selection and explained how an understanding of these could be used by managers to optimize the number of sales. We discussed two primary means for maximizing profits: by pricing products properly and by selling products effectively. We provided illustrations of the three most common approaches to menu pricing and illustrated the two principal means for selling products in a restaurant—the menu, and sales techniques used by the staff. We discussed one useful technique for menu analysis, menu engineering, and explained how it could be used as an aid to profit maximization. We listed the goals of revenue control and explained the most common standard procedures used to achieve the goals. Finally, we illustrated the some uses of computers as sales control tools.

KEY TERMS IN THIS CHAPTER

Sales control	Star
Revenue control	Plowhorse
Differentiated product	Puzzle
Homogeneous product	Guest check
Signature item	Signature book
Price sensitive	Dupe
Menu engineering	Dupe system
Menu mix percent	Sales control sheet
Dog	

QUESTIONS AND PROBLEMS

1. Distinguish between sales control and revenue control.
2. List and explain the three goals of sales control.
3. Given two restaurants offering essentially similar products at similar prices, one of which is located in a city center while the other is in a rural setting, which would you expect to achieve greater dollar sales volume? Why?
4. How can the portion sizes offered by a restaurant affect both the number and type of customers it attracts?
5. Distinguish between homogeneous and differentiated products.
6. What is a price-sensitive product?
7. What is a signature item?
8. List and explain the determinants of customer restaurant selection.
9. Describe the two principal means used by foodservice operators to achieve profit maximization.

10. List and explain the five most important elements in menu preparation.

11. Describe the three most common methods for establishing menu prices.

12. What sales techniques might management suggest that sales personnel use to:
    a. Improve gross revenue and average check?
    b. Increase tips?
    c. Sell a menu item prepared in excess quantity that must be thrown away if not sold?

13. For each of the following, calculate the average sale.

	Number of Covers	Total Sales
a.	20	$ 70.00
b.	87	$ 372.40
c.	142	$ 863.45
d.	463	$2,309.00

14. Why would each of the following adversely affect the average sale in a restaurant?
    a. Deterioration in service standards.
    b. Customer dissatisfaction over food quality.
    c. Inadequate sales promotion.
    d. Changes in portion sizes.

15. Show by example how improper recording of sales affects the food cost percentage.

16.a. A certain restaurant projects labor costs of 36%, fixed costs of 28%, and wants to plan for profit of 12%. What food cost percent should be projected?

   b. Using the food cost percent from (a) above, what menu selling prices would be suitable for each of the following:

	Portion Cost
Item A	$1.94
Item B	2.26
Item C	4.40
Item D	2.88
Item E	2.42

17. The owner of a certain small restaurant realizes that her establishment is offering homogeneous products that are extremely price sensitive. Given its present cost and sales volume, the business is unprofitable, but she does not want to sell out. What suggestions could you make to help this owner make the business profitable?

18. The new manager of a certain restaurant learns that there is always a waiting line of customers on Friday and Saturday nights. Because of the apparent need to serve customers as quickly as possible to make seating available to those waiting in line, to what extent should this new manager suggest the use of selling techniques that tend to prolong service and result in customers spending additional time at tables?

19. Given the following information, determine an appropriate contribution margin to use in setting menu prices and then determine suitable menu selling prices for each of the items.

Gross sales:	$300,000
Cost of food sold:	$100,000
Number of customers served:	50,000

	Portion Costs
Item A	$1.85
Item B	2.60
Item C	3.50
Item D	6.28
Item E	4.12

20a. Given the menu engineering worksheet reproduced in Figure 13.7, fill in the missing information.

20b. Which items, if any, should be removed from the menu? Remain unchanged? Increase in price? Featured or repositioned on the menu? Why?

For Computer Users

21. Using a spreadsheet package of your choice, prepare a menu engineering worksheet following the form illustrated in Figure 13.2.

22. Complete the menu engineering worksheet in Question 20 above, using the worksheet set up in Question 21.

23. Use your spreadsheet program to set up the restaurant sales control sheet illustrated in Figure 13.6 as a worksheet.

FIGURE 13-7
Menu Engineering Worksheet

Date: 3/09/XX

Restaurant: Smuggler's Inn

A Menu Item Name	B No. Sold (MM)	C Menu Mix %	D Item Food Cost	E Item Sales Price	F Item CM (E-D)	G Menu Costs (D*B)	H Menu Revenues (E*B)	L Menu CM (F*B)	P CM Category	R MM Category	S Menu Item Classification
Fried Chicken	175		$3.00	$7.00							
Sirloin Steak	190		$5.50	$13.00							
Baked Ham	40		$4.00	$8.00							
Stuffed Sole	45		$7.00	$13.00							
Broiled Swordfish	80		$8.00	$15.00							
Lobster	60		$7.50	$16.00							
Veal Marsala	90		$5.50	$14.00							
Roast Prime Ribs	145		$6.00	$13.00							
Lamb Chops	125		$6.00	$9.00							
Beef Burgundy	50		$3.50	$7.00							
COLUMN TOTALS	N 1000					I	J	M			

ADDITIONAL COMPUTATIONS

$$K = I/J$$

$$O = M/N$$

$$Q = (1/\text{no. of items})(70\%)$$

part three

Beverage Control

In previous chapters we discussed the need for food, beverage, and labor control procedures and outlined in detail control principles and procedures for food. Beverage control is similar to food control in many ways. It is necessary to develop standards and procedures for purchasing, receiving, storage, issuing, production, and sales. Those standards and procedures are closely akin to those used in food control, only instead of dealing with highly perishable food items, the manager is concerned with liquor items that in many cases can be kept indefinitely. Beverage control is as important as food control because of the nature of the product. The probability that employees will steal or attempt to become silent partners with management is greatest with beverages. Interestingly enough, although it is recognized that beverage control is most needed, it is an area where only limited controls can be successfully instituted.

chapter 14

Beverage Purchasing Control

Learning Objectives

After reading and studying this chapter, the student should be able to:

1. List and describe the three principal classifications of beverages.
2. Identify the two broad classifications of beers and distinguish between them.
3. Identify the three color classifications of wines.
4. Describe the fermentation process and explain its significance in the making of alcoholic beverages.
5. Explain the purpose of the distillation process.
6. Distinguish between call brands and pouring brands.
7. List the primary purposes for establishing beverage purchasing controls.
8. Identify the principal considerations used to establish quality standards for beverage purchasing.
9. List and explain the principal factors used to establish quantity standards for beverage purchasing.
10. Distinguish between license states and control states.
11. Identify the two principal methods for determining order quantities and calculate order quantities using both methods.
12. Describe one standard procedure for processing beverage orders in large operations.
13. Describe a step-by-step process for training beverage purchasing personnel and suggest ways of monitoring their performance.
14. Describe the use of computers to determine order quantities for beverages.
15. Define each of the Key Terms listed at the end of the chapter.

CONTROL PROCESS AND PURCHASING

In Chapter 2, **control** was defined as a process by which managers attempt to direct, regulate, and restrain the actions of people in order to achieve desired goals. The control process was described as having four steps: establishment of standards and standard procedures, training employees to follow those standards and standard procedures, monitoring employees' output and comparing it with established standards, and taking remedial actions as needed.

In previous chapters, we illustrated the application of this process to purchasing, receiving, storing, issuing, producing, and selling food. In this part of the text, we will apply the process to beverages. In the present chapter, our objective will be the application of the control process to beverage purchasing.

BEVERAGES DEFINED

The term *beverage* requires some definition. Technically, any liquid intended for drinking is a beverage, a word derived from the French verb *vivre,* to drink. In a sense, all beverages can be divided into two groups—those that contain some measure of alcohol and those that contain no alcohol at all.

Alcoholic Beverages

Alcoholic beverages, obviously, are those that contain alcohol. They contain one particular type of alcohol—ethyl alcohol, which is produced naturally in the process of making the various alcoholic beverages. Other types of alcohol are unsuitable for human consumption. The amount of alcohol contained in alcoholic beverages varies considerably from one to another. Some have a very small percentage, as little .5%; others have substantially more.

There are three classifications of alcoholic beverages: beers, wines, and spirits. These are substantially different from one another, and it will be useful to describe them and to show how they differ.

Beers

Beers are beverages produced by the fermentation of malted grain, flavored with hops. The grain used is usually barley. **Malted grain** is grain that has been mashed and then steeped in water. **Hops** are the dried blossoms of the hop vine, used to impart the typical bitter flavor to beer. Hops may be either domestic or imported; imported hops are commonly considered superior to domestic.

Fermentation is a natural process resulting from the addition of yeast to a liquid containing malted grain and hops. By complex chemical processes, the starches in the liquid are converted to sugars. These, in turn, are converted to carbon dioxide, which is dispersed, and to alcohol, which remains in the liquid. The remaining liquid containing the alcohol is strained and then stored for varying periods of time to mature and develop flavor. Because natural carbonation is seldom retained during the storage process, most beers are carbonated just before being bottled, canned, or kegged.

Beer does not keep well unless the producer takes steps to eliminate bacteria and other natural impurities that cause spoilage. Essentially, producers do this by one of two methods: high filtration (often coupled with refrigeration), or pasteurization. Pasteurized beer tends to last longer, but most agree that pasteurizing harms flavor. Regardless of the method used to improve shelf life, most beers should be refrigerated as soon as they are received. Low temperatures help retain flavor and lengthen shelf life.

While the term "beer" suggests that all products so named are much the same, this is not the case. Beers are normally divided into two broad classifications: lager beers and ales. They differ in taste, alcohol content, body, and processing method. Lager beer, the type most commonly consumed in the United States, is a category that includes the popular brands of regular and light beer—Budweiser, Miller, Coors, and many others. Bock beers and malt liquors are also classified as lager beers. Compared to lager beer, ale is typically stronger and has a higher alcohol content. Porter and stout, more popular in Europe than in the United States, are both ales.

A comparatively new product is the nonalcoholic beer, produced in much the same way as regular beer, but with the alcohol removed. The popularity of these beers is growing faster than most individuals would have thought possible just a few years ago. In any event, these should be stored and served like other beers.

Wines

Wines are beverages normally produced by the fermentation of grapes, although various other fruits and one grain—rice—are also fermented to produce relatively small quantities of wine.

The fermentation process for wine differs considerably from that used for beers. Traditionally, grapes are crushed, then placed in tanks where the yeasts occurring naturally on the grapes begin the fermentation process. By natural chemical processes, the sugars in the crushed grape mixture are converted to carbon dioxide and alcohol. Left unchecked, conversion will continue until the level of alcohol reaches 14%, at which point the yeast is killed by the alcohol and the process ceases.

Grapes contain varying amounts of sugar, depending on the type of grape and when it is picked. Grapes with less natural sugar produce wines that are not as sweet as those with more natural sugar. The difference has to do with the amount of sugar, if any, remaining in the mixture when the yeasts are killed. If sugar remains unprocessed, the resulting wine will have a sweetness in the flavor. If none remains, the wine will be *dry*, a term used to describe wines that lack sweetness.

When fermentation ends, the resulting liquid is drawn off and stored in fresh wood casks to permit any residue to settle so that the new wine will be clear. When the wines have "cleared" sufficiently, they are drawn off and stored to mature. The nature of the containers used for storing and the length of storage time varies from one wine to another. When the new wine is mature, it is filtered and then bottled. Once bottled, the wine is either shipped for immediate consumption or stored under carefully controlled conditions (or **aged**) for a period of time. The type of wine produced will determine whether it is shipped or aged, and if aged, the length of time appropriate for aging.

The above is a very abbreviated description of the traditional method for making wine, used today primarily by those wineries producing high quality, expensive wines. It should be noted that some makers, typically those producing large quantities of comparatively inexpensive wines, use such modern adaptations of traditional methods as producing wines in vast steel tanks, rather than individual wood casks. Some pasteurize their wines—a process the traditional winemaker would never consider.

Wines are normally classified as red, white, or rose. The color of wine is determined by the variety of grape used and the manner in which is it processed. Red wines range from hearty and full-bodied to light and fruity, and they tend to be drier than most whites. By contrast, white wines tend to be lighter-bodied than reds, and they range from very dry to very sweet. Red wines, normally served at room temperature, are often considered better accompaniments to red meat, while white wines, typically served chilled, more commonly accompany fish, poultry, and veal. Rose wines, served chilled, may be used to accompany any entree. However, while experts tend to follow these general rules, customers' tastes vary, and one often sees exceptions, such as diners drinking white wine with beef.

In addition to the color classifications described above, there are four other terms commonly used to identify wines:

1. *Varietal:* a wine may be identified by the predominant variety of grape it contains. For example, Chardonnay, Zinfadel, Cabernet Sauvignon, and Pinot Noir are grape varieties that lend their names to varietal wines.

2. *Brand name:* many winemakers—some superior; others less so—produce wines under their own names. These are normally blended wines, carefully produced so their characteristics are the same from bottle to bottle, year after year. Lancers Vin Rose is an excellent example.

3. *Geographic:* many wines are identified by their place of origin—the region, district, or other geographic location where the wine is produced. The location may be as small as a particular vineyard, known in France as a *chateau*. Producers in the geographic area are normally required to follow standards and regulations established by some authority, usually a governmental agency, so that the wine produced in the particular location, given the climate and soil there, has identifiable and presumably desirable characteristics. One example of a geographic wine is Chateau Margaux.

4. *Generic:* generic wines take their names from geographic areas, most commonly in France or Italy. Generic wines attempt to replicate the characteristics of the better-known geographic wines after which they are named. For example, certain wines produced in California are known as "burgandy," a name borrowed from the Burgundy region of France. A generic wine may be excellent, very poor, or anything in between. One must taste the wine to determine.

There are several types of wines and wine-based beverages with characteristics that are sufficiently different to warrant separate discussion:

1. *Sparkling wines* are carbonated. They may be red, white, or rose, and the carbonation may be natural or artificial. Champagne, Asti Spumonte, and sparkling burgundy are the three best-known examples.
2. *Fortified wines* are wines to which small quantities of brandy or other spirits have been added to increase the alcoholic content. Port and sherry are the two best-known examples.
3. *Wine coolers* are blends of wine and fruit juice, and are consequently rather low in alcoholic content—commonly about 5%. They are becoming increasingly popular with the growing trend to lighter drinks.
4. *Blush wines* are a comparatively new category. One way to make a blush wine is to ferment red and white grapes together, yielding a wine similar in appearance to a rose. They tend to be light-bodied and sweet and are growing in popularity with Americans.

Spirits

Spirits are beverages produced by the distillation of a fermented liquid. The fermented liquid may be made from grain, fruit, or any of a number of other food products, including sugar cane and potatoes. A list of the possibilities would be almost endless, although most spirits come from the items listed above.

Distillation is the process by means of which alcohol is removed from a fermented liquid. The process takes place in a device known as a *still*. In the still, liquid is heated to change the alcohol to a gas, which is then condensed. The resulting distillate is principally alcohol, accompanied by various impurities that are important in giving essential character to the spirits. Two primary factors determine the nature of the final product:

1. The food ingredient that forms the basis of the fermented liquid.
2. The alcoholic content of the distillate.

Figure 14.1 lists some of the major alcoholic beverages produced by distillation and the primary food ingredients used to produce each.

FIGURE 14.1
Primary Ingredients in Distilled Beverages

Distilled Beverage	Primary Ingredient
Bourbon	Corn
Brandy	Grapes
Gin	Any grain
Rum, dark	Molasses
Rum, light	Sugar cane
Rye	Rye
Scotch	Barley
Vodka	Potatoes; any grain

The alcoholic content of the distillate is stated in terms of *proof.* Proof in the United States is measured on a scale from 0 to 200, with 0 being the complete absence of alcohol and 200 being pure alcohol. One proof is equal to .5% alcohol. Thus, 80 proof is 40% alcohol. The higher the proof of a distillate, the more pure it is, and the fewer the impurities it contains. Higher proof distillates are also clearer to the eye than those of lower proof; a 200-proof distillate would look like water but would actually be pure alcohol.

The distiller can control the proof of a distillate by regulating the temperature, duration, and other elements of the distillation process. In general, the lighter and clearer the final product, the higher has been the proof of the distillate. To produce vodka, for example, the process must be regulated so that the proof of the distillate is 190 or higher; for bourbon, by contrast, the proof is normally between 110 and 130.

With the exception of vodkas and some gins, spirits are stored in wooden barrels for some period of time before being bottled. This aging mellows and brings out the flavor of the final product. The longer the aging, the better and more costly the final product. Thus twelve-year-old scotch is considered better than six-year-old scotch and is more expensive. Just before bottling, all spirits are diluted, or *cut,* with distilled water to lower their proof and thus reduce their potency. When bottled for sale, most spirits are between 80 and 100 proof. Once spirits are bottled, they can be stored at normal temperatures indefinitely.

One particularly interesting group of spirits is that known as **liqueurs**, or cordials. Liqueurs are spirits, typically brandies or neutral spirits, that have been sweetened and combined with flavoring agents. Some, such as Drambuie, come from carefully guarded recipes; others, such as creme de menthe, are produced from well-known recipes by numerous distillers. Because they are sweet, they are commonly consumed as after-dinner drinks or combined with other ingredients in cocktails. Grasshoppers and Brandy Alexanders are examples of cocktails in which liqueurs are vital ingredients. The proof range for liqueurs is wider than spirits, ranging from a low of about 30 proof to a high of just above 100.

Nonalcoholic Beverages

Nonalcoholic beverages commonly include those normally found listed in restaurant menus under the "beverage" category—coffee, tea, and milk, as well as a host of others, some carbonated and some not. Carbonated nonalcoholic beverages include club soda, ginger ale, and a wide range of other flavored beverages. Nonalcoholic beverages that are not carbonated include fruit and vegetable juices, such as orange juice, tomato juice, and V-8. Many of the nonalcoholic beverages are used to dilute alcoholic beverages and to produce a vast number of drinks with a wide variety of flavors. When so used, these nonalcoholic beverages are called **mixers** and most commonly include club soda, ginger ale, lemon-lime soda, cola, tonic water, orange juice, tomato juice, and grapefruit juice.

For purposes of these chapters, we will use the term *beverage* alone to refer to alcoholic beverages, and the term *mixers* to refer to those nonalcoholic beverages that are typically used with alcoholic beverages to produce a variety of mixed drinks. Some mixed drinks, usually produced according to recipe, require additional items, and they will be referred to simply as other ingredients. They typically include olives, pearl onions, sugar, cream, lime juice, and lemon juice.

RESPONSIBILITY FOR BEVERAGE PURCHASING

The nature and size of an operation often dictates who is responsible for purchasing beverages. In small, owner-operated establishments, the responsibility will fall to the owner. In others, it may be held by the manager. In some large operations, the purchasing responsibility is delegated to a purchasing agent, a steward, or even a beverage manager. The job title of the individual responsible for purchasing is of little consequence. The important point is that one individual should be held responsible and accountable for all beverage purchasing. For control purposes, it is desirable to assign the responsibility to someone who is not involved in either the preparation or sale of drinks.

DEVELOPING STANDARDS AND STANDARD PROCEDURES FOR PURCHASING

The primary purposes of establishing beverage purchasing controls are to maintain an appropriate supply of ingredients for producing beverage products, and to ensure that the quality of each is appropriate to its intended use and that each is purchased at the optimum price. As with all control, the key is the establishment of standards and standard procedures.

Standards must be developed for:

1. Quality of beverages purchased.

2. Quantity of beverages purchased.

3. Prices at which beverages are purchased.

Establishing Quality Standards

Alcoholic beverages used by a bar may be divided into two classes according to use: **call brands** and **pouring brands**. A call brand is used only if specifically requested by the customer; a pouring brand is used whenever the customer does not request a call brand. If a customer simply orders a "scotch and soda," she should be given the pouring brand. On the other hand, if the customer orders a specific brand of scotch with soda, she is always given the call brand specifically requested (if it is available). The usual practice is to designate one low- to medium-priced brand in each category of spirits as the pouring brand. The choice will vary with the clientele and the price structure. Once this is done, all other brands become call brands. The selection of pouring brands is an important first step in establishing both quality and cost standards. Although management usually does this, it is important that the beverage controller recognize its significance and check to see that the selection has been made and that the proper brands are being used at the bar.

Establishing quality standards for alcoholic beverages requires one to weigh a number of factors, including product cost, customer preference, product popularity, and age of the beverage, among others. Most people will agree on the extremes— that certain twenty-five-year-old scotches are of high quality, and that various cheap gins are of very low quality—but there remains a vast area between the extremes for possible and legitimate differences of opinion.

The extent of the need for each of the three different types of alcoholic beverages must be determined before any purchase decisions can be made. Needs will differ from place to place, depending on clientele and inherent differences in the nature of operations. Some neighborhood bars cater to customers whose tastes run primarily to domestic beer, inexpensive wines, and comparatively few whiskies. On the other hand, cocktail lounges serving an upper-middle-income business clientele may offer imported beer, a large assortment of spirits, and a few fine wines, while some relatively expensive restaurants may specialize in the finest of imported wines. And these are but a few of the infinite number of possibilities. Because all alcoholic beverages are comparatively expensive, carefully defining customer tastes is particularly important in an attempt to eliminate the purchase of beverages that will not sell. Purchasing beverages involves the outlay of cash for merchandise that must be carried as inventory until sold. It is usually undesirable to maintain an inventory of items that move very slowly. Once the operation is open and control procedures are in effect, a manager can identify slow-moving items and restrict or eliminate their purchase. However, this is a partial solution at best. It is of the utmost importance to restrict initial purchases to items that will meet customer tastes. Thus, quality determination becomes a matter for decision by the individual operator.

Establishing Quantity Standards

Because beverage products are not highly perishable if properly stored, beverages can be purchased far less frequently than perishable foods. This is not to say that beverages are nonperishable, however. Canned and bottled beers should be used within approximately three months of packaging. Draft beer should be consumed within one month. Some wines have comparatively limited lives, while others, those that improve with age, can and should be stored for long periods before use. Most spirits can be stored almost indefinitely. Thus perishability is not a critical factor in establishing quantity standards. Other factors are far more significant.

The principal factors used to establish quantity standards for beverage purchasing are

1. Frequency with which management chooses to place orders.
2. Storage space available.
3. Funds available for inventory purchases.
4. Delivery schedules set by purveyors.
5. Minimum order requirements set by purveyors.
6. Price discounts for volume orders.
7. Price specials available.
8. Limited availability of some items.

Some of these are often more important than others. Most establishments have limited storage space, for example, and finite storage space is clearly a limiting factor in establishing quantity standards. So is the number of times management will permit orders to be placed. No one wants a given item ordered too frequently, so quantity standards must be such that the number of orders placed over time is kept to a minimum. Availability of funds can be another severely limiting factor: beverage purchases require relatively large cash outlay either at the time of delivery or very soon thereafter, depending on local regulations. Thus, if the necessary cash is not available for a purchase of the desired quantity, an adjustment to the purchase quantity may be required. And while management may choose to order a given item very frequently, the purveyor may be willing to deliver no more than once a week. Purveyors may establish minimum order quantities for some items, typically wines, which must usually be purchased in full cases. It is sometimes possible to obtain a discounted price or to receive merchandise dividends by purchasing a quantity somewhat larger than one would normally order. From time to time, some beverage products are available at discounted prices for limited periods, and it may be desirable to increase a current order beyond the normal order quantity. In some instances, beverage products, especially wines, may not be readily available in the market, and it may be necessary to purchase a very large quantity when the item is available if one is to ensure an adequate supply for continuing needs.

To establish quantity standards for beverages, then, management must take all of these factors into account. This is best done by those who have considerable experience with beverage management and are fully informed about all aspects of the beverage operation, including its financial status.

Establishing Standards for Price

Assuming that quality standards have been established and appropriate purchase quantities are known, the next step is to ensure that all beverage purchases are made at the optimum price. The establishment of price standards is somewhat complicated by laws that vary from state to state. The fifty states may be divided into two groups:

1. **License states**, where beverage wholesalers (and sometimes manufacturers and distributors as well) are permitted to sell directly to hotels and restaurants, often resulting in competitive pricing of brands in the market.

2. **Control states**, where the state government actually sells some or all alcoholic beverages through its own network of stores, thus exercising complete control over prices of the items it sells. Control states vary considerably in established practices. Some sell virtually all alcoholic beverages; others sell spirits and wines but permit beer to be sold through beer distributors. In control states, it is typically illegal for hotels and restaurants to buy out of state.

Obtaining optimum price is simple in a control state: there is only one price for each brand, the price set by the state. Because all available brands are sold by the state outlet, one need only determine whether or not to buy a particular brand at the established price. Control states offer special prices on some items from time to time, and the beverage buyer should be alert for these.

By contrast, obtaining optimum price in a license state can be more complicated for the buyer. In license states, hotel and restaurant operators can purchase beverages from wholesale organizations, which may or may not induce price competition, depending on state laws and on such complicating factors as exclusive distributorships granted by some manufacturers.

In general, anyone responsible for purchasing alcoholic beverages must become familiar with the laws, restrictions, and industry practices in effect in his area. If competitive pricing is the rule, the buyer should clearly take full advantage of it. If competition is minimal or nonexistent, the buyer must simply accept the fact and watch for special offers, if any, on approriate beverages.

ESTABLISHING STANDARD PROCEDURES FOR PURCHASING

Having established standards for purchasing beverages, the next step is to establish standard procedures. In beverage purchasing, the need exists for standard procedures to:

1. Determine order quantities.
2. Process orders.

Determining Order Quantities

There are two basic methods for determining order quantities. One, known as the **periodic order method**, is based on fixed order dates and variable order quantities; the second, the **perpetual order method**, uses variable order dates and fixed reorder quantities. These are discussed separately.

Periodic Order Method

The periodic order method requires that order dates be fixed so that there are equal operating periods between order dates. Ordering may be done weekly, bi-weekly, or on any other regular schedule, depending on the decisions of management with respect to frequency of ordering, storage space to be devoted to beverages, and funds available for inventory purchases, as well as on purveyors' delivery schedules and anticipated consumption of beverages.

Determination of anticipated consumption is a key element: the person who sets order quantities must have some reasonable knowledge of the quantity of each beverage that is likely to be consumed in the interval between fixed order dates. There are two ways to determine this. The first and by far the best is to keep records of the quantity of each beverage sold during one period. If bar requisitions of the sort discussed in the following chapter are used, this is comparatively easy; without bar requisitions, some appropriate record-keeping system must be set up for one period. The second method is simply to estimate consumption, based on experience in the particular operation, experience in other similar operations, or on both.

Having established for each beverage the anticipated consumption for one period, one increases that number by some amount that will allow for such unanticipated occurrences as increases in business volume, time required to receive delivery, and possible delay in receiving delivery. Some multiply the usage figure by 150%; others use some other percentage. Many round the results to whole case lots for pouring brands and other high-volume items. In the periodic system, the number so determined for each beverage item is defined as the **par stock** for that item—the maximum quantity of the item that should be on hand at any given time.

There are now two figures established for each beverage: anticipated usage and par stock. For each item in the inventory, both of these figures should be recorded on a label affixed to the shelf where the item is kept in the beverage storeroom, as illustrated in Figure 14.2. On each established order date, the person responsible for determining order quantities must go through the beverage storeroom carefully to check each item in the inventory, using the following procedure:

1. Count the number of units on the shelf.

FIGURE 14.2
Shelf Label

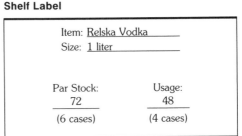

Item: <u>Relska Vodka</u>

Size: <u>1 liter</u>

Par Stock:	Usage:
72	48
(6 cases)	(4 cases)

2. Subtract the inventory from the par stock to determine the order quantity. For example, if there were 24 units of Relska Vodka on the shelf, that number would be subtracted from the par stock of 72 to determine the proper order quantity: 48 units, or 4 cases.

If the actual usage is the same as the usage figure on the label, the order quantity determined in this manner will be the same as the usage figure. If the subtraction results in an order quantity that is substantially different from the usage figure on the label, that is the signal that actual usage is not as anticipated, and the figures on the shelf label must be reviewed for possible change. For example, if one finds 42 units of vodka on the shelf, the order quantity would appear to be 30. However, the fact that there are 42 units on the shelf means that usage has been considerably less than anticipated; thus one should assess the need for a par stock of 72. If the decrease in business volume is other than a temporary phenomenon, par stock and usage figures on the label should be changed for future periods. In general, if the number of units inventoried differs markedly from the difference between par stock and usage, the adequacy of these two figures for ordering purposes must be reviewed.

Perpetual Order Method

The perpetual order method is based on the establishment of a perpetual inventory system for beverages, requiring the use of perpetual inventory cards on which all purchases and issues are recorded carefully and in a timely manner. These are normally maintained in an office away from the beverage storeroom, although, as an alternative, some managers attach these cards to the shelves on which the beverages are stored.

To use the perpetual order method, several key figures must be established and recorded on the cards: par stock, reorder point, and reorder quantity. Par stock is the maximum quantity management wants to have on hand at any given time. It takes into account the storage space to be allocated to the item, the desired frequency of ordering, anticipated usage, and a safety factor to cover such considerations as unanticipated increases in volume. **Reorder point** is the number of units to which the inventory should decrease before an order is placed, and must take into account the time required to obtain delivery of the order. **Reorder quantity** is the amount that should be ordered each time an order is placed, and is equal to the difference between par stock and reorder point, plus the number of units consumed between order date and delivery date.

Figure 14.3 illustrates a perpetual inventory card for a pouring gin consumed at the rate of five bottles per day in an establishment open seven days per week. Management has determined that orders are to be placed at approximately two-week intervals, and experience has shown that it takes five days to obtain delivery. Therefore, par stock is calculated as 5 bottles per day multiplied by 14 days, multiplied by 150% (to include a safety factor), or 105 units, which is rounded off to an even 9 cases. Reorder point is determined by multiplying the number of units used in the 5 days required for delivery—25—by 150% to include a safety factor, and rounding off to the nearest whole case. Reorder quantity is determined by subtracting reorder point from par stock, then adding the number of units used in the five-day period before receiving delivery.

The standard procedures suggested above for determining order quantities assume that supplies of the needed items are readily available. While this is normally true for all mixers, most spirits and beers, and some wines, it is not universally true for all beverages. Complications arise. For example, some wines— especially vintage wines, both imported and domestic—may be unavailable, either

FIGURE 14.3
Perpetual Inventory Card

ITEM	Greys Gin		PAR STOCK		108 (9 cases)
SIZE	1 liter		REORDER POINT		36 (3 cases)
			REORDER QUANTITY		96 (8 cases)

Date	Order #	Quantity	In	Out	Balance
8/25	#7	108			
8/31			108		108
9/1				5	103
9/2				5	98
9/3				4	94
9/4				5	89

temporarily or permanently. In some control states, supplies of various items may not always be adequate to fill an order completely, making adjustments necessary. The beverage buyer must be prepared to meet contingencies as they arise and must be able to deviate from established purchasing procedures when required. Sometimes one can anticipate problems, as with particular wines that one knows will be available at an appropriate price for only a short time. This is often the case with fine wines. In such instances, one must be prepared to place one order for the total amount required over a very long period, possibly several years.

Processing Orders

Whenever practical, it is advisable to establish a purchasing routine that requires formal written purchase orders. In large establishments, formal purchase requests serve as the basis for ordering.

In a large hotel, the purchasing routine might be the following: the wine steward, the person in charge of maintaining the beverage inventory and stockroom, would make up a purchase request such as that illustrated in Figure 14.4 just after the first of the month. These are prepared in duplicate, and the original is forwarded to the purchasing agent in the accounting department. In some establishments, the purchasing agent is required to secure management's written approval on the purchase request before placing any orders. The orders placed are recorded on purchase orders, shown in Figure 14.5, made up in quadruplicate. The copies are distributed as follows: the original is sent to the firm from which the beverages have been ordered; a copy is sent to the wine steward to confirm that the orders have been placed; a second copy is sent to the receiving clerk so that she will know what deliveries to expect and can determine the correctness of the quantities and brands delivered; the third copy is kept by the purchasing agent.

FIGURE 14.4
Purchase Request Form

Quantity	Item	Size	Supplier	Unit Price	Total Price
6 cases	Old Crow	750 ml	A.&C. Suppliers	$95.00	$570.00
2 cases	Beefeater Gin	750 ml	A.&C. Suppliers	$105.00	$210.00

Requested by _S.S. Smith_   Approved by _D. Fogg_
Date _9/29/xx_

FIGURE 14.5
Purchase Order

Henry Hilson Hotel New York City			Date 10/1/XX	
M A.&C. Suppliers			ORDER # C 267	
Please Ship The Following Supplies VIA Your Truck.				
Quantity	Size	Item	Price	Amount
6 cases	750 ml	Old Crow	$95.00	$570.00
2 cases	750 ml	Beefeater Gin	105.00	210.00
				$780.00
			Ordered by	T. C. Chen

Obviously not all establishments follow such detailed purchasing routines. Nevertheless, written records reduce misunderstandings and disputes, and, it is advisable in all instances to maintain some written record of purchases, preferably on a purchase order, to compare with the goods delivered. Written purchase orders eliminate disputes over brands and quantities ordered, prices quoted, and delivery dates. Because the purchase of alcoholic beverages involves the outlay of considerable amounts of cash, it is wise to establish a system such as the purchase order method to reduce or eliminate the possibilities for error.

In many establishments when state law permits, salespeople call on the buyer, and it is common for purchase requests to be made on the basis of these meetings. In some states, dealers offer special discounts from time to time, and a buyer can frequently save a considerable amount by taking advantage of them. In addition, in locations where prices are allowed to fluctuate, this kind of procedure enables the buyer to list a quoted price on the purchase request. By listing a particular dealer's name, in states where this is possible, some of the purchasing work is simplified.

TRAINING FOR PURCHASING

Training an employee means teaching her to perform her job in the manner expected by management. It should be obvious that this can best be done if standard procedures for the job have been established. It is, after all, comparatively easy to train someone to follow an established system; it is virtually impossible to train someone if there is no system to follow.

If management has established standard procedures for beverage purchasing—the periodic method, or the perpetual method, or some other method more appropriate for a given operation—it should be possible for an intelligent and willing manager to explain the standard procedures to the employee who is to follow them. In most operations, this must be done at the work site during the course of the normal working day; few but the largest corporations can set up extended training periods for employees away from their jobs. The training must be carried out on the job, but some time must be set aside when trainer and trainee can concentrate on the task.

The following represents one typical approach. On a day when orders are normally to be placed, trainer and trainee work together in the beverage storage area to determine the proper quantities of the various beverages to purchase. The trainer explains in general terms how the job is to be done and then determines the purchase quantities for the first few beverages to be considered. He does this slowly, explaining each step in detail. The trainee is encouraged to ask as many questions as necessary; as the trainer answers the questions, he uses them to evaluate the extent of the trainee's comprehension. When the trainer judges the trainee to be ready, the trainee be is asked to determine the purchase quantity for the next beverage item alone. The accuracy of trainee's work and the trainer's judgment about the trainee's progress dictate the next step. The trainer might have the employee continue with the work; he might also explain one or more steps again. Finally, the trainer and the trainee arrive at a point at which both are confident of the latter's ability to perform the job as required by management. This might take a comparatively short time, depending on the intelligence, ability, and previous experience of the employee, or a very long time, and the trainee may ultimately be unable to master the job.

Training employee in an operation to follow the standard procedures established for her job can be tedious and time-consuming. However, without that training, management will not have full assurance that employees will perform their jobs in the stipulated manner.

MONITORING PURCHASING PERFORMANCE AND TAKING CORRECTIVE ACTION

Once training has been completed and the employee begins to do the job for which he has been trained, management must monitor performance. With beverage purchasing, there are a number of possibilities for monitoring.

One way of monitoring, which is *not* recommended, is to assume that the employee is doing the right job unless the manager's attention is called to some problem or situation that clearly indicates the contrary. For example, one might learn that there was no pouring gin left in the beverage storeroom, a clear sign that standard procedures for beverage purchasing were not being observed, at least for pouring gin. Most managers would agree that improved monitoring could have prevented this. A better approach is required.

If the periodic order method has been established as the standard procedures for beverage purchasing, a manager would have several means of monitoring employee performance. One possibility would be to create a form for the employee to use when taking inventory is taken on the regular day for determining order quantities and placing orders, as described previously. The employee would be asked to record the inventory count for each item on the form, which would be turned in to management. This provides reasonable assurance that the employee counted units in inventory before determining purchase quantities. This approach could be refined to the development of a worksheet showing, for every item in inventory, par stock, normal usage, amount on hand, and quantity ordered. After orders were placed, the employee would give a copy of this worksheet to a manager, who could quickly evaluate the employee's orders. These are but a few of the possibilities for monitoring performance using the periodic order method.

The perpetual order method also provides many possible means for monitoring. The simplest is to consult the perpetual inventory cards to see that orders have been placed for the proper quantities as items reached their reorder points. These comparisons can be made at any time during the course of an operating period and will quickly reveal an employee's adherence to the standard procedures established.

To the extent that employees are not following the standard procedures established for their jobs, action is required to improve performance. The action selected will vary with the nature of the problem. The possibilities include explaining one or two small points that were misunderstood; completely retraining an employee who misunderstood the entire procedure; and laying off or otherwise disciplining an employee who willfully ignored some or all of the standard procedures established for the job. It is incumbent upon the manager to determine the appropriate action to take in a given situation. However, some action to improve employee performance must be taken, or the job will not be done in the manner expected by management.

COMPUTER APPLICATIONS

Computers can be used to remove much of the tedious work associated with determining purchase quantities for beverages. There are numerous possibilities, determined, in part, by the method selected for purchasing, the periodic or the perpetual.

With the periodic method, it is comparatively simple to use a standard spreadsheet package to develop a worksheet to calculate purchase quantities. As illustrated in Figure 14.6, it requires five columns, the first of which is a list of all the beverages in inventory. The second and third columns list the par stock and normal usage figures for each of the items. The fourth records the quantity on hand for each item, as counted on the order date. The fifth column shows the proper order quantity for each of the items, calculated as column 2 minus column 4. One then prints out the worksheet examines the figures carefully to be sure that the figures in

FIGURE 14.6
Flagg's Bar / Beverage Purchasing Worksheet

Beverage Inventory GINS	Par Stock	Normal Usage	Quantity on Hand	Order Quantity
Beefeater's	18	12	6	12
Booth's	12	8	6	6
Gilbey's	108	72	42	66
Gordon's	54	36	12	42
Plymouth	12	8	8	4
Tanqueray	18	12	2	16

column 3 approximate those in column 5. Significant differences between these two might indicate the need for future adjustments to par stock, usage, or both.

If the perpetual method is in use, the manager would first up a complete perpetual inventory, then add such necessary data as par stock, reorder point, and reorder quantity. A database package would be excellent for this. Once the perpetual inventory was established, it would be necessary to input all purchases and issues to maintain currency. Each day, after current data has been input, one would request a report showing the items that had reached reorder point. These would be the items for which orders should be placed.

Regardless of whether one uses the periodic or perpetual method, it would be possible to input and store all purchase data and develop a variety of reports showing total purchases of each inventory item in units, dollars, or both, totals for categories of items, such as gins or Italian wines, and so on. The information would be of great value for analysis and planning.

CHAPTER ESSENTIALS

In this chapter, we defined beverages, distinguished between alcoholic and nonalcoholic beverages, and classified beverages into four categories: beers, wines, spirits, and mixers. We described basic methods for producing each of the three classes of alcoholic beverages and described the differences among them. We discussed the quality, quantity, and price standards required to establish control over beverage purchasing and identified the principal factors governing the establishment of these standards. We described two common standard procedures for determining purchase quantities and the most common standard procedure for processing purchase requests. We discussed one typical approach to training purchasing employees and several methods for monitoring their performance. We outlined several possible means for correcting deviations from standards. Finally, we described several possible uses of computers for beverage purchasing.

KEY TERMS IN THIS CHAPTER

Beverage   Blush wines

Beers   Proof

Wines   Liqueur

Spirits   Mixer

Fermentation   Call brand

Distillation   Pouring brand

Aging   Control state

Varietal wines   License state

Generic wines   Periodic order method

Brand-name wines   Perpetual order method

Geographic wines   Par stock

Sparkling wines   Reorder point

Fortified wines   Reorder quantity

Wine coolers

QUESTIONS AND PROBLEMS

1. What are the three classifications of alcoholic beverages?

2. What the two broad classifications of beers, and how do they differ?

3. What are the three color classifications of wines?

4. Of what significance is the fermentation process in the making of alcoholic beverages?

5. Define each of the following: varietal wines; brand-name wines; geographic wines; generic wines; sparkling wines; fortified wines; wine coolers; blush wines.

6. What is the distillation process?

7. In the United States, what percentage of alcohol is found in a 100-proof bottle of vodka? in a 90-proof bottle of gin? in an 86-proof bottle of bourbon?

8. How do liqueurs differ from other spirits?

9. Explain the importance of fixing responsibility for beverage purchasing, and the identify the person(s) responsible for that job.

10. Distinguish between call brands and pouring brands.

11. What are the primary purposes of establishing beverage purchasing controls?

12. What considerations should a beverage operator take into account in establishing quality standards for the purchase of beverages?

13. List and explain the principal factors used to establish quantity standards for beverage purchases.

14. Distinguish between a license state and a control state.

15. Name the two principal methods for determining order quantities and state the principal differences between them.

16. a. Given the following information, determine the proper order quantity for each item if the periodic order method is used.

Item	Par Stock	Usage	Quantity On Hand
Smirnoff Vodka	72	48	24
Gordon's Gin	36	24	3
Jack Daniels	5	3	4
Canadian Club	9	6	4
Dewar's White Label	36	24	10

   b. Should any adjustments to par stock or usage figures be considered for any of the listed beverages? Which? Why?

17. The new manager of a nearby hotel plans to do the beverage purchasing for her property using the perpetual inventory method. She wants to reorder the items listed below approximately every two weeks and plans to use a safety factor of 50% for calculating par stock and reorder point. Delivery requires six days. Storage space is ample. Given the daily usage figures below, determine par stock, reorder point, and reorder quantity for each item:

Item	Daily Usage
Gilbey's Gin	4
Relska Vodka	8
Ron Rico Light Rum	2
Cutty Sark Scotch	3
Bushmill's Irish	1

18. The training director of a large hotel is due to begin training a new employee to fill out purchase request forms (illustrated in Fig. 14.4) daily for those items in the perpetual inventory of beverages that have just reached reorder point. The employee has been trained as a bartender but has never before worked with a perpetual inventory.

   a. Describe in detail one suitable step-by-step procedure for the training director to follow.

   b. How could the beverage manager monitor the job performance of this new employee after the training period?

For Computer Users

19. Using any spreadsheet package of your choice, devise a worksheet for Question 16 above.

20. Set up a spreadsheet to complete Question 17 above.

chapter 15

Beverage Receiving, Storing, and Issuing Control

Learning Objectives

After reading and studying this chapter, the student should be able to:

1. Identify the objectives of receiving, storing, and issuing controls for beverages.
2. List and explain the various standards necessary for establishing control over the receiving, storing, and issuing of beverages.
3. Describe the standard receiving procedure for beverages.
4. Identify the beverage receiving report and explain its use.
5. Describe two ways of maintaining security in beverage storage facilities.
6. Explain the measures employed to organize beverage storage facilities.
7. Describe the significance of temperature, humidity, light, handling techniques, and storing methods on the shelf life of beverages.
8. List the three types of bars and describe their differences.
9. Define a requisition system and describe its use in beverage control.
10. Compare training methods and techniques for receiving, storing, and issuing used in small beverage operations with those used by large organizations.
11. List and describe three means of monitoring the performance of employees responsible for receiving, storing, and issuing beverages.
12. Discuss the use of computers in beverage receiving, storing, and issuing control.
13. Define each of the key terms listed at the end of the chapter.

As was illustrated in preceding chapters, establishing control over any phase of a food and beverage operation is dependent upon application of the four-step control process. The previous chapter presented some of the common standards and standard procedures established by owners and managers to gain control over the beverage purchasing function to ensure that adequate quantities of beverages of the proper quality are purchased at optimum prices.

When a beverage manager selects particular qualities and quantities of beverages and places orders at particular prices, he is, in effect, identifying the cost of the beverages that will be served in the establishment. By placing orders, he is accepting those costs, and they may be viewed as planned or budgeted costs. It is therefore clearly in the interest of the enterprise to take appropriate steps to ensure that no unwarranted, unbudgeted costs develop before the beverages are sold to customers.

In this chapter, we will examine the application of control process to three critical areas of beverage operations in which excessive costs can develop: receiving, storing, and issuing. We will begin by describing standards and standard procedures for each of these areas.

RECEIVING

Establishing Standards

The primary goal of receiving control is to ensure that deliveries received conform exactly to orders. In practice, this means that deliveries must be compared to orders placed with respect to quantity, quality, and price. The standards established for receiving are quite simple:

1. The quantity of an item delivered must equal the quantity ordered. This may simply require the counting of bottles or cases, but it might involve weighing kegs of beer to verify the standard of fill or checking container sizes to ensure that containers of the size ordered have been received.

2. The quality of an item delivered must the same as the quality ordered. With wine, this may require verifying vintages or checking bottling dates of wines that are best when young. With beer, it may require checking bottling or canning dates to ascertain freshness. With spirits, as with wines and beers, one would check to be certain that the brand delivered was the same as the brand ordered.

3. The price on the invoice for the item delivered should be the same as the price quoted or listed when the order was placed.

Because the standards for receiving beverages are reasonably straightforward, any honest individual of reasonable intelligence and ability can be trained for the job.

Establishing Standard Procedures

Standard procedures must be established to ensure that standards will be met. In order to meet receiving standards, many operators have established a standard receiving procedure for beverages consisting of the following steps:

1. Maintain an up-to-date file of all beverage orders placed. Depending on the operation, these orders may be formal or informal or some combination of the two. Large hotels, for example, often use a formal purchase order system. By contrast, the only record of an order in a small establishment may be some notes taken during a telephone conversation between the owner and a salesperson. Regardless of the size of an establishment, there can be no effective receiving procedure without written records of the orders placed, and the receiving clerk must have these records available.

2. Remove the record of the order from the file when a delivery arrives and compare it to the invoice presented by the delivery driver to verify that quantities, qualities, and prices on the invoice conform to the order. (Fig. 15.1 illustrates a typical beverage invoice.)

3. Complete the following verifying steps in the presence of the delivery driver before he leaves the premises:

    a. Check brands, dates, or both, as appropriate, to verify that the quality of goods delivered conforms to the invoice.

FIGURE 15.1
Beverage Invoice

ABC SUPPLIERS
427-83 Front Street
Nearville, NY

TO: **Henry Hilson Hotel**   **Invoice No**
    East River Plaza   **639-A142**
    New York City

Date	Order No.	Acct. No.	Terms	Ship Via
10/3/XX	C267	H108	C. O. D	Truck

Item No.	Quantity Ordered	Quantity Shipped	Package	Unit	Description	Unit Price	Total Price
3628	6	6	case	750 ml	Old Crow	$95.00	$570.00
27441	2	2	case	750 ml	Beefeater's	$105.00	$210.00
					TOTAL		$780.00

    b. Count or weigh goods delivered to verify that the quantity received also conforms to the invoice.

4. Call to the attention of both management and the delivery driver any broken or leaking containers or bottles with broken seals or missing labels.

5. Note all discrepancies between delivered goods and the invoice on the invoice itself. Call to management's attention immediately any discrepancy between an order and the delivery. Such discrepancies may require management to decide whether to accept delivery of the questionable items.

6. Sign the original invoice to acknowledge receipt of the goods, and return the signed copy to the driver. Retain the duplicate copy for internal record keeping.

7. Record the invoice on the beverage receiving report, as discussed below.

8. Notify the person responsible for storing beverages that a delivery has been received.

Beverage Receiving Report

In many establishments, a **beverage receiving report** is filled out daily by the person responsible for receiving beverages. The beverage receiving report can take any of several forms, one of which is illustrated in Figure 15.2. It summarizes the invoices for all beverages received on a given day, indicates both quantities received and their values, and provides columns for dividing purchases into essential categories—wines, beers, spirits, and mixers—for purchase journal distribution. In states that require deposits on bottles and cans of beers and mixers the beverage receiving report provides columns for recording the charges and credits attributable to such deposits. The need for separating purchases into these categories will be evident in Chapter 17, on costs and management reports.

Filling out the beverage receiving report is a comparatively simple matter, merely requiring that essential data be transferred from the invoice to the Report. Figures 15.1 and 15.2 show how this is done. Because the beverage receiving report is an accounting document, its specific makeup will vary considerably from place to place, depending on the nature and degree of complexity of the accounting practices in effect. However, it is generally desirable to establish a separate receiving report for beverages and then to design a report form tailored to an individual establishment's needs. In the case of beverages received, it is generally good practice to require not only that the receiving clerk sign a daily report but that the wine steward sign it as well, thus acknowledging receipt of the beverage items listed on the report.

FIGURE 15.2
Beverage Receiving Report

HENRY HILSON HOTEL
BEVERAGE RECEIVING REPORT

Date: 10/3/XX

Distributor	Item	Quantity Received	Package	Unit Size	Package Cost	Total Cost	PURCHASE JOURNAL DISTRIBUTION			
							Wines	Beers	Spirits	Mixers
ABC Suppliers	Old Crow	6	case	750 ml	$95.00	$570.00			$570.00	
ABC Suppliers	Beefeater	2	case	750 ml	$105.00	$210.00			$210.00	
Blue Distrib.	Budweiser	12	case	12 oz	$11.95	$143.40		$143.40		
Canada Dry	Tonic	7	case	8 oz	$9.00	$63.00				$63.00
Krumpf Imports	Moselle	4	case	750 ml	$60.00	$240.00	$240.00			
Krumpf Imports	Chateau Rue	2	case	750 ml	$105.00	$210.00	$210.00			
TOTALS						$1436.40	$450.00	$143.40	$780.00	$63.00

Prepared by: _Joe Blott_

STORING

Establishing Standards

Storing control is established in beverage operations in order to achieve several important objectives:

1. To prevent pilferage.
2. To ensure accessibility of products when needed.
3. To maintain product quality.

In order to accomplish these objectives, standards must be established. The following standards are critical to effective storing control:

1. To prevent pilferage, it is clearly necessary to make all beverage storage areas secure. To establish the proper degree of security, access to storage areas must be restricted to authorized individuals, and steps must be taken to guard against unauthorized use of beverages by those who are permitted access to the storage areas.

   Alcoholic beverages are among the items in a hotel or restaurant that are most highly sought after by those who are inclined to steal. Unless appropriate steps are taken, beverage products disappear. There are many reasons for this, including the dollar value of the products, alcohol addiction, and impulsive behavior, among others.

2. To ensure accessibility of products when needed, the storage facility must be organized so that each particular beverage product can be found when needed. In practice, this means assigning a specific storage location—shelf or bin number—to each item in the beverage inventory.

   Once appropriate supplies of beverage products have been purchased, it is important that they be stored in such a way that they can be found readily in order to be issued when needed.

3. To maintain product quality, each item in the beverage inventory must be stored appropriately: under conditions that will maximize its shelf life. This will require taking into account such important elements as temperature, humidity, and the manner in which items are stored.

   While the quality of spirits will not be adversely affected in storage under most conditions, wines and beers are subject to rapid deterioration if improperly stored.

Establishing Standard Procedures

In order to achieve any standards, standard procedures are required. The standard procedures required to achieve control over the storing of beverages normally include the following:

Procedures to Make Beverage Areas Secure

All beverages must be stored in secure facilities. Because beverage products are so prone to pilferage, it should be obvious that keeping them in a secure facility is an urgent requirement.

There are two ways to maintain the necessary degree of security. The first is to assign one person the responsibility for guarding the stored items. This can mean literally keeping watch over them. This is done in some operations by assigning a steward to work in the storage facility, maintaining the stock and issuing beverages as needed. Typically, this steward is the only person permitted in the facility, except for authorized managers. In operations that are open for long hours, this responsibility may be shared by two or more persons working different shifts, or the hours for storing and issuing beverages may be restricted so that one person can be held accountable for the beverage inventory.

The second way to maintain security is to keep the beverage storage facility locked and to issue a single key to one person who will be held accountable for all beverages in the inventory. The person with the key would be required to open the lock and issue the needed beverages. If she were not available, some provision would be required for obtaining the needed beverages: one or more other persons would have to be provided with the means of gaining access to the beverage storage facility.

The difficulty with both of these procedures is, of course, that the responsible person is not likely to be available twenty-four hours a day. At some point, the storage facility would be inaccessible, and no one would be able to obtain items that might be urgently needed. One way to prepare for this eventuality is to place a second key in a safe or some similar secure location and require that anyone who uses it sign for it and write a short explanation of its use. Some managers require both an explanation and a list of the items removed from the facility. However, making a second key available reduces both the degree of security and the possibility of fixing responsibility. In general, the common standard procedure is to keep the number of keys to the minimum management deems appropriate for efficient operation and maximum security. If there is more than one key, or more than one person has access to the single key, it is normally advisable to change locks frequently to minimize the possibility that some persons may obtain and use duplicate keys. It is also advisable to change locks when a worker with access to the beverage storage facility leaves the employ of the establishment.

Some large operations, principally hotels, take the additional precaution of installing closed-circuit television cameras to keep various facilities under observation. These would include the doors to beverage storage areas. A guard in some remote area would be responsible for observing traffic into and out of the area on a monitor. As an alternative, activity in the area might be recorded on videotape for later monitoring.

Another means of monitoring is to install special locks that print on paper tape the times at which the doors on which they are installed are unlocked and relocked, thus telling management exactly when the door to the facility was unlocked and how long it remained so. This is less costly than a closed-circuit television system, but it provides less information.

Maintaining the security of the beverage inventory is a clear imperative for any hotel or restaurant that requires continual vigilance and careful monitoring.

Procedures to Organize the Beverage Storage Facility

Ensuring accessibility means storing beverage products in an organized manner, so that each stored item is always kept in the same place and thus can readily be found when needed. The physical arrangement of the storage area is important. Like items should be kept together. All gins, for example, should be kept in one area, rye whiskies in another, and scotch whiskies in a third. This kind of arrangement simplifies finding an item when needed. It is helpful, too, for a floor plan of the storage area to be affixed to the door, so that authorized personnel can easily locate items.

One way of ensuring that items will always be found in the same location is to institute the use of bin cards like the one illustrated in Figure 15.3. The **bin card**, a standard form available from stationery suppliers, is affixed to the shelf and serves as a label. It lists pertinent information concerning each item—type of beverage, brand name, and bottle size. It also may include provision for an identification number. Some establishments assign each beverage item a code number from a master list (see Fig. 15.4) and record that code number on the bin card. In many instances, the number is stamped by a mechanical stamping device on each bottle received.

This technique serves several purposes. In the case of wines, many of whose names are not easily pronounced or spelled, it simplifies ordering by both

FIGURE 15.3
Bin Card

Item Old Crow				Stock Number 153			
Date	In	Out	Balance	Date	In	Out	Balance
10/1			4				
10/3		1	3				
10/7		1	2				
10/11		1	1				
10/12	4		5				

FIGURE 15.4
Illustration of Beverage Code Numbers

Sample Numbering Code for Wines, Spirits, and Beers

American Whiskies: 100 series
  Blended Rye: 100–139
  Straight Rye: 140–149
  Bourbon: 150–179
  Sour Mash: 180–189

Imported Whiskies: 200 series
  Scotch: 200–239
  Canadian: 240–249
  Irish: 250–259
  Other: 260–269

Gins & Vodkas: 300 series
  Gins: domestic 300–329
      imported 330–349
  Vodka: domestic 350–379
        imported 380–399

Rums and Brandies: 400 series
  Rum: 400–449
  Brandy: domestic 450–459
        imported: 460–479
  Cognac: 480–499

Cordials and Liqueurs: 500 series

Red Wines: 600 series

White wines (still): 700 series

Other Wines: 800 series
  Sparkling, Rosé, Dessert, Aperitif

Beers and Ales: 900 series

customers and employees. In many instances, wine lists are printed with bin numbers. This is frequently a boon to wine sales, which can be highly profitable.

In the case of all alcoholic beverages, this technique provides an additional measure of control. The number stamped on each bottle identifies the bottle as the property of the establishment. Thus, an employee cannot claim a bottle as personal property if one is found in his possession. In addition, empty bottles can be checked for numbers before they are replaced by full bottles, thus ensuring that no one is bringing empties in from outside and using them to get bottles from the establishment's stores.

The use of bin cards also permits the wine steward to maintain her own perpetual inventory record of quantities on hand. By using this card carefully to record the number of units received as they are placed on the shelves, as well as the number of units issued as they are given out, the wine steward has a way of determining the balance on hand without counting bottles. In addition, the wine steward who carefully maintains such records has a way of determining that bottles are missing so that this important fact can be brought immediately to management's attention.

Internally, the storage area should be kept free of debris that can pile up as the result of emptying cases and stocking shelves. Once opened, cases should be completely emptied. All units in a case should be stored on the appropriate shelf and the empty carton removed at once. Control must be exercised to ensure that some personnel do not remove cartons that are not completely empty.

Procedures to Maximize Shelf Life of Stored Beverages

Procedures for maximizing the shelf life of stored beverages may be divided into two categories: temperature, humidity, and light in the storage facilities; and the manner in which bottles and other containers are handled and shelved.

Temperature, Humidity, and Light in the Storage Facilities   For every beverage product, there is a temperature range appropriate for storage. For some, the range is extremely broad; for others it is quite limited. Spirits, for example, can be stored indefinitely at normal room temperatures without deterioration of product quality. If necessary, they can be stored well above or well below room temperatures for considerable periods. As long as the storage temperature does not become extreme, they will not suffer loss of quality. On the other hand, carefully controlled storage temperatures are critical for maintaining the quality of beers and wines, and the problem of maintaining product quality for these items is complicated by the fact that various wines and beers require different treatments, depending on how they were made and the containers in which they are purchased.

It is normally advisable to learn from the maker, brewer, or distributor of each specific brand the temperature range recommended for the proper storage of the product. As a general rule, red wines should be stored at about 55° F. White wines and sparkling wines should be kept at slightly lower temperatures. Pasteurized beers can be stored for limited periods at normal room temperature without great harm, but they are normally kept under refrigeration, closer to the temperature at which they will be served. However, beer that has once been chilled should be kept chilled thereafter to maintain quality. Unpasteurized beers, including all draft and some bottled and canned beers, should be kept at about 40° F. to reduce the risk of deterioration.

The degree of moisture in the air is of significance only for those beverages purchased in corked bottles. In general, most beverages in corked bottles are wines, and the better the wine, the more likely the bottle is to have a cork rather than a screw top. Low humidity will cause corks to dry out, thus permitting air to reach the wine or other product, and product quality is likely to suffer. Thus, wines are likely to be stored either in rooms that are naturally cool and damp, or in special facilities, such as refrigerated rooms, where both temperature and humidity can be controlled.

Bottled wines and beers should be kept away from light, which adversely affects product quality. Natural light is more harmful than artificial, but all light will affect these products.

Vintners and brewers package their products in colored glass bottles, commonly dark green or dark brown, to minimize the negative effects of light. However, while the dark glass reduces the impact, it merely slows the inevitable deterioration light will cause if these products are not properly stored.

Shelving and Handling Bottles and Other Containers   Spirits can be stored upright on horizontal shelves for unlimited periods. Wines and other corked beverages cannot safely be so stored; if they are to be kept for any length of time, they must be stored on their sides, parallel to the floor. There are special racks designed to store wines in the proper position. In this position, the beverage in the bottled is kept in constant contact with the cork, helping to keep the cork moist and thus keeping the bottle tightly sealed.

Canned and bottled beers are not usually shelved at all. They are delivered in cases and are stored in those cases. The cases are typically stacked in the storage facility to save space. Handling is an important factor in maintaining the quality of beers and wines. Once wines are positioned in their racks, they should be handled with care. Many wines, especially finer reds, develop a natural sediment that settles in the bottle. If the bottle is improperly handled, this sediment will be dispersed through the wine, destroying its clarity and rendering it unpalatable. For all practical purposes, the wine becomes unusable until the sediment has resettled. Sparkling wines—those containing natural or artificial carbonation—must also be handled carefully for obvious reasons. Beers require careful handling as well. They are carbonated beverages, and shaking will cause them to foam excessively.

ISSUING

Establishing Standards

Issuing control is established in hotel and restaurant beverage operations to achieve two important objectives: to ensure the timely release of beverages from inventory in the needed quantities, and to prevent the misuse of alcoholic beverages between release from inventory and delivery to the bar. It is imperative for management to control the quantities of alcoholic beverages issued and to make sure that issued amounts reach their intended destinations.

To achieve these objectives, management must establish two essential standards for issuing beverages:

1. Issue quantities must be carefully set.
2. All beverages are issued to authorized persons.

By authorized persons, we mean those who have been assigned responsibility for the security of the issued beverages and will be held accountable for their disposition.

Establishing Standard Procedures

In order to ensure that issuing standards will be met, it is necessary to establish appropriate standard procedures for issuing beverages. They are establishing par stock for each bar and setting up a requisition system for ordering.

Establish par stock for each bar

Essentially, there are three kinds of bars:

1. **Front bars**, where bartenders serve the public face to face.
2. **Service bars**, where customers' orders are given to the bartender by waiters and waitresses who serve the drinks to the customer.
3. **Special-purpose bars**, usually set up for one particular event, such as a banquet.

As used in bar operations, the meaning of the term *par stock* is somewhat different from the definition previously given. In storeroom operations, par stock means the maximum quantity that may be on hand at any one time; it is a limit which the quantity on hand should never exceed. In bar operations, **par stock** is the precise quantity, stated in numbers of bottles or other containers, that must be on hand at all times for each beverage at the bar.

For example, the stock of gin should be listed according to brand names; it should include bottle sizes for each, as well as an exact number of bottles that should be at the bar at all times. One particular brand of gin, stocked in 750 ml bottles, might have a par stock of five bottles at a certain bar. This implies that someone could check the stock at any time and expect to find five bottles of that particular brand on hand. Not all would necessarily be full, but at least the number of bottles would be under control.

Obviously, par stocks vary greatly from bar to bar. In every case, however, the par stock figures should be related to quantities used and should be changed from time to time as customer demand varies. Drinks may go in and out of fashion for seasonal as well as for other reasons, and par stocks at the bar should be adjusted to meet customer demand without being overstocked. In addition, since storage space at a bar is limited, the quantity of any item should be limited to the amount necessary to meet no more than two days' demand.

In the case of front bars and service bars, par stocks should be established for each bar. However, this is not possible in the case of special-purpose bars, which present unique problems. When these bars are set up, sufficient stocks must be issued to carry the bartender through the banquet. Typically, the quantities established are greater than needed, and the remainder must be returned to the beverage storeroom at the conclusion of the event.

Set up a requisition system for issuing

A **requisition system** is a highly structured method for issuing goods. In beverage control, a key element in the system is the requisition form, on which both the beverages issued and their quantities are recorded. No bottles should ever be issued without a written requisition signed by an authorized person, often the head bartender.

A very simple requisition form is illustrated in Figure 15.5. In the simplest operations, one type of requisition form is normally sufficient for maintaining the desired degree of control over issues. In complex beverage operations, such as those found in many hotels, several kinds of requisitions may be required for specialized bars.

The requisition form is filled out by either a head bartender or some other authorized person who determines the quantities needed at the bar to replenish the par stock. For a special-purpose bar, the quantities would be those established as the par stock for the specific occasion. The signed and dated requisition is given to a wine steward or beverage storeroom clerk (jobs and titles vary from one operation to another). This person is responsible for obtaining the listed items and quantities from inventory and issuing them to the worker authorized to receive them, normally the person who has signed the requisition. In some establishments, the worker who receives the beverages is required to sign the requisition to acknowledge that she has received all listed items. Later, unit costs are entered on the

FIGURE 15.5
Bar Requisition

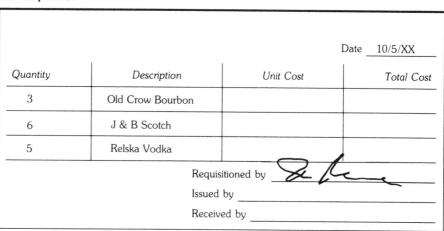

			Date 10/5/XX
Quantity	Description	Unit Cost	Total Cost
3	Old Crow Bourbon		
6	J & B Scotch		
5	Relska Vodka		

Requisitioned by _____

Issued by _____

Received by _____

requisition, which is then extended (each unit cost is multiplied by the number of units to determine the dollar value of the quantity issued). By adding the values of the items issued, the total value of the beverages listed on the requisition is obtained.

Many establishments further their control by requiring that each requisition be accompanied by empty bottles from the bar, so that the units issued replace quantities the bartender has used. When this system is used, a par stock can be maintained at the bar. For example, five bottles of a particular brand of scotch might constitute par stock. When one bottle is emptied, the bartender puts it aside until the end of the night, when it is listed on a requisition form. This form is left for the morning bartender, who sees to it that the empty bottles, together with the requisition on which they are listed, are delivered to the wine steward. The wine steward checks each bottle against the requisition and replenishes the bar stock before the beginning of business. This would bring the stock at the bar back up to par. Such a system ensures a constant and well-controlled supply of beverage items at the bar. In addition, occasional spot checks of par stock against the par stock list would ensure that items are not missing from the bar. This affords an additional measure of control.

Establishments that operate more than one bar must prepare separate requisitions for each, so that bars may be controlled separately. For example, special banquet requisitions are often used that make provision for all bottles issued, whether consumed or returned. An example is illustrated in Figure 15.6.

Such requisitions are often made out by the banquet manager, particularly in hotels. They are given to the wine steward, who issues the items listed in time for the bar to be set up for the event. Provision is made for recording additional issues that may be required. At the end of the event, some other person, such as the beverage controller, checks that all full, empty, and partially used bottles are accounted for. Thus, the correct amount for the quantities actually consumed can be charged to cost, and unused quantities can be returned to stock. Perpetual inventory and bin card entries are made from the Consumed column on the banquet requisition.

Establishments in which most wines are sold by the bottle institute additional procedures for control purposes. In some, small stocks of the most popular wines are maintained at a front or servcie bar to eliminate the need for going to the wine cellar each time a bottle is ordered. Once the bottle of wine is taken form the bar and served to a customer at a table, it is effectively away from the bartender's control. The bartender may not have an empty bottle to turn in with his requisition on the following day to bring his stock up to par. Therefore, many establishments maintain additional control over full-bottle sales by requiring that a form be filled out each time a bottle of wine is delivered to a table. One example is illustrated in Figure 15.7.

Such a form is useful in hotels that serve full bottles of wines and spirits to guests in their rooms, as well as in situations where par stocks of wines are not maintained at the bar and each bottle must come directly from the wine cellar. The

FIGURE 15.6
Banquet Bar Requisition

Function	Lions Club				Bartender	Joe		
Location	Green Room				Date	10/15/XX		

Item	Quantity	Original Issue	Additional Issue	Returns	Con-sumed	Unit Cost	Total Cost
Scotch	2	2					
Gin	2	2					
Vodka	2	2					
Bourbon	1	1					
Canadian	1	1					
S. Vermouth	1	1					
Dry Vermouth	1	1					

Requisition by *B. Berry*

Issued by _____

Received by _____

Returns Checked by _____

FIGURE 15.7
Full Bottle Sales Slip

Date 10/5/XX	Table # 8		Check # 1230	
Code #	Description	Quantity	Size	Cost
602	Chateau LaGrim	1	Full	$95.00

Served by *D. Feat*

Issued by _____

full-bottle sales slip serves as a requisition in such instances. When such a form is used, it is important to require that the server fill it out completely before the bottle is issued to guard against potential problems. When completely filled out, the form provides an excellent means for verifying each sale. It is possible to check them against the guest check numbers indicated and to hold the servers accountable for errors.

TRAINING FOR RECEIVING, STORING, AND ISSUING

In an establishment that offers both food and beverage products for sale, one normally finds fewer employees involved with beverages than with food. In some beverages operations only one person, often the owner, is responsible for all aspects. In such operations, the establishment of control procedures in the usual sense is not a critical concern; the owner, by taking responsibility for all purchasing, receiving, storing, issuing, production, and sometimes sales, is eliminating the need for those control procedures that would be critical to the success of a larger establishment. In this small operation, there may be no training because there are neither employees to train nor control mechanisms.

When the size of an establishment increases to the point at which the owner can no longer perform all tasks alone and it becomes necessary to hire an employee to help, it becomes desirable to set up certain basic work routines. If the new employee can be assigned responsibility for certain specific tasks, the owner can devote time to other tasks that she deems more important, more appropriate, or more complex.

An owner might decide to make the new employee responsible for all beverage receiving, storing, and issuing. The obvious next step would be for the owner to explain the methods and procedures for accomplishing these tasks in an organized manner and in sufficient detail so that the employee could do the work. However, if there are no organized methods and procedures in use, it is necessary for the owner first to establish a certain minimum number so that the new employee can perform the job effectively. Without these standards and standard procedures, little useful training is possible, and it is probably unreasonable to expect an employee to accomplish a job for which he has not been adequately trained.

Before the owner can train anyone, she must define the nature and extent of the job. In small operations, the definition of the job is likely to exist only in the owner's mind. In large, formal organizations, it is probably committed to writing, and is called a **job description**. A job description is a formal definition of a job, including a summary of work to be performed, often accompanied by a list of specific tasks and duties. The more complete the job description, the simpler the task of training, because both trainer and trainee have access to detailed information.

Large organizations typically establish standards and standard procedures in all areas of operation, including the receiving, storing, and issuing of beverages. Many have departments responsible for developing training programs, complete with manuals that include job descriptions, standard procedures, illustrations of forms the employee will be expected to use, and other pertinent information for the new employee. The larger and more complex the organization, the more likely it is that the new employee will be provided with full information about his responsibilities and the employer's expectations.

Regardless of the size of an organization, training cannot proceed effectively without carefully conceived standards and standard procedures. Once these are established, appropriate training programs can be designed to ensure that employees are equipped to carry out the necessary tasks. For receiving, this means being able to maintain up-to-date files of beverages orders; to verify that quantities, qualities, and prices of beverages received conform to the orders placed; and to record necessary information on a beverage receiving report. For storing, it means being able to organize the storage facility; to maintain the beverages appropriately to maximize their shelf life; and to preserve the security of the stored beverages. For issuing, it means being able to fill requisitions properly.

MONITORING RECEIVING, STORING, AND ISSUING PERFORMANCE, AND TAKING CORRECTIVE ACTION.

Unless employees' performance is monitored, management will have less than the desirable amount of information about the extent to which standards and standard procedures are being followed. If, for example, the person responsible for receiving wines fails to count bottles and cases, to check labels and vintages, and to compare invoice prices with order prices, some beverages received may not be the same as those ordered, and some invoice prices may be incorrect. If wines and beers are improperly stored, their shelf life may be minimized, resulting in unsalable beverages and excessive costs. If improper quantities are issued, bars may be inadequately supplied, leading to lost sales. On the other hand, if excessive quantities are issued, pilferage may occur.

It is unwise for management to assume that all employees are performing their jobs correctly. Some amount of auditing is both necessary and desirable. If work is being done carelessly or improperly, it is important that this be discovered as quickly as possible. And even in establishments where management has found employees to be trustworthy and reliable, it is desirable regularly to reconfirm the adequacy of their performance.

There are many possible means for checking employees' performance. Their selection depends on many factors, including the size and complexity of the enterprise, the specific standards and standard procedures established, and the availability of managers to do the monitoring. However, a number of approaches to monitoring beverage receiving, storing, and issuing activities are fairly common.

One technique that is all but universal in organized beverage operations is management's monthly physical inventory of stored beverages. A primary purpose for taking this inventory is to determine cost of beverages sold for the month. At the same time, management can monitor receiving, storing, and issuing procedures by verifying quantities received and issued, checking the organization of the storage facility, and evaluating such considerations as the temperature and cleanliness of the storage area and manner in which the beverages are stored. Checking performance in these areas monthly is basic. Most well-managed operations take additional steps.

The many other possible monitoring techniques for receiving include spot-checking the work of the employee responsible by directly overseeing the work, observing the employee over closed-circuit television, or verifying receiving records before beverages are sent to storage. Similar methods can readily be devised for monitoring storing and issuing by anyone who is familiar with the physical layout of an establishment and its standards and standard procedures.

In beverage operations, corrective action must be taken immediately if monitoring reveals any deviations from the standards.

COMPUTER APPLICATIONS

Increasing numbers of managers are recognizing the extent to which computers can be used to organize and thus to simplify essential record keeping in food and beverage operations. Effective beverage management requires regular maintenance of numerous important records, including orders placed and deliveries anticipated, beverages received and stored, and beverages issued. Computers are particularly useful for these purposes.

If a computer has been used to set up a perpetual beverage inventory (as discussed in Chapter 14), it is necessary to incorporate the computerized inventory into the receiving, storing, and issuing procedures. Once deliveries were received and verified, the quantities received and stored should be added to the perpetual inventory. This could be done from invoices or from the daily receiving report, depending on the system and the procedures established in a given operation. Data from beverage requisitions showing issues from inventory should also be recorded. If all data are recorded in a timely manner, it is simple to check the current quantity of any particular beverage item by viewing the appropriate file on a computer monitor. If necessary, one could print the file for a particular beverage or the perpetual inventory files for all beverages.

No perpetual inventory, whether manually or electronically maintained, is of any value unless the data recorded is both accurate and timely. Any decision to maintain a computer-based perpetual inventory must be accompanied by a commitment to providing the time and staff necessary to update the records carefully and frequently. Daily updates are the most desirable; every other day might be acceptable to some. Infrequent updating tends to make for inaccurate and thus useless records.

CHAPTER ESSENTIALS

In this chapter, we examined the application of control process to the receiving, storing, and issuing phases of beverage operations. We identified management's objectives in establishing control over process and described the standards and standard procedures commonly employed to achieve the stated objectives. For receiving, deliveries received must conform to orders placed in three critical areas: quality, quantity, and price. Standard receiving procedure includes maintaining records of orders placed, verifying that beverages received conform to those orders, and making necessary entries on a receiving report. For storing, the objectives are to prevent pilferage, to ensure product accessibility when needed, and to maintain product quality. Standard storing procedures include assigning responsibility to one person, keeping the storage facility locked when unattended, organizing the storage facility, and maintaining appropriate conditions for temperature, humidity, and light in the facility. For issuing, the objectives are to ensure the timely release of needed quantities and to prevent their misuse between issue from inventory and delivery to the bar. Standard issuing procedures include establishing par stocks for bars and setting up requisition systems to replenish the par stocks.

We described the extent of training in operations of various sizes, indicating the principal differences between small and large establishments. We discussed several approaches to monitoring the performance of employees responsible for receiving, storing, and issuing. Finally, we discussed the updating of data in computer-based perpetual inventory systems as part of receiving, storing, and issuing procedures.

KEY TERMS IN THIS CHAPTER

Beverage receiving report	Special-purpose bar
Bin card	Requisition system
Par stock for bars	Beverage requisition
Front bar	Full-bottle sales slip
Service bar	Job description

QUESTIONS AND PROBLEMS

1. What is the primary goal of receiving control in beverage operations?
2. List and explain the three standards for beverage receiving.
3. Identify the steps in the standard procedure for receiving beverages and explain the importance of each in achieving the primary goal of beverage receiving control.
4. List and explain the three objectives of storing control in beverage operations.
5. Discuss the importance of storeroom security, storeroom organization, and appropriate storage conditions in achieving the objectives of beverage storing control.
6. Describe two methods for maintaining security in the beverage storeroom.
7. What are the purposes of bin cards in beverage storerooms?
8. Explain the reasons for using beverage code numbers.
9. Of what importance is each of the following in a beverage storage facility?
   a. Temperature
   b. Humidity
   c. Light
10. Why should wine bottles normally be stored on their sides?
11. What are the immediate effects of shaking a bottle of fine red wine? A container of beer? A bottle of spirits?
12. Identify the two objectives of issuing control in beverage operations.
13. What standards must be established for issuing beverages to achieve the objectives in Question 12?
14. List and describe the three types of bars.
15. Define the term **par stock** as it is used in bar operations. How does this differ from the definition of par stock used in a storeroom?
16. What is a requisition system?
17. Why are written requisitions necessary in beverage control?
18. What is a full-bottle sales slip, and why is it used?
19. How might training for beverage receiving, storing, and issuing in a small owner-operated bar differ from the training required in a major hotel or restaurant organization?
20. List and describe three means for monitoring the performance of employees responsible for receiving, storing, and issuing beverages.

For Computer Users

21. Using any spreadsheet program of your choice, develop a computer-based beverage receiving report similar to that illustrated in Figure 15.2.

chapter 16

Beverage Production Control

Learning Objectives

After reading and studying this chapter, the student should be able to:

1. Identify the two primary objectives of beverage production control.
2. Describe the standards and standard procedures necessary for establishing control over beverage production.
3. List four devices used to standardize quantities of alcoholic beverages used in beverage production.
4. Describe the role of standardized glassware in beverage control, and the importance of stipulating specific glassware for each drink.
5. Discuss the significance of standard drink recipes in beverage control.
6. Calculate the standard cost of one standard drink, given a recipe and a list of the current market prices of ingredients.
7. Calculate the standard cost-to-sales ratio for one drink, given the standard cost and the selling price.
8. Determine the standard number of straight shots in bottles of various sizes, given the quantity standard for the straight shot.
9. Describe two approaches commonly used to train bartenders to follow established standards and standard procedures.
10. Explain the need for frequent monitoring of bar operations.
11. List four techniques for observing the performance of bartenders.
12. Identify three types of computer programs that can be used by management to maintain standard drink recipes.
13. Define each of the Key Terms listed at the end of the chapter.

Having established standards and standard procedures for purchasing, receiving, storing, and issuing beverages, the next logical step is to establish appropriate standards and standard procedures to control the production of drinks. After all, failure to establish control in this area could lessen the overall impact of the controls carefully designed in the other areas. In addition, neglecting production control can lead to customer dissatisfaction over improperly prepared drinks, as well as to unwarranted costs. Customers, sales, and profits may all be decreased if drinks are produced without control.

Control over beverage production is established to achieve two primary objectives:

1. To ensure that all drinks are prepared according to management's specifications. These specifications for drink production must take into account both the tastes of the expected clientele and management's desire to prepare drinks of appropriate quality and size. After all, a customer who orders a drink often has a preconceived idea of how the drink will taste. The customer orders a daiquiri, for example, because she has enjoyed the taste sensations experienced in the past from the subtle blending of lime juice, sugar, and rum by skillful bartenders. A customer who is served a cocktail that does not meet expectations may be dissatisfied and complain or simply not return. Therefore, any establishment that offers drinks must recognize and accept certain standards of customer expectation and drink preparation, and establish procedures to ensure that these standards will be met.

2. To guard against excessive costs that can develop in the production process.

In order to achieve these objectives, management must establish appropriate standards.

ESTABLISHING STANDARDS AND STANDARD PROCEDURES FOR PRODUCTION

Standards must be established for the quantities of ingredients used in preparation, as well as for the proportions of each ingredient in a drink. In addition, drink sizes must be standardized. When standards are set for ingredients, portions, and drink sizes, the customer has reasonable assurance that the drink will meet expectations each time it is ordered. When these standards are set and enforced by management, they can be held to even in the face of a high rate of employee turnover.

By establishing and maintaining these standards, management also provides a means for controlling costs. When drinks are prepared by formula and served in predetermined portion sizes, each daiquiri prepared should cost the same as every other daiquiri. Because the selling price is fixed, the cost-to-sales ratio for daiquiris should be the same for each daiquiri prepared. If all other drinks also are prepared according to standards appropriate for those drinks, the cost-to-sales ratio for other drinks should also be stable. When this is true, the cost-to-sales ratio for the overall operation should be stabilized, provided that the sales mix does not change greatly.

Simply stated, it becomes possible to develop a standard cost percentage for operation to which the actual cost percentage can be compared. This will be discussed in more detail in the next chapter.

Establishing Quantity Standards and Standard Procedures

One of the first steps in establishing control over production is to standardize the quantities of the most costly ingredients used: the alcoholic beverages. The amounts the bartender uses must be controlled. This involves predetermining the quantities to be used and providing a means of measuring those quantities.

In most beverage operations, the majority of drinks prepared involve combining one kind of liquor with a mixer. Scotch and soda, gin and tonic, rye and ginger ale, and rum and Coke are all examples of this type of drink. Management must determine the quantity of the expensive ingredient: the liquor. The amount varies from bar to bar, from three-quarters of an ounce in some places to as much as two ounces in others. This amount is set in advance by management and should be considered the amount management is willing to give in return for the selling price of the drink. Once the amount is settled, management must provide the bartender with the means for measuring this quantity each time a drink is prepared.*

Devices for Measuring Standard Quantities

There are four commonly used measuring devices: shot glasses, jiggers, pourers, and automated dispensers.

The Shot Glass   In some places, the bartender is provided with small glasses, called **shot glasses**, that are used for measuring. There are two kinds: plain and lined.

Plain shot glasses hold a predetermined quantity when filled to the brim. They are available in a number of sizes, from fractions of an ounce to several ounces. At any given bar, all should be the same size. In many places where these are used, the bartender is told to fill the shot glass and pour the exact measure into the drink. In others, the bartender is provided with shot glasses that hold slightly less than management is willing to give (three-quarters of an ounce, for example, if one ounce is the agreed on measure). The bartender is instructed to pour the three-quarters of an ounce into the drink and then, in view of the customer, add an additional small amount directly from the bottle to the glass. There is a psychological advantage to this method: customers think they are getting more than they are entitled to.

---

* Although wines and spirits are now purchased in metric units, most bars continue to measure and serve in ounces.

A **lined shot glass** is similar to a plain one, but a line is etched in it somewhere below the brim. In some places, the standard of fill is to the line, which is in full view of both the customer and the bartender. Other establishments use shot glasses that have deceptive lines so that when the bartender fills to the line on the inside of the glass, it appears to the customer to go above the line on the outside. This is an optical illusion, but it gives the customer a sense of getting something for nothing. Another variation on the lined-glass approach involves using glasses that hold the standard measure when filled to the brim but have lines etched somewhere below the brim. These are used for the same psychological reasons.

The Jigger   The **jigger** is a double-ended stainless steel measuring device, each end of which resembles a shot glass. They are of different sizes—one may hold 1.0 ounce and the other 1.5 ounces. Many believe the jigger is necessary for the accurate measuring that ensures perfect cocktails. It can be used for measuring straight shots as well, but is more useful for preparing cocktails calling for varying quantities of ingredients. For measuring these drinks, shot glasses are inappropriate. Some cocktails call for such varied measures as one ounce of one ingredient and one-and-one-half ounces of a second. To measure exact quantities of each ingredient, it is necessary to use the jigger.

The Pourer   Another way to control the quantity of liquor used in preparing drinks is by use of a **pourer**, a device that is fitted on top of a bottle and permits the pouring of only a predetermined amount. A number of different types are available, but all operate on the principle of controlling the quantity poured each time the bottle is used. In an establishment where one ounce is the standard measure, the bottles can be fitted with devices that dispense just one ounce. Each time the bartender tips the bottle to pour, exactly one ounce is dispensed. The psychological effect of these pouring devices is widely disputed. Some feel that the customer is given the illusion of the bartender pouring freely; others argue that the customer can feel resentful of management that neither trusts the bartender nor permits an extra drop to be dispensed to the customer. Still others feel that such attachments are useful at a service bar, which customers never see, but should never be used in a front bar, where the customer watches the bartender mix the drink.

The Automated Dispenser   In recent years, numerous companies have developed and successfully marketed various automated devices for dispensing predetermined measures of liquor. These range from comparatively simple systems for controlling only the pouring brands to highly elaborate control systems that not only control ounces but also mix drinks at the push of a button. These complex systems, costing thousands of dollars, are usually connected to a cash register in such a way that the sale is recorded on a guest check as the drink is prepared. In addition, meters record the quantities used and permit elaborate inventory control procedures. Many believe that these systems should be used in service bars but never at front bars except in cases where repeat customers are rare, as in the case of an airport bar.

Free Pour

Another means of measuring quantity is to allow bartenders to **free pour**. In effect, management relies on the experienced bartender to gauge by eye the quantities poured.

Although an experienced bartender can do this with great accuracy, the procedure clearly reduces management's control over the bar operation. In addition, in cases of rapid employee turnover, management is likely to find that it has no control at all over operations. In any bar operation, free pouring is likely to be abused by all but the most dedicated employees, leaving the door wide open for bartenders to operate more for their own advantage than for the general good of the business. However, many owners who permit free pouring seek to offset its disadvantages by raising selling prices to ensure the desired level of profit.

Glassware

In addition to controlling the quantity of liquor used in preparing each drink, it is desirable to control the overall size of the drinks. Standardizing the glassware used for service makes this comparatively simple. It is management's responsibility to predetermine the size of each drink and to provide the bartender with appropriate glassware.

Beverage glassware is available in a wide variety of shapes and sizes. Therefore, management can furnish the bar with particular glassware for particular drinks. For example, stemmed cocktail glasses, holding 2½ ounces, may be used for all cocktails in a particular bar. Because the bartender cannot fill the glass beyond the brim, it is impossible to serve a portion size greater than 2½ ounces without changing glasses or giving the customer a "dividend." By furnishing the bar with 2½ ounce cocktail glassware, directing that all cocktails be served in these glasses, and declaring that no dividend will be given to customers, management can effectively control the portion size. Many fine hotels and restaurants consider the 2½ ounce cocktail glass too small. Management is willing to give a more generous portion for the posted selling price. In such cases, bartenders use lined cocktail glasses—those holding 4½ ounces, with a line etched around the glass indicating a three-ounce measure.

In order to establish effective portion control, then, it is important to purchase glassware in appropriate sizes. Management must determine the kinds of glassware that will be needed (based on present or anticipated clientele and their prefer-ences), then determine portion sizes. The purchasing of glassware must be based on portion sizes determined by management, and bartenders must be instructed what glasses are to be used for serving particular drinks. While a neighborhood bar may be able to get by with just four or five types of glasses of as many sizes, a fine restaurant cannot. Neither can a hotel. Both may require as many as ten to fifteen different types and sizes of glassware for beverage service. Typically, a fine metropolitan hotel or restaurant requires a supply of glassware similar to that listed in Figure 16.1. Samples of common glasses are pictured in Figure 16.2.

Thus, management standardizes portion sizes by purchasing particular glassware for particular purposes and carefully instructing bar personnel in its use. While the standardization of portion sizes helps control beverage costs, that alone is not enough. It is useful to stipulate that a gin and tonic will be served in an eight-ounce glass, yet this alone does not tell bar personnel what part of the standard portion should be gin and what part mixer. This consideration is important in cost control for, after all, the cost of gin is greater per ounce than the cost of mixer, and the relative amounts of each used in making the drink will affect the cost. The following two examples clearly show the difference in the cost of ingredients effected by changing proportions.

Cost of Gin: $.15/oz.   Cost of Mixer:
                                          $.02/oz.

Gin and Tonic A   Gin and Tonic B
Gin—2 oz.   = .30   Gin—1 oz.   = .15
Mixer—6 oz. = .12   Mixer—7 oz. = .14
              .42   .29

FIGURE 16.1

Standard Glassware Sturnley's Restaurant		
Item	Size	Par Stock at Bar
Shot Glass	1.25 oz.	72
Cordial	2 oz.	36
Cocktail	3.5 oz.	72
Cocktail	4.5 oz.	72
Champagne	4.5 oz.	72
Sour	5.25 oz.	72
Rocks	5.5 oz.	144
Brandy	5.5 oz.	36
Wine	8.5 oz.	72
Wine	6.5 oz.	72
Hi-Ball	8 oz.	48
Hi-Ball	10 oz.	144
Pilsner	10 oz.	72

FIGURE 16.2
Standard Glassware for Bars

Shot Glass
1¼ oz.

Cordial
1¼oz.

Whiskey Sour
4½ oz.

Brandy
6 oz.

Cocktail
6 oz.

Old Fashioned
6½ oz.

White Wine
7 3/4 oz.

Hi-Ball
8 oz.

Rocks
8¼ oz.

Red Wine
9 oz.

Footed Pilsner
8 oz.

Tulip Champagne
9 oz.

In both cases, the result is eight ounces of gin and tonic. However, by varying the proportion, the costs differ considerably. If this particular drink is offered at a posted selling price of $2.00, there will be considerable difference between the cost-to-sales ratios as well.

$$\frac{Cost\ .42}{Sales\ 2.00} = Cost\ \%\ 21.0 \qquad \frac{Cost\ .29}{Sales\ 2.00} = Cost\ \%\ 14.5$$

Establishing Quality Standards and Standard Procedures

Standard Recipes

Clearly, if costs are to be controlled, the same control must be established over the proportions of ingredients that go into each drink. In other words, standard recipes must be established so that bar personnel will know how much of each ingredient to use to produce a certain drink.

Generally speaking, bartenders prepare and serve two kinds of drinks that require liquor: straight shots with mixers, such as the gin and tonic, and mixed drinks or cocktails, many of which involve a number of ingredients that must be combined in a certain way for the drink to be right.

In the case of the former, the standard drink is controlled by providing the bartender with appropriate glassware of predetermined size, as well as a jigger or other device for measuring the liquor content. The standard drink size is measured, poured over ice in the right glass, and the glass is then filled with the mixer. In effect, this constitutes the standard recipe. Each time a customer orders a scotch and soda, the bartender places a certain number of ice cubes in the right-sized glass, measures in the standard quantity of the pouring brand of scotch, and fills the glass nearly to the brim with soda. Every scotch and soda prepared in this way will be the same. The customer's second drink will be the same as the first, and on returning to the bar in two weeks, he will receive the same drink for the same price, barring changes in management policy. This is a major factor in establishing customer satisfaction and developing repeat business.

Accomplishing the same end in the case of cocktails is somewhat more complicated. There are often two or more recipes for making any cocktail, the results of which are somewhat different. For example, two different mixing guides might list the following ingredients under recipes for the Manhattan cocktail:

A	B
2-½ oz. blended rye whiskey	1-½ oz. blended rye whiskey
¾ oz. sweet vermouth	¾ oz. sweet vermouth
Dash bitters	Dash bitters

While mixing the ingredients in the prescribed way will produce a Manhattan cocktail in each case, there are substantial differences between them. In cocktail A, the ratio of whiskey to vermouth is 3-to-1; in B, it is 2-to-1. In addition, the recipe A makes a drink that is one ounce larger than the second. Finally, the first costs more to make because it contains an additional ounce of blended rye whiskey.

It is apparent that management must decide which of several recipes will be the standard used to prepare the Manhattan. Similar decisions must be made for all cocktails. While the most frequent approach is to adopt one of the standard recipe guides for use at the bar, it is by no means uncommon, particularly in chain operations, to prepare a special recipe book. In every case, the standard recipe includes not only the measures of alcoholic beverages to be used in preparation but the quantities of all other ingredients, including garnishes, as well as mixing and serving instructions. In some cases, pictures of the drinks are provided to ensure uniformity, particularly in the face of high rates of employee turnover. Figure 16.3 gives examples of typical standard recipes for the Manhattan and the Brandy Alexander, two common cocktails.

The book of standard recipes also provides the bartender with instructions for preparing the unusual cocktails that are requested only on rare occasions. Although a number of bartenders are able to mix virtually any drink requested, many have few occasions to mix a Taxco Fizz, an Opal, or an Earthquake. Thus a standard recipe guide can help ensure the satisfaction of the customer requesting the unusual drink. Although standard bar recipes are a necessity from the point of view of someone interested in control, many bartenders and some managers view them with disdain. In some places, therefore, they are a controversial subject.

FIGURE 16.3
Standard Drink Recipes

Manhattan   S. P. _____

2-1/2 ounces blended rye whiskey
3/4 ounce sweet vermouth
dash of bitters
4 ice cubes
stem cherry

Combine the whiskey, vermouth and ice cubes in a mixing glass and stir well. Strain into a 4-ounce stem cocktail glass. Garnish with the cherry.

Brandy Alexander   S. P. _____

3/4 ounce brandy
3/4 ounce Creme de Cacao
3/4 ounce heavy cream
3 ice cubes

Combine all ingredients in a cocktail shaker and shake vigorously. Strain into a 4-ounce cocktail glass.

It is theoretically possible to establish a standard recipe for every drink served by any bar, indicating the size of the drink and the quantities of each ingredient. As a practical matter, it is not possible to enforce standard recipes in all instances at all bars. One illustration of the problem should suffice.

Most people are familiar with the martini, a cocktail made of gin and dry vermouth, stirred with ice, strained into a cocktail glass, and served garnished with an olive. For some, the best mixture for a three-ounce martini is two ounces of gin to one of vermouth; for others, it is three ounces of gin to one drop of vermouth. And there are an infinite number of variations. Because the bar business seeks to satisfy customer tastes, it is very difficult to set up an inflexible standard recipe for the martini for a particular bar. One single standard recipe might satisfy some customers but make others very unhappy. In many instances, bartenders must be permitted a certain amount of freedom to alter standard recipes, not at their own whims, but at the request of customers. In such cases, the standard recipe should be a kind of average of all the martinis mixed in a certain bar over a period of time.

When standard recipes are established and standard portion sizes have been set, it becomes possible to calculate the standard cost of any drink.

Establishing Standard Portion Costs

Straight Drinks

The cost of straight drinks, served with or without mixers, can be determined by first dividing the standard portion size in ounces into the number of ounces in the bottle to find the number of standard drinks contained in each bottle. This number is then divided into the cost of the bottle to find the standard cost of the drink.

With the introduction of the metric system for beverage packaging, it has become necessary to convert the metric contents of bottles as purchased into their ounce equivalents. A simple table for conversion is shown in Figure 16.4.

For example, the standard portion size for the pouring brand of scotch in a certain bar is 1½ ounces. The bar uses 750 ml bottles of scotch. Figure 16.4 shows that a 750 ml bottle contains 25.4 ounces. Dividing the 1½ ounce standard drink into the 25.4 ounces contained in each bottle, one determines that each bottle contains 16.9 drinks, rounded off to the nearest tenth of a drink.

$$\frac{25.4 \text{ oz.}}{1.5 \text{ oz.}} = 16.9 \text{ Drinks}$$

Because there is a small amount of spillage and evaporation in all bar operations, this can be further rounded off to an average of 16.5 drinks per bottle. If the purchase price of the bottle is $5.55, then each of the 16.5 drinks it contains has a standard cost of $5.55 divided by 16.5, or $.34, when rounded off to the nearest cent.

$$\frac{\$5.55}{16.5} = \$.33636$$

This same bar would normally offer a number of call brands of scotch as well, and the same technique can be used to determine the standard cost of the standard drink of each. In the case of the premium scotch costing $9.20 per 750 ml bottle yielding 16.5 drinks, the standard cost of each drink is somewhat higher.

$$\frac{\$9.20}{16.5} = \$.5575 = \$.56 \text{ per Drink}$$

An alternative procedure for finding the standard cost per drink requires that one divide the cost of the bottle by the number of ounces it contains to find the cost per ounce, then multiplying the ounce cost by the standard drink size. For example, if the pouring brand of gin costs $6.20 per liter, the equivalent of 33.8 ounces, each ounce would cost $.1834, or $.183.

FIGURE 16.4
Relationship of Approved Metric Sizes to U.S. Standards of Fill

DISTILLED SPIRITS			
OLD SIZES *U.S. STANDARDS OF FILL*	*U.S. OUNCES*	*STANDARD METRIC SIZES*	
		LITERS	*MILLILITERS*
Gallon	128		
Half-Gallon	64		
	59.2	1.75	1750
Quart	33.8 32	1.00	1000
Fifth	25.6		
	25.4	3/4 liter	750
3/4 Quart (Cordials)	24		
	17	1/2 liter	500
Pint	16		
4/5 Pint	12.8		
3/4 Pint (Cordials)	12		
Half Pint	8		
	6.8	1/5 liter	200
1/4 Pint	4		
1/8 Pint	2		
	1.7	1/20 liter	50
1/10 Pint (Miniature)	1.6		

(continued)

FIGURE 16.4 (*continued*)

WINES			
OLD SIZES		*STANDARD METRIC SIZES*	
U.S. STANDARDS OF FILL	*U.S. OUNCES*	*LITERS*	*MILLILITERS*
4.9 Gallon	627.2		
3 Gallon	384		
1 Gallon	128		
Jeroboam (4/5 Gallon)	102.4		
	101	3	3000
Half-Gallon	64		
Magnum (2/5 Gallon)	51.2		
	50.7	1.5	1500
	33.8	1	1000
Quart	32		
Fifth	25.6		
	25.4	3/4 liter	750
Pint	16		
4/5 Pint	12.8		
	12.7	3/8 liter	375
1/2 Pint	8		
Split (2/5 Pint)	6.4		
	6.3	3/16 liter	187.5
4 Oz.	4		
	3.4	1/10 liter	100
3 Oz. Miniature	3		
2 Oz.	2		

$$\frac{\$6.20}{33.8 \text{ oz.}} = \$.183$$

This ounce cost, multiplied by the standard 1½-ounce drink size for gin in this particular bar, shows a standard cost for the standard measure of $.2745, or $.27.

1.5-ounce standard Size × $.183 per Ounce = $.27 per Drink

FIGURE 16.5
Standard Costs for Straight Drinks

Bottle Code	Item	Bottle Size ml	Bottle Size oz.	Bottle Cost	Ounce Cost	Drink Size	Drink Cost
201	Old Bagpipe	750	25.4	6.80	.268	1.5 oz.	.40
206	Highland Hiatus	750	25.4	8.45	.333	1.5 oz.	.50
302	Gimby's Gin	1000	33.8	5.84	.173	1.5 oz.	.26

Some who employ this method prefer to divide the bottle size into ounces, but by one ounce less. This has the effect of allowing for the usual evaporation and spillage.

The use of one method rather than another is purely a matter of the preferences of those who perform the calculations. Once these calculations have been performed, the usual practice is to record the results on a form similar to that illustrated in Figure 16.5. These are updated whenever prices change. In this way, up-to-date cost figures are always available for management to use in several ways. One use for the figures is in calculating the cost of mixed drinks and cocktails.

Mixed Drinks and Cocktails

It is particularly important to determine the standard cost of a drink made by standard recipe in the case of cocktails and other mixed drinks. These drinks typically involve several ingredients and often require two or more alcoholic beverages. Consequently, mixed drinks are usually more expensive to make than straight drinks. Knowledge of the cost per drink is important in making intelligent pricing decisions.

To determine the standard cost of cocktails and other mixed drinks and to maintain records of the information, it is useful to obtain a supply of recipe detail and cost forms similar to those illustrated in figures 16.6 and 16.7. Both are used commonly and can be made up either by a printer or by a secretary who has access to a duplicating machine.

The first step in determining the standard cost of the drink is to record on the form all the information from the standard recipe for each drink. It is essential to take into account all ingredients used by the bartender in preparing the drink. The cost of any of these drinks should and does include the cost of all the various nonalcoholic ingredients that are used. Fruit juices, eggs, and heavy cream are but a few of the other ingredients that must be considered. In addition, garnishes for the drinks must be included where appropriate. These might include olives, stem cherries, cocktail onions, and slices of various fruits. To arrive at the true cost of the drink, the cost of all of these must be added to the cost of the basic alcoholic ingredients.

FIGURE 16.6
Standard Recipe / Detail and Cost

Item Martini		Bar Recipe # 53

Selling Price _____$2.00_____
Cost _____$ .42_____
Cost Percentage _____21.0%_____

Ingredients	Quantity	Cost
Gimby's gin	2 oz.	.35
Dry vermouth	1/2 oz.	.05
Martini olive		.02
Totals:	2-1/2 oz.	$.42

Procedure: Pour gin and vermouth into glass mixer. Add cracked ice and stir gently. Pour into 3-oz. cocktail glass. Add olive and serve. Glassware: 3 oz. Cocktail

FIGURE 16.7
Standard Recipe: Detail and Cost

Item: Maurice Cocktail		Bar Recipe: 77	
Date	9/11		
Selling Price	$1.75		
Cost	.31		
Cost Percentage	17.7%		
Bottle Data:			
Date	9/11		
Ingredient Cost			
Gimby's gin	$5.84		
Drink Data:			
Date	9/11		
Ingredient Cost			
Juice of 1/4 orange	.03		
1/2 oz. sweet vermouth	.05		
1/2 oz dry vermouth	.05		
1 oz. gin	.17		
Dash bitters	.01		
Totals	$ .31		

Procedure: Combine all ingredients in glass shaker. Add cracked ice and stir. Strain into 4-oz. cocktail glass.

Standard Glassware _____4-Oz. Cocktail_____

Both the forms given contain space near the bottom for including the standard preparation procedure and the standard glassware. If this information is recorded from the bartenders' guide, management is provided with a complete set of the standard recipes for ready reference, either in a looseleaf book or in a card file.

Once the basic information has been recorded from the standard recipe, it is necessary to find the cost of each ingredient, both alcoholic and nonalcoholic. It is particularly helpful to have the information in a form such as that shown in Figure 16.5. In some large establishments, the beverage controller will have the cost of beverages in perpetual inventory records or in an up-to-date price book.

In some small operations, managers may find it necessary to refer to invoices, receiving sheets, or inventory books. In the case of nonbeverage items, such as the food items transferred from the kitchen, it may be necessary to refer to the relevant transfer memos. In other cases, the steward might be asked for the most recent purchase prices for each item. Here, too, the procedure will vary considerably from place to place. In general, the exact procedure followed is of no particular importance, so long as it results in the correct cost figures for each item in the recipe.

The techniques for recording the data are different from the two forms illustrated. In the first instance, one must calculate the cost of the quantity used before recording any cost information on the form. In the example given (Fig. 16.6), the cost of the two ounces of gin is recorded as $.35. This is determined by referring to the chart in Figure 16.5, which shows that one ounce of the pouring brand costs $.173. This multiplied by the two ounces in the recipe and rounded off to the nearest cent, gives the cost figure to record.

If a form similar to Figure 16.7 is used, the first step is to record the size and cost of a bottle of the pouring brand. In the example shown, the 33.8-ounce bottle of gin is recorded as costing $5.85. The next step is to divide the number of ounces into the cost of the bottle and to multiply the result by the number of ounces of gin in the recipe. This is exactly the same kind of calculating that one would have already performed in compiling the figures illustrated in Figure 16.5.

The only real advantage of the form shown in Figure 16.7 is that it provides space to recalculate drink costs as the costs of the ingredients change. When this form is adopted, it may thus be used for a relatively longer period of time before it becomes necessary to rewrite the cost records.

Once the costs of all ingredients have been determined, the figures are totaled and the result is the standard cost for preparing the drink according to the standard recipe. This cost is recorded at the top on the line provided and divided by the selling price to determine the cost-to-sales ratio for the drink. This is recorded as the cost percentage for that particular drink. If selling prices have not yet been determined, the cost per drink should certainly be one of the chief considerations in arriving at a reasonable figure. Even if selling prices have been set before costs are calculated, all the selling prices should be reviewed in the light of the newly developed cost figures.

Establishing Standard Selling Prices

Once standard costs for standard drinks are known and listed, a similar list of selling prices should be established. One obvious reason for doing this is to enable management to post selling prices at the bar or to list them in a menu, depending on the type of establishment. It is generally good practice to maintain a complete list of standard selling prices in the beverage controller's office. Many of the techniques to be discussed in Chapter 17 depend heavily on selling prices.

The techniques for maintaining such lists of standard selling prices are many and varied. As in so many other cases, the simplest is often the best, and for that reason it is recommended that selling prices for cocktails and mixed drinks be maintained on the recipe detail and cost cards, and the prices for straight drinks be kept on an expanded version of the list first shown in Figure 16.5, which is shown in its expanded form in Figure 16.8.

It is absolutely essential in any bar operation that the selling prices be standardized for each drink sold, for straight drinks as well as for cocktails and other mixed drinks. When selling prices are standardized, customers can be properly charged for the drinks they order, and the prices will not vary from day to day. The possibilities for customer satisfaction are increased, for the customer who has been charged $1.25 for a particular drink on Tuesday has reasonable assurance that an identical charge will be made for the same drink on Wednesday.

FIGURE 16.8
Standard Costs and Selling Prices
Straight Drinks: Scotch

Bottle Code	Item	Bottle Size ml	Bottle Size oz.	Bottle Cost	Ounce Cost	Drink Size	Drink Cost	Drink S.P.
200	Nessie's Blended	750	25.4	5.35	.21	1.5 oz.	.32	1.50
202	Old MacLeod	750	25.4	8.10	.319	1.5 oz.	.48	2.00
203	Purple Heather	750	25.4	8.14	.32	1.5 oz.	.48	2.00
206	Highland Hifios	750	25.4	8.45	.333	1.5 oz.	.50	2.00
207	Grant's	750	25.4	9.20	.362	1.5 oz.	.54	2.00
210	Teacher's	750	25.4	8.90	.35	1.5 oz.	.53	2.00
212	Dewar's White Label	750	25.4	12.10	.476	1.5 oz.	.71	2.50
213	Bell's	750	25.4	14.20	.559	1.5 oz.	.84	2.75

In some places, the list of standardized drink prices is posted on signs over the bar or printed in a menu. Such postings and listings have the additional effect of eliminating many possible arguments over drink prices.

Perhaps the most important purpose behind the standardization of selling prices is the maintenance of a planned cost-to-sales ratio for each drink sold. The drink that costs $.30 when prepared according to standard formula, and that sells for $1.50, has a cost-to-sales ratio of $.30 to $1.50, more commonly expressed as 20%. The sale of each such drink results in the addition of $1.50 to daily sales figures and $.30 to daily cost figures, the net effect being a gross profit on the sale of $1.20. In the case of this particular drink, this is the desired, preplanned effect of each sale. The net effect is not a matter of the bartender's whim; it is planned by management. Ingredients, and consequently costs, are planned. With this in mind, selling prices are set and have a predetermined relationship to the costs. In addition, each sale has a predetermined impact on the operation's overall gross profit. In effect, the profit on each sale is planned when management sets both cost and selling prices. Thus planning and maintaining profit levels becomes possible.

TRAINING FOR PRODUCTION

After management has completed the first step in the control process by establishing the standards and standard procedures necessary for controlling production, it is important to devote appropriate time and energy to the second step: training production employees to follow the standards and standard procedures.

For the purposes of the following discussion, we will assume that the bartenders hired are qualified for their positions by some combination of training and experience. Teaching basic bartending skills will not be required. Training will be restricted to the specific standards and standard procedures established for use in the establishment. It should be noted that many new employees, including bartenders, bring to their jobs methods and procedures learned in previous jobs. To the extent that these are inapplicable, management must see that the necessary retraining is done.

A suitable first step in training in many operations is to show the employee around relevant parts of the establishment, then to focus on the specific station at which he will be working. At this work station, the manager would devote an appropriate amount of time to showing the employee where supplies and equipment are kept. She might then explain the standard procedures established for replenishing supplies. Next, the standards and standard procedures for producing drinks would be explained. These would include such important details as pouring methods, mixing methods, call brands and pouring brands, standard drink recipes, standard drink sizes, standard glassware for drinks, and standard garnishing techniques. The manager would probably explain such additional topics as serving techniques, opening and closing procedures, inventory procedures, and specific rules for registering sales and handling cash, even though these are not formally part of beverage production. This would be done at a time when it would not interfere with normal business, and the bartender would be given ample opportunity to ask questions.

The difficulty with this approach to training is its heavy reliance on the memories of both trainer and trainee. The trainer may forget to include some topics; the trainee may not remember every one of the many topics covered in the short training period. To reduce these problems, many large organizations employ specialized personnel to prepare manuals that specify the standards and standard procedures established for each job in the organization, including bartending. In such organizations, a manual is given to the new employee as the job is explained, and the employee keeps the manual for study and for reference. This approach reduces the need for quick memorization on the part of the trainee and helps eliminate the possibility that the trainer will neglect important topics. Such manuals provide the additional advantage of enabling management to standardize both training and job performance in all units of the organization.

MONITORING PRODUCTION PERFORMANCE AND TAKING CORRECTIVE ACTION

Once standards and standard procedures for beverage production have been established and employees have been suitably trained, management can and must institute the final steps in control process in the production phase of the beverage operation: monitoring employee performance, and taking corrective action as needed.

Before discussing the specifics of monitoring performance in this area, we should note that bar operations present unique opportunities for employees to deviate from established standards and standard procedures without management becoming aware until well after the fact. For example, a bartender who has been instructed to pour 1¼ ounces for a straight shot may instead pour 1½ ounces for many customers for as much as a month—one full accounting period—before management obtains information suggesting that excessive costs have developed in the beverage area. The bartender may have simply misunderstood instructions or may be pouring the larger shots purposely to increase tips. In either event, beverage costs will be excessive, but this fact will not be known until cost figures are determined and investigation can locate the cause. This is but one example of numerous possible deviations that can best be noted quickly through observation. More complete discussion of other possible deviations and methods for detecting them will be found in Chapter 17.

One common approach to monitoring beverage production is to observe the activities of the bartenders as they proceed with their daily work. The frequency of the observations may range from continual to occasional, depending on management's perception of need. Some employees—those whose honesty, ability, or willingness to accept training is open to question—should probably be observed frequently. In making these frequent observations, management attempts to determine the type of corrective action, if any, that may lead to improvement in performance. Other employees, whose loyalty, interest, honesty, and openness to follow standards and standard procedures have been demonstrated amply in their daily work, need be observed far less frequently. At most, management will spot check their work to confirm previous evaluations. When, from time to time, the spot check suggests that performance has fallen below its previous acceptable level, management will find it prudent to focus attention more closely on the particular employee and increase the frequency of observation.

A principal task in monitoring beverage production is to select the means of observing employee performance. There are four possible techniques:

1. The manager observes bar operations on a regular basis.
2. A designated employee, such as a head bartender, observes others working at the bar and reports deviations from standard procedures to management.
3. Persons unknown to the bartenders may be hired to patronize the bar, observe the employee, note deviations, and report to management.
4. Closed-circuit television systems may be installed to permit observation of bar operations from a remote location.

By using one or more of these techniques, management has at its command a reasonable means of assessing employee performance and uncovering operating problems. However, we are not suggesting that the manager of any bar operation can maintain perfect control merely by adopting these techniques. As Chapter 17 will show, the opportunities for employees purposely to deviate from established standards are too many and too varied to be discovered by mere observation.

COMPUTER APPLICATIONS

Computers can be used in beverage production control to maintain standard drink recipes and to determine standard costs for drinks. If maintaining standard recipes were the only objective, one could do so with any simple word processing program. One method would be to treat each standard drink as a document, give it an appropriate file name, and store it on a hard disk or a diskette. The individual documents could be loaded, edited if necessary, the filed or printed, depending on need. Alternatively, all standard recipes could be filed together as one document, which would make it easier to print all of them at once for use in training.

A more practical approach would be to maintain the standard recipes with one of the two more flexible programs—spreadsheet or database. Both permit the user to print the recipes for training and would offer such other useful possibilities as determining standard costs of drinks and updating standard costs when ingredient costs changed. With both the spreadsheet and database programs, all the information could be filed and printed selectively. For example, management would certainly want bartenders to have the recipes, but would probably not want to give them cost data. Using the "report" function common to spreadsheet programs, the computer could be directed to print that portion of the spreadsheet containing the recipe, but not the portion containing the cost information. Using a database would permit an even greater degree of flexibility.

Whether using a word processing program, a spreadsheet, or a database program, maintaining standard recipes in a useful manner is both simpler and easier with a computer.

CHAPTER ESSENTIALS

In this chapter, we identified the two primary objectives for establishing beverage production control: to ensure that all drinks are prepared according to the management's specifications, and to guard against the development of excessive production costs. We described the standards and standard procedures commonly established to achieve these objectives, discussing the meaning and significance of measuring devices, pouring and other dispensing techniques, and standard recipes. We identified methods for determining standard costs for straight drinks and for mixed drinks, including cocktails, and explained the importance of determining standard costs as one basis for establishing selling prices. We described common methods for training bartenders to follow established standards and standard procedures and discussed the importance of monitoring employee performance at bars. We identified four monitoring techniques used to observe employee performance and cautioned against total reliance on these as the sole means of controlling production. Finally, we suggested several ways that computers can be used to maintain standard drink recipes.

KEY TERMS IN THIS CHAPTER

Shot glass	Mixed drink
Lined shot glass	Cocktail
Jigger	Mixer
Pourer	Standard drink recipe
Free pouring	Standard drink cost
Straight drink	Standard selling price

QUESTIONS AND PROBLEMS

1. Identify the two primary objectives of beverage production control.
2. List four devices used to standardize quantities of alcoholic beverages used in beverage production.

3. For what purposes are standard drink recipes established?

4. Why are standard selling prices necessary?

5. The cost of the liquor in a certain drink is $.18 per ounce and the cost of the mixer is $.03 per ounce. Determine the cost of the drink in the following cases.

   a. One ounce of liquor and six ounces of mixer are used.

   b. 1½ ounces of liquor and seven ounces of mixer are used.

   c. Two ounces of liquor and six ounces of mixer are used.

6. In each of the examples in Question 1 above, determine selling price if:

   a. A desired liquor cost of 20% is used.

   b. A desired liquor cost of 25% is used.

   c. A desired liquor cost of 18% is used.

7. In a certain drink, a one-ounce shot of liquor is used, which represents the entire cost of the drink. How much does the drink cost if a one-liter bottle of the liquor costs $5.76?

8. If the desired cost-to-sales ratio is 20% for a certain drink, determine the selling price if a 1½ ounce shot is used and the cost of the liter of liquor is $8.00.

9. If the desired cost-to-sales ratio is 20% for a certain drink, determine the selling price if a 1½ ounce shot is used and the cost of the liter of liquor is $6.40.

10. If the desired cost-to-sales ratio is 25% for a certain drink, determine the selling price if a 1½ ounce shot is used. The cost of the liter of liquor is $6.72 and the cost of the mixer is $.04.

11. How may portion control be instituted in bar operations?

12. Why is production control necessary in bar operations? What are some of the measures which can be taken to institute control?

13. Select recipes for any four common drinks from a book of drink recipes; then determine the standard cost of one standard drink of each using current prices for your calculations.

14. Describe two approaches commonly used to train beverage production employees to follow established standards and standard procedures.

15. Why is frequent monitoring of bar operations essential?

16. List four techniques for observing the performance of beverage production employees.

17. Define each of the key terms for this chapter.

18. Assume that you are manager of a cocktail lounge that uses an electronic sales terminal with automatic pricing as a bar register. There is no other register in the establishment. It is 5:00 P.M. on a busy Friday afternoon, and the terminal

suddenly stops working. What instructions would you give the bartender to follow until the terminal was repaired?

For Computer Users

19. Using a spreadsheet program of your choice, determine the standard cost for one standard portion of each of six cocktails. Select recipes for the cocktails from any bartenders guide.

chapter 17

Monitoring Beverage Operations

Learning Objectives

After reading and studying this chapter, the student should be able to:

1. Name the three general approaches to measuring the effectiveness of beverage controls.
2. Calculate value of liquor issued to a bar, bar inventory differential, and cost of liquor consumed.
3. Calculate cost of beverage sales and beverage cost percent, both daily and monthly.
4. Calculate the above costs and cost percents for wines, spirits, and beers separately.
5. Determine standard beverage cost for a period.
6. List five possible reasons for differences between actual and standard beverage costs.
7. Calculate beverage inventory turnover and discuss its interpretation.
8. Calculate potential sales value per bottle of beverage sold by the straight drink.
9. Calculate a mixed drink differential and use it to adjust potential sales values.
10. Calculate potential sales values by the average sales value method.
11. Calculate potential sales values by the standard deviation method.
12. Identify a generic computer program that can be used in monitoring beverage operations and name the beverage monitoring methods for which computers are most necessary.
13. Define the Key Terms at the end of the chapter.

One important part of the control process is the regular monitoring of operations to determine whether results conform to management's plans. In previous chapters, we illustrated techniques and approaches for the regular monitoring of the performance of employees engaged in beverage purchasing, receiving, storing, issuing, and production. Clearly, the monitoring of individual performance is necessary. However, we must also assess the overall effectiveness of control procedures which, taken together, constitute the control system. That is to say, we must evaluate the entire control process—the standards and standard procedures established, the training methods employed for the staff, and the monitoring techniques of management—to determine whether the controls instituted are effective in producing the desired results.

There are three general approaches to measuring the effectiveness of beverage controls. The decision of which to use depends on the size and scope of operations, and as well as management philosophy. The first is based on cost: determination of cost of beverages sold, and comparison of that figure with either actual cost or standard cost. The second is based on liquid measure: comparison of the number of ounces of beverages sold with the number of ounces of beverages consumed. The third is based on sales values: comparison of the potential sales value of beverages consumed with the actual sales revenue recorded. Many operators use just one of these methods; some use more than one. Each method will be discussed in detail below.

THE COST APPROACH

Cost Percent Methods

Monthly Calculations

It is useful to compare cost and sales figures on a regular basis to see if the anticipated cost-to-sales ratio is being maintained. Methods for doing this vary considerably from operation to operation, so we shall look at several that might be used in operations of different sizes.

Small operations, often owner-managed with few employees, usually have no beverage controller. However, the owner must determine the cost-to-sales ratio. In many places, this is done monthly, with or without the help of an accountant. Cost is determined from inventory and purchase figures in the following manner.

A physical inventory of the storage area is taken, usually immediately after the close of business on the last day of the month. The number of bottles of each item in stock is counted and its value is determined by one of the five methods for inventory valuation discussed in Chapter 10. When the value of each item in stock is known, the values are added, and the result is the total dollar value of the closing inventory for the period. Because the closing inventory figure for any period is, by definition, the opening inventory for the following period, it is necessary to look back at the records to determine the closing inventory for the preceding period. To this opening inventory valuation, the owner adds the cost of all purchases for the month from bookkeeping records. The opening inventory plus the purchases shows the dollar value of all the stock available for sale during the period. To illustrate, consider the following example:

Closing inventory valuation—preceding period	$ 5,000
+ Purchases (from accounting records) this month	8,000
Total stock available for sale during month	$13,000

Of the stock available for sale, some has been issued to the bar and some has not. To find the value of the stock issued to the bar, the ending inventory figure this month is subtracted from the total stock available figure previously determined. Thus:

Total stock available for sale during month	$13,000
− Closing inventory valuation—this month	6,000
Value of stock issued this month	$ 7,000

While the $7,000 figure represents the value of liquor going to the bar, it does not necessarily represent the true cost of liquor sold at the bar. To determine that figure, the $7,000 must be adjusted by the change in inventory at the bar from the beginning to the end of the month. To illustrate:

Bar inventory valuation at the beginning of month	$1,500
− Bar inventory valuation at the end of the month	800
Bar inventory differential	$ 700

That figure must be added to the $7,000 figure to compute the cost of liquor consumed for the month. Thus:

Issues to bar	$7,000
± Inventory differential	700
Cost of liquor consumed	$7,700

If the differential at the bar were a negative figure, that amount would be subtracted, rather than added, to the value of issues to the bar.

Having determined the cost of liquor consumed at the bar, the cost percentage, or cost-to-sales ratio, is determined in the usual manner:

$$\text{Cost percentage} = \frac{\text{Cost}}{\text{Sales}}$$

To illustrate:

$$\text{Cost percentage} = \frac{\$7,700}{\$29,389.30}$$

$$\text{Cost percentage} = 26.2\%$$

The above procedure may be employed by even the smallest of bars and will require the barest minimum of paperwork on the manager's part. It merely requires that some basic bookkeeping records of purchases be maintained and that a par stock be maintained at the bar by issuing full bottles in exchange for empties. From the point of view of control, it is not the best possible procedure, but it does enable the manager to determine the cost-to-sales ratio for a period in establishments where no staff is available for maintaining daily records of issues.

Many managers find that these simple procedures result in determinations of beverage costs and beverage cost percentages that are not suitably accurate for their particular operations, and thus they require some or all of the possible adjustments to cost of beverages issued, described below.

Adjustment to Cost

Food and Beverage Transfers   Some operations do not consider the figures so derived accurate enough, because they do not reflect the cost of such food items as oranges, lemons, eggs, and heavy cream that are often used for beverage preparation but that are typically purchased by the food department and transferred to the bar. The cost of these items is significant and should be included in the beverage cost figures, not in the food cost figures. For this reason, such establishments maintain records of the transfer of these food items from the kitchen to the bar and add the cost to the beverage cost, while subtracting them from the food cost. In the case of food items issued directly from food stores to the bar (such as cocktail cherries and olives), separate bar requisitions are prepared, often on a different color paper from food requisitions. When such is the case, provision must be made for adding the cost of these items to the beverage cost. The effect of their use is reflected in beverage sales, so their cost should properly be reflected in beverage cost.

Many operations use certain beverages in the preparation of food products for sale and send them from the bar to the kitchen when needed. When the amount involved is deemed significant, separate records of these transfers are maintained as well. In the case of an establishment that features a different parfait each day and uses a certain amount of a different cordial from the bar to prepare it, records could be kept on transfer memos of the amounts of each cordial sent to the kitchen for food preparation; the value of the cordial is subtracted from the beverage cost figures.

Other Adjustments   Possible additions to cost include:

1. Any food item used in beverage preparation but not included in transfer memos.
2. Cost of mixers, if not included as transfers.

Possible credits to cost include:

1. Cost of any officers' drinks that should more properly be charged to entertainment or to business promotion. In the event that sales revenue has been recorded for such drinks, this revenue should be subtracted from beverage sales figures and probably written off.
2. Cost of the beverages used in other promotional activities, such as free drinks to couples celebrating fiftieth wedding anniversaries, complimentary drinks offered to diners ordering before 5:30 P.M., and so on.

Using all such adjustments, the cost of beverages sold would be determined as illustrated in figure 17.1. As shown, beverage cost percent equals $7,640.00 ÷ $29,389.30, or 26.0%.

Once determined, the cost-to-sales ratio for a period may be compared to the ratio for other periods to see how results measure up to those of similar periods in the past. If, for example, the cost percentage for the current period is 26.0%, and the records reveal that the cost percentage for the last six months has fluctuated between 25.8% and 27.0%, a manager would likely conclude that the measured results were satisfactory, provided that the past results have been considered satisfactory. If, however, some dramatic change in the cost-to-sales ratio were revealed, and the change was both unexpected and undesirable, the manager would try to determine the reasons for the change and attempt to effect changes in the operation so that the undesirable results would not be repeated.

FIGURE 17.1
Calculation of Cost with Adjustments

Cost of Liquor Consumed		$7,700
Add:		
Food to bar (Directs)		220
Storeroom issues		105
Mixers		525
	Subtotal	$8,550
Less:		
Cooking liquor		335
Officers' drinks		110
Special promotions		465
Cost of Beverages Sold		$7,640

Cost Calculations by Category

Some managers consider the foregoing cost and cost percentage figures too general to be of maximum value for their operations. Many prefer to see both cost and sales figures divided into spirits, wines, and beers, principally because the cost-to-sales ratios for these three categories may differ significantly from one another, and changes from one period to another are not apparent in one cost percent figure that reflects all three. Assuming that appropriate records are available, a form such as that illustrated in Figure 17.2 may be devised both to distribute cost and sales figures for these three major categories and to reflect the various adjustments previously discussed as they affect the major cost and sales categories.

In Chapter 16, standard drink recipes were developed, partly to determine standard portion cost for pricing purposes. If, for example, sales prices for drinks made with spirits had been established with a target cost percent of 20.0%, the overall cost-to-sales ratio of 26.0% determined in the earlier part of the chapter would not tell management whether the target was being achieved. However,

FIGURE 17.2
Cost Calculation by Category

Beverage Sales:

	Sales	Adjustments	Net Sales
Spirits	$20,572.50	$260.00	$20,312.50
Wine	5,877.80	50.00	5,827.80
Beer	2,939.00	50.00	2,879.00
Total sales	$29,389.30	$370.00	$29,019.30

Cost of Beverages Sold:

	Spirits	Wines	Beer	Total
Cost of issues	$3,496.30	$3,250.00	$953.70	$7,700.00
Adjustments:				
Additions				
Food to bar (Directs)	220.00	—	—	220.00
Storeroom issues	105.00	—	—	105.00
Mixers	525.00	—	—	525.00
Subtotal	850.00	- 0 -	- 0 -	850.00
Subtractions				
Bar to kitchen	45.00	220.00	70.00	335.00
Officers' drinks	65.00	25.00	20.00	110.00
Special promotions	105.00	360.00	—	465.00
Subtotal	215.00	605.00	90.00	910.00
Net adjustments	635.00	(605.00)	(90.00)	(60.00)
Net cost of sales	4,131.30	2,645.00	863.70	7,640.00
Cost percent	20.3%	45.4%	30.0%	26.3%
Cost per dollar sale	$.203	$.454	$.30	$.263

when sales and cost figures, as well as adjustments for both wines and beers, are factored out, it becomes possible to determine, as in Figure 17.2, that the cost percent for spirits for the period was 20.3%, and a judgment can be made about the effectiveness of the cost control measures instituted.

The analysis of the cost-to-sales ratio just once each month presents some obvious problems. A month is an accumulation of thirty yesterdays, and by the time the results of all those days are known, it is too late to do anything about them. If the figures indicate that October was a disaster, nothing can be done to change the results of October's operation. It may be possible to reduce the effects over the course of a year by improving results in other months, but nothing can be done to change the past. The best a manager can hope for is to show improvement in the operation for November and December and thus offset the poor results for October. It is preferable to have some knowledge of the cost-to-sales ratio before the period has passed, so that efforts can be made to improve operations while there is still time for the improvements to affect the figures for the current period.

Daily Calculations

If the manager could have figures for the first ten days of the month, changes could conceivably be effected in the operation in time for their positive effect to be reflected in the figures for the period. Some large operations, in which there are staff members to maintain the necessary records, do this. If beverages are issued to the bar daily on the basis of requisitions that accompany the empty bottles, it is possible to determine costs daily. After beverages are issued, the requisitions are numbered and totaled to determine the cost of the issues for the day. This figure is taken as the cost of beverages sold on the preceding day and may be compared to sales for the day to determine a cost percentage. It is obvious that this is less than completely accurate. The assumption is made that every ounce in every empty bottle was sold on the preceding day; this does not account for the possibility that the contents of a bottle might have been sold over a period of several days. The daily cost percentage is therefore unreliable. However, if the cost of daily issues is accumulated daily and compared to the accumulated sales over all the days so far in a period, a more accurate picture emerges. The inaccuracies inherent in the figures for one day tend to be eliminated, and a reasonably reliable picture of overall operations is provided, as illustrated in Figure 17.3.

An even more reliable picture of daily operations can be obtained if management could take daily inventory of the stock at the bar and thus determine an inventory differential for each day similar to that discussed earlier in this chapter. If the manager were able to subtract each day's closing bar inventory from the opening bar inventory, the bar differential obtained could be subtracted (or added, in the case of a negative figure) to the daily issue figure to determine daily cost with greater accuracy.

If such daily differential figures are available, two more columns can be added to the form illustrated in Figure 17.3, between the two columns headed Date and

FIGURE 17.3
Daily Cost Calculations

	Cost		Sales		Cost Percent	
Date	Today	To Date	Today	To Date	Today	To Date
11/1	$300		$900		33.4%	
11/2	$240	$ 540	$970	$1,870	24.8%	28.4%
11/3	$220	$ 760	$920	$2,790	23.8%	27.3%
11/4	$225	$ 985	$995	$3,785	22.6%	26.0%
11/5	$170	$1,155	$930	$4,715	18.3%	24.5%
11/6	$190	$1,345	$920	$5,635	20.7%	23.9%

Cost Today. These would be headed Beverage Issues and Bar Inventory Differential. With the addition of these two, Cost Today would become a net figure, incorporating daily issues and bar differential, and the daily calculation of cost percent for the day and for the period to date would result in a greater degree of accuracy.

The cost percent to date reflects the net effect of all costs and all sales for the number of days that have passed in the period, and it may be fairly judged in the light of comparable figures from the recent past. When comparison reveals undesirable results, attempts may be made to reverse their effect during the current period so the total figures for the period will show more desirable results. An undesirable trend may be reversed well before the end of the period.

Adjustments to Cost   Just as monthly figures can be adjusted in a variety of ways, so daily figures can be adjusted by the manager or beverage cost controller who seeks a more precise picture of operations. If records are available in the form of transfer memos, sales checks, and the like, the form illustrated in Figure 17.3 could be expanded to resemble that in Figure 17.4.

Figure 17.4 provides for increasing the daily issues figure by recording in the Additions column such items as transfers of Directs from the kitchen to the bar, mixers purchased directly for the bar, and food storeroom issues to the bar. If bar inventory were taken daily, positive differential could also be included in this

FIGURE 17.4
Daily Cost Calculations with Adjustments

Date	Beverages Issued	Additions	Subtractions	Total Cost		Sales		Cost Percent	
				Today	To Date	Today	To Date	Today	To Date
11/1	$300	$10	$35	$275		$900		30.6%	
11/2	$240	$20	$25	$235	$ 510	$970	$1,870	24.2%	27.3%
11/3	$220	$10	$20	$210	$ 720	$920	$2,790	22.8%	25.8%
11/4	$225	$ 5	$10	$220	$ 940	$995	$3,785	22.1%	24.8%
11/5	$170	$10	$15	$165	$1,105	$930	$4,715	17.7%	23.4%
11/6	$190	$ 5	$ 5	$190	$1,295	$920	$5,635	20.7%	23.0%

column. In the Subtractions column, one could include transfers of beverages to the kitchen (cooking liquor), the cost of officers' drinks used for entertainment or promotion, and the cost of complimentary drinks used for special promotions. Negative bar differentials could be subtracted here, also. If one preferred, individual columns for each of the above could be included in place of the two columns illustrated.

Using one or another of these forms, a manager can monitor employee performance, note significant deviations from acceptable norms, and take the necessary corrective action while events are still fresh in the minds of participants and investigations are feasible.

Standard Cost Method

In each method of maintaining cost figures discussed so far, the object has been to compare current figures with historical figures—the current cost-to-sales ratio with that ratio for a previous period. Judgments are made on the basis of the acceptability of previous figures and the degree to which current figures measure up. Various kinds of efforts are made to determine actual costs, and these actual costs are compared to actual sales. This is probably the most common approach to the problem of controlling beverage costs, but it is not necessarily the most desirable. After all, current figures may compare favorably to figures for a number of previous periods, but there is no adequate way of determining the extent to which the figures for previous periods were acceptable. Very often this is not the case. The figures for previous periods may reflect any number of unknown problems, and the comparison of current to past figures may merely confirm that past problems continue to exist. Some method must be found for determining the extent to which problems exist. In short, some more accurate standard for judging the cost-to-sales ratio is needed.

There is a more accurate way of evaluating performance and judging the effectiveness of control procedures. It is suitable for those willing to maintain very detailed records of drink sales and able to devote time to the necessary calculations. It presupposes the existence of standard recipes and standard costs for all drinks.

To calculate standard cost for a given operating period, one needs records of the number of sales of each specific drink during the period. For example, the records of spirit sales would have to show type of drink and brand of liquor. Types of drinks would include cocktails, mixed drinks, and straight shots. Records of beer sales would have to show both bottle sales and draft sales by brand. Equivalent detailed records of wine sales would also be needed.

With the necessary sales records and standard costs available, it is possible to determine standard cost of beverages sold for the operating period. First, one multiplies the number of sales of each drink by the standard cost of that drink to find total standard cost for that one item. This must be done for each specific drink sold during the period, with the total standard costs for all drinks added together. Figure 17.5 illustrates the method for calculating standard cost. The final total would be standard cost for the period.

FIGURE 17.5
Determination of Standard Beverage Cost

Item	Number Sold	Standard Cost	Total
Beer:			
Bottled			
Miller	1178	$.38	$447.64
Budweiser	1483	.38	563.54
Coors	674	.39	262.86
Draft			
Miller	2005	.21	495.81
Budweiser	2361	.21	495.81
Total (Beers)			$2,190.90

Once total standard cost for the period is known, it can be compared to actual cost for the same period, calculated as described previously. For example, assume that the actual cost of beer sold for March 19—, the period for which standard cost is determined in Figure 17.5, was $2,341.95. Comparison of the two reveals a difference between actual and standard cost. The amount of the difference can readily be determined by subtracting one from the other:

Actual cost	$2,341.95
− Standard cost	2,190.90
= Difference	$ 151.05

Obviously actual cost is greater than it should be, and this difference of $151.05 can be considered excessive cost. Knowing that the cost of beer sold was excessive for the period, management would immediately begin to determine the reason for the difference. Possible reasons include breakage, pilferage, improper storage and handling of draft beers, and failure to record revenue from sales. It would be important to determine the reasons so that corrective action could be taken, resulting in improvements in operating performance in the future.

Inventory Turnover Method

Management treats excessive cost as wasted money, and for good reason. After all, the $151.05 in excess cost determined above should not have been required to produce these beer sales. This money could have been used for some other purpose. Excess operating costs are not the only examples of dollars used unproductively in beverage operations. Additional examples can often be found by examining the amounts of money tied up in beverage inventories.

If too much money has been spent to purchase large quantities of beverages, such excess amounts can be viewed as unproductive. These dollars could have been used more productively for other purposes. To the extent that excessive quantities of beers have been purchased for inventory, management will risk serving older beer of lesser quality. On the other hand, if inventories are not large enough, more frequent ordering of comparatively small quantities is necessary, and this often means paying higher unit prices. It can also lead to higher labor costs and increased costs for processing orders.

Beverage managers need to be able to determine whether the size of the inventory is appropriate. The size of an inventory should be related to consumption. For example, it is inappropriate to keep 300 cases of one brand of beer in inventory if normal useage is 30 cases a month. Given this level of consumption, inventory should be much smaller.

Inventory turnover for beverages is calculated by means of the same formulas used for calculating inventory turnover for food, as discussed in Chapter 10. The formula is the following:

$$\text{Inventory Turnover} = \frac{\text{Cost of Beverages Sold for the Month}}{\text{Average Inventory}}$$

$$\text{Average Inventory} = \frac{\text{Opening Inventory} + \text{Closing Inventory*}}{2}$$

For example, given opening inventory of $4,800, closing inventory of $5,400, and cost of beverages sold of $5,720, inventory turnover would be calculated as follows:

$$\text{Average Inventory} = \frac{\$4,800 + \$5,400}{2} = \$5,200$$

$$\text{Inventory Turnover} = \frac{\$5,720}{\$5,200} = 1.1$$

This calculation yields the turnover rate for the month, indicating that the average inventory is purchased and used up at the approximate rate of 13.2 times per year, or slightly less than once a month. Some individual items are used more frequently, while others are used less frequently. However, on average, the inventory is consumed 1.1 times per month.

While many operators use this single inventory turnover figure, calculated for the entire beverage inventory, taken as a whole, many others find it useful to calculate separate turnover rates for the three principal components of the

---

* For greatest accuracy, both opening inventory and closing inventory figures should include the values of all inventories in storerooms and bars.

beverage inventory—spirits, beers, and wines. Generally accepted turnover rates for spirits and beers are:

Spirits   1.5
Beers   2.0

For spirits, an inventory turnover rate of 1.0 or less normally indicates an inventory larger than necessary for the volume of business, suggesting that too many dollars have been used to purchase unneeded bottles of spirits—dollars which might better have been used for some other purpose. If the turnover rate is 2.0 or higher, it is probable that the inventory is smaller than it should be, leading to the need for frequent purchasing, possibly at higher prices than might have been obtained by purchasing larger quantities at one time.

For beers—perishable products that lose quality with age—turnover rate should be higher. Many operators prefer to purchase weekly, resulting in higher turnover rates and fewer dollars tied up in inventory at any one time. Most would deem a turnover rate of 2.0 acceptable.

There is no accepted turnover rate for wines: the range of differences among wines is too great. Some restaurants maintain extensive inventories of vintage wines, purchased young and stored to maturity in their wine cellars; others offer more common wines, purchased for immediate use and turned over frequently; many stock a great variety of wines, some fine, others mere table wines. The numbers of possibilities and differences is too great for any accepted turnover rate to be determined.

THE LIQUID MEASURE APPROACH

Ounce-Control Method

Another technique for beverage control is the quantity- or ounce-control method. Some years ago it involved taking daily physical inventory of bar stock in order to determine the number of ounces consumed, and calculating from detailed sales records the number of ounces sold. Ideally, of course, the number of ounces consumed should equal the number of ounces sold; in practice, they never do equal one another because of spillage, evaporation, and breakage. However, when a bar is operated carefully, paying strict attention to the standards set by management, the difference can be kept to a minimum.

In this form, the ounce-control method has virtually disappeared from the field, since the cost of maintaining the procedure daily far outweighs the benefits to be derived from it. However, modern technology has made possible the reappearance of ounce-control procedures in a variety of forms. Some involve meters attached to bottles to measure quantities used daily, and others require the purchase and use of expensive, sophisticated computerized devices that dispense ingredients, mix drinks, record sales, and maintain bar inventory records automatically. Because such sophisticated equipment generally becomes comparatively less expensive in the several years after its introduction, it is probably that more of this equipment will be used in the future.

THE SALES VALUE APPROACH

In some beverage operations, efforts are made to determine what sales should result from the issuing of full bottles of various liquors from the storeroom. For example, if the standard drink of gin is one ounce, and gin is issued in one-liter bottles, then each bottle potentially contains 33.8 drinks. If the standard drink sells for a standard price of $1, then the potential sales value of the bottle issued is 33.8 drinks times $1 per drink, or $33.80. Hypothetically, then, each bottle of gin issued should produce $33.80 in sales. By extension, given standard drink sizes and standard selling prices, the total revenue that will be produced can be determined by issuing one bottle of any item kept at the bar. Therefore, when an empty bottle of any item is turned in with a requisition for replacement, it should be possible to find the potential sales value for the bottle reflected in actual sales. In a simple, hypothetical bar, for example, using only liter bottles and serving only straight drinks in one-ounce shots for $1 per drink, the consumption of one bottle each of gin, rye, and scotch should produce $101.40 in sales. Theoretically, one should find $101.40 recorded in the cash register at the end of the day.

It is possible to develop a chart of the standard sales values of bottles sold only by the straight drink (see Fig. 17.6). In practice, such a chart would necessarily include all brands so sold at the bar and would obviously be considerably longer than that in the figure. However, beverage operations are seldom, if ever, quite this simple. Most bars do not sell spirits only in straight shots. Cocktails and other mixed drinks, involving varying quantities of spirits and other ingredients, account for some portion of sales in most establishments. Therefore, if control is to involve the use of potential sales values of bottles, some way must be found to account for the differences that arise from the production of various mixed drinks. The potential sales value of each bottle must be adjusted according to some formula that takes into consideration variations in both quantities of spirits used and selling prices.

FIGURE 17.6
Calculation of Bottle Sales Values

Bottle Code #	Item	Bottle Size	Drink Size	Drinks per Bottle	$\times$	Drink Price	$=$	Sales Value Per Bottle
301	Gin	1 liter	1 oz.	33.8		$1.00		$33.80
107	Rye	1 liter	1 oz.	33.8		1.00		33.80
217	Scotch	750 ml	1 oz.	25.4		1.00		25.40
352	Vodka	1 liter	1 oz.	33.8		.90		30.42
456	Brandy	750 ml	1 oz.	25.4		1.10		27.94

In fact, control procedures involving potential sales values are generally quite complex and require considerable time and calculation. For these and other related reasons, they are not commonly used except in some very large operations. However, some basic understanding of these procedures is necessary for anyone who seeks to acquire a complete overview of beverage control. Three different methods will be discussed here.

The major problem is to establish the sales values. This may be done in one of three ways. The first involves setting potential sales values based on sales of straight shots only and adjusting these figures daily or periodically by the so-called mixed drink differential. These adjustments to the values of bottles issued and consumed are made after sales have taken place. The second method involves analyzing sales during a test period and determining weighted average values per bottle in advance, based on historical sales records. The third method is really a modification of the second and is generally easier and more practical to use. However, it is sufficiently different from the second to warrant separate discussion.

Actual Sales Record Method

When detailed sales records are available and drinks are prepared according to standard recipes, one can calculate the sales value of the ingredients in each type of drink sold. For example, the preparation of a martini in a certain bar may require two ounces of gin and one-half ounce of dry vermouth. Assuming that gin as a straight drink is sold in two-ounce measures for $2.00, and the martini sells for $2.25, $2.00 represents the sales value of the gin, and the remaining $.25 is called the mixed drink differential. Once the sales value of the primary ingredients has been calculated in this way, it is possible to determine the mixed drink differential for each drink sold. If the sales value of the primary ingredient in a drink is $.90, and the actual selling price is $1.50, each sale of that particular drink must be accounted for by the use of a differential of an additional $.60. On the other hand, if the drink with two ounces of primary ingredient with sales value of $1.80 were sold for $1.75, a differential of minus $.05 would be required. These differentials must be calculated for each drink sold and recorded for frequent reference.

Each day after sales have been analyzed from guest checks, the number of drinks of each type sold is multiplied by the differential for that drink, and the total bottle sales value for spirits consumed is increased by the total of all plus differentials and decreased by the total of all minus differentials.

Figure 17.7 illustrates the calculation of potential sales values based on this method. Sales values per bottle are recorded from a chart similar to that shown in Figure 17.6; multiplying the number of empty bottles of each primary ingredient by the recorded potential sales value per bottle determines total sales value of each primary ingredient. These are totaled to find sales values of the empty bottles from the bar. Next, this total is adjusted for mixed drink sales, as shown in the lower half of the form. Mixed drink differential for each type of drink is multiplied by the number sold to determine total differential per item. These, in turn, are added to

FIGURE 17.7
Daily Analysis of Potential Sales Values

Date _____11/11/XX_____

Bottle Code No.	Item	Bottles Consumed	Sales Value per Bottle	Total Sales Value
301	Gin	3	$33.80	$101.40
107	Rye	2	33.80	67.60
352	Vodka	2	30.42	60.84
			Total	$229.84

Adjustments for Mixed Drink Differentials:

Mixed Drink	Primary Ingredient	Ounces of Primary Ingredient	Straight Drink Price	Mixed Drink Price	Mixed Drink Differential	Number Sold	Total Differential
Martini	gin	2	$2.00	$2.25	+ $.25	22	+ $ 5.50
Screwdriver	vodka	1	.90	1.50	+ .60	18	+ 10.80
Martini	vodka	2	1.80	1.75	– .05	8	– .40
						Total	+ $15.90

Sales Values adjusted by differentials:

Sales Values of empty bottles from bar $229.84
Adjustments for mixed drink differentials + 15.90
$245.74

determine net differential for the day, which is typically added to the sales values of empty bottles to determine an adjusted sales value. In rare instances the differential figure is a negative, in which case it is subtracted from bottle sales values. The resulting potential sales value should be very close to the actual sales figure recorded in the bar register.

Determining differentials by analysis of drink sales must be done daily, and the sales values of bottles issued to replace empties at the bar must be adjusted accordingly to determine the sales value of the spirits consumed. Although this method results in the development of useful and often highly accurate control data, it is somewhat cumbersome for day-to-day use in most establishments. To many, some simplification of the procedures seems necessary and desirable. Therefore, a method for determining average potential sales values of bottles has been developed.

Average Sales Value Method

This method eliminates the need for determining mixed drink differentials daily. It requires establishing a test period during which careful records are kept of the number of each type of drink sold. These records serve as the basis for determining the average potential sales value of each bottle. Such records of actual sales are analyzed in Figure 17.8.

Assuming that the test period truly represents the sales mix, a determination of the average sales value for one ounce of gin can be made by dividing 330 ounces sold into $352.50 total sales. In this case the average sales value for one ounce of gin is $1.07. Because this primary ingredient is purchased and used by the liter, the average sales value of each liter is 33.8 ounces multiplied by the average sales value of each ounce, or $36.17. In some places, the person performing these calculations reduces the bottle size by one ounce in order to account for unavoidable spillage and evaporation, thus assigning a more realistic average sales value to each bottle. Once these calculations have been completed for all primary ingredients consumed during the test period, a chart is prepared of the average sales value of each item used in the bar, as illustrated in Figure 17.9. It replaces the chart of standard sales values of bottles sold only by the straight drink, illustrated previously in figure 17.6.

FIGURE 17.8
Analysis of Actual Sales (Gin)

Primary Ingredient	Gin				
Drinks Prepared	# Sold	Oz./Drink	Total Oz.	Drink Price	Total Sales
Martini	90	2	180	$2.25	$202.50
Straight shots	150	1	150	1.00	150.00
		Totals	330		$352.50

FIGURE 17.9
Chart of Average Potential Sales Values of Bottles

Bottle Code #	Item	Bottle Size	Sales Value
301	Gin	1 liter	$36.17
107	Rye	1 liter	37.73
217	Scotch	750 ml	29.60
352	Vodka	1 liter	30.90
456	Brandy	750 ml	28.35

With such a chart available, the potential sales value of the bottles consumed at the bar can be determined daily by multiplying the number of empty bottles of each brand by the potential sales value per bottle as shown on the chart. The procedure for doing this is illustrated in Figure 17.10. This total potential sales figure would then be compared to actual sales records for the day, as previously described, to uncover any remarkable deviations from standards based on experience during a test period.

Although average potential sales values per bottle are used more often than daily determination of differentials, it is by no means universal. The average method still requires many calculations and can be used only in establishments where one or more persons is available to perform the necessary calculations regularly. In many places this is not practical. Moreover, the average method is useful only if the sales mix at the bar remains relatively stable. Major changes in the sales mix because of changing times and changing customer preferences render the calculated averages unreliable and require the calculation of new average potentials based on a new test period.

Standard Deviation Method

In the interest of further simplifying and eliminating frequent and time-consuming sales analysis of the types discussed, some managers have attempted to adapt to beverage control some of the techniques of statistics. The technique that follows

FIGURE 17.10
Procedure for Determining Total Sales Value

Bottle Code #	Item	Bottles Consumed	Sales Value per Bottle	Total Sales Value
301	Gin	3	$36.17	$108.51
107	Rye	2	37.73	75.46
352	Vodka	2	30.90	61.80
			Total	$245.77

has a growing number of strong defenders but has so far not gained wide acceptance in the industry.

This approach requires the establishment of a test period during which management takes all appropriate steps to ensure strict employee adherence to all standards and standard procedures. In addition, all phases of the bar operation are kept under observation during the period in a further effort to ensure compliance. At the conclusion of the test period, bottle consumption is carefully determined on the basis of inventories and issues, and is translated into potential sales value by drink, as previously discussed. In effect, a potential sales value is determined that indicates what the total sales value might have been if all spirits consumed had been sold by the straight drink. Next, actual sales recorded are compared with the calculated potential sales. Typically, the potential sales figure is greater than the actual sales, and the difference between the two is taken to reflect the sale of cocktails and other mixed drinks as well as the normal spillage to be expected at the bar. Because the operation has been under careful observation throughout the test period, this difference is taken as a standard difference, which can be used for purposes of comparison in the future. The difference is divided by the potential sales figure to determine, as a percentage, the extent of the deviation from the potential. If, for example, potential sales value were $1,000, and actual sales were $950, the difference would be $50 divided by $1,000, or 5%. Expressed in another way, it could be said that during the test period actual sales were 5% less than potential sales. By reducing the potential sales figure by 5% to account for normal spillage and the sales of cocktails and other mixed drinks, it is possible to develop an adjusted potential sales figure, which can be useful in measuring bar operations in the future as long as the sales mix remains fairly constant.

With this in mind, one can calculate adjusted potential sales figures in the future and use these figures to determine the extent to which bar operations are measuring up to expectations. As long as the sales mix does not change greatly, this can be done without resort to the elaborate analytical techniques described earlier. However, if major discrepancies appear between actual sales and adjusted potential, sales analysis may be both necessary and desirable in the process of determining causes.

One important advantage of this approach is the ease with which differentials can be recalculated from time to time. As customers' tastes change and the sales mix changes accordingly, it is comparatively simple to establish a new test period and calculate a new differential for use in measuring operations. Also, as costs or selling prices change, the percentage deviation should remain fairly constant.

Regardless of the techniques involved in their calculation, potential sales figures can be useful in judging the bar operation. When compared to actual sales figures, they provide a means of measuring the extent to which actual operations are meeting management's expectations. For example, if actual sales of $1,400 are compared to potential sales of $1,500, it is apparent that the actual falls short of the potential by $100, or 6.7%. It is incumbent upon management in a particular operation to determine how great a deviation is to be tolerated. Assuming that the potential figure is reasonably accurate, the difference means that the staff is not using the raw materials of production in the manner prescribed by management. This difference reflects operational problems of all sorts, including failure to mix according to standard recipes, excessive spillage, errors in filling orders, overpouring, general waste, and even outright theft. All such problems are of concern to management and should be eliminated. However, in actual and potential sales figures, the amount to be tolerated will differ considerably from operation to operation. In some places, a discrepancy of 1% between actual and potential sales may cause extreme concern and lead to careful and detailed analysis of all phases of the operation. In others, a 3% deviation may be considered within the limits of tolerance. Such determinations are obviously within the province of management. In general, management is usually less tolerant of differences arising from failure to record sales than it is of any other cause. Poor pouring and mixing techniques may often be ascribed to, and tolerated as, the pressures of business at the bar. But failure to record sales often reflects the intention to steal. For this reason, effective managers never accept it as a tolerable reason for the discrepancy between actual and potential sales.

COMPUTER APPLICATIONS

All of the methods for monitoring beverage operations illustrated and discussed in this chapter may be integrated into a computer-based control system. In fact, many chain organizations, franchisers, and independent operators use computers to one extent or another to monitor bar operations. Some merely monitor sales, a topic that will be discussed in Chapter 18. A growing number of others use computers to monitor the cost of beverage operation.

Some maintain computer-based perpetual inventories of beverages, as discussed previously. This may be done by means of a database program. A major organization might hire a programming firm to develop a database for its specific needs; an individual operator might simply use one of the many generic programs available. Assuming timely and accurate data entry for purchases and issues during a period, a printout of the inventory could be obtained for comparison with the monthly physical inventory. Differences would show the extent of deviations from standard control procedures.

To determine monthly cost, it is necessary to value the monthly physical inventory, a time-consuming task if done manually. However, any standard spreadsheet program could be used both to maintain and to value the physical inventory.

Spreadsheets can also be used for calculating daily cost percents, as illustrated in figures 17.3 and 17.4. Once the spreadsheet is set up, one merely inputs figures daily for issues, adjustments, and sales. Printing a daily report for management is the obvious next step.

The standard cost method would be particularly difficult to use if one did not have a computer-based file of standard drink recipes and their costs, along with detailed records of sales showing the number of drinks of each type sold daily and for the period. The latter is best obtained from a computerized sales terminal.

The ounce-control and sales value methods, which have been infrequently used in recent years because of the high labor costs they require, may be in more common use because of computers. Manual calculations consume far too many hours to justify the adoption of these methods, but spreadsheet programs substantially improve the outlook for their increased use.

CHAPTER ESSENTIALS

In this chapter, we identified the three general approaches to measuring the effectiveness of beverage controls: cost, liquid measure, and sales values. We described and illustrated calculations for several cost-based methods, including monthly cost and cost percent, daily cost and cost percent, standard cost, and inventory turnover. We described the ounce-control method and discussed its limitations. We explained three methods for using potential sales values to monitor beverage operations: actual sales record, average sales value, and standard deviation. Finally, we discussed computer-based applications of the various methods illustrated in the chapter and pointed out the impracticality of attempting several of the methods without a computer.

KEY TERMS IN THIS CHAPTER

Inventory differential	Inventory turnover method
Beverage cost percent	Potential sales value
Food and beverage transfers	Actual sales record method
Standard cost method	Mixed drink differential
Actual beverage cost	Average sales value method
Inventory turnover	Average potential sales value
Average inventory	Standard deviation method
Ounce-control method	Primary ingredient

QUESTIONS AND PROBLEMS

1. Given the following information, compute the cost of liquor sold in each case.

Storeroom Inventory Information

	Opening Inventory	Purchases During Month	Closing Inventory
a.	$5,000	$ 8,000	$7,000
b.	8,325	10,666	9,327
c.	4,872	7,454	3,856

Bar Information

	Opening Inventory	Closing Inventory
a.	$1,000	$1,000
b.	2,325	2,050
c.	1,867	1,988

2. From the information obtained in Problem #1, compute the cost-to-sales ratio if:

   a. Sales are $20,000

   b. Sales are $41,412.50

   c. Sales are $29,817.85

3. Using the figures from Questions 1 and 2 as well as the adjustments given below, calculate adjusted cost of beverages sold following the format of Figure 17.1, then calculate cost-to-sales ratio based on adjusted cost.

   a. Food to bar (Directs) $200
      Storeroom issues   150
      Mixers   475
      Cooking liquor   110
      Officers' drinks   120
      Special promotions   160

   b. Mixers $925
      Food to bar (Directs)   500
      Cooking liquor   335
      Special promotions   320

   c. Special promotions $285
      Storeroom issues   235
      Officers' drinks   165
      Mixers   695
      Cooking liquor   185

4. Use the information given below to prepare a report in the form illustrated in Figure 17.2, showing costs, sales, and adjustments by category.

Total beverage sales—$42,320, of which 10% represents beer sales, 18% represents wine sales, and the balance, spirits sales.

Total adjustments to sales—$424, of which 8% is allocated to beer sales, 12% to wine sales, and the balance to spirits sales.

Total cost of issues—$10,500, of which 55% is allocated to spirits, 35% to wines, and the balance to beer.

Mixers	$865
Food to bar (Directs)	305
Bar to kitchen	440
Special promotions	520

Mixers and food to bar (Directs) are all adjustments to spirits alone, but bar to kitchen and special promotions must be allocated as follows:

Bar to kitchen: 70% to wines, 10% to beer, and the balance to spirits.

Special promotions: 60% to wines and 40% to spirits.

5. Using Figure 17.3 as a guide, prepare a cumulative and daily cost-to-sales ratio chart given the following information:

Date	Cost	Sales
10/1	$250	$ 910
10/2	225	850
10/3	270	920
10/4	290	1,070
10/5	240	900

6. Using the figures in Question 5, prepare a chart like that illustrated in Figure 17.4 if the following additional information is given.

Date	Food Transferred to Bar	Liquor Transferred to Kitchen
10/1	$15	$25
10/2	10	30
10/3	12	45
10/4	20	10
10/5	8	18

7. Determine the potential sales value of the following issues assuming only one-ounce shots were poured, liter bottles were issued, and all straight shots sell for $1.30.

Liquor	Number of Bottles Issued
Gin	5
Scotch whiskey	3
Canadian whiskey	4
Blended whiskey	3
Vodka	4
Bourbon whiskey	2

8. During the period of time in Question 7, the following mixed drinks were served.

> Gin martinis: 20
>
> Vodka martinis: 10
>
> Manhattan cocktails (prepared with blended whiskey): 25
>
> Whiskey sours: 18
>
> Rob Roys: 16

The price for each mixed drink is $3.00. However, each martini and Manhattan contains three ounces of liquor, and each whiskey sour and Rob Roy contains two ounces of liquor. Use this information and needed data from Question 7 above to prepare a chart like the one in Figure 17.7.

9. Prepare a chart similar to Figure 17.8. Using the average potential sales value method, determine the potential sales value of twelve-liter bottles of gin given the following information from a test period.

Drinks Prepared	Number Sold	Oz./Drink	Drink Price
Martinis	20	2	$1.40
Straight shots	120	1½	1.10

10. a. Compute the deviation from potential as suggested in the text given the following information.

> Test Period
>
> Actual Sales for period = $1,200
>
> Potential Sales based on straight shots = $1,250

b. What should actual sales be if the potential sales based on straight shots in 10(a) above were $900?

11. Refer to the figures in Question 1 above. Calculate inventory turnover for each of the three set of figures. Be sure to include both bar and storeroom inventories in determining average inventory.

12. What are the three approaches to measuring the effectiveness of beverage controls?

13. Managers of most bar operations use monthly cost percents. To what purpose?

14. Why is it necessary to take bar inventory differential into account when calculating monthly cost of beverages sold?

15. Assume that the beverage manager of a hotel calculates a single cost percent each month for the entire beverage operation. What are the disadvantages of relying exclusively on this figure, with or without adjustments, to monitor the beverage operation?

16. Would you advise the beverage manager cited in Question 13 above to adopt a daily cost percent calculation? Why? What would be the advantages and disadvantages of the daily method, compared to the monthly?

17. Is the standard cost method more useful or less useful than cost percent methods for monitoring operations? Why?

18. Compare and contrast the advantages of the average sales value method with those of the standard deviation method for measuring the effectiveness of beverage controls.

For Computer Users

19. Using any spreadsheet program of your choice, prepare a worksheet using the dollar values and the format of Figure 17.4.

20. Use the worksheet template prepared for Question 19 above to solve Questions 5 and 6.

chapter 18

Beverage Sales Control

Learning Objectives

After reading and studying this chapter, the student should be able to:

1. List and explain the three goals of beverage sales control.
2. List and explain five reasons customers use to patronize an establishment that offers alcoholic beverages for sale.
3. Describe the specific steps that bar managers can take to attract particular market segments.
4. Describe two methods that can be used to maximize profits in beverage operations.
5. List the principal considerations used by managers to establish beverage selling prices.
6. List ten working habits of bartenders that limit management's ability to institute effective revenue control.
7. Compare and contrast the two operating patterns used in bars to establish revenue control.
8. Describe the essential features of a pre-check system.
9. List the advantages and disadvantages of automated bars compared to more traditional methods of mixing and pouring drinks.
10. Explain how the division of labor improves the effectiveness of revenue control.
11. Define the Key Terms at the end of the chapter.

In previous chapters, we pointed out that establishment of control over any phase of food and beverage operations can best proceed from an understanding of management's goals and objectives. The controls set up by management must be carefully designed to ensure that the goals can be achieved, and a clear view of those goals is a desirable starting point for the discussion of the particular techniques and procedures established to control any phase of operation. This is no less true for sales control than for any other. A good beginning point, then, is an analysis of the goals of beverage sales control.

In an earlier discussion of food sales control, we pointed out that many consider the goal of sales control to be revenue control—ensuring that each individual sale to a customer results in appropriate revenue to the establishment. In the earlier discussion, we took the position that sales control is more than a mere synonym for revenue control. Revenue control is clearly one goal of sales control, but it is not the only one. Sales control is a broad area, encompassing other goals as well. There are at least two others. In this chapter, we will discuss the following goals of beverage sales control:

1. Optimizing the number of sales.
2. Maximizing profit
3. Controlling revenue

While these are identical to the goals of food sales control, there are special considerations in bar operation—some legal, some ethical and moral—that lead to significant differences in the meaning of some of the terms. For example, in food sales control, profit maximization is taken to include selling the maximum number of products to each customer—an approach that no reasonable beverage manager should attempt. At the same time, bar operators who attempt to optimize the number of sales will find their efforts restricted by various local, state, and federal laws and regulations affecting such considerations as customer age and hours of operation. A number of special concerns give rise to differences in the interpretation of the meaning of sales optimization and profit maximization in beverage sales control.

OPTIMIZING THE NUMBER OF BEVERAGE SALES

In beverage operations, optimizing the number of sales means engaging in activities that will increase the number of customers to the desired level, as defined by the individual operator. However, anyone seeking to increase beverage sales volume must first understand why people patronize establishments that serve beverages, including both restaurants and bars. At first glance, it might appear that people are usually motivated to patronize these establishments by a desire to consume alcoholic beverages. While this may be true for some customers, it is probably not the principal reason for most. After all, alcoholic beverages can be obtained for home consumption in most communities, and drinking at home is considerably less expensive. It is necessary, then, to understand some of the many other possible reasons for a customer to decide to patronize an establishment that sells alcoholic beverages. People patronize these establishments for the following reasons:

1. For social purposes.
2. For food.
3. For entertainment.
4. To kill time.

For Social Purposes

Perhaps the most significant motivating factors for patronizing beverage operations are social: meeting and conversing with other people. The possibilities are almost endless: meeting friends after work; meeting neighbors after dinner; meeting associates to discuss business; attempting to make new friends. Consuming alcoholic beverages is almost incidental; it is an accepted and expected part of the social setting. The incidental nature of the drinking may help to explain the trend to drinks with lower alcohol content, including white wine, spritzers, wine coolers, and light beers.

For Food

Many customers patronize food and beverage establishments primarily to eat and order alcoholic beverages as desirable enhancements to their meal. Beverages purchased for this reason include cocktails or other drinks before the meal, wines to accompany one or more of the courses, and such after-dinner drinks as brandy, liqueur, and dessert wine. The primary motivator is the desire to dine, and beverage purchases may be incidental. However, for some customers, the availability of beverages may be an important factor in selecting one dining establishment over another, and most successful restaurants that serve evening meals would probably lose considerable business volume if they did not make alcoholic beverages available.

For Entertainment

Many people go out to seek entertainment and consume alcoholic beverages while enjoying the entertainment. From a beverage standpoint, there are two types of establishments that offer entertainment: those deriving their primary revenue from beverage sales, and those deriving their primary revenue from ticket sales for the entertainment. The former include night clubs, discos, and piano bars—establishments that offer entertainment to increase the number of customers and thus to increase beverage sales volume. The latter include sports facilities, many so-called legitimate theaters, and some concert halls—establishments that offer alcoholic beverages as a convenience to patrons.

To Kill Time

There are many occasions when people must wait: at airports, at train stations, when meeting someone. Time must be killed—some hours or minutes must somehow be consumed. For many people, a bar is a suitable place to kill time. It is convenient, and it offers shelter, a place to sit, a television set to watch, and something to do: drink. Bars and cocktails lounges at airports are examples of establishments that cater almost exclusively to this type of trade.

Clearly, anyone who operates a beverage-selling establishment must be aware of the various reasons people have for patronizing those establishments and must take them into account when planning activities designed to increase the number of customers to the desired level. It is also important to point out that the beverage business includes many types of markets based on reasons for customer patronage of beverage operations. Furthermore, any customer may be included in one type of market one day and another type the next. The reasons for patronage change from day to day. For example, the person who patronizes a neighborhood bar for social reasons on one evening may be killing time at an airport the following afternoon, and then may go out to dinner with his spouse to celebrate some special occasion.

Each type of market can be subdivided. For example, those who patronize beverage establishments for social reasons can be divided into vast numbers of subgroups, each with special reasons for patronizing particular kinds of establishments. Each of these subgroups is called a **market segment**.

The owner or manager of a beverage operation must determine which market segment or segments she intends to attract, or target. Once the target segments have been identified, numerous decisions must be made as to brands and types of drinks, portion sizes, selling prices, entertainment, lighting, decor, ambiance, dress codes, giveaways, advertising, promotions, hours and days of operation, extent of service, classifications of employees, and suitable uniforms, among others. The decisions made will have significant impact on whether or not the target market will be attracted to the establishment in sufficient numbers to achieve the desired level of sales. For example, the owner of a bar attempting to attract a late-afternoon clientele of white-collar workers might decide to offer moderately priced large drinks made with high-quality liquor, to maintain an informal atmosphere, to provide free hot and cold hors d'oeuvres, to advertise by means of handbills distributed through neighboring office buildings, and to make a conscious effort to learn and to use customers' names. By contrast, the management of a fine hotel, targeting a different market segment for the late-afternoon cocktail hour, might prefer to offer expensive, high-quality drinks in a more formal atmosphere, with formal waiter service, and to provide such amenities as soft piano music and elegant hors d'oeuvres, while restricting advertising to small, tasteful signs in the elevators and guest rooms.

It should be apparent that optimizing beverages sales is a complex process, requiring not only substantial amounts of time and effort but also considerable experience in the beverage business and some reasonable knowledge of both the principles of marketing and techniques of market research.

MAXIMIZING PROFITS

In food sales control, one element of profit maximization is increasing customer purchases, an approach that is of only limited use in beverage sales control. It is important to understand the reasons for this.

Many people reject the notion that the amount of alcohol an individual consumes is wholly his own affair. They point out that those who have consumed excessive amounts of alcohol frequently behave in ways that have adverse, sometimes lethal, effects on others. Drunk drivers are the most common examples. As a consequence, there is a growing tendency to hold both the consumer of alcohol and those who are responsible for serving him accountable for any harm he may do as a result of excessive drinking. Many states have passed relevant laws, known as **dram shop** laws, that hold the serving establishment and the server financially liable for damages if any employee in the establishment has served an alcoholic drink to a customer who is intoxicated and that intoxicated customer, in turn, causes harm to a third party. In some states without dram shop laws, third parties can still recover damages under common-law liability. In addition, some states have now passed laws to eliminate the use of the term ''happy hour'' and to prohibit such practices as offering two drinks for the price of one. Because of changes in society's outlook and the passage of various laws, it is both advisable and necessary for beverage operators and their employees to restrict customers' purchases of alcoholic beverages rather than to attempt to increase them in the usual sense. Beverage operators can, however, adopt various merchandising techniques to influence the customer to select one drink—a drink with a greater contribution margin—rather than another.

In beverage operation, **profit maximization** is accomplished by establishing drink prices that will maximize gross profit and by influencing customers' selections. These must be discussed separately.

Establishing Drink Prices

Unlike food sales prices, drink prices are not primarily determined by the costs of ingredients and labor. Beverage ingredient and labor costs per dollar sale are normally lower than those for food, so they are not as significant in establishing selling prices. This is not to say that labor costs can or should be wholly ignored; many operators tend to charge more for drinks that require more labor to produce. However, the ingredient and labor costs associated with a particular drink tend to be similar from one operation to another. Drink prices are based primarily on other considerations. These include overhead costs, including occupation costs, insurance premiums, license fees, and entertainment expenses, and significant market considerations.

Overhead costs for a beverage operation typically represent a large percentage of total costs, although the dollar amounts vary considerably from one operation to another, even if the number of sales are similar. For example, airport rents tend to be compatively high, forcing beverage operators to set high sales prices for drinks. By contrast, neighborhood bars in low-rent areas can charge considerably lower prices and still be profitable. Insurance premiums vary dramatically from one area to another, depending in part on the legal climate in the region. The passage of dram shop laws, for example, normally raises the cost of liability insurance for a bar owner. The costs associated with purchasing and maintaining licenses are considerably different from one locale to another. Establishments that offer live entertainment must either charge drink prices high enough to cover these costs or charge an admission fee to avoid raising prices.

There are market considerations that must be taken into account in setting drink prices. Chief among these is the clientele targeted. Many operators rely heavily on regular customers—those who patronize an establishment frequently, often because they live or work close by. Such customers tend to be concerned with the prices charged, and operators serving this kind of clientele are usually careful to charge prices their customers consider reasonable and to avoid price increases unless necessary. By these means, they attempt to maintain as large a group of regular customers as possible, thus maximizing profits. By contrast, other beverage operations cater to transient, rather than regular, customers. The transient customer may have no practical choice of establishments—at an airport, for instance—and her choice may be limited to paying the high price or not drinking. Some transient customers are traveling on expense accounts and may be unconcerned about the specific prices changed for drinks. In general, those serving transient customers can change high drink prices.

Other market considerations that a beverage operator would take into account in establishing drink prices include such questions as average income in the area served, prices charged by the competition, special advantages offered by prime location—such as the top floor of the world's tallest building—and even management's desire to maintain exclusivity through pricing, among others. For the above reasons, selling prices for drinks must be established by each individual operator after he has carefully weighed both cost structure and market considerations relevant to the particular establishment.

No discussion of drink prices could be concluded without bringing up pricing differences between call brands and pouring brands. Call brands, selected by the customer, are normally of higher quality and cost and are thus given higher selling prices. Pouring brands, selected by the bar operator for the customer who expresses no preference, are typically of somewhat lower quality, less costly, and are therefore given lower sales prices. In general, the contribution margins of drinks made with pouring brands are lower than those of drinks made with call brands. While it is to the operator's advantage for customers to request specific call brands, most customers do not.

Influencing Customer Selections

As with food products, contribution margins vary greatly from one drink to another. From the viewpoint of the bar operator, it is desirable to sell more drinks with high contribution margins and fewer drinks with low contribution margin. If a customer were having difficulty deciding which of two identically priced drinks to order, it would clearly be to the bar operator's advantage for the customer to select the one with the higher contribution margin.

Some bar operators attempt to maximize profits by featuring and promoting selected drinks, often drinks specially created for the purpose. They may be given enticing names, or be served in unusual ways—in hollowed fruits, or with exotic garnishes, for example—or be made from unusual combinations of ingredients. These special drinks are normally sold for high prices, and they normally produce higher-than-average contribution margins.

Another technique for influencing customer selections is to produce a carefully designed beverage menu that includes pictures of the drinks management would prefer to sell, along with appropriate descriptive language to entice customers. Customers' orders would not necessarily be restricted to the listed drinks, but the drink menu would include only those drinks management preferred to sell.

Understanding and using the many creative possibilities for influencing customer selections is a key element in maximizing profits that is ignored by many bar operators and used wisely and to full advantage by others.

CONTROLLING REVENUE

Revenue control consists of those activities established to ensure that each sale to a customer results in appropriate revenue to the operation. In beverage operations, the opportunities for revenue control are often somewhat limited. To a great extent, effective control procedures depend on division of work among several employees, a condition not found in many bars. In many instances, one employee, the bartender, is responsible for taking orders from customers, filling those orders, recording the sales, and collecting cash or securing signatures on charge vouchers. This dependence on one person tends to reduce the opportunities for control and often sets the stage for the development of a number of operational problems.

One indication that problems exist can often be found in certain work habits of some bartenders, as listed below. Most of the following are considered unacceptable in most well-managed bars, because the owners or managers are aware of the problems likely to develop.

1. **Working with the cash drawer open**. This enables dishonest employees to make sales transactions without recording the sales in the register. This is a serious problem if the bartender is responsible at the end of the shift for only those sales recorded on the register tape.

2. **Under-ringing sales**, either as No Sale or as some amount less than the actual sale. This could enable an employee to pocket the difference between the cash in the register drawer and the sales recorded on the tape.

3. **Overcharging customers, but ringing correct amounts in the register**. This too provides a source of pocketable cash amounting to the difference between the amounts collected and amounts rung in the register.

4. **Undercharging customers**. This may be done to accommodate a bartender's personal friends or in an attempt to increase tips. It may be done in several ways, including giving call brands but charging for pouring brands, or by overpouring.

5. **Overpouring**. Giving the customer more than he or she pays for, often through willful failure to measure, typically results in unfavorable cost-to-sales ratios and in reduced profits from operation.

6. **Underpouring**. This technique is sometimes adopted by bartenders who selectively overpour, in an effort to prevent detection of the overpouring. Too, the bartender who keeps mental records of the extent of his underpouring may later use the reserved amounts to prepare drinks. These drinks may then be given to friends or sold to customers with the sales revenue being pocketed by the bartender.

7. **Diluting bottle contents**. This practice involves pouring off some of a bottle's contents to reserve for later use and replacing it with an equal amount of water. The liquor poured off is typically used in drinks for which the money is pocketed.

8. **Bringing own bottles into the bar**. This practice permits a bartender to become a "silent partner" in the operation. He can prepare drinks using his own bottles and pocket the sales revenue without his performance being detected through changes in cost and sales figures.

9. **Charging for drinks not served**. This enables a bartender to sell for his own benefit a drink previously paid for by a customer who did not receive it.

10. **Drinking on the job**. In addition to the unprofessional appearance and performance caused by this practice, an employee who is drinking is more likely to make mistakes in pouring, mixing, and properly recording sales than one who does not drink on the job.

In order to reduce the number of revenue control problems to a minimum, management must establish techniques and procedures for bar operation. Effective revenue control requires that employees adhere strictly to these techniques and procedures and that their performance be monitored by management. Over the years, bar operators have developed various approaches to revenue control. They follow one of the following operating patterns:

Bars without Guest Checks

Many bars, especially small, owner-operated neighborhood bars, do not use guest checks. These establishments do not normally have any charge sales. Customers pay cash, the owner is normally the bartender, and she collects all cash personally. This owner/bartender does not perceive any revenue control problem, and sees no need for guest checks. Some owners require each customer to pay for each drink as it is served; others serve customers more than one drink without paying, somehow remembering what the customer has drunk, and collecting the cash after the customer has finished the last drink. The system offers the advantage of simplicity, saves time that would be required to write guest checks, and is clearly inexpensive to operate. It works well enough as long as the owner is the bartender.

If the owner does not tend the bar and collect the cash personally, someone else must be given the responsibility, either a family member or a hired bartender. In either case, the person who tends bar may have some or all of the unacceptable work habits listed above. If so, revenues will be misrecorded or not recorded at all. To reduce the number of such problems, the owner will spend some amount of time at the bar observing the bartender, depending on the extent to which the bartender is trusted. Someone other than the owner may also be stationed at the bar to monitor the bartender, with or without his knowledge. This system, with some variations, works well in many establishments. However, if there is no one available to monitor the bartender, some other operating procedure must be found.

Bars Using Guest Checks

When the visual control methods described above are impossible or impractical, some degree of control is introduced with numbered guest checks. A standard procedure is established that requires that all drink orders be written or otherwise recorded on numbered checks. If all employees follow the procedure, records of all sales are available for daily audit. In its simplest form, such an audit would consist of verifying that no numbered checks are missing, that correct prices were charged for all drinks, and that total sales recorded on the checks equalled the total of cash and charge revenues recorded by the bartender or the person responsible for operating the cash register. With written records of sales available, it becomes possible for an owner or manager to monitor revenue.

The system is has some disadvantages. Essentially, there are two. First, writing orders on guest checks takes time. In addition, unless bartenders dry their hands thoroughly before writing an order, the check may be illegible, and the drying of hands also takes time. In either case, customer service will be slow during busy periods, possibly reducing sales volume and annoying customers who must wait for their drinks. This disadvantage affects only front bars; if a service bar is in use, drink orders are written on the numbered checks by servers, who then relay the orders to a bartender for preparation. In some service bars, the bartender is still required to record the sale in a register and must handle the written check for that purpose, which is a minor disadvantage; in others, the bartender merely prepares the drink, and the sale is recorded in a register by someone else. This latter approach permits better control by dividing the work, but may lead to slower service, depending in part on the location of the person operating the register.

Second, the cost of checks varies with the type, size, number of parts, and design. Some offered by stationers as standard forms are quite inexpensive; many printed to detailed specifications are much more expensive. The use of numbered guest checks does reduce the profit on a drink. The owners and manager of most well-organized bars agree that both disadvantages cited here are more than offset by the measure of control made possible by the use of numbered guest checks.

There are many variations on the way in which guest checks may be used. The following are some common examples.

Pre-Check System

There are registers available that enable bartenders to record each sale as drinks are served and to accumulate all the sales for one customer on one check. Such registers make it possible to require that a guest check be placed in front of each customer. When the customer is ready to leave, the check is rung up in the register as either a cash sale or a charge sale, and at the end of the day's operation, the total of the drink sales recorded in the register, plus any taxes, should equal the total of cash and charge sales. Readings taken from such a register at the end of a day would resemble those in Figure 18.1. The void key would be used to record such cases as drinks rejected by customers or unserved because a customer walks out. In

FIGURE 18.1
Cash Register Reconciliation

Register #1		6-12-XX
Liquor	$375.00	
Beer	45.00	
Wine	30.00	
Tax	18.00	
Tip	5.00	
Total		$473.00
Cash	$420.00	
Charge	42.00	
Voids	11.00	
Total		$473.00

any case, each void entry would be investigated by the beverage controller. The accountant or bookkeeper would adjust sales figures to reflect voids before making entries in the accounting records for the day's sales.

Automated Systems

Another approach to controlling revenue, particularly when close supervision by management is either impossible or impractical, is to install one of the many automated bars available. An **automated bar** is both an electronic sales terminal and an computerized dispensing device for beverages. The dispensing device is controlled by the sales terminal. Bottles are connected to the system, which may be in view of the customers or in some nearby location, out of sight. In either case, the bartender cannot pour directly from the bottles; their contents may be dispensed only by depressing keys on the terminal.

When a drink is ordered, the bartender obtains it by placing the proper glassware under the dispensing device, inserting a guest check in the terminal or in a separate printer controlled by the terminal, and depressing the terminal key with the name of the drink on it. When the key is depressed, the name of the drink and its preassigned sales price are printed on the check. Simultaneously, the terminal signals the release of the proper quantities of the correct ingredients, which are automatically dispensed. Both the drink and the check are given to the customer or to a server to takes them to the customer, depending on the type of bar.

At the end of each day, management obtains a report showing the number of each type of drink sold, as well as the total dollar sales recorded in the terminal. With some systems, a perpetual inventory is maintained for beverages connected to the system, and the number of ounces in the inventory is reduced appropriately with each drink order recorded.

Automated systems are available in a variety of sizes and configurations. Some hold a comparatively small number of bottles and can prepare only a limited number of drinks. Others can accommodate many bottles and produce hundreds of different drinks.

There are some significant advantages to automated systems over traditional methods of preparing drinks: the proportions of ingredients are exactly the same each time a given drink is prepared, and the drinks are thus of uniform quality, prepared according to the standard recipes programmed; the quantity of each ingredient is measured exactly, and the size of each drink of any given type is uniform. However, it must be noted that these systems only reduce the possibilities for the development of excessive costs through pilferage, spillage, and various bartender errors. The possibilities for charging incorrect prices are greatly reduced.

There are also some important disadvantages to these systems. None of them can accommodate customers' requests for variations of standard recipes. Because of this, they are more commonly used at service bars than front bars. At front bars, many customers react negatively to them. They are accustomed to watching bartender go through the ritual of mixing drinks—many are accomplished artists who enjoy displaying their showmanship—and having drinks prepared by a machine takes something away from the experience. In addition, traditional methods of drink preparation by bartenders often give the impression to the customer that he or she is receiving more than the standard measure—a dividend, so to speak. This may or may not be true, depending on the bar and the bartender, but the customer who believes that it is true does not react well to machine-prepared drinks, feeling that the measure is stingy, or the preparation is too exact to result in a good drink.

Systems Relying on Division of Labor

In many large operations where table service only is offered, particularly in major metropolitan hotels, sales control procedures may be easier to institute because labor is divided among many employees, including the full-time cashier and the service bartender. Whenever such division of labor exists and effective controls have been instituted, cheating becomes more difficult. While any effective control system must be designed to meet a particular establishment's needs, one possible control system is the following.

The server takes orders for drinks from customers at tables, records the items on a check, then proceeds to the service bar and orders the drinks from the service bartender. When the drinks are made and placed on a tray, the waiter goes to a beverage checker, who records on the guest check through a register the price of each drink. After serving the drinks, the waiter leaves the check with the customer at the table. A separate cashier is stationed near the door of the lounge, and the customer presents the check to this cashier on leaving. The casher either collects cash or prepares an appropriate charge voucher and rings the values into a register. At the end of the day, the readings from both the checker's and the cashier's machines are compared and any discrepancies investigated. Any missing checks can be traced to the servers responsible, provided that checks are distributed according to serial numbers and servers are required to sign for checks issued as well as to return unused checks. Other systems for larger operations typically are variations of these procedures.

Although none of these systems guarantees that all sales will result in appropriate revenue for the establishment, each adds some measure of control. Any procedure established to control revenue will add costs to an operation and reduce the speed of service. Some balance must be achieved between the need for revenue control, on the one hand, and the reluctance to incur cost, delay service, increase customer discontent, and possibly lower sales volume on the other.

CHAPTER ESSENTIALS

In this chapter, we defined the scope of beverage sales control and explained essential differences between food sales control and beverage sales control. We identified the three goals of beverage sales control as optimizing the number of sales, maximizing profit, and controlling revenue. We pointed out various special considerations in beverage operations that lead to significant differences in the meaning of these goals. We stated the principal reasons that customers patronize establishments that offer alcoholic beverages for sale. We discussed some of the market segments that beverage operators attempt to target and suggested some specific steps management can take to reach these target markets. We identified the two means considered appropriate to maximizing beverage profits—setting suitable drink prices and influencing customer selection of drinks. We listed a number of poor work habits that bartenders may exhibit and explained how these limit management's ability to institute revenue controls. Finally, we identified two basic operating patterns for beverage revenue control and described variations on both.

KEY TERMS IN THIS CHAPTER

Beverage sales control

Optimizing the number of beverage sales

Profit maximization

Controlling beverage revenue

Dram shop laws

Market type

Market segment

Pre-check system

Automated bar

QUESTIONS AND PROBLEMS

1. What are the three goals of beverage sales control?
2. Why is selling the maximum number of drinks to each customer an improper goal for a bar operator?
3. List and explain five possible reasons for a customer to patronize an establishment that offers alcoholic beverages for sale.
4. Identify two ways in which profit may be maximized in a beverage operation.
5. How do dram shop laws typically affect the cost of bar operation?
6. What are the principal considerations in determining beverage selling prices?
7. Select one beverage operation in your area, list the target markets it attempts to reach, and describe features of the operation that attract the market. If possible, identify specific steps management has taken to increase the appeal of the operation for that market.
8. Select a beverage operation in your area and list the market considerations that have influenced the selling prices management has established for drinks.

9. Two months ago Fred Sneed became the owner of a small bar in Springfield. When he assumed ownership, beverage cost percent was 24.5%. Since Fred assumed ownership, beverage cost percent has increased to 29.5%, although increases in purchase prices have been negligible, as have been changes in the sales mix. The bartender has been employed in the establishment for the last eight years. Fred has concluded that the increase is somehow related to the bartender's work and has decided to observe his performance closely. Rank in order the five most important work habits that he should observe.

10. If a beverage operation does not use guest checks, how can some degree of control be established over revenue?

11. What are the essential features of a pre-check system?

12. List the possible advantages and disadvantages of automated bars as compared to traditional methods for pouring and mixing drinks.

13. How does division of labor improve the effectiveness of revenue control?

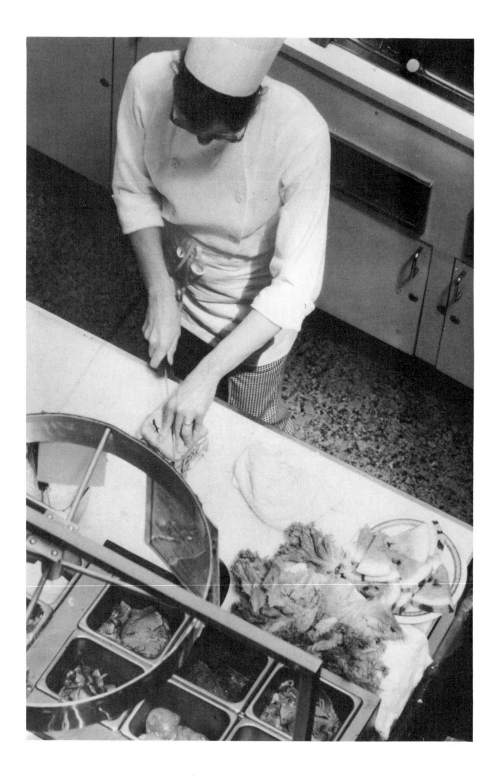

part four

Labor Control

Anyone who visits restaurants has witnessed situations that suggest the need for labor control. Sometimes it seems nearly impossible to get any service; the few servers in sight clearly have more customers to serve than they can possibly handle, and even when a customer has managed to place an order, it seems an eternity before the food is served. At other times, there seem to be more servers on duty than there are customers in the dining room, and one wonders how the management can afford to have all that help around when there appears to be no business to support it.

In the first example, one can readily imagine the number of customers who walk out in disgust without ordering at all, as well as those who silently resolve never to return after waiting perhaps fifteen minutes to order and another forty-five minutes to be served. The gross sales for the day are clearly less than they might have been if adequate service staff had been provided; gross sales for future days may be affected because of customers who have taken their business elsewhere.

In the restaurant where more staff members are on duty than are warranted by current business, the wages paid to unneeded staff increase payroll costs. At the very least, this will lead to owner dissatisfaction on the one hand, and, on the other, dissatisfaction among employees whose incomes depend largely on the tips they receive from customers.

In either case, one certain effect will be the reduction of net profit from current operations, from lower sales in the first instance, and from increased costs in the second. Clearly there is a need to control labor in such a way as to maximize sales while at the same time minimizing costs.

Labor control represents an attempt to obtain maximum efficiency from all employees without compromising standards of operating performance. We shall see that it is most difficult to achieve because of the relative unpredictability of the number of customers in a restaurant at any given time, and other factors. These will be discussed in the following chapters.

chapter 19

Labor Cost Determinants

Learning Objectives

After reading and studying this chapter, the student should be able to:

1. Explain why labor costs and labor cost percentages vary from one establishment to another.
2. Define labor cost control.
3. Explain why the minimizing of dollar wages is not necessarily the same as labor cost control.
4. Explain why each of the following is a determinant of labor cost:

weather	layout
labor legislation	preparation
labor contracts	service
labor turnover	menu
sales volume	hours of operation
location	management ability
equipment	

5. Define the key terms listed at the end of the chapter.

In all food and beverage establishments, including hotels and restaurants, the cost of labor accounts for considerable sums of money. Taken as a percentage of sales, the cost of labor typically ranges from 15% to 45%. In some special instances, labor cost percentages are as high as 60%, but only in establishment operated on a not-for-profit basis.

It will be worthwhile, at this point, to restate an important point made in the first section of this text, namely that the three basic categories of cost—fixed, directly variable, and semivariable—taken together must add up to a figure that is less than total sales if the operation is to show a profit. These costs must total less than 100% of sales. Therefore, the proportion of total sales that must be allocated to cover each of the three types of costs partly depends on the proportion required to cover the other two. If fixed and directly variable costs account for a high percentage of the income dollar, semivariable costs (primarily labor costs) must be kept down. By the same token, if fixed and directly variable costs are comparatively low, semivariable costs can be proportionally higher. Stated another way, assuming fixed costs as a constant 30% of sales in a particular restaurant that seeks to show a profit of 10% of sales, 60% of the sales dollars remain to cover directly variable and semivariable costs. If directly variable costs run regularly in the 20% range, then semivariable costs may be as high as 40% without disturbing the profit picture. On the other hand, if food and beverage costs are in the 45% range, then semivariable costs must be held to 15% of the sales dollar in order that the 10% desired profit be maintained. Figure 19.1 illustrates this point.

It should be obvious that an increase in the percentage of sales attributable to any cost category will have an effect on the remaining cost categories, on profit, or on both. If the semivariable cost of labor increases from 20% to 25%, then management must somehow reduce the percentages for the remaining costs or be prepared to accept a decreased percentage of profit. Similarly, if the percentage of variable costs increases, then management must be prepared to exercise some restraining influence on fixed or semivariable cost percentages if the percentage of profit is to be held constant.

The objective in this section of the text is to acquaint the student with accepted procedures and techniques for controlling the semivariable cost of labor in foodservice establishments. We will begin by defining labor cost control.

FIGURE 19.1
Cost Comparison: Two Restaurants

| | Restaurant A | | Restaurant B | |
	Dollars	Percentage	Dollars	Percentage
Sales	$300,000	100%	$300,000	100%
Fixed Costs	90,000	30%	90,000	30%
Semivariable Costs	60,000	20%	105,000	35%
Directly Variable Costs	120,000	40%	75,000	25%
Profit	30,000	10%	30,000	10%

LABOR COST CONTROL DEFINED

Labor cost control is a process by which management attempts to direct, regulate, and restrain employees' actions in order to obtain a desired level of performance at an appropriate level of cost. To the inexperienced, labor cost control is sometimes taken to suggest the mere reduction of payroll costs to their irreducible minimum, which might be achieved by employing a bare minimum number of people paid the minimum legal wage. But there is more to labor cost control than just minimizing dollar wages—a fact sometimes unknown to owners and managers who take the short-term view of operations, thinking only of immediate profits and not taking into account the long-term effects of their policies and actions.

Short-term policies geared strictly to minimizing immediate costs may have long-term undesirable effects, including decreased dollar sales, increased operating costs, and even business failure. For example, hiring a full staff of employees at minimum wage may minimize immediate labor costs but lead to poor-quality products, high labor turnover, customer dissatisfaction, decreasing sales volume, and a host of other long-term problems. Obviously, management should not pay beyond the wages necessary to attract and retain qualified personnel. To overpay may make for an operation that cannot be profitable.

Appropriate performance levels differ from establishment to establishment. For some—fast-food restaurants serving frozen, portioned products that need only be heated and served by comparatively unskilled labor—desired levels of performance may be such that minimum-wage employees are appropriate; for others—fine restaurants attempting to offer the finest in products and services available in their areas—appropriate levels of performance may be such that wages considerably above those prevailing in the area may be required.

But level of performance is not simply a function of wage rates. Unskilled employees in fast-food establishments cannot perform at appropriate levels unless they are provided with appropriate equipment, given suitable training, placed in a working environment conducive to working, and supervised in a manner that will inspire them to work and remain on the staff. This is also true for highly skilled employees in the finest restaurants. Suitable wage levels do not guarantee appropriate performance. Many other factors are involved in ensuring suitable levels of performance.

In the author's view, the discussion of techniques and procedures for controlling labor cost must be prefaced by an examination of some of the many determinants of labor cost. Some of them are essentially not controllable by a manager, but many—the majority, certainly—can be controlled to a greater or lesser extent. Although the following discussion treats each briefly and singly, one must keep in mind that the determinants of labor cost are so interdependent and intertwined that managers do not normally have the luxury of dealing with them one at a time in this fashion.

LABOR COST DETERMINANTS
Weather

Of all the determinants of labor cost, weather is surely the least controllable. Weather often affects sales volume, which in turn affects staffing levels in our industry. Bad weather, such as snowstorms or heavy rain, deters potential customers from venturing out to restaurants. Interestingly, identical weather conditions typically increase sales volume in hotel restaurants for the very same reason—those who might have gone out to other restaurants remain in the hotel to avoid the weather. To the extent one can obtain accurate weather forecasts, one can plan staffing levels suitable for anticipated demand. The problem, of course, is that weather forecasts are not always accurate, and unforeseen weather changes may render planned staffing levels inappropriate. When this occurs, it is often too late to modify the employee schedule. Sometimes employees can be sent home early if the restaurant is overstaffed, although this may have negative consequences, particularly on employee morale, turnover, and performance. On the other hand, weather changes that render planned staffing levels inadequate may cause other types of problems, including poor service and even lost sales, as well as an overworked staff. These consequences can sometimes be avoided by maintaining a list of employees willing to come to work on call.

Labor Legislation

Labor legislation differs considerably from state to state, and thus the net effect of legislation on labor cost for any particular food operation must be discussed in terms of the legislation in effect in the particular state where the operation is located. However, it is possible to generalize a discussion of a significant area covered by legislation in all states: minimum wages and provision for overtime.

A **minimum wage** is the gross dollar wage before deductions that an employer must pay each employee in covered categories. It is usually expressed as a dollar figure per hour. Minimum-wage legislation normally defines a maximum number of hours per day for work beyond which overtime must be paid, and a maximum number of consecutive working days per week beyond which overtime must also be paid. As a labor intensive industry, the foodservice industry has traditionally employed a large number of unskilled persons, many of whom have been paid the prevailing minimum wage. Thus, as state legislatures have steadily increased minimum wages, labor cost in the restaurant industry has been significantly affected.

In addition, some states meet the cost of unemployment insurance by levying a tax on an employer's gross dollar payroll. This usually takes the form of a percentage of that payroll, and the percentage is governed by an experience factor such that the higher the employee turnover rate, the higher the percentage that must be paid. Because the foodservice industry traditionally experiences a higher rate of employee turnover than almost any other industry, this extra expense, categorized as wage expense, has been of considerable importance in calculating overall labor cost. In an effort to reduce the percentage levied against gross payroll, some restaurant employers have made special efforts to reduce the rate of employee turnover and thus reduce at least one aspect of labor cost.

Labor Contracts

The presence or absence of labor contracts will always be an important factor affecting labor cost. Where employees are organized and labor contracts exist, wages for each category of employee tend to be high. For purposes of this discussion, such fringe benefits as vacation pay, sick pay, employees meals, and health insurance are included in the term **wages.** These fringe benefits are most likely to be found where union organizations and contracts exist.

Although the effects of wages and fringe benefits on labor cost are apparent, in situations where labor contracts exist there are often other factors that also have a significant effect. Of primary concern are provisions in labor contracts that limit management's freedom to change work rules. Such contracts typically restrict management's ability to alter the duties of an employee in a particular job category. An effect of this may be to force the employer to hire someone for a job when existing employees have the time and ability to do it, with the effect of increasing the overall labor cost and the labor cost per unit. In one hotel in a certain large city, the work rules mandate that every station in the main kitchen be manned whenever the kitchen is open, regardless of business volume and menu changes. Such a restrictive rule has great impact on the overall labor cost.

Labor Turnover

Labor turnover, a ratio relating the number of departing employees to the total number of employees on the staff and usually expressed as a percentage, is unfortunately high in the foodservice industry. It has been commonly measured at 100% per year across the industry, with some specific establishments showing rates as high as 300%. This does not compare favorably with turnover rates in American industry in general, which tend to range between 10% and 20%. The effect of high labor turnover on labor cost is often enormous, for it places managers in positions of facing two interdependent problems:

1. Filling vacant positions.
2. Training newly hired employees.

When jobs become vacant and management deems it desirable to fill those jobs, it is typically the responsibility of management itself to see to the recruiting, interviewing, selecting, and hiring of the replacement personnel. Large organizations may employ a personnel department or a single personnel officer who is assigned to much of this work; but small restaurants have no personnel department, and the work falls to the restaurant manager and possibly to various department heads. It can be time-consuming, depending in part on the nature and extent of the skills sought in a new employee; and to the degree that a manager or department head is engaged in recruiting and hiring, that manager must defer some other tasks. If turnover is so great that it becomes necessary to hire someone full-time to fill vacancies, the additional cost is obvious. If such work consumes a great portion of the manager's time, it may become necessary to hire some assistance for the manager, also at considerable cost.

The need for some degree of training exists in all foodservice establishments. Managers, after all, are not typically able to hire employees with a thorough knowledge of the job for which they are hired. On the most elementary level, training may entail merely showing a new dishwasher the location of the machine and explaining the operation of the controls, or it may involve a meeting with a new chef who needs to be familiarized with the nature of the menu or the restaurant's clientele. On another level, training may include daily meetings with sales personnel to make sure that each understands the menu fully and is aware of the items management is most anxious to sell. Then again, training may mean taking completely inexperienced persons and teaching them everything they need to know to perform some particular job, either completely on premises, or partly with the aid of some outside agencies, including public, private, and proprietary schools. For a server, this complete training might include instruction in procedures for waiting on customers; methods of serving and removing dishes, flatware, and glassware from tables; standard setups for tables; napkin-folding techniques; and methods for presenting and pouring wines.

Training should be conducted on an ongoing basis and need not be restricted to the new employee. Management should maintain certain standards for the performance of each job in the establishment, and to the extent that employees are not performing up to these levels, management may use many opportunities for training to improve overall performance. In addition, if management changes some aspect of operations, such as introducing a new item on the menu that requires special presentation to the customer, the staff must be trained to deal with the change.

Training, even in its simplest form, is not accomplished without cost, however. Both trainer and trainee are being paid while training is being carried out, and frequently neither is as productive as a completely trained individual would be. Viewed as an investment in time, money, or both, training will over the long term provide a more efficient, more effective, and more knowledgeable staff. As a result, customers will probably be better satisfied, and revenue is likely to be higher.

Some establishments do little training, sometimes because managers do not realize its importance, and sometimes because managers are unwilling to incur costs that do not provide immediate returns in higher revenue. In such places, it may be apparent to customers that employees are not performing their jobs in the most satisfactory manner. Service may be slow, personnel may be impolite, the quality of food and beverage items may be below customers' expectations, and the overall impression may be entirely unsatisfactory. For these reasons revenue is likely to decrease or at least be lower than it might have been under better conditions.

Establishments that neglect training frequently develop other problems. Managers who are not particularly understanding or articulate tend to become angry with employees who are not performing satisfactorily, often without realizing that the poor performance is largely the result of never having explained the employee's job in sufficient detail. Employees quit or are fired and are replaced by others, who repeat the entire cycle. Not only do such establishments suffer for failing to satisfy customers, but they must bear the often hidden costs of high employee turnover rates, including advertising costs in classified sections of newspapers, employment agency fees, higher contribution rates for state unemployment insurance costs based on experience factors, and revenue lost while some position was vacant.

From a labor control viewpoint, it is apparent that employees operate more efficiently and effectively if they are suitably trained for their work. In the long run, this leads to lower labor costs and potentially higher gross receipts for the establishment. The extent of training carried on in any particular establishment is an important determinant of the overall cost of labor.

Sales Volume

For a restaurant of any given size, increases in sales volume will result in increased productivity per employee up to his or her maximum capacity to perform. For example, in a certain restaurant selling only hamburgers and employing only one cook, 100 hamburgers are typically prepared and sold during one busy hour of the lunch period. During the slack period of the afternoon, the same cook prepares only 10 hamburgers during a one-hour period. If the cook is being paid $8 per hour, the labor cost per unit produced during the peak period is equal to his hourly wage of $8 divided by the 100 hamburgers produced during that period, or $.08 per unit. On the other hand, the labor cost per unit for hamburgers prepared during the slow period is equal to his $8 wage divided by the 10 hamburgers sold, or $.80.

It is clear from the foregoing that the cook in question is working at less than his proven capacity during the slack hour, obviously because of the absence of customers. We can see that as the sales volume increases, the cook's labor is used more efficiently. At the same time, as his efficiency increased, the cost of labor per unit produced decreased. Therefore, it is apparent that an increase in sales volume results in greater employee efficiency at lower labor cost per unit.

In the previous example, one employee is the minimum number that can be hired for that particular job. However, in larger establishments that require greater numbers of employees as the minimum, it is possible to better schedule employees for greater efficiency, thus keeping each employee more of the time. It is desirable to schedule fewer employees during slack periods and more during busy periods, thus increasing individual efficiency.

In addition, large restaurants are often able to take advantage of the economies of large-scale production. In simplest terms, this also might be described as the division of labor, assigning individuals to the tasks they are best qualified to complete and paying each of them a wage commensurate with his level of ability and training. For example, the single cook cited above might be required as part of his job to wash dishes, keep the counter clear, or act as cashier, all for the single wage of $8 per hour. In effect, the jobs of cook, dishwasher, counterman, and cashier are all being paid $8 per hour. Furthermore, the particular individual in the job may not be very good at the side jobs assigned, and his performance at those tasks may be less efficient than that of someone hired perhaps at a lower hourly wage, but specifically trained for the job. The small restaurant can usually do nothing about this, but the large restaurant frequently can hire dishwashers and countermen at considerably lower wages.

In large establishments where there is enough work to keep a specialist in any category busy most of the time, it is usually cheaper to hire the specialist at the prevailing wage for his or her job category, thus reducing the labor cost per unit produced. As an illustration, if the hamburger restaurant cited above were large enough, it could hire cooks at $8 per hour, dishwashers at $5.00 per hour, and a counterman at $4.50 per hour, thus resulting in a reduction of the overall labor cost per unit produced. As an additional benefit, each of the specialists should be more efficient at his job and capable of performing higher quality work. In the long run, this should reduce the labor cost per unit still further.

Location

It is well known that the cost of labor varies from one part of the country to another. In many rural areas, particularly those where jobs are scarce and competition for jobs is severe, employers can often pay comparatively low hourly rates, and so keep labor costs down. This same condition often can be noted outside rural areas, particularly in depressed areas and in areas where living costs are low. However, while such conditions as these may result in lower labor costs in dollars, labor costs as percentages of sales may not be lower at all. The reason for this may be the lower menu prices in effect in such areas.

On the other hand, the opposite effect often can be noted in metropolitan areas where living costs are greater and wage scales higher. Under such conditions, labor costs in dollars may be quite high by some standards, but as percentages of sales may be identical to those found in rural and depressed areas. To illustrate, one might consider a certain item produced in a kitchen in one area at a labor cost of $1.50 and sold at a menu price of $5, contrasted with that same item produced in another area at a labor cost of $3 and sold for $10. In the second instance, the labor cost in dollars is twice what it is in the first, but in both cases the relationship between labor cost and selling price is identical.

Equipment

Assuming that certain tasks such as peeling potatoes, washing dishes, and slicing meats must be accomplished in a particular kitchen, lower labor costs will result from accomplishing those tasks with modern equipment rather than by traditional

- who are your
  competitors?
- what are they doing.

hand methods. For example, a machine can peel 100 pounds of potatoes in less than twenty minutes, while the same job done by hand might require many hours. Slicing a round of beef with modern slicing equipment may take less than five minutes, while doing the same job manually could require more than fifteen minutes. Chopping cabbage for cole slaw by hand might require four to six times the amount of time needed to do the job with up-to-date machinery. In addition, old equipment in poor condition often requires more time to accomplish a given job than equipment that is newer or in better condition. In general, from the point of view of labor cost, doing work by machine is cheaper than doing it by hand, and doing a job with good equipment is cheaper than doing it with poor equipment. The amount of equipment in use, as well as its variety and condition, has considerable effect on labor cost.

Layout

Labor cost is directly affected by the manner in which space is used. Within the work area, equipment must be arranged to facilitate, rather than impede, employees' ability to perform their tasks. In new establishments, equipment and facilities can be suitably arranged during construction; in converted properties, arrangement is often less than satisfactory because of walls that cannot be moved, plumbing that is not readily moved, and room sizes that are less than ideal for a given purpose. If equipment is poorly arranged, employees may have to walk excessive distances. In extreme cases, it may even be necessary to hire employees who might not have been required had the equipment and facilities been better arranged. For example, if the person working at the broiler does not have ready access to a reach-in refrigerator, she may have to walk a considerable distance each time a broiler order is placed. If the broiler were extremely busy, it might be necessary to assign one person to bring items from a refrigerator when they were required at the broiler station. In some hotels, the kitchen is so far removed from the dining room that a larger than necessary staff of servers is required.

In all of the above instances, equipment and facilities have been so arranged that labor costs are higher than they might have been. It is not a question of the workers being inefficient; the poor layout of the restaurant virtually forces them to be so.

Preparation

Theoretically one could rate all foodservice operations on a scale of zero to 100 to reflect the amount of preparation required on the premises. At the zero end of the scale would be any establishment that purchased all items precooked, fully prepared and preportioned, thus requiring minimal preparation beyond reheating prior to sale. At the opposite end would appear those establishments that prepared everything on the premises, including such basic ingredients as mayonnaise and catsup. In places falling near the zero end of the scale, labor costs could clearly be kept minimal. Foods could be served in the disposable packages in which they were purchased, thus eliminating the need for dishwashing. Clearly, this type of establishment would require largely unskilled personnel in the kitchen. "Cooking" would merely be a matter of reheating, and the services of a traditional chef would not be required. Conversely, restaurants at the other end of the scale would require kitchen personnel with special talents for comparatively complex and conceivably elaborate preparations, probably under the expert guidance of a highly trained and highly paid executive chef. In addition, such an establishment would require additional personnel to take charge of the many responsibilities involved in the purchasing, receiving, storing, and issuing of the expensive and highly perishable basic ingredients required for many of the preparations.

While few, if any, restaurants would appear at either absolute end of such a scale, a reasonable number would be near either end. Typical fast-food restaurants would appear at the lower end, and traditional restaurants offering haute cuisine would appear at the higher end. Clearly fast-food restaurants have a considerably lower labor cost than those offering continental dishes to customers with gourmet tastes.

Service

Foodservice establishments could also be charted on a scale of zero to 100, based on the amount of service offered to the customer. At the lower end of the scale might appear vending machine operations offering no service. At the other end are continental establishments that offer French service involving the completion of the cooking of food in the dining room on a gueridon. In the middle range, one could find typical American restaurants where food is plated in the kitchen and served by a server, whose station includes a number of tables.

For those establishments at the lower end of the scale, labor costs for service tend to be minimal. On the other hand, establishments near the opposite end of the scale require not only considerable numbers of servers but also personnel who can demonstrate considerable skill in preparations and service. Clearly, labor costs would be lower in restaurants in the former category and higher in those in the latter category.

Menu

From the point of view of labor cost, it is less costly to prepare 300 portions of one item than it is to prepare 30 portions each of 10 different items, especially if those 10 items require several types of preparation, such as braising, broiling, baking, roasting, and boiling. This is because one employee could conceivably prepare all 300 portions of the single item, but the preparation of 10 different items by several different methods would probably require employees in several different job categories, particularly if all portions were needed at one time, as in the case of a banquet. This is one of the primary reasons that many establishments restrict their menus to only a few items. In the case of certain fast-food operations, the menu may even be restricted to one basic entree: the hamburger. Clearly, the limiting of numbers and varieties of menu items is one factor of considerable importance in the control of labor cost.

Hours of Operation

Obviously, the number of hours a restaurant operates will have significant impact on labor cost. A restaurant open only for dinner will have lower labor costs than that same operation open for three meals each day. However, decisions concerning numbers of hours of operation involve more considerations than the mere cost of labor.

Every operation has overhead costs that exist regardless of whether the restaurant is open or closed. These typically include rent or mortgage payments, salaries not based on hours of work (managers' salaries as distinguished from those of service personnel paid hourly wages), insurance premiums, depreciation, property taxes, and so on. These fixed costs are independent of business volume. As a general rule, as long as additional revenue gained by staying open is greater than the additional cost incurred during that period of time, remaining open is desirable from a financial viewpoint.

For example, assume a restaurateur is trying to determine whether to extend the dinner hours from 9:00 P.M. to 10:00 P.M. He calculates that additional wages for that hour will be $148; heat and light are estimated at $11. These additional costs can be considered fixed once the decision to remain open for the extra hour is made. Variable costs, including food, beverages, linen, and miscellaneous, are estimated at 38% of each dollar of sale. Thus, from the formulas in Chapter 3:

$$\text{Breakeven for the addition hour} = \frac{FC}{CR \text{ (which is } 1 - VR)}$$

$$BE = \frac{\$159}{.62}$$

$$BE = \$256.45$$

If management can project sales volume in excess of $256.45, it will be financially advantageous to remain open. Thus, assume a sales volume of $350 for the additional hour. Costs for that period would include the $159 previously cited plus 38% of $350, or $133. Total costs for the additional hour at the projected sales level would be $292, leaving a net revenue of $58 ($350 − $292) that would be available to cover overhead costs of the restaurant and additional profit. Management must decide if the $58 additional net revenue is worth the time and effort required. Employee morale and long-term effects on overall sales volume must also be considered.

Management Ability

The cost of labor is greatly determined by management's ability to plan, organize, control, direct, and lead the organization in such a way that the desired level of employee performance is obtained at an appropriate level of cost. This requires, among other things, that the manager understand what work is to be done, the number and types of employees required to do it, what constitutes suitable performance, how employees should be scheduled to optimize performance level, what training, facilities, equipment, and other materials will be required, and how and when these are to be obtained and in what quantities. The manager's ability to motivate, direct, and lead will determine the quality of work and level of performance.

This might be summed up by saying that good management will have positive effects on labor costs while poor management will have negative effects. A good manager, merely by being a good manager, will create a work environment conducive to optimal performance at minimal cost. The student who has studied management methods and leadership styles will recognize that these topics are beyond the scope of a control text.

In the light of the foregoing discussion, it is apparent that each of these factors must be taken into account in any intelligent analysis of labor cost. Moreover, because of the many differences that exist among establishments within this industry, which includes operations ranging from hotdog stands to the finest hotels, and from fast-food chains to award-winning gourmet-style restaurants, it is impossible to arrive at industrywide standards or averages for a particular manager to use as guides for his own establishment.

Each owner or manager must base the desired and optimal labor cost and labor cost percentage for her operation on a host of factors and must recognize that labor cost in a particular operation will be affected to a greater or lesser extent by the various determinants discussed above (weather, labor legislation, labor contracts, labor turnover, training, sales volume, location, equipment, layout, preparation, service, menu, hours of operation, as well as her own ability). Clearly, the effect of each of these factors varies considerably from restaurant to restaurant. Indeed, two identical restaurants located in different areas do not, and probably should not, have the same labor costs or the same labor cost percentages. In fact, two such restaurants will normally be found to have significantly different cost structures for food, beverages, and overhead, as well as for labor.

In the final analysis, every restaurant owner or manager must control combined food, beverage, and labor so that the operation earns a satisfactory profit. That combined figure typically should not exceed 60% to 70% of sales, depending on overhead, if overhead is to be met and profits are to result.

Having discussed the determinants of labor cost, it will now be appropriate to examine specific techniques and procedures that managers employ in attempting to control labor costs. These will be the subjects of the next two chapters.

CHAPTER ESSENTIALS

In this chapter, we explained why labor costs and labor cost percentages vary from one establishment to another by illustrating the comparative cost structures of two common types of restaurants. We defined labor cost control and explained why minimal labor costs are not necessarily optimal labor costs. Finally, we listed and explained thirteen major determinants of labor cost: weather, labor legislation, labor contracts, labor turnover, sales volume, location, equipment, layout, preparation, service, menu, hours of operation, and management ability.

KEY TERMS IN THIS CHAPTER

Fixed cost

Directly variable cost

Semivariable cost

Labor cost control

Minimum wage

Wages

Labor turnover

QUESTIONS AND PROBLEMS

1. A restaurant's income statement shows the following cost and sales structure:

Sales	$450,000
Fixed Costs	$135,000
Directly Variable Costs	120,000

   What must the semivariable cost figure be if the restaurant is to show a profit of $30,000?

2. A restaurant's cost structure, expressed as a percentage of sales, is as follows:

Fixed costs	30%
Directly variable costs	25%

   As a percentage of sales, what must the semivariable costs be if the restaurant is to show a 10% profit?

3. Rank the type of restaurants listed below in order by percentage of labor cost, from low to high. In each case, discuss the effect of preparation on labor cost.

   a. An industrial cafeteria using primarily convenience foods.

   b. A seafood restaurant advertising "strictly fresh fish."

   c. A diner specializing in hot meals served to truck drivers.

   d. An elaborate French restaurant.

4. A restaurant that employs one cook sells only hamburgers. During the peak lunch hour, he is able to produce 120 hamburgers per hour. During the slack afternoon period, he produces only 30 hamburgers per hour. If each hamburger sells for sixty cents and the cook is paid $8.00 per hour, calculate the labor cost per hamburger for one hour during each period.

5. In a paragraph of at least fifty words, discuss the possible effects on labor cost of a newly negotiated labor contract.

6. Select and describe a reasonably well-known restaurant in your area. Then discuss the effect of at least five of the factors analyzed in this chapter on that particular restaurant's labor cost.

7. What are some of the hidden costs of high labor turnover?

8. Research the various types of dining room service (American, French, Russian, English, and cafeteria); then rank them according to the labor costs they create. Justify the order in which you have ranked them.

9. Under what circumstances might it be cheaper to use employees to perform certain kitchen work typically performed by machine?

10. What labor legislation exists in your area, and what effect does it have on labor cost? Include in your answer federal minimum wage and overtime provisions.

11. The Aliby Restaurant is normally open for business until 8:00 P.M. Recently business has been getting better during the time period just before closing, and the manager is attempting to determine the viability of remaining open until 9:00 P.M. She estimates her additional costs for the extra hour as follows:

    Labor = $75
    Heat, light, and gas = $12
    Variable cost of food, beverage, etc. = 40% of sales

    a. What additional sales are necessary for the manager to break even exactly on the extra hour of opening?

    b. If the manager were able to obtain $280 in sales volume for the extra hour, what income could be applied to normal overhead expenses?

chapter 20

Controlling Labor Costs I

Learning Objectives

After reading and studying this chapter, the student should be able to:

1. Identify the primary purpose of labor control.
2. Distinguish between variable cost personnel and fixed cost personnel.
3. Explain the nature of demand for restaurant products, and differentiate it from the demand for other manufactured products.
4. List the preliminary steps necessary for work organization.
5. Prepare an organization chart.
6. Write a job description.
7. Develop an analysis of business volume.
8. Distinguish between the scheduling of variable cost personnel and that of fixed cost personnel.
9. Prepare a table of manpower requirements and an hourly schedule for variable cost personnel from an analysis of business volume.
10. Identify the means by which the cost of fixed cost employees may be adjusted on a temporary or on a permanent basis.
11. Explain how the computer can aid management in analyzing business volume and in determining manpower requirements.
12. Define each of the Key Terms at the end of the chapter.

Our discussion of the factors affecting labor cost in the previous chapter showed that job categories and numbers of personnel involved in each vary greatly from restaurant to restaurant. As the extent of preparation increases, the numbers of job categories and the degrees of specialization in each increase as well. In addition, as service becomes more complicated, going from self-service to elaborate French service, the number of personnel required to perform the service and the degree of expertise necessary both increase. Regardless of the extent of preparation and the type and extent of service, however, managers should work to ensure that the workers in their establishments are performing as effectively as possible.

THE PURPOSE OF LABOR CONTROL

The primary purpose of labor control is to maximize the efficiency of the labor force in a manner consistent with the established standards of quality and service. Ideally, each employee's services will be utilized as effectively as possible. There should be a sufficient number of dishwashers working to ensure that dishes are washed as efficiently as possible, but there should be no time when dishwashers stand around with nothing to do. Similarly, a sufficient number of servers should ensure that all customers are served as quickly as possible while standards of service are maintained, but at no time should there be more than a sufficient number on hand to serve the customers then in the restaurant.

NATURE OF DEMAND FOR RESTAURANT PRODUCTS

In all efforts to maximize efficiency and control labor cost, management must recognize that a basic difference between the food business and other manufacturing industries makes it more difficult to control labor costs. The manufacturer and the restaurant operator can anticipate demand for their products at future times. The restaurant operator knows with some degree of certainty that the busy season will bring significantly more business than slow periods. Similarly, the manufacturer has busy and slow times. However, the manufacturer can utilize labor now in preparing products for sale at a later time. The restaurant operator *cannot* utilize labor now for a future demand, except to a very limited degree. For example, salad dressings can be prepared in quantity so that sufficient amounts are on hand to last a week or so, and possibly certain meat items can be precut and stored for future use, depending on standards. However, because of the perishability of food products, they cannot be prepared for demand six months hence. The furniture manufacturer, on the other hand, can gear the production of his present labor to demand six months in the future.

Thus, production in a restaurant must be geared for immediate sale of the items produced, and labor must be hired and available to meet that demand. Further, the demand for the items produced fluctuates not only daily but also hourly, so that to achieve ultimate efficiency in the utilization of labor, it is necessary to predict and prepare for the hourly demand for products and schedule accordingly—a difficult task at best.

LABOR CLASSIFICATIONS FOR CONTROL PURPOSES

It is important for any manager attempting to maximize efficiency and to control the labor cost percentage to recognize the existence of two classifications of employees:

1. Variable cost personnel.
2. Fixed cost personnel.

Taken as a whole, labor cost becomes a semivariable cost, increasing with increasing volume of business and decreasing with decreasing volume of business, but not in direct proportion to changes in volume.

Because the treatment of each category of employees is significantly different in the establishment of a labor control system, they will be discussed separately.

Variable Cost Personnel

Variable cost personnel are those whose numbers are related to the volume of business. As business volume increases, hiring more personnel in this category becomes necessary; consequently, the labor cost in dollars increases for this classification of employee. The reverse also should be true: as business volume decreases, it is possible to decrease the number of employees in this category and thus to decrease the dollar cost of labor.

Typical examples of these kinds of employees are servers and busboys. When business volume reaches a peak, as it typically does during normal meal hours, comparatively large numbers of these workers must be available. During nonpeak times, such as the middle of the afternoon, reduced business volume can be handled with comparatively fewer employees in these categories.Clearly, for employees in these categories the dollar cost of labor is higher during peak hours than it is during nonpeak hours.

Other examples of employees who typically fall into the variable cost category are dishwashers and certain food preparation personnel. As business volume increases, so does the work for these employees; although their hours of work do not necessarily coincide with the hours of peak sales. Preparation personnel, for example, are needed in comparatively large numbers before the hours of anticipated peak sales so that food will be ready when needed.

A time lapse normally exists between the onset of peak sales in the dining room and the beginning of peak dishwashing needs in the kitchen. In addition, the period of peak dishwashing usually continues for some time after peak food sales have ended. Thus, an increase or decrease in business volume will dictate the need for an increase or decrease in the number of variable cost personnel; but their hours of work does not necessarily coincide with the hours of peak business volume.

It is important to recognize that the points made in the foregoing discussion also apply to periodic or seasonal changes in business volume. During slow periods, fewer variable cost personnel are needed to handle reduced business volume; as volume increases during busier periods, more of these employees must be hired. One typical example is a restaurant at a well-known eastern seashore resort, which does comparatively little business during the winter months but operates at near capacity during the summer. The number of variable cost personnel is kept to a minimum during the slow season and greatly expanded during the busy summer season.

Fixed Cost Personnel

Fixed cost personnel are those whose numbers have little relation to the volume of business. As business volume increases and decreases, the number of these employees remains relatively constant. Because of this, the cost of their services in dollars also remains relatively constant. Typical examples include the manager, the bookkeeper, the chef, and the steward, as well as maintenance personnel and cashiers. Regardless of the increases and decreases in business volume, there will be only one manager. The same is true for the chef. As business volume changes, it becomes necessary to vary the number of personnel working under the chef's jurisdiction, but the chef, whose job as a result will vary in difficulty, will be the single constant factor in the kitchen. The same is usually true of the bookkeeper. During a slow period, the sales figure entered in the accounting records of the business may be only $1,000 for a given day, but it takes neither more nor less time to make that entry than it does to enter a sales figure of $10,000 for a single day during a busy period. Depending on the particular duties assigned to the bookkeeper, preparation for making the bookkeeping entry may take longer in the case of $10,000 in sales, but it is highly unlikely that any additional bookkeeping help will be hired during the busy period.

WORK ORGANIZATION

For the manager to have labor efficiency, employees' work must be organized. To do that properly, the following preliminary steps are advisable:

1. Establish an operational plan.
2. Prepare job descriptions for all positions in the organizational plan.
3. Prepare an analysis of business volume.

Establishing an Operational Plan

Establishing an operational plan requires the owner or manager first to develop a clear idea of the nature of her operation, including the type of clientele, the nature of the products offered, and the extent and type of service rendered. In addition, she must anticipate with some accuracy the number of meals to be prepared and served. Once the owner or manager has formulated an idea of the nature and scope of the operation, she can begin to think in terms of specific jobs that must be performed.

As an illustration, consider the case of a comparatively small establishment serving fast foods from a limited menu and offering counter service rather than table service to a working clientele. The manager could order the comparatively small selection of frozen, preportioned foods and oversee the simple cooking of these items by a small number of cooks of limited ability, who would also serve as counter help. If the items were all served in disposable containers, the services of dishwasher might not be needed. And if the manager were also able to handle the cash register, a cashier would not be necessary. The restaurant could exist with only two categories of employees—manager and cook/counter help—and with that idea clearly in mind, the manager could begin to think of hiring a staff.

In contrast, a large restaurant offering continental cuisine prepared from raw materials by highly skilled kitchen personnel, and highly professional French service, would require a large staff consisting of a number of specialists. The kitchen staff might consist of skilled professionals, carefully trained in the arts of butchering meats, preparing soups and sauces, decorating cold platters, and doing other jobs appropriate to such a restaurant. Typically, the manager could not handle any of the other tasks in addition to her own job and hence would require the services of receiving clerks, stewards, storeroom clerks, hosts, cashiers, and a bookkeeper.

In addition to establishing the categories of employees needed to operate an establishment as she sees it, a manager must also think in terms of the relationships that should exist between and among employees in various job classifications. Briefly stated, the manager must decide which employees will be responsible for seeing to it that other employees do certain work. The manager must decide, for example, that the chef will have complete jurisdiction over the production of food items, and that to carry out this responsibility, the chef must be placed in charge of the specialists who will serve under his direction and guidance, such as the sous chef, the saucier, the legumier, and the garde manager, among others. The chef will supervise these other workers, and it is important that they know this and fully understand all the implications of it. In turn, the chef must know that he is responsible to the manager and works under the manager's direction. The chef must also realize that a certain special working relationship must exist between him and the steward; that while they are equals in the organizational structure, they must be cooperate fully if the best interests of the restaurant and its customers are to be served.

So that all of these distinctions and relationships may be seen in their proper perspectives, the owner or manager of a restaurant is usually advised to set them down on paper in the form of a **functional organization chart**, such as that illustrated in Figure 20.1. A functional organization chart shows the positions according to function within the operation. The lines drawn from one position to another signify the lines of authority and cooperation. An unbroken line from one position to another indicates that the person below reports to and takes direction

FIGURE 20.1
Table of Organization

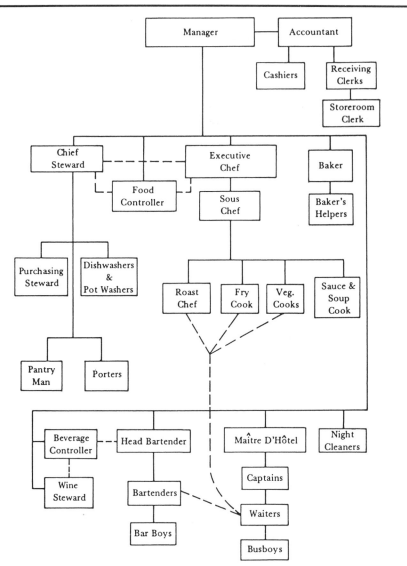

from the person immediately above on the chart. The dotted lines show communication and cooperation between the two positions, but one does not have authority over or the responsibility for the actions of the other. Thus, on the chart in Figure 20.1, the unbroken connecting line shows that the position of executive chef is next above that of sous chef. This, of course, means that the sous chef reports to the executive chef and takes direction from him. On the other hand, the lateral dotted line between the executive chef and the chief steward shows that the two are expected to cooperate in every possible way in accomplishing their respective tasks, but that neither takes direction from the other.

Once the functional organization chart is completed to accurately reflect the operational plan of the owner or manager, particularly with respect to the job titles necessary for successful operation, it is desirable to prepare an appropriate job description for each job title on the chart.

Preparing Job Descriptions

A primary purpose of creating a job description for each position on the organizational chart is to list in detail the duties each employee with any given title will be expected to perform. The writing of job descriptions forces management to determine in advance which jobs are to be done by which employees. This ensures that each task is assigned to some position. In addition, by reviewing the completed job descriptions, management has the opportunity to see that an appropriate collection of tasks has been grouped under one job title in such a way that no employee will be asked to perform a series of unrelated tasks requiring very different skills.

In some instances, job descriptions go one step further by specifying particular methods for performing particular tasks. The job description illustrated in Figure 20.2, for example, includes instructions on how certain jobs are to be done. In this case, the job description not only shows the dishwasher's duties and responsibilities in a general way but also gives instructions on the operation of the dishwashing machine, including a full explanation of the washing and rinsing temperature requirements. It also includes a detailed discussion of which items are to be washed by machine and which by hand.

Once the job descriptions are complete—once management has completely reviewed all tasks and assigned each to a particular job title in an orderly and logical way—a copy of the appropriate job description can be given to each employee in each job category. By this means, every employee on the staff can have a complete and thorough understanding of the nature of his or her job, as well as complete instructions for performing it. With these specifications for each job set down in writing, there can be no question of who is responsible for doing what within the framework of the organization.

Once a complete job description has been placed in the hands of each employee, management has a means for holding each employee accountable for performing a particular job in a particular way. One cannot hold an employee responsible for successfully completing a job unless she has been assigned it by management. The written job description is an important and useful means of assigning specific work. In addition, when work is well organized in this manner, it is more likely that costs will be kept to a minimum.

FIGURE 20.2
Sample Job Description

Job Description

Title: Dishwasher

Summary of Work Performed: Washes all dishes, glassware, and silver. Maintains dishwashing machine cleanliness. Keeps dishwashing area clean.

Duties:
1. Washes all dishes, silver, and glassware in automatic dishwasher as follows:
   a. Wash hands and put on clean apron before starting work.
   b. Scrape all dishes into garbage can.
   c. Stack dishes, silver and glassware in separate containers, making sure no container is overloaded.
   d. Obtain instructions for operating dishwasher from steward, taking care that following temperatures are maintained.
      (1) Wash cycle: 140 degrees.
      (2) Rinse cycle: 180 degrees.
   e. Change wash water after each hour of use.
   f. Check each item for cleanliness. Wipe dry with clean dishcloth if necessary and stack in proper place.
2. Keep area immediately around dishwasher clean and dry.
3. Empty garbage at dishwasher after each meal.
4. Clean out dishwasher after each meal.
5. Perform other duties that are required from time to time.

Analyzing Business Volume

The third important step the manager must take before scheduling employees in such a way that labor costs are effectively controlled involves preparing an analysis of business volume. This analysis of volume typically takes the form of tallies of numbers of covers served. These tallies should be made on both a daily and an hourly basis.

Daily Analysis

Several techniques are commonly used for determining the number of covers served daily. Perhaps the simplest is to take the information from records being prepared for a sales history, as discussed in Part Two on food control. If a cashier, for example, is developing records of the number of portions of each entree served in the dining room, one could determine the total number of covers served during the day by totaling the number of portions of all items served. In small restaurants, where sales histories are not developed but where guest checks are used, it is reasonably simple to record from the checks the number of persons served, after the close of business for the day. A third approach may be found in some establishments, particularly fast-food establishments, which use modern electronic registers to record sales. These registers give readings at the end of the day of the number of persons or covers served. In the last analysis, each restaurant manager must find a technique appropriate to his operation to determine the number of covers served daily.

With the development of the figures, business volume can be accurately forecasted in terms of the number of anticipated customers. In many restaurants, for example, volume of customers served varies from day to day during the week. As an illustration, many managers have found that Monday is slower than Friday. Knowing this in advance enables a manager to schedule an appropriate number of employees for each of the days, with a lesser number on a Monday and a higher number on a Friday.

In addition to helping forecast the appropriate numbers of employees needed to meet anticipated sales volume on various days of the week, such records also enable a careful manager to spot such things as seasonal variations in business volume, which should be taken into account in scheduling staff. Obviously nontypical days and weeks resulting from such unforeseen circumstances as bad weather, strikes, and gas shortages must be dealt with as they occur. A graphic illustration of the analysis of business volume by day of the week appears in Figure 20.3.

Hourly Analysis

The daily analysis of business volume described above helps in controlling labor cost by permitting the manager to schedule employees' workdays and days off in accordance with anticipated needs, but it does not help with problems posed by hourly fluctuation of demand. Many establishments, for example, find that the middle of the afternoon is a very slack period between two periods of peak volume—the luncheon and dinner hours. In such cases the maximum number of dining room personnel on duty are clearly necessary during the luncheon and dinner hours. However, from the standpoint of keeping labor cost at the optimum level, it is undesirable for the dining room personnel who were on duty during the busy lunch hour to stand around idle through the slack afternoon in anticipation of the busy dinner hour. Appropriate scheduling frequently eliminates the resulting excessive labor cost if management knows in advance which are busy times and which are comparatively slow. In cases that are not clear-cut, management can prepare an hourly analysis of business volume, which can be an important aid in establishing employee schedules designed to maximize employee efficiency and minimize excessive labor cost.

There are several ways to develop hourly analyses of business volume. One common way for determining hourly volume of business is to require the hostess to count and record the number of customers seated in the dining room every hour on the hour. While this is by far the simplest system, it is not the most accurate. Many customers order several cocktails before ordering food and others linger over coffee

FIGURE 20.3
Analysis of Number of Covers Served Per Day

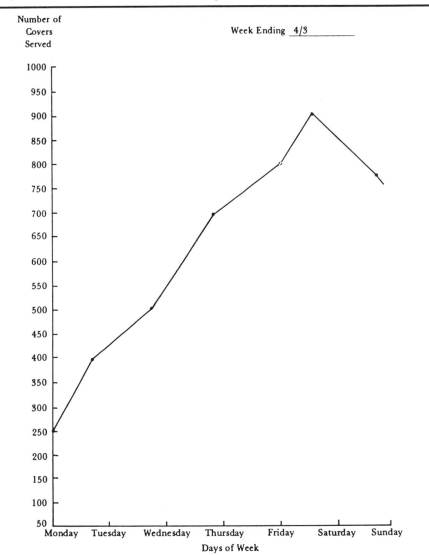

after eating. In either case, the hourly count does not accurately reflect the number of covers served during any particular period. To the extent that this count is used to schedule preparation personnel as well as dining room personnel, it may be misleading and consequently cause the manager to prepare inefficient work schedules.

To offset the inadequacy of this hourly counting procedure, some managers have instituted a system that involves time-stamping either guest checks or dupes in the kitchen as orders are given to the cooks. The checks or dupes are then analyzed at the end of the day; these results more accurately reflect when service personnel take orders, as well as when preparation personnel receive them.

A third system for analyzing hourly volume of business requires that the cashier in the dining room record the number of covers served as customers pay or charge guest checks. Each guest check reaches the cashier as the customer leaves the restaurant. Therefore, a simple system can be instituted, whereby the cashier makes marks on a form like the one illustrated in Figure 20.4. When the guest check has been paid or charged and the transaction is completed, the cashier determines how many covers are reflected on the check and records that number in the space on the form for the one-hour period then current. This system is not as completely accurate with respect to preparation and service as is the one involving time stamps in the kitchen, but it has the advantage of being relatively simple and inexpensive.

By one or another of these means, the owner or manager can accumulate in a relatively short period a useful set of figures reflecting the hourly volume of business. By developing and maintaining this information on a regular basis, the manager can better schedule variable cost employees and thus control labor cost more effectively.

The first step in using this information is to tabulate the hourly volume of business for a given day, as has been done in Figure 20.4. These tabulated figures are shown on the graph in Figure 20.5. In this graph, the degree of fluctuation in hourly volume of business for this particular restaurant is readily apparent. However, this graph represents only one day, a certain Friday in April, and the manager has way of knowing whether this day is typical. Clearly, it would be unwise to base general scheduling on the information reflecting only one day's operation. Therefore, is be necessary to accumulate similar data for other Fridays, and for other days of the week as well. A broader picture of operations will form a better basis or making these decisions.

A second step in scheduling is to tabulate the hourly volume data or a series of Fridays, for example, in a form similar to that shown in Figure 20.6. Charts of this nature may be prepared for each day of the business week. Taken together, they present a history of the hourly volume of business that management can use to plan work activity to control the cost of labor. One of the keys to labor cost control is effective manpower planning, and it is vital that the manager institute this control by scheduling labor according to anticipated requirements based on experience.

An important third step in scheduling to translate the raw numbers such as those in Figure 20.6 into a graphic presentation that reflects the experienced hourly volume of business over a reasonable period of time. The graph shown in Figure 20.7 presents a picture of the hourly volume of business for Fridays in the month of April. With the figures on the vertical axis showing volume of business and those along the horizontal axis showing hourly periods of the operating day, three lines

FIGURE 20.4
Hourly Volume of Business

Weather Clear   Date 4/1

External Conditions Affecting Sales Strong Breeze

Hourly Period		Number of Covers
11:00–Noon	ɪɪɪɪ ɪɪɪɪ ɪɪɪɪ ɪɪɪɪ ɪɪɪɪ ɪɪɪɪ 111	33
Noon–1 PM	ɪɪɪɪ ɪɪɪɪ ɪɪɪɪ ɪɪɪɪ ɪɪɪɪ ɪɪɪɪ 1111 ɪɪɪɪ ɪɪɪɪ ɪɪɪɪ ɪɪɪɪ ɪɪɪɪ ɪɪɪɪ ɪɪɪɪ ɪɪɪɪ ɪɪɪɪ ɪɪɪɪ ɪɪɪɪ	90
1PM–2PM	ɪɪɪɪ ɪɪɪɪ ɪɪɪɪ ɪɪɪɪ ɪɪɪɪ ɪɪɪɪ ɪɪɪɪ ɪɪɪɪ ɪɪɪɪ ɪɪɪɪ ɪɪɪɪ ɪɪɪɪ ɪɪɪɪ ɪɪɪɪ ɪɪɪɪ ɪɪɪɪ ɪɪɪɪ 1111	89
2PM–3PM	ɪɪɪɪ ɪɪɪɪ ɪɪɪɪ ɪɪɪɪ ɪɪɪɪ ɪɪɪɪ ɪɪɪɪ ɪɪɪɪ ɪɪɪɪ ɪɪɪɪ 1	51
3PM–4PM	ɪɪɪɪ 1	6
4PM–5PM	ɪɪɪɪ 11	7
5PM–6PM	ɪɪɪɪ ɪɪɪɪ ɪɪɪɪ ɪɪɪɪ ɪɪɪɪ ɪɪɪɪ ɪɪɪɪ ɪɪɪɪ ɪɪɪɪ	45
6PM–7PM	ɪɪɪɪ ɪɪɪɪ ɪɪɪɪ ɪɪɪɪ ɪɪɪɪ ɪɪɪɪ ɪɪɪɪ ɪɪɪɪ ɪɪɪɪ ɪɪɪɪ ɪɪɪɪ ɪɪɪɪ ɪɪɪɪ ɪɪɪɪ ɪɪɪɪ 111	78
7PM–8PM	ɪɪɪɪ ɪɪɪɪ ɪɪɪɪ ɪɪɪɪ ɪɪɪɪ ɪɪɪɪ ɪɪɪɪ ɪɪɪɪ ɪɪɪɪ ɪɪɪɪ ɪɪɪɪ ɪɪɪɪ ɪɪɪɪ ɪɪɪɪ ɪɪɪɪ ɪɪɪɪ ɪɪɪɪ ɪɪɪɪ ɪɪɪɪ	95
8PM–9PM	ɪɪɪɪ ɪɪɪɪ ɪɪɪɪ ɪɪɪɪ ɪɪɪɪ ɪɪɪɪ ɪɪɪɪ ɪɪɪɪ ɪɪɪɪ ɪɪɪɪ ɪɪɪɪ ɪɪɪɪ ɪɪɪɪ ɪɪɪɪ ɪɪɪɪ ɪɪɪɪ ɪɪɪɪ ɪɪɪɪ ɪɪɪɪ	95
9PM–10PM	ɪɪɪɪ ɪɪɪɪ ɪɪɪɪ ɪɪɪɪ ɪɪɪɪ ɪɪɪɪ ɪɪɪɪ ɪɪɪɪ ɪɪɪɪ ɪɪɪɪ ɪɪɪɪ ɪɪɪɪ ɪɪɪɪ ɪɪɪɪ 111	73
10PM–11PM	ɪɪɪɪ ɪɪɪɪ ɪɪɪɪ ɪɪɪɪ ɪɪɪɪ ɪɪɪɪ ɪɪɪɪ ɪɪɪɪ ɪɪɪɪ 111	48

are plotted on the graph to show volume at particular times. The upper dotted line shows the maximum volume of business experienced at each hour during the period covered by the graph. The lower dotted line shows the minimum volume. These are the extremes to which the hourly volume has gone during the hours shown. The solid middle line shows the median.

FIGURE 20.5
Hourly Analysis of Business Volume

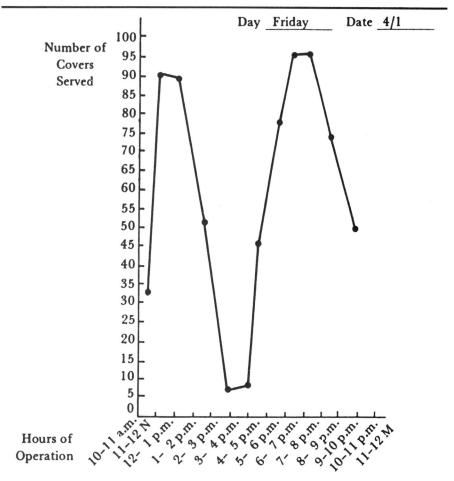

The **median** is the value of the middle item in a group. It is not an average, but a middle point. Figure 20.7 shows that business volume on the five successive Fridays between the hours of noon and 1:00 P.M. ranged from 85 to 107 covers. The numbers of covers at that time for the five days, taken in ascending order, were 85, 90, 100, 105, and 107. From this list of five days, the two with the highest values were the days when it reached 105 and 107 covers per hour. The two days with the lowest volume were those on which it was 85 and 90 covers per hour. By eliminating the two highest and lowest values, one is left with the value in the middle, the median. If the list of values had included hourly volume for fifteen days, eliminating the seven highest and seven lowest values would leave the middle value, the median hourly volume of business during the period.

FIGURE 20.6
Tabulation of Hourly Volume Data

Hourly Time Periods	Hourly Volume of Business (number of covers): Fridays Dates				
	4/1/XX	4/8/XX	4/15/XX	4/22/XX	4/29/XX
11 a.m. to Noon	33	30	50	40	60
Noon to 1 p.m.	90	85	105	100	107
1 p.m. to 2 p.m.	89	85	105	100	105
2 p.m. to 3 p.m.	51	50	63	60	65
3 p.m. to 4 p.m.	6	5	15	10	18
4 p.m. to 5 p.m.	7	5	12	10	18
5 p.m. to 6 p.m.	45	45	55	50	60
6 p.m. to 7 p.m.	78	75	96	90	100
7 p.m. to 8 p.m.	95	95	100	100	105
8 p.m. to 9 p.m.	95	85	95	95	100
9 p.m. to 10 p.m.	73	70	77	75	85
10 p.m. to 11 p.m.	48	45	55	50	60

The advantage of determining the median number of covers served during an hour rather than the arithmetic mean, commonly known as the average, is that the median shows the central tendency unaffected by either high or low extremes. For example, if the number of covers served between 1:00 and 2:00 P.M. on five successive Fridays were 65, 66, 68, 71, and 25, the arithmetic mean, or average number, would be the total of 295 divided by the five periods represented, or 59 covers. The median is 66, however, which is clearly more representative of the typical number of covers served. In this case, the average is weighed too heavily by the one extremely low number of covers served during one hour on one particular day. Since these figures are to be used for staff scheduling, it would be far safer to plan on the basis of the median number of covers served than on the average. The median offers a better idea of the typical number of covers to be served. By adding to the graph both the maximum and minimum numbers that have been served, as discussed above, the manager has a complete picture of the hourly volume of sales, including the typical number of covers served as well as the maximum and minimum extremes.

FIGURE 20.7
Graph of Hourly Volume

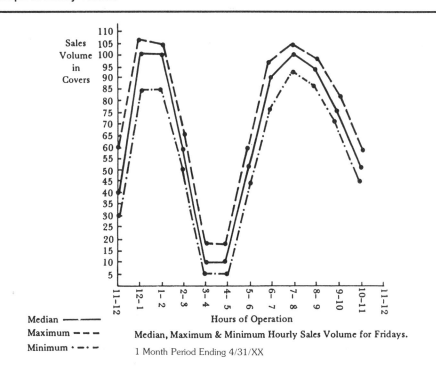

Median, Maximum & Minimum Hourly Sales Volume for Fridays.

1 Month Period Ending 4/31/XX

SCHEDULING

With appropriate information from the formal analysis of the daily and hourly volume of business, a manager is then prepared to address the next step in controlling labor costs—scheduling employees. Earlier in this chapter, employees were divided into two categories: variable cost employees and fixed cost employees. Because of marked differences in the scheduling of these two categories, particularly with reference to the use of daily and hourly analysis of business volume, scheduling techniques and procedures for employees in these groups will be discussed separately.

Scheduling Variable Cost Employees

With the completion of the daily and hourly analyses of business volume, a manager is in a highly favorable position to schedule variable cost employees, the need for whom varies directly with business volume. A first step is to forecast total volume of business on a daily basis for each day in an upcoming period for which employees are to be scheduled, typically a work week. Because of conditions peculiar to a certain establishment or to a certain geographical area, or to both, this scheduling may be done on a biweekly basis instead, but the same principles would apply.

Any manager or owner is in a better business position if he or she can determine today what conditions and sales volume are likely to be encountered in a future period. For this reason forecasts are made. Since experience has shown that history tends to repeat itself in food and beverage service businesses, an owner or manager can use historical records to predict what is likely to occur at some time in the near future. In food and beverage purchasing and production, such forecasts enable the manager to exercise degree of control over costs. Similarly, a manager can better control labor cost if she is able to predict with reasonable accuracy the restaurant's labor requirements for a certain volume of business and then schedule an appropriate number of variable cost personnel on those days and times when they are needed. Looking back to Figure 20.3, one sees a greater daily volume of business on Fridays and Saturdays than on Mondays and Tuesdays. Assuming that the graph represents the historical record of median business volume over an appropriate period, and also that similar conditions are expected for the week to be scheduled, it would be advisable to plan a schedule for variable cost employees geared to the experiences graphed in Figure 20.3. A manager should also use, to the extent possible, the recorded analysis of hourly volume of business so that all variable cost employees do not work the same schedule. Their working hours should be staggered to meet anticipated hourly demand. However, before this anticipated hourly volume can be of the fullest use in scheduling, the manager must judge the number of employees needed in each job classification of variable cost employees affected by hourly volume. For servers, she must determine how many covers each can serve in a given hour and still maintain the established service standards. For dishwashers, she must determine how many dishes each can wash per hour. Similar judgments must be made for each job category.

Manpower requirements are typically determined by intuitive judgments based on the manager's experience. (A more sophisticated approach used by many large operations will be discussed in the next chapter.) In the manpower requirement chart (Fig. 20.8), the manager first judged that each server could serve twenty covers per hour, and then referred to Figure 20.3, the number of covers served per week, and to Figure 20.7, the median number of covers served per hour on a particular day. For purposes of this discussion, we are assuming that the median figures given are those that are expected to occur in the future. Obviously, the manpower requirements would vary if conditions on the date forecasted more nearly approximated the maximum or minimum figure shown. Referring to Figure 20.7, it can be seen that 100 covers are expected between 12:00 and 1:00 P.M. If one server can serve twenty covers per hour, five servers are needed for that time period. Similar calculations are made for the other hours of the business day.

The manager can then prepare a schedule showing the total number of servers needed for the day and the time periods they will work. In Figure 20.9, the manager has scheduled waiters one hour before opening and one hour after

FIGURE 20.8
Manpower Requirements for Servers—
Friday, September, 2, 19XX
(Based on Median Sales)

Hours of Operation	Anticipated Sales Volume in Covers	Manpower Requirements for Waiters
10 a.m. to 11 a.m.	—	2
11 a.m. to Noon	40	2
Noon to 1 p.m.	100	5
1 p.m. to 2 p.m.	100	5
2 p.m. to 3 p.m.	60	3
3 p.m. to 4 p.m.	10	1
4 p.m. to 5 p.m.	10	1
5 p.m. to 6 p.m.	50	3
6 p.m. to 7 p.m.	90	5
7 p.m. to 8 p.m.	100	5
8 p.m. to 9 p.m.	95	5
9 p.m. to 10 p.m.	75	4
10 p.m. to 11 p.m.	50	3
11 p.m. to 12 p.m.	—	2

closing for purposes of preparation and cleanup. To increase efficiency, she has also taken advantage of part-time employees. It is apparent that seven waiters are needed, three of them part-time and four full-time, of whom three are working split shifts. Other possible working schedules could be devised. For example, employee B could become a full-time employee by working his normal shift and, in addition, taking on the shift of employee G. This would reduce the number of waiters from seven to six.

By following this procedure for all days and hours of operation during the work week being planned, while keeping in mind the number of days and hours that each employee could or would work, the manager could devise a work schedule based on both anticipated sales volume by day and hour and the her judgments concerning servers' ability to meet these anticipated sales without sacrificing the standard of service. In addition, because the schedule would be based on these realistically anticipated needs, it could be set up in such a way that labor costs would be maintained at the minimum level needed for forecasted sales. Once complete, a schedule like the one shown in Figure 20.10 would be made up and posted, so that each employee would know his or her scheduled work hours in advance.

Scheduling Fixed Cost Employees

While the scheduling of variable cost employees is tied directly to the daily and hourly analysis of business volume, the scheduling of fixed cost employees is

FIGURE 20.9
Sample Schedule Worksheet: Hourly Schedule for Servers

Day: _____ Friday _____

Date: _____ September 2, 19XX _____

Waiter	AM						PM								
	10-11	11-12	12-1	1-2	2-3	3-4	4-5	5-6	6-7	7-8	8-9	9-10	10-11	11-12
A														
B														
C														
D														
E														
F														
G														

FIGURE 20.10
Sample Schedule For Waiters

Waiter	Mon.	Tues.	Wed.	Thurs.	Fri.	Sat.	Sun.
A	Off	Off	10–6	10–6	10–6	10–6	10–6
B	Off	10–6	10–2	10–2	10–2	10–2	10–2
C	Off	Off	12–3 5–10	12–3 5–10	12–3 5–10	12–3 5–10	12–3 5–10
D	12–3 6–11	Off	Off	12–3 6–11	12–3 6–11	12–3 6–11	12–3 6–11
E	10–2 5–9	10–2 5–9	Off	Off	12–2 6–12	12–2 6–12	12–2 6–12
F	10–6	6–12	Off	Off	6–12	6–12 6–12	
G	Off	5–9	5–12	5–12	5–9	5–9	Off
H						6–10	

related to such an ananlsys only indirectly and usually only in extreme circumstances.

Before fixed cost personnel can be scheduled with any degree of certainty, the manager must determine what factors of operation affect each job and take all such factors into account. In the case of a storeroom clerk, such factors as the need to have the storeroom open so that commodities can be issued to the production staff during hours of preparation, and the need to have the storeroom clerk available to accept commodities taken in by the receiving clerk, must be considered before establishing the work schedule for the job. When all such factors have been considered, a manager can establish and post a schedule for fixed cost personnel that would resemble Figure 20.11. While schedules for fixed cost employees tend to be relatively permanent, changes in business volume extended over a considerable period may cause the manager to reassess both schedules and costs for fixed cost personnel. Substantial decreases in business, for example, may suggest the need for a substantial decrease in labor costs generally, including a reduction in fixed cost personnel. In such instances, means must be found for instituting appropriate cost reductions without substantial reduction in the efficiency of the operation.

FIGURE 20.11
Sample Schedule For Fixed Cost Employees

Employee	Mon.	Tues.	Wed.	Thurs.	Fri.	Sat.	Sun.
Purchasing Steward	9–5	9–5	9–5	9–5	9–5	9–5	Off
Storeroom Clerk	Off	8–4	8–4	8–4	8–4	8–4	8–4
Receiving Clerk	7–3	7–3	7–3	7–3	7–3	7–3	Off
Porter	Off	12–8	12–8	12–8	12–8	12–8	12–8
Vegetable Man	Off	8–4	8–4	8–4	8–4	8–4	8–4
Cashier 1	Off	5–12	10–5	10–5	10–5	10–5	10–5
Cashier 2	5–12	Off	5–12	5–12	5–12	5–12	5–12

One means of lowering this cost is to take advantage of part-time help. During a slow period, a manager might employ a receiving clerk to work fewer than thirty-five hours per week, and accordingly reduce the payroll. In some areas of the country, certain fixed cost employees look forward to slow periods so that they may reduce their work weeks and devote more time to other outside interests; they may even take jobs in other industries for a change of pace. Such arrangements are clearly to the advantage of the manager, who must keep overall labor costs in line.

During slow periods in some establishments, the manager reduces the work weeks for such employees as cashiers to part-time status and personally fills the position during the other hours of the week. When business is slow enough, managers can often effectively perform two jobs at one time without diminishing their effectiveness, thereby effecting a labor cost saving, or payroll saving, of the dollar cost of the cashier.

A related technique employed by managers whose payroll costs must be reduced during slack periods involves combining jobs. If, for example, a manager determined that a period of reduced business volume dictates reducing by half the hours of both the receiving clerk and the steward, he might eliminate one of them from the payroll entirely and retain the other to perform the needed work in both job categories, serving half the time as receiving clerk and the other half as steward. The manager will not only reduce payroll costs at the approximate time and for the appropriate duration but also retain the more able of the two employees, thus strengthening the staff.

In some instances, although management may be determined to reduce the cost of labor in proportion to the reduction in sales, turning some jobs into part-time positions or reducing the size of the fixed cost staff by combining jobs becomes impractical. In these cases, the normal work routines of fixed cost employees can be added to the work responsibilities of variable cost employees. Under these circumstances, certain positions carry augmented duties for the duration of the slack period, but duties revert to normal when the volume of business returned to normal. While this approach does not reduce the dollar cost of the fixed cost employees involved, it does reduce the number of dollars expended for variable cost employees, and the net effect on overall labor cost is the same.

A fourth method of reducing the cost of certain fixed cost personnel has become feasible in recent years with the increasing popularity of convenience foods of all sorts. Many establishments substantially reduce the payroll expense for fixed cost employees, particularly specialized food preparation staff, by using a variety of items that require little or no preparation other than heating or chilling in the restaurant kitchen. While both advantages and disadvantages accompany the use of such products, their use does simplify certain purchasing, receiving, and preparation tasks. This frequently enables a manager to reduce the size of the fixed cost work force, to employ persons with less skill at lower wages, or both. For example, purchasing frozen, portioned meat might result in the elimination of a butcher from the kitchen staff, as well as make possible the hiring at a lower salary of a receiving clerk with a limited knowledge of meats.

It must be pointed out that deciding whether to keep a butcher on the staff or to buy frozen, portioned meats is not always simple. When a manager decides to purchase frozen, portioned meats, she is deciding, wittingly or unwittingly, to reduce the cost for fixed labor in exchange for an increase in food cost. After all, any item purchased already prepared must include the cost of the producer's labor; in effect, the higher food cost includes a labor cost. Assuming qualities to be equal, which may or may not be true, one factor in the "make-or-buy" decision must be a determination of the extent to which the increased food cost will be offset by the reduction in labor cost. A rule of thumb in the industry has been that it is normally cheaper to employ a butcher as long as there is sufficient work to keep one busy for the full number of working hours. However, this does not take into account such varying factors as labor contracts in different parts of the country or how butchering on the premises affects other steps in kitchen production.

A manager can use one or more of these techniques to reduce the payroll expenditure for fixed cost personnel for a limited period. With a return of business volume to a normal pattern, decisions can be reversed, and the staff of fixed cost personnel returned to former size. However, in the light of changing conditions, permanent changes in staffing become necessary. In these cases, the manager must address himself to the problem of total reorganization—a process that may involve changing not only the size and quality of the staff of fixed cost personnel but also number and calibre of variable cost personnel and even the entire character of the operation. In the face of drastic problems, drastic measures are often required if the operation is to remain in business profitably. Total reorganization is often the sum of the drastic measures required.

REORGANIZATION

It would be impossible to compose a complete list of the conditions that have led restaurant owners and managers to decide to reorganize their establishments. However, in most cases, the conditions include either increases in costs, decreases in sales, or both.

Increases in costs may be noted in any of the three areas discussed in previous chapters: fixed, directly variable, or semivariable. Fixed costs, which are normally noncontrollable, may be increased when a new lease is negotiated with a landlord. In the case of a restaurant that occupies a building owned by the restaurant owner, local government may dramatically increase real estate taxes.

Directly variable costs, primarily those for food and beverage items, may increase to such an extent that a manager cannot maintain a stable cost-to-sales ratio without raising selling prices beyond the amounts that customers are willing to pay. Labor costs may go up because of general economic conditions or because of a new labor contract negotiated by some management organization to which the restaurant owner belongs, and this cost increase might be greater than what could be offset by an increase in selling prices. On the other hand, the same kinds of effects—increases in cost-to-sales ratios—might result from decreases in dollar sales.

Despite the reasons for these increases in costs or decreases in sales, because of an increase in the cost-to-sales ratio for fixed, semivariable, or directly variable costs, or any combination of these three, the owner or manager must take drastic action to ensure favorable cost-to-sales ratios for each cost area and, consequently, for the entire operation. While it is frequently possible to affect the food and beverage cost ratios and thereby ensure profit, and sometimes possible to take a variety of steps to affect fixed costs in the long run, neither of these possibilities need concern us in a discussion of labor control. Rather, we will address ourselves to a need for total reorganization and consequent restructuring of the labor force, on the assumption that all other possibilities have been ruled out. This will enable us to make certain points about reorganization in general, as well as to continue pertinent discussion of labor cost control.

Any manager who proposes to undertake a reorganization must remember two principal points:

1. Any resulting increase in cost-to-sales ratio for any cost category must be more than offset by a decrease in the ratio for another.
2. Any resulting increase or decrease in overall dollar sales volume must result in increased profit to the operation.

With these two points in mind, the manager planning reorganization has certain basic objectives against which to measure and judge any plans for change. Assuming that changes in fixed and directly variable costs have been ruled out, the manager will address himself to the subject of possible changes in the area of semivariable costs—labor costs.

The techniques for reducing labor costs as part of a reorganization program do not differ markedly from those employed by managers seeking to reduce costs temporarily. As discussed previously, they include combining jobs, hiring part-time rather than full-time employees where possible, adding duties of variable cost employees to the normal work of fixed cost personnel, and making appropriate use of various preprepared food and beverage items to reduce the labor cost of preparation.

The chief differences between a temporary reduction of labor cost and a permanent reduction through reorganization typically involve degree of change, as well as impact on the labor force as a whole and on particular jobs. Clearly, the manager who decides in favor of reorganization is reacting to a situation that has become untenable, one that dictates the need for a steady and reasoned reversal from insupportable financial statements to an acceptable profit picture. The manager knows what he must do: reduce the cost of labor to the extent necessary to ensure profit, particularly if there can be no increase in either directly variable or fixed costs. To the extent to which the manager can do this, each dollar reduction in the labor cost should be a dollar increase in profit, assuming no change in overall dollar sales.

As an example of what might be done, Figure 20.12 shows the effect of studied change on the organization chart of that hypothetical restaurant first presented in Figure 20.1. It will be noted that reorganization has had major impact on a number of positions in the kitchen. For example, the sous chef has been eliminated, and the executive chef is now a working chef. In addition, the work of the purchasing steward has been taken over by the chief steward. Both the fry cook and the vegetable cook have been eliminated and replaced by a new worker whose duties include those of both the former job titles. The entire baking department has been eliminated, probably because of a decision to buy rather than make bakery products. These and other changes have resulted in a net reduction of five fixed cost employees, as well as an indeterminable number of variable cost employees. This reorganization represents an annual payroll saving of thousands of dollars, by which amount net profits should be increased.

It will be noted in the foregoing that management decided to eliminate the jobs of both the fry cook and the vegetable cook in favor of creating a new position for a combination vegetable/fry cook. This new worker could probably not perform all the duties of the former employees, so management would need to undertake another important facet in reorganizing: writing new job descriptions. As a result of the reorganization and the consequent elimination of some jobs and combining of others, new areas of responsibility have been created, and it is important that each be clearly and concisely covered by job description.

After a major reorganization in the operation, it is to be assumed that maximum efficiency has been achieved, with every dollar of labor cost having a positive impact on the profit dollar.

FIGURE 20.12
Organization Chart After Reorganization

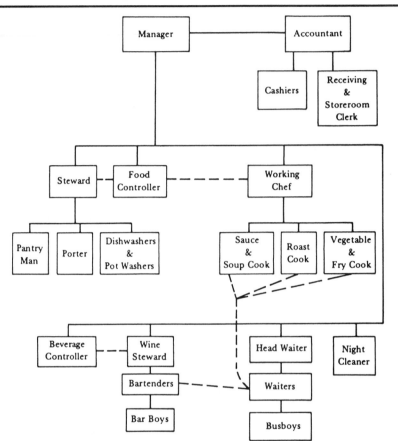

END NOTE

It should be noted that all the procedures previously discussed for controlling labor cost are found particularly useful by establishments that are able to predict consumer demand with reasonable accuracy. Industrial, college, school, and institutional foodservice operations have this advantage. However, many operations do not enjoy the luxury of being able to forecast demand. Among them are numerous owner-operated and other commercial restaurants. Although they maintain sales histories, attempt to discern patterns in sales, and continue to strive for accurate forecasting, they find it impossible to predict what their customers are likely to do on any given day. Some have found it possible to predict likely sales for a week but have not been able to forecast for any one particular day in that week with any high degree of accuracy. Such factors as weather, holidays, long weekends, and other events in the area all appear to affect sales, but not in a manner sufficiently consistent to allow for a forecast. These operators must recognize that they are at some disadvantage in attempting to devise systems and procedures for the strict control of labor cost and must be prepared to modify accepted control systems to their special conditions.

In general, such operators must be prepared to accept some degree of inefficiency in order to be able to meet customer demand when it occurs. Some are able to offset their disadvantage partially by keeping some personnel on call for possible part-time work if demand develops on some particular day. Others typically staff their operations at level suitable for meeting minimum demand and stand ready to work alongside their employees when business warrants. Any student planning to own or manage a small commercial operation should be aware of the possible limitations on the use of labor cost control techniques, and should keep in mind any possibilities for maintaining a list of willing part-time workers or for becoming a working manager when conditions demand it.

COMPUTER APPLICATIONS

In Chapter 13 we described terminals that servers use at side stands in a dining room for a number of purposes, including placing orders in the kitchen. These terminals are employed in conjunction with a CPU that includes a real-time clock. This clock notes the time at which any order is placed. Additional possibilities include determining both the time at which any party placed its first order and the time at which it settled the check. With all of this information stored in the computer, analyzing business volume by day, meal, or hour is merely a matter of requesting a printout of the requisite data. These data can be used to prepare a table of manpower requirements that would help management schedule variable cost personnel.

CHAPTER ESSENTIALS

In this chapter, we identified the primary purpose of labor control. We described the special characteristics of the restaurant industry that prevent implementation of labor cost controls to the extent found in other industries. For purposes of labor cost control, we distinguished between variable cost personnel and fixed cost personnel. We listed and discussed three preliminary steps in scheduling employees and showed how both variable and fixed cost employees may be scheduled. We discussed how adjustments or reorganization can reduce excessive costs of fixed cost personnel. Finally, we suggested how computers could assist managers in analyzing business volume to determine manpower requirements.

KEY TERMS IN THIS CHAPTER

Variable cost personnel

Fixed cost personnel

Operational plan

Functional organization chart

Job description

Daily analysis of business volume

Hourly analysis of business volume

Median

Manpower requirements

Work schedule

QUESTIONS AND PROBLEMS

1. What is the primary purpose of labor control?

2. What are the differences between fixed cost personnel and variable cost personnel?

3. In what respects does the demand for restaurant products differ from the demand for most other manufactured products?

4. What preliminary steps should be taken before work can be organized?

5. Prepare a job description for a receiving clerk.

6. The chart below is an hourly analysis of business volume for a typical day in a nearby restaurant. Each server in the restaurant can take care of twenty-five covers per hour, and each is scheduled for an eight-hour work day whenever possible. Part time help is often used, and split shifts are permitted. Two servers are required to come in one hour before the 11:00 A.M. opening to set up the dining room, and two remain from 10:00 P.M. to 11:00 P.M. for cleanup.

Time Period	Covers Served
11:00 A.M.–Noon	50
Noon–1:00 P.M.	200
1:00 P.M.–2:00 P.M.	100
2:00 P.M.–3:00 P.M.	25
3:00 P.M.–4:00 P.M.	10
4:00 P.M.–5:00 P.M.	10
5:00 P.M.–6:00 P.M.	60
6:00 P.M.–7:00 P.M.	150
7:00 P.M.–8:00 P.M.	100
8:00 P.M.–9:00 P.M.	50
9:00 P.M.–10:00 P.M.	20

a. Prepare a chart similar to Figure 20.5 showing an hourly analysis of the volume of business on a typical day.

b. Prepare an hourly schedule for servers similar to that found in Figure 20.9.

7. Refer to the analysis of business volume in Question 6 above. Assume that the restaurant is open seven days per week and that the first five days follow the pattern of business indicated above, but the last two days of the week normally show business volume equal to 50% of that seen on other days. Full-time servers work a five-day week; part-time servers work four-hour days, and the manager prefers to use as few part-time servers as possible. Given this information, prepare a weekly schedule for servers similar to that found in Figure 20.10.

8. In what ways do schedules for fixed cost personnel differ from schedules for variable cost personnel?

9. What conditions would necessitate temporary changes in staffing levels and costs of fixed cost personnel? What conditions might make permanent changes necessary?

10. Define each of the following terms.

Variable cost personnel	Fixed cost personnel
Job description	Organization chart
Work schedule	Manpower requirements
Reorganization	Median

11. How can computers be used to analyze business volume and determine manpower requirements?

chapter 21

Controlling Labor Costs II

Learning Objectives

After reading and studying this chapter, the student should be able to:

1. Explain the significance of quality and quantity standards in labor control.
2. Explain why foodservice operators cannot normally adopt typical industrial procedures for controlling labor cost.
3. List and describe three methods for establishing performance standards.
4. Prepare a table of standard man-hour requirements, and forecast staffing requirements for a given level of sales.
5. Prepare a reconciliation of standard and actual man-hours based on the number of covers served.
6. Explain how the computer can help management develop standard manpower requirements.
7. Define each of the Key Terms at the end of this chapter.

The last chapter showed how management can determine manpower requirements for variable cost personnel, based on the number of covers anticipated, taking into account the number of employees in each category needed to service a given number of customers. Daily schedules were then prepared that took advantage of part-time employees and split shifts to create maximum efficiency. Manpower requirements for fixed cost personnel were based on factors other than the number of covers anticipated, and schedules were prepared to meet the needs of the establishment. Maximum efficiency was achieved through reevaluation of needs using the techniques of combining jobs, hiring part-time employees, adding to work routines the jobs of variable cost employees, and using preportioned or precooked foods to eliminate jobs.

This approach to labor control is useful and widespread throughout the industry. However, many large restaurants and chain operations have found it desirable to take the process one step further; they try to determine on an ongoing basis how well department heads and individual restaurants are scheduling employees to maintain maximum efficiency. Standards of performance for departments and units have been determined and means have been found to compare these standards with actual performance. That is the subject of this concluding chapter.

STANDARDS OF PERFORMANCE

In Chapter 2 we defined standards as rules or measures established for making comparisons or judgments. Management sets standards to determine the extent to which the results of activity meet preliminary expectations or plans. Other chapters illustrated the importance of the standards in judging the effectiveness of procedures set up to control food and beverage costs. Now it will be appropriate to discuss and illustrate the importance of setting up and using standards to control and measure labor costs.

Previous chapters showed that standards can be divided into two primary categories: *quality* standards and *quantity* standards. Standards for the control of labor cost fall into these same two classifications.

The Development of Quality Standards

Before attempting to develop any quality standards for employee performance, the manager must first have in mind a clear and detailed image of the restaurant, which includes an understanding of the quality standards for food and beverage items offered, as well as the nature of the clientele. Only then can quality standards for employee performance be set. For example, a manager would be in a better position to establish quality standards if she knew that the restaurant would be serving sandwiches to a hurried clientele of business people and shoppers, rather than steak Diane to a relaxed group of corporate executives celebrating the conclusion of a multi-million-dollar business deal. The quality standards for performance in the first instance need not be so exacting as those in the second. Sandwich service need not be so polished as the French service appropriate to serving steak Diane.

The Development of Quantity Standards

Once appropriate quality standards have been established, corresponding quantity standards must be developed. The manager must determine the number of times that a task of a given level of quality can performed within a certain time period. The typical time period is the same as that used for payroll purposes, the hour. In effect, the manager must determine the quantity of performance to be expected per hour, per meal, per day from employees in each job classification.

In the business world, a number of sophisticated techniques have been developed for the establishment of these standards. These approaches have been successful in setting up performance standards for a variety of factory and office jobs that are essentially repetitive in nature. On an assembly line, for example, one person is typically responsible for one task and can reasonably be expected to perform that task a certain number of times per hour. Each job may be analyzed by such techniques as a time and motion study, which involves breaking a job down into component parts and particular body movements. Each job may be re-evaluated from time to time, and the most efficient means of performance must be clearly defined and taught to the workers. The key to this approach lies in the repetitive nature of the tasks to be performed, as well as in the nonperishable nature of the manufactured product.

In a typical manufacturing business, production is tied to demand in the long run, but need not be tied to demand on a day-by-day basis. A factory can turn out items that can be stored in inventory for appreciable periods. In the long run, management must schedule production in such a way that the supply of an item produced does not exceed demand, and this can be done by increasing and decreasing—or even by ceasing—production for a period of time.

Some fast-food chains have made significant progress in defining jobs and scheduling production so that they come close to approaching the efficiency of many manufacturing operations. For example, several nationally known hamburger chains produce various kinds of sandwiches for anticipated demand based on ongoing business volume analysis. The sandwiches are stored in inventory for a very short period, usually not more than ten minutes, after which they are discarded.

While these industrial techniques can be used in the restaurant business, they have not been widely applied. For example, a time and motion study might be performed to determine appropriate techniques for a cook to use in making omelettes of acceptable quality at peak efficiency for one hour. Such a study might result in a determination that the cook could produce thirty omelettes per hour by following certain carefully specified procedures. However, this would be of little use unless the cook actually had to produce thirty omelettes per hour for each hour of work. Generally, this is not the case.

In the restaurant business, production must be closely related to immediate customer demand, not to projected demand as in other manufacturing businesses. In part, this is due to the perishable nature of the product. In most instances, items can be stored for only limited times before sale. Many items, such as omelettes, cannot be stored at all.

The products of the restaurant kitchen are highly perishable. In addition, the tasks involved in their production must be governed to a great extent by the perishable nature of the product and also by the fluctuation of customer demand. Further, unlike typical factory workers, restaurant personnel do not usually repeat the same tasks hour after hour, day after day. The cook who makes omelettes one minute may be called on to produce some other item the next. If and when the menu changes, the tasks assigned to the cook may change as well; if omelettes are not on the menu, the cook will be producing something else.

Some fast-food operators and a number of food processors that cater to fast-food restaurants have been able to take advantage of certain production techniques used in typical manufacturing enterprises and have thus been able to employ such techniques as time and motion studies in establishing quantity standards for production. Certain preportioned fast-food items can be produced, frozen, and stored for projected sale, either by the processor or by the fast-food operator. In some instances, such items as hamburgers can be produced by employees doing repetitive assembly-line jobs and stored in their cooked state for limited periods until sold. However, most restaurants are not able to use these assembly-line techniques. Even those that do use them to a limited extent find that they are applicable only to a limited number of personnel, many of them fixed cost personnel. Therefore, food and beverage service operations must find other ways to establish quantity standards for employee performance.

ESTABLISHING PERFORMANCE STANDARDS

While many disagree about what constitutes the best method for establishing realistic quantity standards for performance and scheduling, several methods have received acceptance in the restaurant industry. Because of their differing emphases, they must be discussed separately.

One popular approach is commonly found in restaurants whose menus seldom vary and whose sales change little from week to week. Managers of these establishments routinely review the staffing of the restaurant in the most recent weeks. Purely on the basis of recollection, they decide whether sufficient staff was on duty to meet customer needs. Then, to the extent to which previous schedules were adequate, they are repeated, thus becoming standards of sorts. If recollection suggests that staffing was excessive or inadequate, changes are made and an amended schedule is prepared. It should be noted that the entire scheduling process depends on remembering the details of past performance; pure guesswork is the essential factor in determining increases or decreases in scheduled work hours. Because this approach fails to make use of any recorded data on sales volume, it is usually not a reliable way to maximize efficiency and thus control labor cost.

A second method attempts to set realistic standards by approaching the problem in a pragmatic, orderly manner. A test period of a particular number of days or weeks is established for gathering data. During this period, sales volume records are kept, detailing the number of covers sold per day or per meal, depending on the type of restaurant under analysis. Management also records the number of persons on duty in each fixed and variable cost job category, and reviews each category, making intuitive judgments about the sufficiency of the numbers and the efficiency of employee performance in each category.

Variable Cost Personnel

Figure 21.1 relates numbers of variable cost personnel to sales volume in covers for a particular test period and shows one manager's judgments about staffing during that period. As the chart shows, with sales of 300 covers and seven waiters scheduled for lunch on May 1, the manager judged performance to be highly inefficient because of overstaffing and recorded his observations for future reference. As the one-week period progressed, he continued to note his estimates of labor efficiency, relating the number of waiters working to the total number of covers served. While figure 21.1 has been set up to record estimates of labor efficiency for an entire meal period, it would be possible to do this on an hourly basis if a more detailed view were required.

FIGURE 21.1
Evaluation of Employee Efficiency

NOON MEAL 11:00 A.M.–2:00 P.M.							
Date	5/1	5/2	5/3	5/4	5/5	5/6	5/7
No. of Covers Served	275	450	400	350	400	425	500
Waiters Scheduled	7	7	7	7	7	7	7
Efficiency of Performance	Poor— Only 5 Waiters Needed	Excellent	Very Good	Poor— Only 6 Waiters Needed	Very Good	Excellent	Poor— 8 Waiters Needed
Warewashers Scheduled	3	3	3	3	3	3	3
Efficiency of Performance	Poor— Only 2 Needed	Excellent	Good— Some Inefficiency	Poor— Only 2 Needed	Good— Some Inefficiency	Excellent	Poor— Overtime Required
Preparation Personnel Scheduled	4	4	4	4	4	4	4
Efficiency of Performance	Poor— Only 3 Needed	Excellent	Good— 1 Less Needed	Not Good— 1 Less Needed	Good	Excellent	Excellent

Fixed Cost Personnel

It also is feasible to prepare a similar chart that relates numbers of fixed cost personnel to numbers of covers sold for a period and to make provision for the manager to estimate employee efficiency by the day or meal, or even by the hour. However, as has been noted, the nature of the work of fixed cost personnel is such that the numbers on duty in any category cannot be varied in normal circumstances. Under extraordinary conditions—for example, when sales increase or decrease abnormally for protracted periods—such charts could reflect the need for either augmenting staff or laying off staff and combining jobs. However, such volume/staffing review charts are normally prepared only for variable cost personnel.

MANPOWER REQUIREMENTS

Once these charts have been prepared for the test period and the manager has a record of sales volume, numbers of variable cost employees working, and personal estimates of the employees' efficiency, he can begin to take the next logical step: to develop a table of manpower requirements for variable cost personnel at several levels of business volume. Figure 21.2, a typical example, shows manpower requirements for variable cost personnel in each category. It is apparent from a comparison of figures 21.1 and 21.2 that this manager judged seven servers excessive for serving 300 covers on May 1 and therefore set five as a more appropriate number. Similarly, he judged seven as insufficient for serving 500 covers on May 7 and determined that this number of covers could be satisfactorily served by eight servers. Thus, by judging performance carefully and recording these judgments over a period of time, a manager can set standards for staffing. Referring to both of these tables of standard manpower requirements and forecasts of anticipated sales for a coming week enables the manager to better control labor cost by more accurately scheduling only that amount of manpower necessary to meet the preparation and service standard of the establishment. This technique can be refined to reflect hourly standards for manpower performance. When hourly tables are used, the manager can achieve an even greater degree of control over labor cost. Clearly, hourly analysis and appropriate tables abstracted from them, as discussed in the previous chapter, would present a more complete and detailed view of labor efficiency.

FIGURE 21.2
Standard Manpower Requirements Luncheon

Covers	200–299	300–399	400–499	500–599
Waiters	5	6	7	8
Warewashers	2	2	3	4
Preparation Personnel	3	3	4	4

Although this second approach to developing quantity standards for labor performance is an improvement over the first, particularly in providing a useful approach to the scheduling of variable cost employees for forecasted sales, it does not provide a means of measuring either how well scheduling has been done based on established standards or how efficient labor actually was. If a way could be found to compare actual performance with the standards for performance set by management, differences could be noted, particularly those that reflect inefficiencies in labor productivity. Once these differences, or variances, have been noted, it is possible for management to make efforts to eliminate them in future planning, bringing labor productivity up to the standards set and potentially reducing labor inefficiencies to the lowest possible point.

In order to accomplish this goal, it is necessary to discuss another way of looking at standards for labor productivity. We will discuss **standard man-hours**: the number of employee work hours necessary in each job category to perform a given volume of forecasted work.

If, for example, eight servers are needed to serve 500 covers in a given three-hour luncheon period, the standard man-hours required would be calculated as follows: 8 servers $\times$ 3 hours = 24 man-hours of servers' work. The twenty-four-man-hours would become the standard for serving 500 covers over the luncheon period, and any excess of man-hours scheduled would indicate to the manager that some degree of inefficiency exists in the scheduling of servers. Any number of hours less than the twenty-four would indicate that less than satisfactory service (quality standards) was being given to the customers. A different number of standard man-hours would be required for different levels of sales volume, and it would be up to management to determine what these should be. The number of standard man-hours required would not necessarily change in direct proportion with the volume of business. In the previous example, twenty-four man-hours of servers' work was the standard for serving 500 covers during the luncheon period. For the three-hour time period, this works out to 20.83 covers per standard man-hour. At a lesser volume—300 covers, for example—seven servers representing twenty-one standard man-hours may be necessary because of the accepted relative inefficiency at lower volume. During low-volume periods, a server at her station would not have as many customers to wait on but would be kept busy. At the lower volume, this works out to 14.3 covers per standard man-hour. Thus, the number of man-hours required for 300 covers is twenty-one, based on management's judgment of quality service. To the extent that more man-hours than the standard number required are utilized, management will see that greater efficiency is both possible and desirable. If fewer than the standard are utilized, management might judge that the quality of service was not up to standard. By employing the techniques previously discussed, management can develop tables of standard man-hour requirements for various levels of business activity (see Fig. 21.3).

Figure 21.3 is one example of a table of standard man-hour requirements for variable cost personnel for one particular restaurant. Used in conjunction with forecasts of sales volume, these figures are helpful in both forecasting manpower

FIGURE 21.3
Standard Man-Hour Requirements
Variable Cost Personnel: Luncheon

Number of Covers	Service Personnel	Warewashing Personnel	Preparation Personnel
200	15	6	8
300	17	6	8
400	19	8	11
500	21	10	11
600	23	10	11

and scheduling employees as efficiently as possible. In a given restaurant, 450 covers for a given luncheon period have been forecast based on the sales history. Schedules are prepared, and at the conclusion of the meal a report similar to the one in Figure 21.4 is prepared.

It should be noted that the scheduling of the service personnel and the dishwashers was done well, and that proper explanation was given for the excess over standard man-hours for the preparation personnel. This provides the owner or manager with a report indicating how well or how efficiently the variable cost personnel were scheduled. However, it does not tell the manager how efficient the personnel were during actual service, because the report does not take into account the actual numbers of covers served. More than the forecasted number of customers might have been served, in which case the service might not be up to standard quality. Or, on the other hand, if fewer than the forecasted number of covers were served, it can be assumed that labor was not used to its maximum efficiency. Therefore, an additional report like the one shown in Figure 21.5 is necessary so that the manager can determine with some degree of accuracy the efficiency of the labor force.

It is readily apparent that while scheduling has been efficiently accomplished on the basis of the forecast, a degree of inefficiency resulted from the overscheduling of personnel. If the above result were repeated frequently, the owner or

FIGURE 21.4
Daily Comparison of Forecast and Actual Man-Hours Scheduled

Day __6/2/XX__   Date __Tuesday__   Meal __Luncheon__
Number of Covers:
  Forecast __450__

Personnel	Standard Man-Hours	Actual Man-Hours	Difference	Explanation
Service	19	19	- 0 -	
Warewashers	8	8	- 0 -	
Preparation	11	14	3	training new cook

FIGURE 21.5
Daily Reconciliation of Standard and Actual Man-Hours, Based on Actual Covers Served

Day Tuesday	Date 6/2/XX		Meal Luncheon	
Number of Covers: Sold 360			Weather fair	
Personnel	Standard Man-Hours	Actual Man-Hours	Difference	Explanation
Service	17	19	2	covers fewer than forecast
Warewashers	6	8	2	covers fewer than forecast
Preparation	8	14	6	covers fewer than forecast

manager might have to find ways to forecast with greater accuracy. Other possible reasons for differences between standard man-hours and actual hours worked might be unforeseen variations in weather and in other conditions affecting sales, such as the street in front of the restaurant being torn up, improper attention to standard man-hour charts resulting in poor scheduling, and absenteeism. The important point is that management now has some means of determining the efficiency of labor, and thus can better pinpoint inefficiency and take remedial action to improve future performance.

COMPUTER APPLICATIONS

Many fast-food chains are using the computer to establish suitable production rates based on extensive ongoing analysis of sales volume. From the data developed, they have been able to establish standard manpower requirements for all personnel classifications and for all levels of sales volume. This enables the manager of such an establishment to obtain information from the computer to schedule personnel efficiently.

CHAPTER ESSENTIALS

In this chapter we discussed the importance of developing performance standards, both as guides for efficient scheduling and as means for judging performance. We distinguished between quality standards and quantity standards for performance and explained how performance standards may be implemented and expressed as standard manpower requirements. We showed how standard man-hours and actual hours worked may be compared and analyzed. Finally, we showed how computers may be used to forecast standard manpower requirements for given levels of sales volume and can assist in controlling labor cost.

KEY TERMS IN THIS CHAPTER

Quality standards

Quantity standards

Performance standards

Manpower requirements

Standard man-hours

QUESTIONS AND PROBLEMS

1. Of what significance are established quality and quantity performance standards in controlling labor costs?

2. List and describe the methods for establishing performance standards.

3. Which of the methods for establishing performance standards would be most practical for most foodservice establishments? Why? Which would be the least practical for small operations? Why?

4. Why might managers of small restaurants decide not to attempt the standard man-hour approach to controlling labor cost?

5. Many object to the standard man-hour approach to labor cost control on the grounds that it ignores the human relations element in the workplace. What do you believe they mean by this? What possible drawbacks are inherent in this approach?

6. Assume that the figures in Figure 21.3 are applicable to a restaurant you are managing. Prepare a list of staffing requirements for the five days forecasted below:

     Monday, June 7—200 covers
     Tuesday, June 8—350 covers
     Wednesday, June 9—450 covers
     Thursday, June 10—600 covers
     Friday, June 11—800 covers

7. What characteristics of the foodservice industry make it difficult or impossible to pursue the industrial approaches to standard man-hour labor control?

8. In a certain restaurant the manager has determined that six servers are needed for between 320 and 380 covers over a three-hour luncheon period; seven servers are needed for between 381 and 440 covers; eight servers are needed for between 441 and 520 covers; and nine servers are needed for between 521 and 600 covers. Prepare a table of standard man-hours using Figure 21.3 as a guide.

9. Using the chart developed in Question 8 above, prepare a report similar to

Figure 21.4 for servers only, if 460 covers are forecasted and twenty-six hours were scheduled on Tuesday, June 4.

10. Using the data from questions 8 and 9 above, prepare a report similar to Figure 21.5 for servers only, if 420 covers were actually served during the three-hour luncheon period on Tuesday, June 4.

11. How can computers be used to assist management in developing standard manpower requirements?

Afterword

Throughout the text the authors have attempted to provide a structured introduction to food, beverage, and labor controls for the student planning a career in the hospitality service industry. We strongly believe that anyone planning a career on any level of management in this industry should be familiar with these principles of control. Moreover, anyone planning such a career should be prepared to translate these principles into judicious practice whenever and wherever conditions warrant. The operative phrase here is, of course, judicious practice.

In our teaching experience we have both encountered students who planned to impose some prefabricated control system on whatever operations they were hired to manage. They have been warned, by us and by others, of the impossibility of doing so. Most have heeded our warning; some have not, and they have been the ones to reconfirm, through their own hard experiences, the problems inherent in installing preconceived control systems where none have previously been used, or, alternately, changing existing systems to suit some preconceived ideas of what control systems should be used. Some have even been surprised to discover that most establishments have no food controller and no beverage controller and that, in fact, any control procedures put into effect in the average foodservice operation must be both instituted and supervised by the manager, who, in effect, becomes food controller, beverage controller, or both.

Those entering the field should be aware from the outset that comparatively few of the many thousands of foodservice operations maintain anything like complete control systems. Many of large establishments, including chains, do have reasonably complex systems. Some individually owned and managed operations attempt to control some aspects of their businesses, but a substantial number have no conception of the principles or techniques of control. This last may help to explain why the business failure rate among restaurants is so high.

To attempt to impose complex control techniques and procedures on all foodservice operations is probably not the answer. To do so would doubtless be costly and probably uneconomical. On the other hand, carefully and judiciously selected techniques used in certain phases of the operation would probably benefit many.

This is what we hope the student entering the industry will recognize and be able to implement. We hope, for example, that he or she will see the importance of reasonable portion control measures in most situations and will be able to suggest or mandate portion control in some particular kitchen setting without feeling obligated to insist on a complete precost, precontrol system. We hope that each will be able and feel free to modify and adapt the principles, techniques, procedures, forms, devices, and suggestions from this text to use in particular industry settings. If our student-readers across the years are able to do this, the industry will have been well served.

Index